State & Society in Europe
1550 – 1650

STATE & SOCIETY
IN EUROPE
1550 — 1650

V. G. Kiernan

St.Martin's Press   *New York*

ISBN 0-312-75607-0

Library of Congress Cataloging in Publication Data

Kiernan, E   Victor Gordon.
    State and society in Europe, 1550-1650.

    Bibliography: p.
    1. Europe—Politics and government—1517-1648.
2. Europe—Social conditions. I. title.
D234.K53 1980   940.2'3   80-16557
ISBN 0-312-75607-0

To an old friend and fellow-historian,
Alfred Jenkin, from whom I have learned much.

Contents

Preface

This is an attempt to survey the changing social and political structure in early modern times of that familiar but enigmatic entity, Europe, which has imposed so much of itself and its discordance on the world. The continent is covered as comprehensively as space allowed; Turkey is included, as a partaker for centuries of many of its tribulations, and as, with Russia in a lesser degree, a bridge towards understanding of likenesses and unlikenesses between Europe and Asia. Interactions of society and state being the subject, many other things of the epoch – religion and war, the arts, the place of women, and so on – are excluded except where they seem indispensably connected with it. Narrative has been kept to the minimum necessary as framework. References are given only for direct quotations and on points of special indebtedness, but it is evident that any such comparative essay must be dependent on other scholars' researches; also that linguistic obstacles make it less easy to draw on these in some areas than in others.

My endeavour has been to identify some of the ramifying problems involved, and some of the causes of variability among different regions. They are bound up in a diversity of ways with the emergence of a capitalist from a feudal order, intensively debated of late years, but of seemingly inexhaustible complexity. I have no new master-key or set of equations to offer, but have given the best answers I have been able to hit on, or suggestions towards possible answers. My guide through the Inferno or Purgatorio of the past has been Marx, but one cannot go far in his company without finding that, unlike Dante's omniscient conductor, on a journey like this he gives only tentative and fragmentary information. I have learned from many historians, with most sense of gain from those sharing a generally Marxian outlook. The study closest to mine in its purposes is Perry Anderson's *Lineages of the Absolutist State*, which, however, covers much wider ground, in both time and space.

Not a few reasons might be adduced to account for an under-taking like this falling short, after not a few years' toil, of its hopes; but it may be prudent to recall the adage that he who excuses himself accuses himself. In such a labyrinth causes and effects are elusive, and always multiple, and an explorer may often have to be content with a looser kind of explanation, a happening-together of things. Where the authorities so often and widely disagree, he must frequently find it hard to feel solid ground under his feet. He may be reduced to wondering whether any effort to make sense of so huge and remote an expanse of history, on Marxist or any other orderly lines, can be a sensible one. He may even at moments seem to see the past dissolving under his gaze from chaotic pile into mere nebulosity, or taking on the 'spectral' quality that Carlyle felt so acutely in most of 'the generations and their arguments and battle-ments'.[1] Then history-writing becomes a struggle to chart a phantasmagorical cloud-procession, or build with mists and vapours instead of bricks and mortar.

In the end all problems are questions about mankind, with its prodigious capacities and unharmonized impulses, those of a race imperfectly rationalized by its confused struggle for survival, and only partially explicable in the historian's rationalizing terms. Early modern Europe was making a halting, uneven, but epochal advance; if a great proportion of what composed this was morbid and regressive, it may be that change, progress, is not natural to the human collective, and will only come about less painfully and raggedly when humanity attains a higher enlightenment than ever hitherto. In the meantime the student of the past must grope among approximations, or Wordsworth's 'recognitions dim and faint', by the light of whatever his own experience of how men live, think, and behave has taught him to regard as the lantern of common sense.

---

[1] *Historical Sketches*, ed. A. Carlyle (4th edn, London, 1902), pp. 28–9.

1

The Condition of Europe

For study of the relationship between the structure of changing societies and the evolution of the state, the period of European history of a hundred years or so (its limits varying somewhat from country to country) from the middle of the sixteenth century is of exceptional interest. It represents a crucial phase in a long–drawn transition from 'medieval' to 'modern', and in the development of governments and their connexions with social groups or classes. Innovation was accompanied by a dawning national sense, still indistinct and blended with other feelings, primarily religious; there was beginning to emerge the 'nation–state', most dynamic of all Europe's political forms. One manifestation was pride in national languages and literature.[1] Another was an access of interest in history, felt also by smaller areas, provinces like Normandy. European consciousness was expanding in time, as well as, with the voyages of discovery, in space.

Some countries already had, others were acquiring, capital cities like London or Paris. These two were economic centres as well, and London, like Lisbon and the Scandinavian capitals, was a seaport; whereas in an age of expanding maritime trade Madrid lay far inland. So did the eastern capitals Vienna, Cracow, Moscow, though all of them owed some of their importance to being, like Paris and unlike Madrid, river ports. But all states of any size were apt to be conglomerates, comprehending more than one nationality. This complicated the problem of controlling outlying regions, with available means of communication and transport. From the late sixteenth century the growing strength and swelling needs of governments would lead to centralizing programmes, which would provoke resentment, often resistance, on the part of provinces accustomed to a liberal measure of autonomy.

[1] Kohn, p. 153. Where full references are not given in the notes, see the relevant section of the Bibliography.

Map 1   *Europe in the first half of the sixteenth century*

Prodigal of institutions, by contrast with the massive uniformity of most of Asia, medieval Europe gave birth to a wide range of political species, all still extant in 1550 though with uneven vitality. All the half dozen states that counted most were monarchies. Three, those of Spain, France and England, belonged to a western type evolving from the feudal kingship of the middle ages, and were strictly hereditary, unlike the still semi-elective thrones of northern and eastern Europe whose future was far more problematical. There was in addition the ecclesiastical principality, represented by the Papal States and a medley of smaller units mainly in the Germanic region. Here were also to be found the republican Swiss cantons and, as in Italy on a diminishing scale, an array of cities fully or partially self-governing. Europe's endowment included, moreover, side by side with monarchy, a landowning baronage, a thriving municipal life, and strong clerical corporations. They provided the basis for a multitude of assemblies of roughly parliamentary type, upholding the interests of classes or bodies with chartered rights, as against government on the one hand, unprivileged masses on the other.

Much of the future would depend on whether such 'Estates' would prove able to hold their ground and evolve further. They were to show most tenacity in smaller countries, or in provinces where there was a local spirit to sustain them. It was far harder for a country of the size of France or Castile, even with a big metropolis as national forum, to feel enough community of interests to keep them going. In small political entities also, or regions whose sovereigns resided elsewhere, they might retain or acquire administrative duties, raising and spending revenue through committees or agencies. In all such cases the drawback was that the sections of society represented were narrow and exclusive; which helps to explain how small committees were often able to engross most of the rights of their parent bodies. In Franche Comté, that detached fragment of Spain's Burgundian inheritance, when the Estates voted money they set up a committee of nine, three from each order, to decide quotas and arrange for their collection. This could be very lucrative business, and was eagerly sought for its opportunities of self-enrichment;[2] it must have been fairly typical of 'Estates-monarchy' proceedings.

It was in the west that feudalism had taken on its most elaborate shape, too complex and artificial to last for very long; and it was

---

[2] L. Febvre, *Philippe II et la Franche-Comté* (new edn, Paris, 1970), pp. 59–60.

here, towards the close of the middle ages, that a new political epoch was ushered in by manifold instabilities, including rifts within the higher aristocratic groups. Underlying them was the 'crisis of feudalism', today still imperfectly understood, which made older modes of appropriation no longer practicable, or inadequate, and pushed lords into seeking new means of keeping up or improving their position. It might seem that the time had come for burghers to supplant barons as the predominant force, and so they were to do in the exceptional circumstances of the northern Netherlands. But towns were divided from one another by commercial jealousies, and internally by acute frictions between rich and poor, with oligarchies under challenge from both urban middle classes and artisans demanding a voice in civic affairs.

Instead, when feudal nobility proved too factious and irresponsible to wield power directly, there came to the front in western Europe the reorganized, reinvigorated type of royal rule which has been christened the 'new' or 'absolute' monarchy. It is far from easy to define, since it was part and parcel of an intricate pattern of many interacting elements; there were besides marked divergencies from the outset, and it is again not easy to decide which case, if any, was closest to the norm. In all of them old and new methods were combined on novel lines. There was a duality here in key with their own ambiguous character and origin. In the long-established western polities there was no room for new dynasties to arise, but reigning families underwent sharp discontinuities, sharpest of all in England where change was to go furthest.

Marx was foreshortening history when he wrote of 'the great monarchies which established themselves on the downfall of the conflicting feudal classes – the aristocracy and the towns', and which paved the way for 'the general rule of the middle classes' and modern civilized life.[3] There may even appear to be something in his words akin to Augustine's on the Roman empire as the destined cradle of Christianity. This was not yet a society made up of clear-cut 'classes' in the modern sense, itself in part a historical fiction. It was 'grouped into corporations, divided into orders, and linked vertically by powerful ties of kinship and clientage'.[4] No

[3] K. Marx and F. Engels, *Revolution in Spain* (New York edn, 1939), p. 25. Cf. Max Weber's dictum that the competition of national states 'created the largest opportunities for modern western capitalism. . . . Out of this alliance of the state with capital . . . arose the national citizen class, the bourgeoisie in the modern sense of the word.' *General Economic History*, trans. F. H. Knight (London, 1927), p. 337.
[4] Elliott, 'Revolution and Continuity', p. 42.

'bourgeoisie', as a solidary force ready to assert itself, yet existed.
Marx's 'middle classes' would make their advent, as he saw, under
the aegis of the new monarchy, but only by slow degrees, and only
where other factors proved favourable.

Under the new dispensation, much though it owed at the start to
support from townsmen, the higher nobility was still in the ascen-
dant, but it was far less than before a governing class. Its territorial
power was curtailed; at the centre, hereditary constables, high
stewards, and the rest, might continue to strut in the robes of
office, but their functions were taken over by professional men. Far
from being expropriated, however, feudal lords were being treated
so to speak as wards of court, saved from themselves by the king as
head of the whole aristocratic family. As Schopenhauer was to say
of his Germany centuries later, a monarch is the premier nobleman
of his realm, and thinks of all of noble blood as his kinsmen.[5] In
return for delegating political decision, the lords kept their estates
and most of their seigneurial prerogatives.[6] They were freed from
the onerous need to maintain private armies of retainers: their rights
would be upheld for them at the public expense. Aristocracy, high
or low, continued to enjoy immunity from taxation nearly everywhere on the continent, while getting rid of most of the obligation
of military service which formerly went with it. 'Base is the slave
that pays,' as Ancient Pistol says.

Fiscal privilege, shared by many urban patricians, could have
been broken down by a more thorough-going alliance with the
third estate than any crowned head could contemplate. By allowing
it to continue, monarchy doomed the mass of its subjects to chronic
over-taxation, and itself to chronic financial embarrassment.
Instead of the nobility having to pay its share, an appreciable part of
royal expenditure consisted of what were really subsidies to it from
the taxpayer. The current was in the direction of what may be called
'feudal centralism', with analogies in the Ottoman and other Muslim
realms – appropriation of wealth by the élite largely through the
medium of the crown instead of directly from the producers.
'Absolutism' was the highest stage of feudalism much more than
the first stage of bourgeois or middle-class hegemony. To speak of
the new pattern as 'feudal' is, all the same, liable to many con-
fusions; the least misleading designation for it may be 'the aristocratic
state'.

[5] *On Human Nature* (anthology, ed. T. B. Saunders; London, 1897).
[6] Whether the framework of seigneurial control was on the whole recovering, and
even gaining strength, or fading, seems a matter of disagreement.

During the final decades of the fifteenth century and the first half of the sixteenth century peasant discontent at intensified exploitation brought on a series of massive collisions all the way across Europe. They were most widespread and threatening where state power was weakest, in Germany and Hungary. Even there the lords, despite internecine feuds, were victorious. But where a significant development of state power had taken place already, it had an active part in suppression of revolt, as in Austria in 1525 and subsequently in France and England. Its existence also kept revolt to local limits, making it easier to cope with than in Germany in 1525. This does not mean that monarchy, embedded in the feudal milieu yet to some extent lifted above it by responsibility and extraneous resources, was always an unconditional champion of landowner against peasant. In search of balances and counterweights, it might see its own interest as well as a patriarchal duty in a role as moderator between conflicting claims, particularly in the years when it was still finding its feet. Ferdinand of Aragon did so in 1486 when he ended prolonged conflict in the Catalan countryside by dictating the compromise settlement known as the 'sentencia de Guadalupe'.

Extension of state authority included partial transfer of jurisdiction from seigneurial to royal courts, and afforded the cultivator some sort of shelter. This might be remote and ineffectual, but a government like the French which relied heavily on direct taxation of its peasantry had an incentive to shield them from over-much rapacity on the part of their lords. This aspect of western absolutism as social regulator shows more favourably by comparison with agrarian relations further east, whether under feudal oligarchies or under the Muscovite type of despotism. There the peasantry was being reduced to the serfdom that western Europe had on the whole shaken off. It can be said too that in many parts of the west there was a still lively village community, often electing its own headman, and forming the lowest rung of the ladder up to the throne.[7] But even so the villager was dropping behind, failing to secure a place in a society in flux. Only in a few corners of Europe did he have any footing in the Estates. The gulf between town and country, the widest in European life, became harder still to cross as education and printing raised urban cultural standards.

Monarchy's first task was to restore order, by quelling troublesome nobles rather than peasants. How much this purpose underlay all others may be seen from the intertwined meanings of 'police' and

[7] E. Le Roy Ladurie, 'Peasants', in NCMH XIII, pp. 134–5.

'policy', both terms standing for administration in general. Even this elemental duty was fulfilled only imperfectly; breaches of the peace of every private and local kind went on, even where, as in Tudor England, law was coming to have the reinforcement of public opinion. Still, large-scale disorders were being prevented; and while monarchy removed some powers from those hitherto in possession of them, it underwrote all others. By moral encouragement or practical backing it reinforced the authority of town councils over their citizens, prelates over clergy and parishioners, husbands over wives. Religion polished the royal halo, and fostered a conviction of the crown being the linchpin whose removal would mean social dissolution. Shakespeare spoke of the 'general groan' that must follow when a king came to grief. Such a groan had been heard not many years before in Lisbon, when the death of King Sebastian in battle was announced. A visitor saw 'innumerable crowds who wept pitifully and cried aloud: "Oh! what shall we do?" They kicked one another with their feet and tore their hair', or knocked their heads against the walls.[8]

To the masses monarchy had always been 'absolute'; the coronation ceremony sealed a mystic pact between heaven and earth, with the sovereign, like a Chinese emperor, as mediator. Royal display, parade, pageantry were a potent means of impressing or humouring the populace, and its betters as well. Francis I was typical in his 'insatiable delight' in the spectacular.[9] There was a childish element in all the ostentation, but also calculation; and it served to glorify not the monarchy alone but the social order, and consecrate the entire gamut of acquiescence owed by the liegeman. To the better-off classes (outside the court circles), with their secure share of the rights from which commoners were excluded, the personal aspect of monarchy meant less, the institutional more. Political philosophy, expounding their feelings, could go quite far in envisaging kings as constitutional rather than absolute or irresponsible rulers, even if the restraints on them had little formal embodiment. England was groping towards a political rendering of the concept of a ruler as part of a moral order larger than himself, with the doctrine of the sovereignty of 'king-in-parliament'.

But the state in a fuller sense could only mature in the wake of these new or regenerated monarchies, which could operate at first

---

[8] *Fugger News-Letters*, p. 31.
[9] C. Bingham, *James V, King of Scots 1512–1542* (London, 1971), pp. 125–6. Machiavelli advised rulers to regale their subjects with spectacles and festivities. *The Prince*, chap. 21.

only by dint of the ruler's own energy. He was, symbolically at least, chief justiciar, as well as prime minister and commander in chief; only gradually could these attributes be entrusted to others, and government institutionalized. It was a characteristic of the time that so many youthfully self-confident sovereigns were on the scene. In Spain Ferdinand and Isabella, their grandson Charles, his son Philip, all had responsibility thrust on them at a very early age; so had Francis I and his son Henry, all the Tudors and Stuarts, and Sulaiman of Turkey. Only by slow degrees was a throne ceasing to be thought of as a possession, which some individual was entitled to by birth; ordinary men's minds might be seriously exercised over rival claims to it, as they had been in England during the Wars of the Roses. Advances from one stage of political evolution to another are more patent to the historian than to the contemporary, and there have been few spring-cleanings to dispel the litter of the past. A Spanish monarch signed documents with an impersonal 'I the King'. Yet as late as 1625 the Spanish government, appealing to the Cortes for money, could urge that its army in the Netherlands was defending 'the king's patrimony', as well as religion.[10] Such thinking could appeal to all propertied families, because they cherished their own inheritances in the same spirit.

To compel the nobility's acceptance of changes, even on the very advantageous terms offered, monarchy required a certain independence, and therefore backing from other quarters. It welcomed early on the cooperation of elective bodies, which represented largely the towns, indirectly the public as a whole. But the essential need was the forging of administrative cadres. These were recruited from various walks of life, and one use of royal magnificence was to shed lustre on crown servants who might be parvenus and frequently had to face obstruction. The more literate of the gentry or lesser nobility – all over Europe partly led by, partly at loggerheads with, the greater men – supplied numerous office-holders. Many others had to be drawn from outside the boundaries of feudal landownership: without them a centralized landowners' state, in itself fundamentally a contradiction, could not be organized. Churchmen were often useful as civil servants, since they were accustomed to work within a large organization and a chain of command. Townsmen, above all, of the professional or moneyed sort, were eager to hitch their fortunes to that of the new regime. So far as their higher strata were concerned, they were following a line

[10] J. Lynch, *Spain under the Habsburgs* II (Oxford, 1969), p. 3.

of evolution of their own; urban patriciates had come to rely more on the perquisites and privileges of office for their income than on trade.

Sumptuary legislation, designed to preserve social distinctions, was common enough to reveal blue-blooded fears of encroachment by the money-bags; a challenge not to the class as a whole, like that from the peasantry, but to its weaker members. To offer a political challenge, even had they possessed enough coherence, the middle classes would have had to mobilize perilous popular support. It has sometimes been held that by flocking into the bureaucracy they were achieving the same purpose by another route; that the influx amounted to 'a political revolution coupled with a social revolution'.[11] Some such notion had currency at the time. When Perkin Warbeck accused Henry VII of shouldering the nobility aside and employing upstarts who plundered their fellow-commoners, he was invoking a traditional conviction, not confined to the nobility, that it was the nobles who had a natural right, duty, and capacity to help in running a kingdom. In reality the middle-class admixture in administration did not anywhere lead on to the aristocratic state being taken over from within by the middle classes. On the contrary, monarchy and with it aristocracy were fortified by the enlisting of outsiders as managers, and of their money through government borrowing. Thereby the state was 'co-opting the bourgeoisie, buying its support'.[12] Employment of plebeians, so far from subverting the social order, was aristocratizing the higher middle strata. They (and their wives and daughters, whose influence must have been a considerable factor) found it more seductive to aspire to a share in noble privilege, including tax-exemptions, than to seek its abolition.

Centralized authority ought to have brought each country handsome economies, by making a great part of the old feudal and ecclesiastical paraphernalia redundant. Instead, a rage for official employment, as well as the cost of *douceurs* to the aristocracy, cancelled out any saving. Officialdom was growing beyond any rational logic, like ivy round the oak. It distracted many from other avocations, most harmfully from trade and production, and the more these were neglected the less could they blossom and offer opportunity. One consequence of this unhealthy appetite, and of royal improvidence and neediness, was the sale of offices, many of

[11] Braudel, *The Mediterranean*, p. 681.
[12] G. Ardant, 'Financial Policy and Economic Infrastructure', in Tilly, p. 17.

them created only to be sold. Public office conceived of as private speculation harmonized only too well with the rest of the system, and furnishes a clue to its nature. Functionaries were becoming a sort of synthetic class, and the machinery of state something like a vast joint-stock company, in which anyone with means could acquire shares. As such it had too little detachment to be able to fulfil more than fumblingly the bureaucratic mission of defeudalizing public life by depersonalizing it, establishing procedures applicable to all cases and persons – the task imperfectly carried out later on by European nations in their colonies.

Bacon called Henry VII 'an entertainer of fortune by the day', and the same might be said of all his brother-monarchs. Their eyes were usually on immediate successes, or on bare survival, not on distant goals or historic missions; so far as any of them pursued a consistent and meaningful path it was because the contours of the society they belonged to dictated it. After the consolidation of order it was time for more attention to be given to tasks such as in new countries in our age have been called the 'nation-building' activities of government. That authority should exert itself to promote trade, foster industry, regulate economic life, required no fresh revelation; rulers in the later middle ages were quite cognizant of such calls on them.[13] Absolutism set off with some heightened recognition of them; in Spain, for instance, where many of the flood of ordinances issued by Ferdinand and Isabella dealt with commercial affairs, roads and bridges, encouragement of productive skills.

Such regulations were often, it is true, ill-considered and incoherent.[14] In any case, to keep up any momentum on these lines was another matter. Kings incapable of balancing their own accounts were unlikely to be great hands at the hundrum cares of national housekeeping, so antipodean to the courtly existence. As little was officialdom qualified to make good their deficiencies. Administration was entrusted collectively to councils, boards, colleges, out of their depth when they had anything more than routine to grapple with. They were imperfectly specialized; bodies at once judicial and administrative, like the Parlement of Paris or the *audiencias* – provincial courts of appeal in Castile – abounded. Lawmaking might be little more than a declaration of intent, an edifying flourish. At best, what a Frenchman said of his country could have been said of any other: 'for a start all our laws and ordinances are

[13] See   e.g. E. Miller, 'Government Economic Policies and Public Finance 900–1500', in *Fontana Economic History of Europe* I (London, 1970).
[14] Lynch , *op. cit.* I (Oxford, 1964), p. 17.

observed and kept, but after a while neglected and let down.'[15] Gypsies were always being ordered out of Scotland on pain of death.[16]

In place of constructive activity, the monarchies devoted their surplus energies to war. With them came a 'prodigious increase' in the number of soldiers in Europe.[17] This bulks so large in their record that it has been easy to view the new-model state as growing much more out of external aims and needs than out of the social matrix, the country's inner composition; to maintain for instance that 'the development of centralized government in France was primarily the result of foreign pressures'.[18] But competition among states, though the most visible and dramatic aspect of the story, was always entangled in a complexity of ways with the aims and animosities of groups within each one, the relations, in short, among classes. These two planes were inseparable; but logical priority must belong to the social structure and the shifts always going on within it.

All the monarchies entered on life with a bias towards war implanted in them by the situations out of which they arose. Ferdinand and Isabella extricated Spain from its civil broils with the aid of their conquest of Granada, Sweden had to fight for its independence from Denmark. More deep-rooted were the bellicose propensities of their feudal background, a condition they never shook off. Royalty was continuing the old feuding of the great noble houses, concentrating in itself the quarrelsomeness which within their dominions they sought to eradicate. It is a curious sidelight on these common origins that one of Sully's motives for abetting Henry IV's war design in 1609 was his hope of recovering through it some lost family possessions in Flanders.[19] A monarch was a glorified landowner, and nobles trying to accumulate estates, and kings restlessly adding province to province, each influenced the other by their example.

In the bigger military states the interests which benefited, or hoped to benefit, by war were more vocal and harder to disregard than those who suffered by it. War affected the landed strata diversely, and they present a contradictory picture, at times

---

[15] Blaise de Monluc, *Military Memoirs,* ed. I Roy (London, 1971), p. 60.

[16] See D. Macritchie, *Scottish Gypsies under the Stewarts* (Edinburgh, 1894).

[17] See G. Parker, 'Warfare', in NCMH XIII, p. 205, and 'The "Military Revolution 1560–1660" – a Myth?', in his *Spain and the Netherlands 1559–1659* (London, 1979).

[18] D. Buisseret, *Sully* (London, 1968), p. 12.

[19] *ibid.,* p. 53.

seeming bent on pushing their governments into hostilities, at others hanging back and leaving them in the lurch. In general those with adequate sources of income were little inclined to expose themselves in the field, the less so because gunpowder was making warfare more risky. But ambitious individuals like the martial duke of Alva would crave for the command of armies; and even the wealthiest might have younger sons to provide for. Nobility nearly everywhere practised primogeniture.

Those most avid for army service and its chances were the lower, poorer nobility, such as abounded in France, especially in the south, or in Castile. It behoved the monarchies to provide an outlet for feudal pugnacity now superfluous, and they were far better at finding safety-valves than useful channels. America made room for many. In Europe an officer with luck and (a much commoner endowment) freedom from scruples could do very well for himself. Plunder and ransoms were to be had: and the memoirs of Monluc, the Gascon who fought in the Italian wars, go into detail about artful dodges like falsifying muster-rolls and pocketing bribes.[20] In England too a captain 'could swindle with comparative ease and impunity both the government and his men.'[21] Yet with altering technical conditions, and with the necessity of hiring hosts of foreign professionals,[22] warfare represented a very inefficient though a very costly way of keeping hungry swordsmen happy. Such wastefulness was a hallmark of the entire monarchical edifice.

Ordinary folk went to the wars with reluctance. So far as they were concerned, Europe was being militarized against the grain. Part of the function of war was to thin them out, by disposing of unwanted elements, the unemployed or unemployable poor, the vagrants or disorderly. In England, for instance, 'masterless men' thronged the levies for foreign service, among them rogues and vagabonds, swept up especially in the environs of London.[23] Malcontents, or any humble individuals whom their superiors had a grudge against, could be got rid of likewise. Not surprisingly, among the respectable classes there was a habitual assent to war, an assumption voiced by many statesmen and writers, Shakespeare among them, that it was the best guarantee of social tranquillity at home. Peace was felt to be an 'evil good', war a 'good evil'.[24]

---

[20] Monluc, *op. cit.*, pp. 228–30.
[21] C. G. Cruickshank, *Elizabeth's Army* (London, 1946), p. 39.
[22] See V. G. Kiernan, 'Foreign Mercenaries and Absolute Monarchy', in Aston.
[23] Cruickshank, *op. cit.*, pp. 1, n.1, 9–10.
[24] D. Caldecott-Baird, *The Expedition in Holland 1572–1574* (London, 1976), p. 13.

This axiom could find confirmation in what happened when financial exhaustion put an end at last to the dreary futility of the Italian wars, by the peace of Cateau Cambrécy. These wars, fought on and off between France and Spain from 1494 to 1559, were the classic case of dynastic duelling, with a strong dash of light-hearted levity. France lost Italy; what was soon to plunge it into anarchy was not so much failure abroad as cessation of war. Later on too, there was a noble revolt when the government tried to reduce the size of the army in 1619.[25] For Spaniards employment never flagged, because there were always Turks or Moors or rebel Netherlanders and Englishmen to fight; partly as a result, there was no breakdown of order in Spain after 1521, but a collapse of the treasury instead. With its multiple fighting fronts, Spain was out-stripping France in the shift from troops enrolled for specific campaigns to the far more expensive standing army which could be properly trained. Swollen forces and bureaucracies, together with the extravagant upkeep of royalty, were a burden beyond what any sixteenth-century exchequer could sustain. We princes are all hard up nowadays, Cellini's patron, the pope, said to him wrily.[26]

Altogether, the aristocrat state was a very clumsy instrument of progress, a demonstration of how fumblingly Europe was freeing itself from its feudal past. Its ideal condition was still one where everybody had his place and the business of government was to keep him in it. Except beyond the frontiers, rulers and those who did their thinking were much less desirous of guiding change than of slowing or halting it. In his baffled later years Charles V would sit for hours tinkering with pieces of clockwork and, it may be guessed, wishing that a state could run as smoothly. In more philosophical minds was dawning the conception of a universe wound up by God like a great clock to go for ever. Sharing the inability of all dictatorial regimes to go on moving and adapting, absolutism would only be pushed into spasmodic advance by fresh currents of disturbance, like those in France after 1559.

Among disrupting factors, economic ailments were prominent. In its earlier phases the new monarchy had been borne along on the crest of a tide; in some senses, indeed, its advent was a consequence or index of recovery from the low point in European history marked by the Black Death. Very much of what happened remains debatable, but some leading points stand out fairly clearly. Growth

[25] A. D. Lublinskaya, *French Absolutism,* trans. B. Pearce (Cambridge, 1968), pp. 268–9.
[26] Benvenuto Cellini, *Memoirs,* chap. 2.

continued until some time in the second half of the sixteenth century, if very irregularly, and by 1560 Europe may have recovered to its level of 1320. Subsequently recession set in. A very long-term decline in agricultural productivity may indeed have started as early as 1500, and lasted for two centuries.[27] It owed something to climatic change, though even this accident made itself felt through the network of social relations. Europe had been growing colder since about 1300, but from about 1550 to 1700 winters were more severe than they had been for millennia.[28] Worsening conditions and a rising death-rate in the seventeenth century have been plausibly linked with this 'little ice age'.[29] Over most of the continent from 1500 to 1800 there were few improvements in agriculture to counteract it.[30]

Monetary derangements added confusion; there was an epidemic of them around the mid-sixteenth century, thanks in part to currency debasements like Henry VIII's. Import of silver from Spanish America contributed to a persistent inflation of prices. But the phenomenon had started earlier, and it was felt in very far-away parts of Europe, and of the Ottoman empire even beyond Europe. It is clear that contemporaries who traced it exclusively to bullion landed at Seville were hitting on too simple and mechanical an explanation. Historians have sometimes repeated their error.[31] Underlying causes must be looked for in social imbalance, constriction of productive forces and their failure to keep up with the pressure of growing population on goods, and above all on food, where the lag was worst and prices rose faster than those of manufactures. Demography affected everything else. In 1500 Europe's population may have been 60 or 80 million, well below its level before the Black Death.[32] In the next hundred years it was

[27] A. de Maddalena, 'Rural Europe 1500–1700', in Cipolla, pp. 337–40.
[28] H. H. Lamb, 'Trends in the Weather', *Discovery*, Feb. 1964.
[29] J. Dupâquier, 'Population', in NCMH XIII, p. 96. B. H. Slicher van Bath, 'Agriculture in the Vital Revolution', in CEHE, p. 63, discounts the climatic factor. Le Roy Ladurie, 'History and Climate', in Burke, *Economy and Society*, discusses its variable effects. Cf. Braudel, *The Mediterranean*, pp. 267 ff. There are intriguing ideas about epidemics and their causes in this period in W. H. McNeill, *Plagues and Peoples* (Oxford, 1977).
[30] C. Tilly, 'Food Supply and Public Order', in Tilly, p. 415.
[31] See especially E. J. Hamilton, *American Treasure and the Price Revolution in Spain, 1501–1650* (Harvard, 1934). C. M. Cipolla, in Burke, *Economy and Society*, pp. 43 ff., criticizes the explanation of price-rises in monetary terms; A. R. E. Chabert, *ibid.*, pp. 47 ff., defends it.
[32] Dupâquier, *op. cit.*, p. 93. He warns of the very wide divergences in population estimates.

climbing, moving perhaps towards the perilous climax of another cycle. This was happening in spite of the fact that from the fifteenth to the eighteenth century western Europe was learning to put a check on population by a higher age of marriage.[33] Yet population cannot explain things by itself; it too affected them through complex interaction with causes and effects located within the social structure. To make it solely responsible has been aptly called 'demographic determinism'.[34]

Gathering tensions were aggravated by a chapter of dynastic misfortunes, clustering thickly around the mid-sixteenth century but continuing to beset the state throughout the next epoch of its fortunes. Kings still fought, or played at fighting. James V of Scotland was killed at Solway Moss in 1542, Sebastian of Portugal in Morocco in 1578, Henry II of France in a tournament in 1559. Henry III of France was murdered in 1589, Henry IV in 1610. James V left only an infant daughter with a French mother. Henry VIII in 1547 left a weakly son and two daughters, all destined to reign and to die childless. Henry II of France left a brood of youngsters with an Italian mother to fend for them. Women, it should be said, were not always the least successful managers; they might be less hidebound, readier to leave old grooves. Three Habsburg princesses were governors of the Netherlands one after the other. They all proved competent, and may have been regarded by the heads of the family as more dependable than close male relatives. Austria, like France, was a sufferer from a plague of junior princes to which Spain and England were surprisingly immune. That princes in the later sixteenth and early seventeenth centuries were frequently, if frivolously, to be found in opposition to the throne was a mark of the distempered times, and of the instability of personal rule.

At the other end of the scale, dynasties might be dying out. The bodily and mental state of kings and other great men, and the medical treatment they were subjected to, deserve serious consideration as a part of the political history of the age. A king is by definition an unnatural creature, and these beings led intensely unnatural lives. Several of them, like the Emperor Rudolf, the Grand Duke Francesco of Tuscany, or Shakespeare's Glendower,

---

[33] Le Roy Ladurie, in NCMH XIII, p. 128.
[34] G. Bois, 'Against the Neo-Malthusian Orthodoxy', *Past and Present*, no. 79 (1978), p. 61, supporting Brenner's argument against M. Postan and Le Roy Ladurie that the effect of demographic factors always depends on class structures and the balance of class forces.

were addicted to scientific or cabalistic experiments, sometimes including research into poisons, as if impelled to discover the secrets of nature and win the domination over it so hard to attain over mankind. Degeneracy, physical or mental or both, put an end to the Valois in 1589, and the Ruriks in 1598, as to the Spanish Habsburgs a century later. The Jagellon family petered out in 1572; the Braganza in 1580; the Tudor in 1603. All this extinction of native dynasties, and the extreme difficulty of replacing them with other home-grown families because of jealousies among the magnates, meant that more countries – Poland, Portugal, England – were coming, like Spain, Bohemia, Hungary not long before, under the sway of foreigners. In Spain an awkward hiatus threatened in 1568, with the death or disappearance of Philip II's son Don Carlos and the death of his French third wife, leaving only two young daughters. If her Austrian replacement had not provided him with a son and successor, Spain might have fared better, if less peacefully.

From the start the new monarchies left themselves vulnerable on one side by nailing their flags uncompromisingly to partnership with the old church. Spanish sovereigns styled themselves 'Catholic Majesties', French 'Most Christian', Hungarian and then their Austrian heirs 'Apostolic'; English rulers became 'Defenders of the Faith'. Safeguarding the old faith was an obligatory part of the shoring up of the old order; and in persecuting heretics much could be learned of the art of making a country tractable. All these princes had a liberal share of control over the church in their dominions, and made use of it and drew revenues from it. But the connexion deepened the inherent tendency of absolutism towards conservative rigidity.

A measure of ecclesiastical reform was a corollary of the secular reorganization carried out. Stricter clerical discipline was as much in demand as suppression of lawlessness among the nobility – of which most prelates were themselves members. Priestly misbehaviour was the main grievance against the church, and governments could, as in Spain, impose some restraint on it. On the whole far too little was done in this direction, and anti-clerical sentiment was intensifying, along with the social unrest of which heresy might be a symptom. It found its easiest vent in middle Europe, and the result was the Reformation. German princes and patricians were not strong enough to dam it up, nor could they have the whip hand of the cosmopolitan Catholic church in their own territories as greater rulers could do. But they could go with, or even ahead of, popular feeling, and sponsor local churches under their guidance.

Departure from Rome of most of Germany, followed by all
northern Europe, was an immense event bound to have repercussions on the west. Spain stood firm, at the cost of growing more
and more immobile and unadaptable. France, in this as in many
other ways, was the intermediate nation; there was a long era of
indecision before it returned to the fold. Smaller and undergoing
more rapid social and economic transformation, England after
twenty years of wavering came down on the Protestant side. Sub-
stitution of the new spiritual lamp for the old prompted innovation
in other fields too. To carry through and then defend the revolutionary change, support had everywhere to be mobilized on a
broad front, and was likely to be sought from bodies like Parliament. It was a paradox of the time that in the conservative Catholic
realms most representative bodies, those links with the past, were
fading away for want of any compelling purpose to keep them alive;
while in Protestant lands they were taking on a new lease of life, and
continuity from the past and dramatic alteration in the present went
together. With this, a way was open for a move forward from
personal autocracy to impersonal state.

By mid-century Reformation was entering on the new phase
characterized by Calvinism. Its centre of gravity lay in the social
middle; it wanted a more far-reaching reordering than Lutherans
were satisfied with, but was just as firmly opposed to the sweeping
social change aspired to by Anabaptism, the Reformation of the
masses. It could make common cause with a diversity of property
interests, and enable them to follow concerted aims. Its mission,
reflected in an élitist ideology, was to provide a stimulant or
catalyst; it did much to transform northwestern Europe, in one way
or another, more profoundly than Lutheranism its zone. Its
opponent, the Counter-Reformation, shared its faculty of accommodating itself to local or national contexts. It was inextricably
bound up with the Habsburg ambitions which aroused so many
fears, and some hopes, of a universal monarchy to quell and pacify
Europe; and it would carry with it to other parts of the continent the
same programme of fundamentally conservative rebuilding that
western absolutism stood for.

In the meantime, religious controversy was adding fresh fuel to
the already remarkable intellectual activity, with its accompaniment of humanism, the printing-press, and competition for
official posts or professional openings.[35] In England education was

---

[35] On the rapid spread of printing and literacy see Burke, *Popular Culture,*
pp. 250–51.

ballooning as fast as any industry. Spain was chock full of universities and students. A ferment of ideas reacted on all the social discords of the age. On all sides the right of resistance to oppression became the burning question of political theory. Between the Italian wars and the Thirty Years War, or from 1559 to 1618, there was no comparable tourney of kings; what was now to the fore, and had vastly more meaning, was strife within national boundaries, intertwined with the combat between religions, including a last Moorish insurrection in Spain in 1568. External wars might arise from or give rise to meddling by governments in their neighbours' dissensions, a development which spread to eastern Europe as well; though they were often torn between desire to stir up trouble for one another, and fear of the flames of rebellion spreading to their own roofs. Exposed to competing religious and political influences across all its frontiers, as well as to many inner contradictions, France became the grand theatre of civil war and foreign intervention.

2
Spain

Intervals when authority faced a challenge broke in on the history of all the monarchies; Castile went through an early and brief one. Dynastic accident helped to precipitate the 'Revolt of the Comuneros' of 1520–21. Ferdinand and Isabella's grandson, Charles, arrived in Spain in 1517, a foreign-educated youngster surrounded by foreign advisers, and early in 1520 went off abroad to attend to his other realms. Heavy tax-demands on top of this provoked a movement of protest, with a dozen towns ('communes') of Old and New Castile in the lead.

Towns played a considerable part in Spanish life, but they were in many respects collective lordships, with charters empowering them to manage their own affairs and also those of the *tierra*, the surrounding countryside. This combination of urban and rural was more likely to bring feudal influences into the town than to eliminate them from the village; most markedly in Andalusia, where great lords, by comparison with the lesser nobility or *hidalguía*, were more powerful than in the north, while their peasants, descendants largely of subjugated Moors, were more servile. Andalusia held aloof from the rising. Comunero thinking, a medley of two epochs, can be regarded as mostly backward-looking, medieval and localist. More sympathetically it can be credited with a national and constitutional outlook, concern for liberty as distinct from sectional 'liberties'.[1] In medieval times there had been repeated struggles of burghers against feudal overlords, as in other countries, and they had an echo now in townships on some estates. Most of this last flare-up of the burgher spirit was against crown instead of lord; but the enlargement of horizon was confused and indistinct.

Anything like a social programme, for the benefit of the poorer

[1] E. g. Maravall, *Las comunidades,* pp. 54–5, 85, 169.

classes, still lay well beyond the horizon. In the countryside separate risings broke out. By a law of 1480 peasants had been authorized to quit an estate, taking their belongings with them; this ruled out serfdom, and provided a safety-valve, but all who stayed were liable to many exactions.[2] To respectable citizens social agitation was unnerving, still more so when it erupted in their own towns. Food scarcities in 1521 swelled it, and by April street leaders in Valladolid were proclaiming a 'war of fire and blood' against all the higher classes. Support among these for the government grew, while for the resistance it dwindled. Before long the revolt came to an inglorious end, prophetic of how class divisions were to frustrate constitutional ideas throughout the era of absolutism, not in Spain alone.

Alarm had been worsened by the socially more extremist rising in Valencia at the same time of the *Germanías* or brotherhoods of artisans. There too middle-class elements in the movement were estranged by its deepening radicalism; and the Valencian countryside was always bedevilled by rancours of Christian against Moorish cultivators, virtual serfs who were in a way competitors or blacklegs. In all Spain in the later middle ages class strife had been too much overlaid by communal bitterness of Christian, Muslim, Jew, and convert. Absolutism arose more directly out of religious than social division, and hence in a sense prematurely; while the brutal solutions it dictated invested Spanish life permanently with an acrid flavour of bigotry.

After 1521 monarchy was re-established on a still firmer footing. The privileged had succeeded in putting down social rebellion with little assistance from it. But they were professedly acting in the king's name; and they were given a fright, and could better appreciate the value of an imposing edifice of government and its moral as well as physical authority. Charles and those about him understood their motives, and adhered to a policy of excluding aristocrats from positions of trust. On the other hand they had no desire to undermine the status of the aristocracy, whose top families were coming to form a definite peerage, the *grandeza*. In 1537, when Charles was at loggerheads with them over a heavy new excise, the *sisa*, which he wanted all classes to pay, it was the right moment to appeal to nation against nobility; but this was a Rubicon that monarchy could very seldom cross. Charles ceased to summon the nobles to meetings of the Cortes of Castile, whose three houses never again met together.

---

[2] On these see Gutiérrez Nieto, p. 133.

Political and social heartburnings were allayed by Spanish pre-eminence in Europe, and empire overseas, which fostered national pride and with it a sort of unity. Also, in the middle decades of the century what was still essentially a backward, subsistence economy[3] was having a spell of relative prosperity. Manufactures flourished in the Castilian towns; silk-weaving, woollens, and many other crafts were active. At Seville the spoils of America were nourishing businessmen opulent enough to marry into the nobility, and grandees like Medina Sidonia were not above engaging in colonial traffic: commerce was no derogation if its profits were of dignified proportions.[4]

All this ensured buoyant urban markets for agricultural products, whose prices as in Europe generally climbed faster between 1500 and 1575 than those of other commodities. Capital was being invested, in vineyards and olive-groves especially, the cultivated area was enlarged. Busiest of all was the valley of the Guadalquivir where the market pull of Seville and America was strongest. Leases were usually short, and allowed economic rents to be pushed up as price levels rose, bringing in much more than the old uncertain feudal dues. But the agrarian structure was being modified, not transformed. What was taking shape was a variant of the feudal capitalism, or capitalist feudalism, which in diverse forms was a feature of all Europe in that transitional epoch; in Spain the Mesta, the powerful corporation of owners of migratory sheep-flocks, was another specimen of it.

Philip II's reign over Spain began in effect at the age of sixteen, when his father left the country in 1543 and was kept away for years by his problems elsewhere. From 1548 there was a lengthy spell during which both father and son were abroad; and after Charles's abdication in 1556 it was not until 1559 that Philip was able to return from the Netherlands. No other ruling family would have ventured on such prolonged absenteeism; and though there was no open defiance of authority, Philip found things considerably out of joint, and discontent obvious. He set to work to make the royal power impregnable.

He gave Spain for the first time a fixed capital, and chose Madrid. He has been thought to have rejected Toledo as ringleader of the Comuneros. Madrid was a comparatively obscure place, with poor communications. It was difficult to provision, and as it grew

---

[3] Velarde Fuentes, pp. 498ff.
[4] Wright, pp. 65–7; Pike, pp. 32–3.

Toledo decayed; there was not room for both. It lay at the country's centre, but this meant that it lay far inland, when Castile owned a huge maritime empire, still expanding. Thirty years after Philip ceased to be king of England, as Mary Tudor's husband, he became king of Ceylon. It was, however, a perennial contradiction of Spanish history that scarcely any of Iberia's coastal areas were authentically Castilian.

Foreign visitors found Madrid very mediocre, and Spanish writers often deplored its mean aspect.[5] Philip did little to brighten it, and was soon building an abode for himself, the Escorial, well outside. In the course of reasserting his authority he had to tour Castile extensively, but he was not a wanderer by temperament like his father. In later years gout shut him up with his towering projects and his labyrinth of papers in one narrow room. Today the traveller may look down on the Escorial from its hills, and picture the small mind that once inhabited that vast shell moving fleets on distant oceans, its thoughts filling their sails like the breath of heaven.

Bureaucratic centralism, which was in the logic of all absolutism, could now be carried to the limit, at any rate in principle. Most of its machinery had been devised before the advent of the 'new monarchy', and Castile can even be said to have had 'the most advanced version of absolutism to be found in the whole of later medieval Europe'.[6] Now was the time for it to be made to work in good earnest. At the centre business was coordinated by the king's secretaries, half-way towards becoming secretaries of state, occupants of posts with a permanent existence. They were men who worked their way up from modest beginnings, and in the earlier, less self-assured phases of Philip's reign could acquire great influence. Their forerunner was Francisco de los Cobos, who had a strong voice in the government until his death in 1547, and as *contador mayor* dealt with finance, ably enough to accumulate riches for himself if not for his master. Gonzalo Pérez was made a secretary in 1543; when he died in 1566 his duties were portioned out between two men, one of them his son Antonio. Such family successions were among the legacies of the feudal past. Antonio eventually proved too clever by half, and in later years Philip's assistants were apt to be not much better than clerks, like the unobtrusive Mateo Vásquez de Leca. Kings bent on ruling as well as reigning were always inclined to be jealous of men of talent; they were under a

[5] J. A. Gaya Nuño, *Madrid monumental* (Madrid, n. d.), p. 44.
[6] MacKay, p. 121; cf. pp. 5, 143.

compulsion to feel, as well as to appear, omnicompetent.

Philip's reports came to him from or through his councils, accompanied by statements of the members' opinions, collective or individual. At their summit was the Council of State, which had some room for aristocrats, and was restricted as a rule to foreign and military affairs, the spheres that kings felt it safest and most useful to associate their nobles with them in. Far more important for domestic matters was the Royal Council, or Council of Castile, from which others had been hiving off – one for finance, several in charge of possessions in Italy and beyond the Atlantic. Castile's having so many of these dependencies was a factor favouring the 'conciliar' mode of administration, typical of the Europe of that age but more fully elaborated here than anywhere else. It preserved medieval habits of consultation and collective decision; on the other hand a body like the Royal Council was in many ways an assortment of individuals, each with an axe to grind, more than a true meeting-place of minds. As a regulating organ, amid a confusing multiplicity of boards, it was very inadequate.[7] Much of its business was judicial; it had little to do with political decisions of any moment.

All monarchy bred intrigue, deception, an atmosphere of mistrust and slander. It suited Philip's temper not to preside over councils himself, but to work in splendid isolation. To keep his freedom by employing men of divergent opinions, whose disputes would enable him to see both sides of every question, was part of the statecraft taught him by his father, who had balanced Cobos and his faction with a rival one headed by Tavera, archbishop of Toledo. At times this strategy could lead to a tug of war between the nobility of the sword and the newer race of civil servants. Alva spoke for ambitious grandees desirous of spirited foreign policies. They were opposed by a Portuguese, Ruy Gómez de Silva, one of Philip's few confidants, and after his death by his protégé Antonio Pérez; while another secretary, Zayas, was one of Alva's men. There was no consistent 'war party' or 'peace party', but it was the men of action whose ideas were triumphing in Philip's later and more adventurous years, when Castile was called on for enormous exertions and subjected to crippling strains.

His councillors belonged to the genus of *letrados*, college men for whom higher posts in church or state offered glittering prizes.

---

[7] The conciliar method was 'a balancing system between semi-autonomous, if not antagonistic forces': J. Vicens Vives, 'The Administrative Structure of the State', in Cohn, p. 77. Cf. Fernández-Santamaría, p. 241, on its incurable factionalism.

Close relations of patronage linked government circles with the fashionable *colegios mayores*.[8] For any specialized duties these men, mostly law graduates, were as ill-prepared as their Confucian counterparts in China. Few in the Council of the Indies ever set foot in America. Mediocrity and longevity were the safest passports. Bacon spoke of the notorious sluggishness of all Spanish government business, and quoted a saying that if death came from Spain we should all live to a ripe age.[9] In 1586 an attempt was made to improve the Royal Council by adding more members, and in 1598, at the end of Philip's reign, and in 1608, it was somewhat reorganized.

Castile was divided into districts, some seventy by the end of the century, each in the charge of a *corregidor* or prefect, who resided in the chief town but was expected to tour his area regularly. More than a hundred years ahead of France's *intendants*, this organization gave the government some chance at least of a firm hold over the country. Well-qualified men were hard to find, however, or found it hard to make their way up in a society where careers were still far more open to influence than to talent. One cause of the outbreak of 1520, Charles's deputy observed, was the poor calibre of many *corregidores*.[10] This defect was never made good, and the crown's failure to get the right men for what should have been its steel framework was very damaging. Like most others, these officials were poorly paid, so it behoved them to pay themselves. It was a longstanding plea of the Cortes that members of the Royal Council and others should be given better salaries, to compensate for the cost of living. But official place, as all over Europe, or Asia, yielded most of its harvest in perquisites and pickings close to or overstepping a hazy borderline of legality. A *corregidor* was likely to appoint subordinates in consideration of substantial marks of their esteem;[11] such posts were much coveted by the educated, or the half-educated swarm of rapacious understrappers and hangers-on. By the end of the century he might be more an instrument of local faction than of government policy. A functionary of this stamp could make little head against the entrenched interests in his circuit; and it deducted appreciably from royal centralism that some of the biggest landowners, like the duke of Medina Sidonia in Andalusia

[8] Kagan, p. 68.
[9] Quoted by Havelock Ellis, *The Soul of Spain* (new edn, London, 1926), pp. 392–3.
[10] Seaver, p. 297
[11] K. W. Swart, *Sale of Offices in the Seventeenth Century* (Hague, 1949), p. 26.

or the marquis of Mondéjar in Granada, were more or less hereditary captain-generals, or governors, of their provinces.

It was a measure both of Spain's fortitude and of its failings that it
was equal to the prodigious effort of putting the Armada to sea in
1588, but sent it out laden with putrid water, rotten food, and
insufficient munitions. Justice too was frail, and jeremiads about its
quality were never-ending. This was a serious weakness, because
the sacred aura encircling the monarchy owed much to its responsibility for justice. Isabella had taken great pains to improve it,
partly by setting up regional *audiencias* or courts of appeal. To
remedy misconduct by public servants there was the *visita*, or
investigation, and the rule which forbade anyone vacating a post to
go away until there had been time for allegations against him to be
gone into. Credit is due to this first serious endeavour in any
country to curb official misbehaviour. If it also curbed initiative, as
often urged, this would scarcely have appeared to Philip an objec-
tion. But as usual intention and result were far apart. Inspections,
which Charles had wanted officials to undergo every four years,
took place irregularly, and their methods were muddled; account-
ancy was chaotic.[12] Up to date methods of auditing and book-
keeping were familiar in north Italian and some Spanish mercantile
circles; the mandarins knew – perhaps preferred to know – nothing
of them. Inability to enforce passable standards of honesty and
competence was the monarchy's fundamental weakness.[13] It could
subdue heresy, as many dictatorships today can subdue opposition,
but not corruption, any more than they can.

Among all human miseries the worst is lack of money: a king of
Spain could echo this sentiment from Calderón's play as feelingly as
any of his subjects. Just how hard up he was, he never knew; like his
brother monarchs he was always groping in the dark, stumbling on
from year to year.[14] Philip inherited a large debt as well as a large
empire, and had perforce to continue the sale of patents of nobility,
which reduced the number of taxpayers, and of crown rights,
which undermined the royal prerogative. In the first Cortes held
after his return as king there were expostulations against the alien-
ating of crown lands and jurisdictions; he could only plead financial
necessity. Such remonstrances had been heard since the thirteenth

[12] Thompson, pp. 55, 77–8.
[13] *ibid.*, p. 272; cf. Lynch, I, p. 125, on the falsification of cargo records at Seville
through collusion between merchants and officials of the *Casa de Contratación*
which supervised trade with America.
[14] A. W. Lovett, in a comment in *Past and Present*, no. 55 (1972), pp. 156–7.

century;[15] by the seventeenth century probably less than half the country fell within the *realengo*, or territory directly under the crown. True, a *señorío* or lordship was not the same now as in bygone times. Its holder could collect feudal imposts, appoint local office-holders, run petty courts, and some grants included a right to impropriate excise duties; but the sovereignty of the state remained, in principle, unimpaired.[16]

It was one facet of the contradictory nature of absolutism that the cost of building the state and fighting its wars should compel the surrender of so much state authority. There was an analogous tendency in the multiplication and sale by the government of municipal offices, which became hereditary, and left townsmen still more under the thumb of cliques of wealthy individuals, chiefly resident gentlemen concerned to feather their own nests. Yet another parallel can be seen in the reversal, before the close of Philip's reign, of his earlier decision to concentrate war administration and supply in the hands of the government. 'By the 1630s practically the whole of the war machine . . . had passed into private hands, contracted out to entrepreneurs and local authorities.'[17]

In all likelihood no modern empire has been so rewarding to its government as Spain's. Tribute silver from America reached its apogee in the 1590s, when it had a part in inflating Philip's grand designs; but at no period was it nearly big enough to obviate the need for rising taxation. The main direct tax, the *servicio*, voted originally by the Cortes on special occasions, had come to be counted on by the government as a regular standby. Chief among indirect tolls was the *alcabala*, a revenue taken over from the Moors, that is from outside the feudal orbit, and hence forming a special reinforcement to the monarchy. But it had been commuted for a lump sum, payable in quotas by the districts, whose value fell off with the falling value of money; Philip, therefore, like his father was always wrestling with the Cortes to get the figure raised. Their longest wrangle dragged on from 1575 to 1577, and ended with his only partially getting his way.

Extortion and peculation by tax-farmers and revenue-collectors worsened things for government and public alike. Spaniards had rid themselves of the Jews who formerly handled the fisc, but the

[15] Gutiérrez Nieto, p. 263.
[16] Guilarte, pp. 21, 25, 146.
[17] Thompson, p. 7; cf. pp. 165–7, 174. Cf. G. Parker, *Spain and the Netherlands 1559–1659* (London, 1979), chap. 4.

looked-for deliverance proved a mirage. To be able to manipulate local assessments, and shuffle the load on to other shoulders, was a prime reason why the rich wanted to be in the municipal saddle.[18] Meanwhile, one revenue after another had to be mortgaged to cover the interest on loans from foreign bankers, or the great merchants of Seville; in this way too the state was stripping itself of its assets. Annuity bonds or *juros* were always on sale, and underpinned the regime by giving numerous investors a stake in it, but they further widened the gulf between these and the majority who paid and got nothing. Moreover, they changed hands among people in want of ready money, and came to form a sort of depreciating paper currency. Inflation reduced the weight of debt, for the crown as for others; but 1596 saw another of its periodical 'bankruptcies' – not a repudiation of debt but suspension of interest payments, and scaling down of the sums owed, which might be done through conversion into *juros*.[19]

It was a long time since the now truncated Cortes of Castile had met as a trio of Estates. Its first two chambers, of prelates and magnates summoned individually, were set apart by exemption from direct taxation; though as in other countries this concerned them from the point of view that if the government took too much from their vassals there would be too little left for them to take. During the Comunero year there were proposals for an enlargement and reconstruction of the Cortes. Nothing came of them; but there was no move by the restored government to abolish it, and under Philip II it met a dozen times. It had no meeting-place of its own at Madrid; its meagre numbers could be accommodated in any building. Only eighteen towns were represented, each by two deputies, as undemocratically chosen as in most English boroughs.

So scanty a band could not gather the self-confidence that the House of Commons with its hundreds of members was coming to feel, or outgrow parochial habits of thinking. Geographically too the towns nearly all belonged to the provinces of Old and New Castile, so that the Cortes was rather a provincial than a national institution. In 1554 Philip in effect declared the crown competent by itself to make or abolish laws, as well as edicts[20] – a pronounced

[18] Guilarte, pp. 140–41; Domínguez Ortiz, p. 150.
[19] See G. Parker, 'The Emergence of Modern Finance in Europe 1500–1730', in Cipolla, pp. 568–70.
[20] See text in G. Griffiths, *Representative Government in Western Europe in the Sixteenth Century* (Oxford, 1968), p. 43.

departure from the use and wont of old Europe. No doubt some legislation continued to originate in petitions of the Cortes, but it suffered another reverse in 1566 when it took an unusually strong stand on the principle of redress before supply. On his side Philip insisted on the view, only in appearance favourable to parliamentarism, that a Cortes had full discretionary power, untrammelled by any mandates from its constituents: full power, that is, to assent to government requests.

Not to lose ground fatally, the Cortes must learn to play a more prominent part in the national life; but there was no vigorous social force to work through it and turn it into an agency of progress. Deputies grumbled at times about the country being too often and expensively at war. They bewailed the languishing economy, but their notions of a cure were inconsistent. By composition and mentality the Cortes was more responsive to the wants of the rentier or consuming classes than of the productive; it could not desire to see industry protected by tariffs or embargoes. Issues sometimes arose on which it, like other assemblies, voiced popular feeling; but too often, it must be suspected, as a gesture, rather than with any expectation of anything coming of its words.

Philip's monastery-palace was symbolic of an exceptionally close link between the spiritual and temporal powers. Prelates regularly held places in the councils, and the royal confessor had something like the status of a minister without portfolio, or general consultant. But it was very distinctly the monarchy that led, while the church like a dutiful wife followed. Ferdinand and Isabella had secured the right to nominate bishops. In 1557 Philip chose to appoint to the metropolitan see of Toledo a man with no aristocratic connexions, Carranza; in 1559 he allowed him to be arrested by the Inquisition on charges of heresy. Despite papal outcries at this extraordinary act, Carranza was kept in prison for years, while his immense income was impounded by the crown. Even in ultra-Catholic Spain diatribes against the piling up of landed wealth by the clergy were often heard, but the richer they were the more the government could get from them. By the time of Philip's accession they were handing over to it a third of the tithes, besides other refreshers. Philip improved his share of the tithes, but had less success in curtailing clerical exemptions; in the next century all clergy were free of the *alcabala*, or paid at reduced rates.

In the wake of the revolt of 1520 the apparatus of the Inquisition, with its army of 'familiars' spying on the public, was being reinforced. This organization, set up in 1480 to invigilate over converts suspected of backsliding, must be reckoned an integral part, and the most original and remarkable, of the machinery of the new monarchy, which directed its governing body. It is a sidelight on the failure to build a reliable bureaucracy that some tasks like frontier patrolling, for instance to prevent illicit export of horses, might be entrusted to the Inquisition. Even if seldom overtly employed for political purposes,[21] by its presence it fostered a climate of submissiveness, not in the sphere of doctrine alone. Philip's homecoming in 1559 was warmed by the glow of burning faggots and heretics. Chronic dread of heretics, even if few Spaniards ever saw one of those fearsome creatures, supplied the foe within the gates that Spain always had need of to distract attention from its real enemies, the rich. A fresh edition in 1614 of the *Index Librorum Prohibitorum et Expurgatorum* ran to 884 pages, and in his foreword Sandoval, archbishop of Toledo and inquisitor-general, was still lamenting the insidious works entering the country by stealth.

In 1568 the Moriscos of Granada were goaded by inquisitorial zeal into a rebellion which took two years and methods of barbarism to stamp out; 1609 saw the final expulsion of all Moriscos, with heavy loss, heaviest for Valencia, of population and rural labour.[22] On the astral plane of doctrine Spain could at last achieve the unity which in mundane terms of class or region eluded it. Even the victory of faith left it divided in another way, between those who could boast *limpieza de sangre*, 'cleanness of blood' or racial purity, and those tainted with Moorish or Jewish ancestry. All this was part of the price paid for the obstinate persistence of an obsolete social order.

In this setting no government could have much success in grappling with the country's material wants. Promotion of trade and industry might bulk large in diplomatic papers and treaties;[23] in practice the country was a hunting-ground for Genoese and many other foreign businessmen, who had to be granted concessions

---

[21] This is Kamen's view, in *The Spanish Inquisition*. Cf. Fernández-Santamaría, p. 273, on its 'severely deleterious effect on the intellectual and spiritual climate of Spain'.

[22] Estimates of how heavy this loss was vary widely. E.J. Hamilton, 'The Decline of Spain', in E.M. Carus-Wilson (ed.), *Essays in Economic History* (London, 1954), regards it as not a major calamity.

[23] See e. g. A. C. Hess, 'The Battle of Lepanto', *Past and Present*, no. 57 (1972), p. 73 n.

because they had money to lend. Foreign workmen flocked in too. It was an ironic sequel to Spain's feverish efforts to rid itself of all alien blood and brains. Philip was not incurious about the state of his country, and indeed Spain led Europe in official enquiries and surveys: possession of a colonial empire, where such inventories had to be taken, may have helped to create a taste for them at home. A thorough fact-finding was ordered in 1574–5, and testimony collected by *corregidores* through town councils. This, like most Spanish undertakings, was never completed, but enough was brought to light to show that things were already going wrong, at any rate for the mass of a Castilian population which, according to a census in 1591, may have been about six and a half million.

Some sense of a duty to protect the poor and weak went with the conception of monarchy as guardian of justice. There was in addition the prudential motive of forestalling a desperation that might goad the poor into rebellion. Regulation of food prices in time of scarcity was being systematized from 1539.[24] It was more than usually hard to implement in an era of inflation. Clearly also from one point of view it meant cheaper food for towns at the expense of the countryside, and opinion was not at one as to its merits. But this was a sphere, not the only one, where an 'absolute' government was free to issue what orders it liked, and the wealthy were almost as free to ignore them. An edict of 1571 admitted that hitherto instructions had accomplished little, and sought to prevent evasion.[25] Hoarders and profiteers, the churchman Pedro de Valencia declared, were the men with power – *los poderosos*; most flagrantly in densely feudal Andalusia and Extremadura, where he accused the rich of behaving as if there were no laws at all, human or divine.[26] He was an exponent of the Christian-socialist thinking which was an ingredient, if a minor one, of the Catholic revival in Europe, and a warm advocate of regulation as a blessing to the poor, rural as well as urban.

An uncounted multitude of Philip's lieges followed him to the grave; in the two years after his death there was a terrible epidemic, whose deadlines may as in all such cases testify to mass enfeeblement by hunger. Population was already sinking, and this was not halted until some time in the second half of the seventeenth century. A marked decline in the cultivated area had been reported, as the

[24] See Cárdenas, II, pp. 319–20.
[25] E. J. Hamilton, *American Treasure*, p. 245.
[26] Valencia, pp. 21, 103; cf. p. 108.

short-lived economic boom petered out.[27] One stumbling-block
was the prevalence of the *mayorazgo*, or strict entailing of estates, a
practice in which lesser men were impelled by family conceit to
emulate the grandees. Owners went on adding field to field and
piling up land for the sake of social prestige, even when there was no
labour or incentive to cultivate it.[28] A further incalculable acreage
was held in mortmain by the church, so that the land market was far
narrower than in France or England. It was brisker round big cities,
where official and professional families were keen buyers.[29]

Transport, by waggon or mule, was arduous, and clogged
besides by seigneurial tolls; districts for the most part supplied their
own agricultural wants. It was a situation that sustained the prevalent conservatism. Peasant proprietorship was dwindling in most
areas in the sixteenth and seventeenth centuries, though there was a
small middle class of *labradores*, resembling English yeomen.
Whether owning or renting land, they might owe their prosperity
to possession of teams of plough-animals. This was what marked
off the well-to-do peasant from the poor in many parts of Europe;[30]
Justice Shallow's mind turned easily from thoughts of mortality to
the price of a yoke of bullocks at Stamford fair. But the dream of a
labrador, as of a prosperous townsman, was to rise to the status of
hidalgo, or gentleman, and its privileges.

In the mass the cultivators were being crushed down by an
accumulation of burdens, among which old seigneurial dues were
the lightest: royal taxes were much heavier, tithes very much
heavier, and by 1600 rents may have been heaviest of all. In New
Castile a peasant might be deprived of more than half of all he
earned.[31] A great many were reduced to wage labour, with seasonal
earnings eked out by odd jobs. Usury was a scourge of the countryside; and the *censo* type of leasehold which made room for a rustic
middle class also occasioned a tangle of sub-tenures.[32] If active
peasant resistance was slight, then as later, inequalities cutting
across the village must have been one cause. Another can be found

[27] Viñas y Mey, pp. 24–5. Cf. Kamen, 'The Decline of Spain, p. 39, n. 63: 'there is
a massive gap in our knowledge of the agrarian history of modern Spain.'
[28] Viñas y Mey, p. 52.
[29] Salomon, pp. 160–61.
[30] E. Le Roy Ladurie, 'Peasants', in NCMH XIII, p. 115
[31] Salomon, chap. 6; cf. the paper on 'Tithes and Agricultural Production in
Modern Spain' by G. Anes and A. García Sanz at the Seventh World Economic
History Congress, Edinburgh, 1978.
[32] Cárdenas, II, pp. 335–6.

in the common lands, still very extensive in spite of nibbling by big men, and selling off by crown agents in defiance of protests by the Cortes:[33] the narrowness of the land market was thus relieved for those with money to buy. Monastic charity was another cushion; it must also have helped, like the Speenhamland system in early nineteenth-century England, to keep rural wages down. Men dissatisfied with their lot moved off to the towns, or the army, or found their way to the colonies.

American trade was flagging, and industrial prosperity too was brief. Textiles were limping before 1600, even if 'real decadence' did not set in until 1650: by that time some once stirring urban centres had lost half their population.[34] It has been argued that a salient obstacle to capitalist growth was the cost of labour.[35] But in general real wages seem to have fallen appreciably during the sixteenth century;[36] though in 1602 workmen and tradesmen in opulent Madrid were being banned from the theatre on weekdays,[37] while in 1608 there were estimated to be 150,000 vagrants on the roads.[38] An undoubtedly restrictive factor was the *gremio* or guild, whose proliferation in Castile owed much to the Aragonese connexion. As always it sought gain from monopoly instead of improvement, but it was congenial to the authorities as stable and conservative, and was made the vehicle of bureaucratically minute regulation.[39]

Spain's immense unadaptability was stiffened by inflexible religious and imperial attitudes, and no true bourgeoisie was coming forward to confront it. There was no appropriate ideology, such as Puritanism supplied in England, to deter businessmen from the haven of noble rank and idleness. Citizens who were not genuine townsmen and landowners who were not genuine agriculturists converged in a torpid, epicene middle. While politically and militarily Spain dominated so much of Europe, economically it was sinking to the level of a colony.

Yet this was the golden age, or sunset glow, of art and imagination, and there was an intelligentsia whose mind was not yet

---

[33] Salomon, p. 143.

[34] C. H. Wilson, 'Economic Growth and Decline in Early Modern History', in CEHE, p. 29; H. Kellenbenz, 'The Organization of Industrial Production', *ibid.*, p. 516.

[35] Hamilton, *American Treasure*, pp. 279, 281–2.

[36] Lynch, I, p. 127.

[37] Rennart, p. 215, n. 1.

[38] Davies, *The Golden Century*, p. 272.

[39] Uña Sarthou, pp. 183–5, 216, etc.

numb. Education produced at least a reading public, and something like a recognizable public opinion was forming. It found expression in a flood of pamphlets and satires, for in some ways Spaniards enjoyed surprising freedom of speech. Political philosophy was academic and unimpressive, but in their criticism of concrete evils early economists and *arbitristas* or planners often had sensible proposals: fiscal reform, an end to sale of office, a check on the hypertrophy of lay and clerical estates, enforcement of better cultivation. Disquiet whetted by the chaotic state of the currency prodded the Royal Council in 1618 into a wide-ranging enquiry. Next year it presented a report, with the scant result that was to be expected. Still less could come of exhortations by Pedro de Valencia to the new ruler Philip III to play the part of absolute monarch on behalf of the poor instead of the rich, and make a start by cutting up the great estates into small family holdings.[40]

By the time Philip II died the style of government he embodied had exhausted itself, and changes were inevitable, all the more because Philip III (1598–1621) was only twenty at his accession, his son Philip IV (1621–65) only sixteen. There was even a temporary removal of the capital, to Valladolid; to bring the court back Madrid had to pay through the nose. Direct running of affairs by the king gave way to management by a new type of politician, dubbed *privado* or *valido*. In part its advent was a regression towards the sway of royal favourites like those of the fifteenth century. On the other hand there was now a well-established administrative tradition, and the man at the head was necessarily clothed with more of an official character. As time went on he would come to be known by the modern-sounding title of *primer ministro*; though in Spanish conditions the arrangement could not evolve into anything truly modern. All *validos* were hated, not only by envious rivals.[41] Ordinary folk wanted to be able to think of their sovereign himself watching over them, not a mere substitute. In plays like Calderón's the ruler makes an appearance on the stage now and then, as *deus ex machina*, to set things right; one of Lope de Vega's is entitled *The Best Magistrate, the King*.

Very unlike their predecessors, the royal secretaries, those who got to the top now belonged usually to the peerage, and their arrival marked in a sense a return of their class to political power. It was far too anachronistic to rule in any more coherent, rational fashion than

---

[40] Valencia, pp. 67–8; cf. p. 141.
[41] Valiente, p. 110.

through these minister-favourites. It was too effete, rather than too law-abiding, to divide and come to blows as seriously as the French nobility was still capable of doing. Petty disorderliness had never been eradicated by the monarchy, and now worsened; brigandage was rampant in outlying regions, in Madrid nobles and their retinues quarrelled and brawled.[42] Political cliques pullulated, destitute of any principle except of backbiting or flattering the man in office.

Other aristocrats were stepping into high positions from which they had been sternly excluded. Philip II's warlike later years opened the way by giving opportunity to blue blood, and the Council of State had more of the limelight, while the Council of War was enlarged. Noblemen flocked to court, finding life there far more to their taste than in the austere Philip II's day. It was one long fiesta now, with endless sums lavished on receptions, royal birthdays, religious displays. Monarchy was retreating into a world of fantasy. But with dissipation mingled hard-headed calculation, crafty angling for royal favours. There were sinecures and pensions and many other snug things to be had, among them nearly two hundred *encomiendas* or fiefs, now in the gift of the crown, of the military orders which dated from the reconquest of Spain from the Moors.[43] Hard up as he might be, a king still had to keep on giving to these around him; royal largesse was inseparable from true monarchy.

Men of pedigree had been obliged before now to pocket their pride and fawn on upstarts like Pérez,[44] but their necessities were growing more urgent. Absentee landlords left their estates to be run by bailiffs, who doubtless robbed them as well as their tenants and labourers, just as the king as well as the public was robbed by the tax-collector. Entails hindered them from raising money by loans for such purposes as payment of dowries; the crown could come to the rescue by authorizing them to borrow on the security of their rentals, while restraining creditors from foreclosing on their lands.[45] Seventeenth-century Spain, in a word, displayed on a magnified scale the pattern always inherent in absolutism, its existing primarily for the benefit of the landed nobility.

First of the *validos* was Philip III's trusted marquis of Denia, who

[42] Bravo Morata, p. 95.
[43] Wright, pp. 39, 46–9.
[44] Marañón, p. 62.
[45] Jago, p. 222; J. P. Cooper, 'Patterns of inheritance and settlement by great landowners', in Goody, pp. 233, 244.

promptly rose to duke of Lerma and from modest means to prodigious wealth. Formal instructions were issued to the departments to take their cue from him, but most of his energy was always bestowed on manipulation of court groups. To a Venetian envoy it could appear that Spain was being governed by the councils, more like a republic than a kingdom.[46] They, however, could do no more than keep going by force of inertia, and less unwieldy bodies, small juntas or committees, were taking over matters where some initiative was required.

Compared with Lerma, the count-duke of Olivares, at the helm from early in Philip IV's reign until 1643, was a statesman of very superior quality. A glutton for work, he formed a *junta de estado* with some resemblance to a modern cabinet, and set about grandiose schemes of reform. Among these the least unsuccessful was one to bring plain collars into fashion, in place of the ruinously expensive ruff. Most far-reaching was an attempt in 1623 at direct taxation of the propertied classes – the same rock on which the French monarchy was finally to founder in 1789. Always stauncher in defence of property than of the poor, the Cortes blocked this, consenting instead to an extension of Philip II's excise tax, the *millones*. On this occasion many of the towns reverted to their old practice of conferring only limited powers on their deputies. After 1665 the government circumvented it by arranging to get tax votes from each town individually. There had been nine Cortes sessions in Philip IV's reign, following six in his father's; they were the last.

Olivares's effort to make the rich pay shifted to other methods, politically archaizing instead of modernizing. Once more the driving force was war. Lerma had at least been pacific; with the Thirty Years War overspreading Europe from 1618, Spain was sucked into the maelstrom. To an aspiring minister, war promised a greater place in the state and in history. It dangled tempting opportunities before contractors and commanders and other birds of prey. Above all, the entire bias of the aristocratic state was towards war and its spoils. Grandees did well out of Spanish hegemony and the many lucrative posts it provided, as lesser men did out of army service. But a stage was being reached when a deep-seated contradiction showed itself between commitment to war and empire and the escalating costs which made it impossible for blue blood to escape some part of the load. Somewhat similarly, twentieth-century wars have had some democratizing tendency, whatever

---

[46] D. Ogg, *Europe in the Seventeenth Century* (8th edn, London, 1960), p. 44.

hand capitalism may have had in bringing them about.

Olivares got at the landowners largely by resurrecting feudal military obligations. Landowners were called on to furnish contingents for the army at their own charge, and the government abdicated part of its responsibility for defence to them and their still tenacious local influence.[47] Between crown and nobility there had never been complete harmony, and now latent frictions were brought into the open. They found concentrated expression in the detestation felt for Olivares by his fellow-nobles. Deprived long since of their place in a Cortes which seemed needless to them, they had no constitutional means of resisting, such as victims of Stuart money-raising stratagems had in Parliament. Not altogether unlike the Polish landowners, they might come to feel that a state power strong enough to be independent of them, even if some of their assets were bound up with the position it secured for Spain abroad, was no longer to be desired. To soothe them, still more rewards and privileges had to be distributed. Sacrifice fell most heavily, as always, and without any recompense, on the poor; besides taxation, a militia system was being organized from the 1620s, with recruits often obtained by what was in effect conscription, from which blue blood was immune.[48]

Olivares left a Castile sinking fast into decay. Madrid's still accelerating growth was parasitic on court and upper-class spending and artificially cheap food: statecraft was reduced to *pan y toros*, bread and bullfights. This morbid society was mirrored in novels thronged with cheating friars, out-at-elbows gentlemen, professional beggars, all engaged in deception or self-deception. *Don Quixote* allegorized the whole antithesis of reality and illusion. Reality broke in from time to time in the shape of food riots, serious in the south in 1652. Beyond this Spain could not go in protest against its fate. There was no rising class to take the lead, no schismatic creed to instigate revolt.

Swarms of all ranks sought security by entering the church, or its entourage. Lerma got the archbishopric of Toledo for an uncle, and the tremulously pious Philip III had his younger son installed in the same dignity at the age of nine. For the man in the street there was the consolation of religious ceremonies, processions, incantations,

[47] Thompson, pp. 156–7; cf. p. 146: 'By the mid-seventeenth century Spain seemed to have reverted to quasi-medieval forms of raising armies.'
[48] *ibid.*, pp. 123–8, 132. R. Stradling emphasizes that the decline of Spanish military and naval power was a slow, long-drawn process. 'Catastrophe and Recovery: the Defeat of Spain, 1639–43', *History* (June 1979).

with the priest-ridden kings leading actors. Rumours of miraculous happenings abounded;[49] rational hopes like those of the *arbitristas* had come to nothing, and for Spain now miracles were the least improbable salvation. As the mainspring of government wore out, and crown and Cortes sank together into inanition, authority came to lean more and more on the church, and Spain verged on a theocratic regime not without resemblance to Tibet's.

Castile's decline was to a noteworthy extent a displacement of vitality from the central plateau to peripheral areas of Iberia, though not to all of them. This made for a mounting disequilibrium between a region still holding political primacy and others economically more alive. Spain's divisions, regional as well as social, were in the long run deepened instead of assuaged by absolutism. They handicapped the state in sundry ways, besides retarding the growth of a national market; they assisted it, most obviously in 1520–21, by making it impossible for Spain to combine against the government.

At the western end of the Pyrenees the three Basque provinces, though under the Castilian crown, managed most of their own affairs. From having been as disorderly as the Scottish Highlands, they were settling down to better habits, and making advances in shipbuilding and iron-working. In spite of a common language there was no fellow-feeling between them and their neighbour, the 'Most Illustrious' kingdom of Navarre, attached to Castile only since 1512 and left for the most part to its own devices under the watch of a viceroy and a Council of Navarre. A common political ancestry, and occasional joint sessions of their assemblies, imparted scarcely more of a spirit of combination to the three *reinos* of the crown of Aragon. All three came into conflict with the Habsburg monarchy, Valencia in 1520, Aragon in 1590, Catalonia in 1640, but each on its own, and on quite separate issues.

Each had a viceroy, normally chosen from its own nobility, and there was a supervisory Council of Aragon at Madrid with an Aragonese chairman and members from each of the provinces. Otherwise, in their rulers' absence ever since the union of crowns with Castile in 1479, they went on as 'Estates-monarchies' or semi-republics, each dealing with most of its business through standing committees of its Cortes. They were well sheltered from one evil: it was another of many Spanish paradoxes that taxation always fell heaviest on Castile, the metropolis of empire. This was not reflected in any corresponding well-being for ordinary people, who had their

[49] See N. Pérez.

native vampires to batten on them. These principalities were in fact illustrations of how stationary such polities were likely to be, despite freedom from royal despotism, while Castile's record underlined an opposite risk. Only a fusion of the two elements, parliamentary and monarchical, as in England, held a promise of progress.

Aragon proper had a Cortes with four houses, one each for the higher and lower nobles, who always thought of their relationship with the crown as contractual, instead of one of natural allegiance as in Castile.[50] Ferdinand had wished to give a measure of protection to the peasantry, as he did in Catalonia, but had to give way in face of landlord obstinacy. Feudal tyranny, unabated, provoked the same mutinies in the sixteenth century as in the fifteenth. Castilian peasants too were being exploited, but in a less brutally old-fashioned style. Feuds of noble houses were another nuisance. Philip II could not do much to remedy these abuses, but one item in his centralizing policy was the setting up in 1555 of a new Council of Italy, predominantly Castilian, whose jurisdiction included Naples and Sicily, possessions of the crown of Aragon. Both Aragonese nobles and Catalans were indignant. His meeting with the Aragonese Cortes in 1562 was as unfriendly as it was a rarity; he of course wanted money, the pledge of its affections that all monarchs desired from every assembly.

Relations did not improve, and in 1588 Philip provoked tumultuous protest by appointing a Castilian viceroy. Two years later open collision was precipitated by the melodramatic episode of Antonio Pérez, the disgraced secretary, and his escape from prison to Aragon, where he had connexions and could throw himself on the protection of the law. Philip was in no mood to be trifled with; he was smarting under the failure of the Armada, and condign punishment of Pérez would give notice that he was still master at any rate in his own house. But it was an admission of the shackles on royal power that he was only able to strike at his defiant opponent by trumping up a charge of heresy. It was equally an advertisement of the Inquisition's utility as an engine overriding all boundaries and legal barriers. Reactions in Saragossa were riotous. Any capital city abandoned by its sovereign – Edinburgh after 1603 was another – could be expected to nurse a grudge. But its resistance was not seconded by the other towns, nor by the peasantry. Among the nobles there was an often-seen divergence:

[50] MacKay, p. 50.

the lesser men were the more intransigent, while the great lords hung back. Some of the latter had more to hope from royal favour, all had reason to fear mass outbreaks.

Philip had the pretext he required to send troops across the border. Opposition then speedily collapsed. Pérez got away; one or two ringleaders or figureheads were executed, among them the young *justicia*, hereditary marshal of the nobility and guardian of the *privilegio general* or charter of rights which was Aragon's oligarchical constitution. There was no question of an annexation, or abolition of feudal lordships; this would have called for larger forces, and would have alarmed the upper classes in all Spanish dominions. By now the monarchy had outlived any impulse of social reform or revision that it might have set out with. In future the *justicia* would be removable, and Cortes control of money and militia was reduced. Philip's settlement marked accurately enough the length to which any confrontation between crown and entrenched feudalism, with their perennial love-and-hate relation, would go.

In Catalonia, which had no frontier with Castile, the government met other but not less awkward embarrassments. Its viceroy had little armed force at his disposal. His most useful instrument, an unpopular one, was the *audiencia* at Barcelona. As in other fields of action far from Madrid, the faithful Inquisition was too much disposed to make itself a state within the state, hampering law and order by sheltering its 'familiars' from prosecution.[51] Every large organization develops its own corporate interests, which may diverge from those of its employer. On the Catalan side the three-chamber assembly, the *Corts*, had a powerful standing committee, the *Generalitat* or *Diputació*,[52] which had evolved into something like an executive government, but degenerated at the same time into 'an enormous racket run for the benefit of the ruling few',[53] because too little under check or scrutiny either from above or from below. Barcelona had its own constitution, and was ruled by five councillors chosen annually and a *Concell de Cent* where the artisanate had some voice.

In the fifteenth century the great landowners had been weakened both by peasant risings and by quarrels with the towns, while the gentry viewed them as 'natural enemies', and looked

[51] Elliott, *The Revolt of the Catalans*, p. 134.
[52] On its origin and name see Peers, pp. 32–3.
[53] Elliott, *The Revolt of the Catalans*, p. 134.

towards the crown.[54] There was opportunity here for social advance. But materially Catalonia was far past its zenith. In the sixteenth century agriculture was faring well enough,[55] and industry showed some life, but the old wide-ranging Mediterranean enterprise of the seaports was at an end, and the once stirring merchantry was turning away to land-buying, office-seeking, a rentier life. In 1520 the higher classes were afraid of the masses catching the contagion of excitement, and abstained from any action.[56]

Always riddled with social acrimonies, the principality was suffering more and more acutely from them – enmities of coastal plain and hilly interior, town and country, urban rich and poor, peasant and landlord lay or clerical, with the *payeses* emancipated by Ferdinand now hard-handed kulaks. Within the church humble friars were ready to sympathize with the poor, against rich monasteries as well as lay oppressors. There were fewer magnates than in the adjoining provinces; some had moved into Castile and been assimilated. A swarm of minor nobles, often in debt, found some openings for their sons in the army, very few in the more lucrative court careers.[57] Banditry was rife. It may be significant that it reached one of its climaxes in the decade after 1605, when Spain was entering one of its intervals of peace abroad. It had found its material in the poor hillmen who were forced to look for work in the lowlands, and could not always find it; but lords frequently took a hand in the game, which promised booty and an outlet for thwarted energy.[58] Family feuds played a part. In fact the old private warfare of the feudalists can be seen prolonging itself in this patronage of competing brigand bands: as in so many cases, absolutism pushed old evils into disguised forms, instead of uprooting them.

Among the lower classes there could be no such blind trust in the monarchy as it had secured in Castile, but rather ill-will against it as protector of the rich. All classes disliked the Castilianizing pressures at work; the intrusion of non-Catalan carpet-baggers was a grievance keenly felt by the clergy, mostly poorer than in Castile and exposed in addition to government exactions because it was hard to extract any other revenue from the province. Madrid was

[54] Chaytor, pp. 252–3.
[55] See J. de Vries, *The Economy of Europe in an Age of Crisis 1600–1750* (Cambridge, 1976), p. 51.
[56] Vilar, pp. 530–31.
[57] Reglà, p. 114.
[58] *ibid.*, pp. 16, 144.

desirous of strengthening its hold. One incentive was suspicion, strongly felt in Philip II's time, of Huguenot ideas infiltrating through the mountains. More urgent still, after the return to war in 1621, was the wish to make Catalonia and the other fiscally sheltered provinces pay more towards its costs, just as the privileged in Castile had somehow to be made to contribute more. When Philip IV, with Olivares in his train, paid his inaugural visit to the eastern *reinos* in 1625–6, all three were recalcitrant, though Valencia was bullied into giving way. Catalonia's dogged deafness was the more unpalatable because its wealth and population were greatly overestimated.

Olivares must have been recalling Philip II's brush with Aragon when he proposed to Philip IV, in a secret memorandum of 1625, that they should provoke a rising in Catalonia in order to have an excuse for bringing the province to heel. He had a less machiavellian idea in mind too, of winning the Catalan nobility round by encouraging intermarriage and conferring more posts. He was an Andalusian, as Lerma had been a Valencian; their reigns were another symptom of ebbing Castilian energy, and Castilian prejudice must help to explain their unpopularity. Olivares has been commended as 'the champion not of Castile but of Spain'.[59] More precisely he was the champion of Spanish or Habsburg aristocracy. Monarchy was looking for supporters among the classes, to the exclusion of the masses, and Catalonia (like the rebel Netherlands) was obnoxious on account of its tenacious popular elements, as well as its dislike of paying taxes. A more concrete part of Olivares's thinking, the 'Union of Arms' by which every dominion would supply its quota towards a strong standing army, would in practice mean a kind of federal league of nobilities under royal presidency, with a single cosmopolitan cadre of state service. That men were best employed outside their own homelands was an idea in the air.

Northeastern Catalonia was an old Franco-Spanish cockpit, and in 1639 French invasion gave Olivares ground for sending in troops, thus violating the *fueros* which prohibited movement of soldiers either into or out of the province without its consent. He might thus be said to be carrying out the tactics of provocation he had sketched in 1625. Franchises like Catalonia's were by now in many ways behind the times, but they were clung to in default of any acceptable scheme of national unification, instead of the mechanical imposition

[59] Elliott, *The Revolt of the Catalans*, p. 203.

of unity which was all the monarchy could hold out. A cathedral canon, Pau Claris, president of the *Diputació* and a 'passionately conservative' provincialist, [60] came forward as spokesman of the objectors.

More forward-looking leadership was wanted, but not forthcoming, when revolt broke out in 1640, authority collapsed, and all Catalonia's pent-up embitterments exploded. Men like Claris could not think of setting up a republic; instead they turned to France, and at the beginning of 1641 accepted the suzerainty of Louis XIII, at least as much for an insurance against their own people as against Madrid. In 1643 Olivares fell from power. He had helped to stir disaffection in France, and Paris welcomed the chance of a tit for tat; but collaboration with its turbulent new subjects could not be smooth. Within the insurgent ranks class antagonisms persisted. Resistance was gradually worn down, and Barcelona captured late in 1652 after a year's siege. Still at war with France and nearing exhaustion, the government was willing to grant an amnesty and confirm the *fueros*. These no longer had much meaning; and under Charles II the *Corts*, like the Cortes of Castile, never met.

3

The Spanish Dependencies

On the tabula rasa of the American colonies absolutism could set out to build both an administration and a society approximating to the ideal which may be said to have floated before its mind: revered sovereign, well-conducted officials, loyal townsmen, landowners purged of original sin, or feudal vice, and docile peasantry, all tutored by an obedient battalion of priests. Utopian fantasy, so much astir in the Europe of the humanists, could spill over into the New World, and draw pictures of Indian settlements all harmony and bliss.[1] Reality was to prove a dismal caricature of all such dreams. Yet there could be boasted at least the creation of an imperial fabric destined to last for three centuries.

A Council of the Indies took distinct form in 1524; its procedures were standardized by an ordinance of 1571, little altered to the end of the next century; Spanish bureaucracy loved to repose in fixed grooves. Its members were jurists or theologians rather than colonial experts. Innumerable edicts and directives flowed from it to the men on the spot: the sheer bulk of its correspondence with their heads, it has been said, has to be seen to be believed.[2] How much of it they troubled to read may be doubtful. But they were watched with a vigilance proportionate to their remoteness from Spain, and allowed as a rule only short terms of office. An array of checks and balances was part of the huge rusty grandfather-clock mechanism of Spain and its empire. Two viceroys, in charge of Mexico and Peru and the subordinate governorships, had as watchdogs on their doings the *audiencias*, of which seven were set up by 1550; as in Spain they had executive as well as judicial functions. There was no Cortes to make trouble, as England's colonial assem-

---

[1] See S. Zavala, 'Sir Thomas More in New Spain' (London, 1955).
[2] Hanke, *Spanish Viceroys*, pp. 6, 12.

blies were often to do. Municipal self-government was carried across the Atlantic, and attained a degree of vitality, but care was taken to prevent it going too far; popular election of town councils was exceptional. No colonial Comuneros were wanted.

A weighty reinforcement of royal authority was the *Patronato* of the Indies, established with papal consent in 1508, which gave the crown the unrestricted control in ecclesiastical matters that it aspired to with less complete success in its European possessions. As its shield and buckler against both races, the church was even more indispensable than in Europe, and the state's eventual drift into reliance on this church, or the evolution of the church into a pseudo-state, could go still further. In the 1570s the Inquisition was introduced, though the Indians were excluded from its purview. Ecclesiastical headship also greatly expanded the patronage at the crown's disposal, and the more patronage any government had to bestow the more secure its position. On the other hand, here too profligacy and penury, leading to sale of offices, might loosen its hold over its employees. By the end of Philip II's reign sale of colonial posts was a valuable source of revenue. From 1606 incumbents had the right to sell them to others.[3]

In principle, the government regarded itself as the protector of the Indians, as at home of the poor, and its councillors excelled at drafting elaborate codes and regulations. What might be called the implicit apologia of absolutism in Europe became in the colonial sphere more self-conscious and declaratory. In the rules for expeditions of conquest laid down in 1573, and in the pronouncements of a benevolent viceroy like Francisco de Toledo in Peru about the same time, Spain's title to rule was rested on positive benefits to its subjects: religion, civilization, roads. But if the crown was so little able to defend Spanish peasants against their oppressors, or to dream of summoning them to defend themselves, there was very little chance of its being able to defend Indians thousands of miles away; to say nothing of its own peremptory need of forced labour for the silver mines. An investigation in 1542–3 revealed that several members of the Council of the Indies had been in receipt of bribes from the conquistadores.[4]

A dominant class of hereditary landowners was soon sprouting; from the first an absentee, town-dwelling one, for life among

[3] Parry, *The Sale of Public Office*, p. 4.
[4] Hanke, *The Spanish Struggle for Justice*, pp. 93–4; and see his critique of later writings in 'More Heat and Some Light'.

aborigines had even fewer attractions than among Castilian yokels. To arrest this tendency, the 'New Laws' of 1542 banned grants of *encomiendas* or fiefs and the enslavement of the inhabitants that was taking place. This was the signal for the stiffest defiance of crown by colonists in the entire period.[5] Its leader, Pizarro's brother Gonzalo, was defeated and killed, but in 1545 the ban on *encomiendas* had to be revoked, though slavery continued illegal. Apart from the settlers' insubordination there were greedy mouths at home to be filled. To the aristocracy Spain's colonies as much as Spain itself existed for their behoof. Court favours or *mercedes* frequently took the form of drafts on colonial treasuries, or assignments of native labour.[6] But as Spain declined the colonies were growing up; the displacement of energy from the Castilian plateau to the Iberian periphery was being repeated and magnified.

Portugal was the other pioneer of empire, though it did far less colonizing than Castile. From the first it was a state of peculiar mould, conditioned to an unusual degree by external pulls. Its ships scoured the oceans while at home districts cut off by desert or mountains might be scarcely in touch with the capital. Sea trade and merchantry provided from early on a counterweight to the feudal estates, and allowed the monarchy more freedom of action than elsewhere. Between them feudal and mercantile appetites drew Portugal on to a course of overseas adventure, analogous with medieval Catalonia's in the Mediterranean.

Disorders in the fifteenth century resembled those in Castile, and John II (1481–95) must have been mindful of Castilian example when he set about restoring the power of the throne. He went to work, however, in a more bloodthirsty fashion than any other royal architect outside Muscovy; there was a regular massacre of nobles. Such a *coup de main* was practicable because of the relative weakness of feudalism here, and the country's small size. John's successors turned the attack against the towns, whose charters were drastically curtailed in 1525: note had clearly been taken of the lessons of urban rebellion in Castile. Craft guilds sometimes enjoyed representation in municipal councils, as they did at Lisbon;[7] they and the higher ranks might usefully hold each other in check. In the moneyed classes Jews had been still more prominent than in Spain, and even after their expulsion trade and finance remained very much in the

---

[5] Parry, *Seaborne Empire*, pp. 182 ff.
[6] J. Lynch, *Spain under the Habsburgs* II (Oxford, 1969), p. 166.
[7] Cf. Boxer, pp. 278 ff., on a similar colonial municipal pattern.

hands of converts or 'New Christians', often crypto-Jews against whom a never-ending hue and cry was kept up. It was inconceivable that such a class should put itself at the head of the masses, as the urban rich could do in Holland.

From the late fifteenth century the Cortes, similarly constituted to Castile's, was called less and less frequently. Tribute flowing in from overseas helped to make the crown self-sufficient. Lisbon was becoming an imperial metropolis. Elephants marched in parades, marble elephants support the royal sarcophagi in the monastery of Belém. After the East and its spices came the exploitation of sugar in Brazil. From 1505–6 trade with the Indies was a crown monopoly. In 1577, shortly before the loss of independence, individuals or syndicates who contracted to provide ships were admitted to a share.[8] It was a symptom of the government's faltering will, with no corresponding growth of a bourgeoisie. Profits were largely drawn off by foreigners, Italian, German, Flemish, or by the 'converts' with their connexions abroad. 'Portugal ran a vast colonial empire mainly for the benefit of others.'[9] It was being drained of men and resources for the enrichment of a few; debts piled up at home and abroad, food had to be imported. Camoens's vainglorious epic of gold and triumph contrasted strangely with an influx of slave labour from Africa to work land in southern provinces whose own people had gone away. About 1580 an Italian in Lisbon thought one fifth of its population – morbidly swollen like that of so many cities of southern Europe – was composed of slaves, black or Indian or Far Eastern.[10]

Sebastian, who came young to the throne in 1557, grew up with a strong tinge of the mental derangement which haunted European royalty. His invasion of Morocco in 1578 was a last convulsive effort by a sick nation, as well as monarchy, to free itself by a desperate throw of the dice. His crushing defeat and death were a Portuguese Flodden. Two years later the dynasty expired, and the throne was taken by Philip II, who had valid genealogical claims. While Camoens lay dying, an expensive military operation was mounted to make them good, and an army under Alva entered the country and suppressed opposition with an iron hand. He had lately been at work on rebels in the Netherlands, and was an exponent of

[8] K. Glamann, 'European Trade 1500–1750', in Cipolla, pp. 486–7.
[9] Nowell, p. 93.
[10] C. Viñas y Mey, *El problema de la tierra en la España de los siglos XVI–XVII* (Madrid, 1941), p. 165.

the philosophy of terrorism which had a very definite place in the armoury of absolutism.

Resistance did not amount to much; by the upper classes and higher clergy Philip was accepted not too reluctantly. They might not want monarchy too strong, but they needed it as a shield against the sullen masses, and could hope, correctly enough, that an absentee ruler like Philip would provide this while leaving them a good deal of rope: they were of course aware that men of position in the Aragonese lands enjoyed this double advantage. Philip was quite ready to meet them half way. He made a lengthy stay in Lisbon, called the Cortes, and gave assurances that official posts both domestic and colonial would be reserved to them as before. Royal authority in all Spanish dependencies relied on aristocratic, not popular consent. As often, the commonalty were more patriotic, or anti-foreign, than their betters, and a myth lingered among them that their prince lost in Morocco was not really dead, but would return.

The royalism of the well off was of a utilitarian cast; the cult of *Sebastianismo* – of a king who alive had done his people no good – shows how much of wishful thinking or fantasy, derived from ancient magical ideas, entered into the royalism of the masses. There has been noticed in it also a vein of New Christian messianism, which released an outpouring of rhapsodic poetry,[11] and there were prophecies, seductive to high and low, of a wonderful national resurgence.[12] On this rarified level irreconcilable faiths and classes could mingle their feelings. There were parallels to *Sebastianismo* in lands as far off as Russia. Scots hugged a belief that their James IV had not perished at Flodden, but only disappeared, on a pilgrimage it might be, and would come again at his nation's call. Only through a king's resurrection could an illiterate, disoriented populace imagine deliverance.

There was at least as much to be said for political unification of Iberia as of the British Isles; but the Castilian monarchy was even less well qualified for the task than the Tudors. Philip II kept most of his pledges, but his new subjects and their colonies were dragged into his wars with Holland and England. Philip III paid only one visit, late in his reign, and now posts in Portugal were more and more often made use of to reward Castilians. As in Catalonia, a Castilianizing process was at work, less deliberate policy than a

[11] Livermore, p. 165.
[12] Boxer, pp. 369 ff.

consequence of patronage and its lures. Renewed war brought applications for heavier subsidies; in 1636 these provoked disorders. Olivares wanted Portuguese nobles too to provide quotas for the army, or their cash equivalent. There may be some ground for the conjecture that they would not have been averse to complete fusion with Spain, and equal opportunity for themselves within it.[13] They too had need of a paternal ruler to bail them out of financial predicaments. But now it was the onerous side of the Spanish connexion that was obtruding itself. With discontent seething in the streets, the wealthier had to decide whether it would not be safer to swim with the tide than to stand any longer with Madrid.

Revolt when it came in 1640 was partly touched off by that of the Catalans. For a while this seemed to herald a total break-up of Spain. There was a separatist conspiracy in Andalusia, round the duke of Medina Sidonia to whose family the defences of south west Spain had been committed for the past sixty years. The crown was paying the penalty for not having rallied plebeian allies, instead of falling back into dependence on the grandees. Medina Sidonia's brother-in-law was Portugal's premier duke, Braganza, rashly entrusted by Olivares with the army command in his country.[14] He was related to the old ruling family, and made a safely conservative figurehead for the national rising.

Here there were far fewer elements of republicanism than in Catalonia, and even the Catalan movement might have held together better if there had been a native race of princes to head it. In both cases there were national institutions to provide a framework for rebellion, if a cramping one. In 1641 the Cortes came back to life. Its recovery never went far; and it was foreign aid and Spanish weakness, more than Portuguese resolution, that restored in the end a limping independence. There were still the colonies to encourage habits of parasitism, and with them the sway of aristocracy and church. A few enlightened patriots wanted Portugal to turn away from its old ruinous courses to reconstruction at home, and urged landowners to return to their estates and improve them. But these were voices crying in the wilderness.[15]

How much Italy may have lost – and gained – by not having a national government of its own is a matter for speculation. Gramsci thought than an Italian absolutism was possible and would have

[13] Oliveira Martins, p. 408.
[14] I. A. A. Thompson, *War and Government in Habsburg Spain 1560–1620* (London, 1978), p. 156.
[15] Viñas y Mey, *op. cit.*, pp. 140 ff.

been beneficial. But the country may have been too heterogeneous, and its more advanced centres too sophisticated for so crude a remedy. Monarchy would have had to join hands with the church more closely than anywhere else, and much of value would have been suffocated, more completely than befell it under the Spanish hegemony.

Italy's population may have exceeded that of Iberia, and grown during the sixteenth century from 10 and a half to over 13 million.[16] Spanish power rested in the last resort on a mere handful of Spanish troops, scarcely more than 6,000 as a rule;[17] and in 1566 all the veterans were called up to march with Alva to the Netherlands. There was no intention of bringing Italy under a single uniform administration. A tenuous measure of coordination was represented by the Council of Italy, with some members from Sicily, Naples, and Milan, the rest usually Castilians. It made feasible some planning of combined operations against Turkish or Moorish raiders. Protection had to be paid for by a heavy drain in taxation or irregular tolls, made worse by involvement in Spain's irrelevant wars in other spheres. Naples contributed men to the fighting of 1568–71 in Granada.[18] In the same fashion India was to have to contribute men and money towards British colonial campaigns. Italy was at any rate not a colonial market for Spanish goods, as America for a time was; it was rather the other way about.

Grievous as Spanish rule was in some ways, Italy – like Spain – suffered most from the dead weight of its own dominant classes. This was nowhere more true than in Sardinia, which remained attached to the Aragonese crown, with a member in the Council of Aragon. Its condition was the outcome of old feudal conquest, and the parcelling out of the soil among Spanish nobles, whose descendants proved for centuries landlords of the worst stamp, and no more responsive to the wishes of government than Italian or any other aristocracies. They of course had the chief say in a *Parlamento* which had some legislative rights. In Philip II's time there were efforts by the government at improvement, economic as well as administrative; among them a new law code and court of appeal, amenities that a civil service of lawyers was well equipped to confer. Some viceroys showed a constructive turn. But they were blocked by the hostility of the privileged, which at times took violent forms, and

[16] R. Mols, 'Population in Europe 1500–1700', in Cipolla, p. 38.
[17] Thompson, *op. cit.*, p. 104.
[18] *ibid.*, p. 18. Cf. Lynch, *op. cit.* II, p. 31: 'The Italian dependencies contributed much more to imperial expenditure than did the Low Countries.'

against which there was no middle class of any weight to lend support. Rifts between nobility and clergy helped authority to maintain itself, if inertly.

Offshoots of Spanish families were to be found in other provinces, especially in Sicily; in general Spain's upper classes benefited from their country's position indirectly, through the crown, and the Italian plums at its disposal were among its many means of keeping its nobles in good feather. As viceroy or governor a grandee could enjoy the almost sovereign position his ancestors held on their estates. Ordinarily the distant Council of Italy acted more as court of appeal than as overseer. Philip II did supervise his deputies narrowly, and bombarded them with despatches. But this did not interfere with splendid living and pocket-filling. Olivares's *bête noire*, the duke of Medina del Rioseco, asked for Milan as compensation for sums laid out in army service, turned up his nose at Valencia, and accepted Sicily, followed by Naples.[19] Machiavelli noted how prone to pillaging habits were officials in all outlying territories.[20]

There were snuggeries for churchmen too. In Sicily, in face of local dislike of foreign office-holders, benefices were the best things that well-connected Spaniards could look to.[21] This harmonized with Madrid's need of a reliable clerical establishment to supplement its very limited physical resources. It was even more essential than in Spain that all subjects should be unquestioning Catholics, and that the church should understand what it owed to the throne; the Counter-Reformation was adding to its usefulness. Madrid's eagerness to set up everywhere branches of its own trusty Inquisition, instead of having to lean on the papal Holy Office, showed very plainly its estimate of the institution's utility at home. Its menace to all local autonomies was equally patent, and plans to introduce it in Naples in 1547 and Milan in 1563 met with determined and successful opposition, endorsed by Rome. In Sardinia and Sicily, where Spanish rule was older, the Spanish Inquisition had been busy since its birth in the time of Ferdinand the Catholic. In Sicily particularly, with Spaniards in senior posts, it furnished an information service and an auxiliary police, which helped to suppress risings in 1560 and 1565.[22] Indeed it waxed so powerful as to rival the viceroy, and during the 1590s steps had to be taken to

---

[19] Shaw, pp. 5–6, 13–14.
[20] *The Prince*, chap. 3.
[21] Koenisgberger, p. 50.
[22] D. M. Smith, pp. 164–5.

curb it. In Malta similarly it tried to take the upper hand of the Grand Master.

Sicily in the early years of the sixteenth century was the scene of tumults in which aristocratic dislike of royal encroachments played a leading part. In 1516–17 there was graver trouble at Palermo, provoked by food shortages and taxes. As the masses came on the scene, the nobles prepared to quit it, and earn rewards for their loyalty. It was a sequence of events strikingly like that of the Comunero rising a few years later, when Castilian noblemen may have taken a leaf out of the Sicilian book. A balance was arrived at, with the government satisfied with the pre-eminence it had achieved, and no nationwide resistance to it conceivable because the baronage and the privileged ruling groups in the big towns – commercial in Messina, patrician in Palermo – were always at odds with one another, while both feared and distrusted the impoverished masses whom both exploited. They stood in need of royal tutelage; their decrepit feudal society could not produce a new-style monarchy of its own: submission to one from outside was the alternative.

Relations between government and *Parlamento* were an accurate expression of this balance. Consent to taxation required in theory the agreement of all three houses, representing clergy, nobility and the 'domains' or districts directly under the crown, like the *realengo* in Castile. It was the wishes of the nobles that counted most, above all in the standing committee which superintended local affairs and expenditure. They were supposed to pay their share of taxation, but found ways of transferring it to their vassals. Few notables bothered to attend in person, and their procurators might be royal officials; but behind the scenes they knew how to make themselves felt, and to plague any viceroy who displeased them.[23]

An occasional viceroy might try to ginger up the administration, as the duke of Osuna appointed in 1611 did. He came of one of the families with a tradition of such appointments: his grandfather was viceroy of Naples in the 1580s, as he himself was later on, and his son was another viceroy of Sicily. He took stern measures to put down banditry and fend off Barbary corsairs, toured the island and inspected schools and orphanages, and patronized the arts. All this refurbishing was rolling the stone uphill, because there could be no reformation of society to consolidate any gains made. Moreover, a

---

[23] H. G. Koenigsberger, 'The Parliament of Sicily and the Spanish Empire', in *Estates and Revolutions* (Cornell University Press, 1971), p. 86.

preference for 'alternative centres of authority' was inherent in the Spanish system, and ministers were chosen by the metropolitan government, not by the viceroy.[24] For another thing, after Philip II's reign increasing sale of offices, and sale to the nobles of rights of jurisdiction, meant a partial relinquishment of power; as in Castile, monarchical centralism was being reversed or unwound, and neo-feudalism taking its place.

Steadily more effete and useless, the baronage was far from being a united class, since family feuds honeycombed it; along with banditry they made even elementary law and order unattainable. It might be supposed that the natural course for the crown would be to sweep it away, and so make itself really master of the island and its wealth. But this would be too revolutionary a step for any monarchy to take, except after a general mutiny of the landowners like that in Bohemia in 1618–20, which could scarcely happen in Sicily. Besides, it would leave a foreign government face to face with a people it had little notion of how to deal with directly. It was constrained to try to civilize or domesticate noblemen by luring them to live in Palermo, and by a lavish sale of dignities. Men of means in the towns too were taxed obliquely by being induced to buy all sorts of titles and distinctions, each outbidding the other, until the small island was bulging with dukes and princes. With economic decline setting in, many here too came to rely on royal graces and favours to keep them solvent, and their allegiance was all the better assured.

Cultivation, under such ownership, was 'exceedingly primitive';[25] yet export of grain was elaborately organized, and went on as it had done through the ages.[26] It represented imperial tribute, and payment for luxury imports, and could only be taken out of the stock needed for consumption by the people. In 1647 when Madrid had its hands full with rebellions and foreign war, anger at bread shortages and food taxes exploded into revolt at Palermo. It ran a hectic course, a medley of factions and mobs materializing and dissolving, the most that could be expected in a society so demoralized. Craft guilds like those of the tanners and fishermen were the solidest force, a sort of industrial middle class. But artisan mentality was ambivalent, a mixture of anger at noble blood-sucking and

[24] *ibid.*, p. 90.
[25] J. de Vries, *The Economy of Europe in an Age of Crisis 1600–1750* (Cambridge, 1976), p. 52.
[26] F. Braudel, *The Mediterranean . . . in the Age of Philip II* (2nd ed., trans., London, 1972–3), pp. 603–4.

conservative respect for the old social order.[27] Some such blend of feeling was characteristic of the Europe of that age, and in other forms is still to be met with today. Things ended in government and nobility being drawn still closer together. Thanks to this combination, and exhaustion of all forces of protest, Spanish rule dragged on – a monarchy destitute of any national foundations, more year by year a caricature of absolutism.

In the kingdom of Naples the government had a freer hand, though chiefly, as usual, to rob the poor. More could be extracted for imperial uses, including a good deal of manpower, sometimes pressganged and taken in chains to the ports for shipment abroad. With the same composition as Sicily's, the *Parlamento* was weaker still, because more sharply divided; nobles as well as public were irritated by the church's riches and privileges, and not sorry to see Philip II dragooning it.[28] With papal supremacy almost eliminated, the church had no choice but to submit to the government and, in return for protection, become its faithful creature. The chamber of the nobility earned royal approval by voting grants, or *donativi*, usually every two years, to be paid by the third estate. This could not save the treasury from being always hard up, but while revenues were mortgaged to its creditors, tax-gatherers and tax-farmers prospered.[29]

Meanwhile troops plundered, administration was at sixes and sevens, justice was anything but blind. Things were not improved by depreciated currency, or by economic policies many of which belonged to the stock in trade of governments, and were not confined to 'colonial' territories: prohibition or restriction of some exports, monopolies, internal tolls. Naples had its share in the sixteenth-century boom in grain, and as in other countries it was the bigger landowners who fared best. Surpluses of oil, timber, and wool from their estates, as well as food, were actively marketed. They benefited here too by the sale of seigneurial jurisdiction, which went so far that in the seventeenth century scarcely any part of the country was left under direct royal administration; the peasants' unwillingness to be abandoned to the mercies of their lords was ignored. A sprinkling of farmers also did well, chiefly near the coast with access to maritime trade, until they were

---

[27] H. G. Koenigsberger, 'The Revolt of Palermo in 1647', in *Estates and Revolutions, cit. supra*, p. 268.
[28] R. B. Merriman, *The Rise of the Spanish Empire* IV (New York, 1934), pp. 470–72.
[29] Coniglio, pp. 125, 190, 202.

crippled by the fall of prices in the seventeenth century.[30]

The city of Naples had a modicum of self-government, but the right to representation was being cut down, and by 1600 was confined to a few privileged groups such as the tax-collectors and lawyers. The government could play on burgher vanity by conferring titles, and this was a means of dividing and ruling, for the old and new aristocracy were always at loggerheads. Between them by 1650 they mustered 119 princes and 156 dukes. To keep the populace quiet, something was done to check food prices from getting out of hand.[31] Inevitably the prospect of cheaper food helped to suck in more and more hungry mouths, and population may have swelled by the end of the sixteenth century to 280,000. 'Naples had no equivalent in Christendom. . . The whole of southern Italy flocked to the city.'[32] It had silk and other luxury industries, but most of this immoderate growth was, as in southern Europe generally, a result of social decay. With such congestion food supplies could not be ensured, and the city could not be insulated from the currents of desperation sweeping the countryside and taking the form after about 1580 of hunger riots, brigandage, messianic excitement.[33]

In 1585 food riots in the capital combined with middle-class political grievances to start an insurrection which took on an anti-Spanish complexion. It was put down by a combination of food imports and brutal repression, government and aristocracy joining forces. In 1647 there was revolt again in Naples as well as in Palermo, set off by a new tax on fruit. It was directed less against Spain than against the local oppressors who were Spain's clients. Foreign rule had so deepened the antagonism of classes that there could be no national front such as Catalonia and Portugal, however stumblingly, could achieve. Instead, the outbreak had more resemblance to Valencia's in 1520. From the city it spread into the countryside, and there was a dingdong struggle between peasantry on one side, government and landlords on the other, ending in the defeat of the rebels and fierce reprisals.

In the Papal States too the regime was largely foreign, staffed by ecclesiastics from far and wide. Administrative progress was being

[30] A. de Maddalena, 'Rural Europe 1500–1750', in Cipolla, p. 297; Vries, *op. cit.*, p. 52.
[31] Jamison, p. 281.
[32] Braudel, *op. cit.*, p. 345.
[33] R. Villari, 'The Insurrection in Naples of 1585', in Cochrane, *The Late Italian Renaissance*, pp. 305–6.

made, on lines which denoted one more variant of the collegiate or
conciliar model. Within the Curia, 'congregations' headed by cardinals multiplied, with specific duties, under the direction of a
secretary of state; they were overhauled and put on a permanent
basis by Sixtus V (1585–90). It was a defect that posts too often
changed hands with each new pope. Another was the extravagance
which was subsidizing Catholic causes up and down Europe, and
spending liberally on the beautification of Rome, for the sake of
international as well as domestic prestige. Taxation soared: by the
end of the sixteenth century three quarters of all papal income was
being raised at home.[34] Resort was had here too to sale of offices,
mostly sinecures devised to be sold, whose salaries then ate into the
revenue. External loans were raised through bankers, all over Italy
and even abroad. Financial needs saved Jews from molestation.

Excluded from any share in government, nobles took different
paths. Many gravitated to the capital, where they fell helplessly into
debt through trying to live up to its novel style of magnificence.
This splendid Rome, the magnet that drew them, thus paid a
political return for its heavy cost. Meanwhile, economic decline
was overtaking central, like southern, Italy towards 1600, after a
spell of relative prosperity. Landlords tried to recoup their losses at
the expense of the peasantry, by usurpation of village commons and
rights. In this they were imitated by the men of means who rented
or bought up many of their estates.[35] Others reverted, as in
Catalonia and other regions, to still very recent habits of feudal
lawlessness; they connived at or dabbled in the banditry which
erupted in the closing decades of the century, an inarticulate expression of social unrest and peasant impoverishment. The papal hotch-
potch of territories had no sort of historical unity, no such common
tradition as even Naples or Sicily had; and the artificial city of Rome
was peculiarly unfitted to give the village any political ideas or aid.
This helps to explain why agrarian ferment failed to rise to any
higher level. For the higher classes brigandage had the advantage of
diverting the anger of the masses, and splitting the peasantry. Order
was restored by 1595, not through any reforms but by dint of brute
force and mass executions. Rome had the same treatment for its
rebel poor as for heretics abroad. Sterile torpor followed, closely
akin to the Spanish south of the peninsula.

---

[34] ʟ. Delumeau, 'Political and Administrative Centralisation in the Papal State',
ibid., p. 298.
[35] Procaccio, pp. 181–2.

Northern Italy made a good recovery after the wars ended in 1559, but no more than a temporary one. In the first half of the seventeenth century the country's total population may have sagged from 13 to 11 million, that of the north may have fallen by a quarter;[36] exports shrank to little more than agricultural produce, carried by foreign shipping. Spanish overlordship, with its habitual conservative bias, and enforced religious uniformity, was among the enfeebling causes; others must be looked for in the country's own socio-economic structure. Unlike the German free cities, those of northern Italy expanded politically over the countryside, and in so doing lost much of their original nature. Again unlike the German cities, which bred patricians but not despots, many though not all of them were so deeply infected by the feudal spirit of contention for sole power that from republics they turned into autocracies.

Of this, Spain's recent acquisition, Milan, was a prominent example. Charles V and his heirs were dukes of Milan, ruling through governors, not viceroys. It and its province of Lombardy were centrally placed in upper Italy, much of which was a patchwork of Spanish satellites. There was always a force of regulars on the spot, with one eye on the Milanese, the other on the French. A local militia also existed, on a modest scale because of the government's fear, shared by so many others in Europe, of arming its own people.[37] Under Charles there was codification of law, bringing more uniformity to a province whose other towns still preserved many of their own ways. In 1545 detailed regulations concerning official duties were promulgated. They were part of the state-building common to most of Europe, but as everywhere at that early stage much administrative confusion and inefficiency persisted, however lucid the paper scheme.[38]

A small ark of autonomy was a Senate, set up not long since under French auspices and grudgingly allowed to continue. It was the rallying-point of a magistracy sensitive, like its exemplar the Paris Parlement, to any invasion of its domain, and trying with dwindling success to assert a right of registering or vetoing edicts. More effective was the church's defence of its franchises. In extensive kingdoms the church could identify itself with monarchy, but in

[36] Vries, *op. cit.,* pp. 4–5. Cf. C. M. Cipolla, 'The Economic Decline of Italy', in Pullan. He points out that Italy's former large exports were being crippled by foreign competition, and antiquated methods due to excessive guild control.

[37] Visconti, p. 439.

[38] *ibid.*, pp. 407, 436–7.

circumstances like Italy's it might take sides with regional feeling against the new centralism. This attitude was epitomized by the aristocratic archbishop of Milan from 1564 to 1584, canonized as St Carlo Borromeo; an unswerving paladin of orthodoxy, but one who saw little need of Spanish pikes to prop it, none at all of the Spanish Inquisition.

Industry in Milan and other towns was active down to about 1600, to an accompaniment of rising prices. Mining, chiefly of iron, was also brisk. The plain of southern Lombardy was fertilized by a vast irrigation network, which demanded heavy investment and made for large estates,[39] with a more capitalistic bent than the mere feudal rack-renting of southern Italy. An enquiry in 1547 revealed that peasants owned most of the poor hill soil, but scarcely any land on the rich plain. On the estates rice cultivation was coming in, with seasonal labour harshly exploited.[40] Spanish rule lent vigorous support to water control;[41] the neglect of irrigation in Spain itself is one of many evidences of how little exchange of useful ideas and methods took place among the dominions of the crown. Clashes were frequent between the authorities and landowners, who could not be prevented from grabbing water supplies, as elsewhere they grabbed common lands, and could not be forced to submit to measurement and taxing of the water they used, as elsewhere they refused to be taxed on their acres.

Humbler folk could not evade revenue claims rendered exorbitant by wider Spanish interests which had to be satisfied. Billeting of troops on the province was one cause of the food shortage which led to furious rioting in the capital near the end of 1628. Dearth was followed in 1630 by plague, much land went out of cultivation, banditry spread. No political revolt was possible. The masses were leaderless; the upper classes, whatever disagreements there might be between them and the regime, stood far closer to it than to their own people. They paid it the compliment of aping Castilian court manners; 'Spanish etiquette' was still in vogue at Milan when the nineteenth century opened. Alien rule fostered an obsession with petty distinctions of rank, precedence, dress.[42]

In 1530 Charles's army took Florence after a long siege and snuffed out what was left of the republican tradition in favour of his

[39] R. B. Smith II. p. 113.
[40] Braudel, *op cit.*, pp. 74–5.
[41] R. B. Smith, I, p. 202; p. 125.
[42] Visconti, pp. 420–21.

clients, the Medici. Their oligarchic opponents had made small effort to mobilize the commonalty against them, and were now content to accept their protection. Cosimo I reigned until his death in 1574, and proved an able and highly successful ruler. He abolished the old government or *Signoria*, but he and his privy council worked through a senatorial body of forty-eight, drawn from the highest families, and legal norms were usually respected. In 1567 Cosimo made himself grand duke not of Florence but of Tuscany: he had grown up outside the walls, and was free of the assumption of both the old parties that 'the countryside existed to be exploited by the city of Florence.'[43] There was more equitable treatment of city, minor towns, and villages. His reliance on a volunteer rustic militia, with officers raised from the ranks, implies that this earned him some popular good will. He won approval also by taking the church in hand and improving the moral tone of the clergy.

Peace and order restored prosperity, with some assistance from constructive measures of a kind that small principalities might be readier to undertake, like some in Germany, than more exalted ones. Canals were dug, marshland drained, harbours improved. Other economic policies were, as so often, less helpful, and impeded innovation and progress.[44] More harmfully, Cosimo was a true absolutist in indulging in costly external aggrandizement. In the next century Florence was one of many Italian centres whose cloth manufactures were crippled by English and Dutch competition.[45] From about 1620 a prolonged decline set in. The propertied classes were turning away from industry and finance to land, and Florence becoming little but a focus of government.

Medici ambitions were not always palatable to Madrid; those of another client dukedom, Savoy, far less. This was one more of Europe's dual states, if one of the smallest. Savoy, its primitive nucleus, a nest of unruly nobles and their forts, belonged to the medley of small entities rooted in the Alps, as well as along the Pyrenees; they included Swiss cantons and free cities and ecclesiastical principalities. During the middle ages its rulers got possession of Piedmont, with a foothold on the sea at Nice. At first Piedmont had a very subordinate status, with Savoyards monopolizing most offices and benefices; and its Estates gained ground as the province's defender, while ducal poverty and need for tax-votes

[43] Hale, pp. 128, 133.
[44] Cochrane, *Florence*, p. 55.
[45] K. Glamann, 'The Changing Patterns of Trade', in CEHE, p. 225.

enabled them to assert themselves to good effect.[46]

In the sixteenth century a more equal balance was being reached. When, following French precedent, Latin was given up as the language of record, French was adopted for Savoy, Italian for Piedmont. As time went on the realm was growing less French and more Italian, a change marked by the shift of capital in the 1560s from Chambéry to Turin. This diminished Piedmont's need of its Estates. Moreover they were not a compact institution, for as in Castile the three chambers seldom met together; the third figured most, because it had most concern with money. It represented the 'communes', the country's little towns and their districts, but again one-sidedly, because deputies were drawn from an élite of leading families, mostly landowners or merchants.[47]

State-building processes were often most clearly visible in miniature, and Savoy, like Prussia a century later, was palpably building itself up out of very little, by drawing on outside experience and techniques, and emulating the ambitions of its betters. Those of its ruling family and their associates were precociously fanned by geography, and by the bellows of the long-drawn Franco-Spanish struggle. They seemed to have foundered during its later phases, when the little state was virtually partitioned between the two great rivals. Emanuel Filibert, who inherited a vanished throne in 1553, served Spain in the Netherlands, where he rose to be governor-general; thanks to this, with the peace of 1559 he was able to return to his patrimony.

Welcomed by a war-weary country, he was given a generous grant of money by the Estates in 1560, and never called them again. At this stage in the evolution of monarchy his ideal could not be other than autocracy and centralism. His old enemy France was his model, and French institutions were being combined with older home-grown ones. Parlements set up in both provinces during French occupation were retained as Senates. He used his money to enlist soldiers, and his soldiers to extract more taxes – the customary spiral of early modern Europe. To make more wealth available for extraction, he exerted himself to foster the economy. Irrigation was beginning to acquire the value it already had in Lombardy; canals were constructed, and supervison was simplified by ownership of all running water being vested in the state. Industry had to be started from

[46] Koenigsberger, 'The Parliament of Piedmont during the Renaissance 1460–1560', in *Estates and Revolutions, cit. supra,* pp. 30, 49.
[47] *ibid.,* pp. 35–8.

scratch, at first by outsiders induced to settle in Piedmont by the standard bait of tax exemptions and monopolies.

Unluckily the purpose of all this useful activity was to enable the dynasty to join its neighbours again at the gambling-table of war and conquest. Emanuel Filibert could not afford to hire many foreign troops, and to depend on his nobles and their levies was risky. Instead he, like Cosimo, organized a serviceable militia, each parish having to contribute men to the infantry, to be trained by professional drill-masters. They fought well enough. A minor ruler could be closer to the common man than a grand monarch, and pose as father of his people. He tried to improve on his early glow of popularity by issuing decrees in the 1560s against some feudal imposts, to please the peasantry, and by not enforcing them, to please the mostly hard-up nobility. In Piedmont, though far more slowly in Savoy, serfdom was fading, and there was a growing number of small farms occupied by tenants.[48] Also, after his first years Emanuel Filibert abandoned persecution of Protestants, numerous in the upland valleys. His knowledge of the Netherlands must have helped to suggest this prudence. But taxation was grinding, and his successor Charles Emanuel (1580–1630) hazarded the existence of the state, and forfeited part of its soil, and all his subjects' esteem, by reviving the old challenge to France, and then in 1610, still more rashly, trying to seize Milan with French backing.

Unlike Florence, Genoa was not falling under a monarchy, and to this some part of its continuing vitality may be ascribed. It and Venice shared the expansionism of all the city-states, but they were ports, their ambitions drew them seaward, and their territorial acquisitions were sufficiently detached from them to have less repercussions on domestic politics. In addition, financial capital in Genoa, merchant capital in Venice, did less than Florentine industry to call into being democratic forces and a conflict of classes leading towards deadlock and despotism. Social strife in Genoa was bitter enough, but not so deep-seated, being primarily between financial élite and middle-grade businessmen engaged in trade and industry. They were sparring until 1528, when Andrea Doria, the aristocratic chief, carried the city over to the Spanish side. Its naval strength made it a welcome auxiliary to Spain, while Spanish friendship ensured the triumph of the oligarchy.

Under the still more restrictive constitution imposed by Doria,

[48] Maddalena, *op. cit.*, p. 297.

authority was concentrated in a doge and eight governors elected for two years; a Grand Council of four hundred was chosen by lot from the nobility, with some places for the class below it. Friction between older and newer élite went on, and in the 1570s broke out in civil war, each side once more with foreign backing. The third party in the arena, the plebs, was too little organized to count for much, and the opposition was reluctant to mobilize it against the ruling class. Things quietened down in 1576 as the propertied classes coalesced into a single bloc, with some reduction of the taxes payable by the new men. It was one more of many cases of an upper middle class not striking for power with mass support, but preferring to push its way into the ranks of the aristocracy.

Opportunity outside helped to allay internal tensions. The Spanish connexion opened the way for loans and contracts in many lands, so profitable that in some areas Genoa was doing better out of Spanish power than Castile itself, a fact not rare in the history of empires. It was an astonishing display of energy, and cupidity, by a single city. And these Genoese were not businessmen alone. A good many entered Spanish service, and rose high in state or church. Most remarkable was Ambrogio Spinola, scion of the banking dynasty whose palace still stands among the most imposing of old Genoa. He applied his civilian talents to the organization of war in the Netherlands, and quickly became Spain's foremost commander.

Genoa wanted to colonize on its own account as well. Hemmed in on the mainland by Piedmont and Lombardy, it pitched on Corsica as its prize. The island was more a millstone round the city's neck than a useful asset, or an asset only to some individuals, much as the Netherlands were to some Spaniards. A rising in 1564 brought on fierce conflict. Revolts against Genoese tax-collectors persisted. Lack of unity prevented them from being successful. But the governor's authority, supposedly all-embracing, in practice was limited, like that of many a would-be absolute monarch, by some urban privileges and, more constrictingly, by the rights of the lords on their estates. Family feuds kept life disorderly; government efforts to improve agriculture came to as little as in the twin island of Sardinia.

In all Italy the one state stubbornly outside the Spanish sphere of influence (though Rome would very much have liked to be another) was Venice. Its sway extended far over the northeast mainland, where it may have profited by some lessons learned in its Levantine colonies before its unpopularity there helped the Turks to filch them

away. Venetian *podestàs* or governors were often better than most of
their kind. There were times during the Italian wars when plebeians
showed a preference for Venetian rule, against the local aristocracies seeking to restore their towns' independence.[49] Venice was
little inclined to build on this, and chose rather, much as Spain did,
to let local élites keep their place under its tutelage. Nor had it any
more desire than Spain to fuse its possessions together. Nothing
like a states-general to represent them took shape; to the republicans
of Venice such an institution was more alien than to most monarchies.

In Venice itself an old popular assembly disappeared after 1423,
and membership of the Grand Council was limited to the noble
families registered from 1506 in the Golden Book. From it
emanated the Senate or executive body, and, directly or indirectly,
the various councils or committees at work under the Doge. They
formed a closely interlocking machinery, far more so than Spain's
miscellany of councils, and were invested with awe-inspiring
secrecy, sometimes it may be more theatrical than real. Supreme
among them was the annually appointed Council of Ten, whose
duties were more strictly defined in 1582. Public life was notably
more stable than in Genoa; there was still less of any combination of
the disfranchised classes: poorer nobles squeezed out by the
oligarchy, *borghesia* or middle class, and *popolo minuto* or plebs.
Stability, and absence of any personal autocracy, nourished a spirit
of legalism. It was Venetian law that, more than anything else,
'won for the Republic such lasting respect'.[50]

Venetian shipping was handled by government and merchants in
partnership: the first built most of the galleys and decided on
voyages to be undertaken, and then auctioned them to associations
of traders.[51] It was a form of state capitalism natural to a city where
wealth and power were in the same hands, and must have helped to
fortify republican institutions. For seventy years after the victory
over the Turks at Lepanto in 1571, followed so closely by the loss to
them of Cyprus, Venice tried to avoid wars with them or anyone
else; but its shipping and commerce were suffering before 1600
from the irruption, aggressive and often piratical, of those northern
barbarians the English, and still more the Dutch, into the Mediterranean. There was a brief period when Venice seemed to be turning

[49] Procaccio, pp. 125–7. S. J. Woolf is sceptical about this; see 'Venice and the
Terraferma', in Pullan, p. 190.
[50] Molmenti, II, p. 21.
[51] Lane, part 3, p. 45..

towards the big-scale industrial development with which Europe's future lay. But glassware, printing, and above all woollen cloth, failed to sustain their impetus into the seventeenth century. Employers complained of the craft guilds and their conservatism, and of labour costs.[52] Excessive regulation of industry by the government has also been blamed, and it is certainly noteworthy that the regulatory passion was common to bureaucracies both republican and monarchical.

Merchant princes shunned the thickening perils of the sea by acquiring land in occupied Italy. There was a stimulus to cultivation in the need to ensure the city's food supplies, now that imports from the Black Sea could no longer be counted on. Investments were skilfully used in draining, for instance along the Adige river, and in promoting rice culture. Venetia, with Lombardy, formed part of a broad expanse of north Italy known over Europe for its flourishing agriculture. But investors seem to have come from a small circle of the richest Venetian families,[53] so that the ruling class was becoming still more exclusive. And when grain prices fell, further development was unprofitable.

Intrigue and corruption bedevilled the republic as they did the royal courts. Yet some better qualities survived, and Venice could be admired by other Italians, and looked at askance by Spaniards, as a stronghold of liberty. Plots were hatched against it at Milan; Venice refused to be browbeaten.[54] Friction with the Rome of the Counter-Reformation, aligned with Spain, was chronic. It led to an open breach in 1606, when a papal interdict was declared. Venice stood undaunted, with the patriotic monk Paolo Sarpi as its spokesman. He took his ground on the authority of the state, as derived directly from heaven: a republic as well as a king could set up divine right against ecclesiastical meddling. Relaxation of morals, extravagant living in defiance of long-standing sumptuary laws, the reign of glittering courtesans, were in their way another assertion of freedom, and congenial to the arts and to secular thought. Italy as a whole, the first country of Europe to leave the middle ages behind, though failing now to advance towards economic modernity was transmuting accumulated energy into intellectual, and still more into artistic, achievement.

[52] D. Sella, 'The Rise and Fall of the Venetian Woollen Industry', in Pullan, p. 117, stresses the loss of Turkish and Levantine markets, and Anglo-Dutch competiton, as causes of decline. On labour costs, see E. Pullan, 'Wage-earners and the Venetian Economy 1550–1603', *ibid*.

53 Procaccio, p. 173.

54 Hazlitt, pp. 161 ff.

4

The Netherlands

Seven provinces of the congeries making up the Netherlands, furthest outpost of Spanish power in Europe, broke away from it far more decisively than Portugal, into a different historical orbit. This polyglot corner of the Holy Roman Empire was from the late fourteenth century under a single rule, of the dukes of Burgundy and then their Habsburg heirs. Combination was forced on the area from above, but had old foundations in local sentiment, even though particularism remained strong.[1] It facilitated economic growth, and the Netherlands of the sixteenth century, if not yet a fully capitalist society, were exposed like England to much change and ferment. Old Flemish hives of industry were facing difficulties, but Antwerp was blossoming into Europe's busiest financial centre. Holland and Zeeland lived largely from the sea, and were indefatigable in the Baltic trade.

All this engendered social tensions. A true precursor of later absolutism, Burgundian rule gave the towns a helping hand against the nobility, powerful chiefly in the south, but within the towns helped patricians to subdue a still pugnacious democracy. Some of the proud nobles, following another often-repeated zigzag, resisted the first Habsburg, husband of the heiress, but they as well as the urban ruling cliques wanted the turbulent plebs put down; and having failed to prevent the state from overtopping them, they sought to make it their own. Its authority became 'the indispensable condition of the prestige which they enjoyed'.[2]

Charles V enlarged his Burgundian inheritance by dogged frontier fighting, of more interest to him than to his people;

[1] H. Pirenne, 'The Burgundian State', reprinted in A. J. Slavin (ed.), *The 'New Monarchies' and Representative Assemblies* (Boston, 1964), p. 29.
[2] *ibid.*, p. 30.

Map 2   *The Netherlands after the truce of 1609*

Guelders and Zutphen, surrendered by the duke of Cleves in 1543, brought the tally of provinces up to seventeen. After his German triumph in 1547 he was able to constitute them formally as the 'Burgundian Circle' of the Empire, but in reality to detach them from it. Brussels was taking its place as the capital, seat of an expanding bureaucracy surmounted by a Council of State for political matters, a Privy Council for administrative, and a treasury. A prominent place in these bodies, though the government preferred it to be more ornamental than substantial, was held by the great nobles, to whom went also the chief army commands, and the stadholderates or provincial governorships. Charles's sister Mary, widowed queen of Hungary and from 1531 his deputy, had to have regulations drawn up to keep stadholders from getting too big for their boots.[3]

Each province had its own Estates, in most of which only a small part of the public was represented in any direct way; Friesland's were more broadly based. Generally the towns, in this most thoroughly urbanized region of Europe, had most to say. In Holland the clergy had dropped out, the nobles had one voice, to speak in theory for the whole countryside: the biggest towns made up the rest. Most towns were increasingly oligarchical. In Brabant, and in Flanders until the revolt of Ghent in 1539, guild craftsmen had local representation, and might be obstructive when it came to voting money. In Brussels nine chief craft guilds nominated two spokesmen each to 'The Eighteen', a committee with weight in civic affairs.

The States-General was no more than a gathering of delegates from the provincial Estates. It was summoned repeatedly in Charles V's reign, because of his aching need for money from this richest of all his possessions. Under pressure of war crown lands, never at all adequate to sustain the government, were having to be sold off, and as in Spain it was borrowing, and selling annuities, at a ruinous pace.[4] It was simpler, when large sums were wanted, to ask a single assembly for them. It could be hoped that deputies would prove more manageable at the capital, away from their home bases – a calculation not uncommonly made by rulers of fragmented territories, each with its own assembly. Here it was frustrated by the

[3] P. Rosenfeld, 'The Provincial Governors of the Netherlands from the Minority of Charles V to the Revolt', in Cohn, pp. 261–3.
[4] M. Baelde, 'Financial Policy . . . in the Netherlands under Charles V and Philip II (1530–1560)', *ibid.*, p. 216.

tenacity with which Netherlanders stuck to the principle of the mandate, and of reference back to the provinces; members of provincial bodies often had to refer back in the same way to their constituents. Full powers for deputies might easily play into the hands of a government which knew how to bribe or browbeat them. The States-General could not be got to vote away its independence by granting a permanent money supply, the darling wish of every government.

Taxes were paid with all the less alacrity because they were wanted for wars whose purposes in the Netherlanders' eyes went far beyond the sole legitimate one of defence against France. The privileged could spare their pockets by shuffling off most of the burden on to towns without representation, and the countryside.[5] Everywhere in Europe property showed much the same evasiveness. Humbler folk had no such recourse, and life was hard enough for them already. Population was growing, food production was not keeping pace with it. Labour riots were frequent, as among the textile workers at Antwerp where wages, niggardly at the beginning of the century, were being outstripped by prices.[6]

In 1539 the artisans of Ghent rebelled against tax demands, but were speedily suppressed because, with the poor clamouring for food or money, the well off – weavers' guild as well as patricians – rallied to the government.[7] It was a foreshadowing of many events to come. Social rancour was finding vent, as it had done in the older towns for centuries before the Reformation, in stirrings of religious dissent. In 1533 there was a millenarian outbreak in Haarlem, with a communistic tinge. The price rise benefited peasants with food to sell, and may account for their passivity during the German upheaval in 1525, and the fact that few of them joined Anabaptism, 'the craftsman's religion of social protest'.[8] Anabaptism was crippled by persecution, but Lutheranism and Calvinism were also coming in, from Germany and France, and attracting some of the middle classes and lower nobility as well as the poor.

A dismal financial situation faced Philip at his accession, and early in 1557 he was obliged to suspend interest payments, a heavy

[5] J. Lynch, *Spain under the Habsburgs* I (Oxford, 1964), pp. 275, 282.
[6] C. Verlinden *et al.*, 'Price and Wage Movements in Belgium in the Sixteenth Century', in Burke, pp. 56, 59–60, 79–80.
[7] See a contemporary account in Rowen, pp. 17 ff.
[8] H. G. Koenigsberger, *Estates and Revolutions* (Cornell University Press, 1971), p. 162.

blow to Antwerp financiers and to public confidence. The States-General would only agree to a grant on condition of being allowed to supervise its raising and spending. This was not unusual in local finance, and not much objected to by rulers; but central revenue, everywhere for the most part earmarked for war, Philip wanted to have under his own control. Peace in 1559 found the country badly shaken, many districts devastated, the poor embittered, the nobles often in debt and full of the gratitude they felt the government owed them for their services.

Clearly firm measures were called for, and years in the Netherlands made it the only one of Philip's dominions, except Castile, that he had much first-hand knowledge of, and where he could feel confident of hitting on the right tactics. Both his own bent and the momentum of absolutism were towards centralized Castilian control. It was equally a matter of course that ecclesiastical machinery would be brought into play. His scheme, quickly worked out with his advisers, was to raise the scanty number of dioceses to fourteen, with three archbishops. Prelates would be chosen by him, and would stiffen the Council of State and serve as his mouthpiece in the States-General. It was a prospect repugnant to the higher nobles who wanted to be top dogs; the special inquisitorial arrangements to be made in each diocese were a menace to all who feared Spanish despotism, as well as to heretics, and might well have disruptive effects on commercial life. It was for similar reasons that Naples and Milan refused to have the Spanish Inquisition foisted on them.

Philip was moving in the same direction as Charles I sixty years later when he set out to rule England without Parliament. He would have given himself a better chance to master his difficulties by staying at Brussels, but as soon as war ended he had to depart to Spain. To carry out his programme he left the son of his father's quondam chancellor, Granvelle. Appropriately a churchman, and now promoted cardinal-archbishop, this man was detested by the aristocracy as a parvenu, by all as an outsider and as arrogant and heavy-handed. Ill-humour was quickly astir, with a novel national sentiment, reflected in a flood of pamphlets and ballads, breaking through localist feeling.[9] Literacy was well disseminated, and a propaganda battle was to be waged continuously, alongside political and military struggle. But Philip was never to have to face the

---

[9] Geyl, *The Revolt,* p. 89; cf. P. Burke, *Popular Culture in Early Modern Europe* (London, 1978), pp. 260–61.

whole country in revolt. Social divisions cut deeper than geographical. All revolutions have been fired by multiple social forces
and causes, and this one more than most suffered from a diversity of
cross purposes. One result, perhaps, was the emergence amid great
events of few great personalities.

Opposition began, hesitantly, with the magnates, who felt the
new centralism threatening their pre-eminence. Lesser nobles were
ready to follow a lead from them, and then often to go further.
Philip was willing to make concessions to buy the grandees off; in
1564 he removed Granvelle. But agitation had spread to the lower
orders in the crowded southern towns, and was fanned by economic distress and unemployment, exceptionally severe in the
'hunger-year' 1566. Hunger and heresy spread together, and outbreaks of iconoclasm alarmed the higher classes as well as the
government. In brief and confused fighting, the forces of order
gained the upper hand. It was the hackneyed story of an advanced
urban society, such as Florence had been in Italy, paralysed politically by its social antagonisms.

Collision extended as far as Franche Comté, that curious outlier
of the Burgundian kingdom, French-speaking like the Walloon
provinces, important because it lay on the 'Spanish road' from
Milan to Brussels. It was ruled through a governor, a local aristocrat; he was chronically at odds with a Parlement resembling that of
Paris, the citadel of a bourgeoisie which was pushing its way into
landowning, partly by getting nobles and peasants into debt.[10]
Estates voted money, and handled finance through a committee.
Philip's centralizing programme had some benefits to hold out,
judicial reform for instance;[11] but it aimed at restricting local rights,
and especially at clipping the wings of the Parlement. There was a
sharp encounter in 1567; here too religion mingled with other
quarrels.

With the defeat of these first risings, it was the right moment for
Philip to show himself again in the Netherlands, and there was talk
at Madrid of a visitation. Temperament and a bureaucrat's im-
mobility kept him at the centre of his spider-web. Instead he sent his
man of iron, Alva, who arrived in 1567 with a steamroller army.
Egmont and Hoorn, the heads of the aristocratic faction, were
executed. Other executions, fines, and confiscations had their due
effect; the diocesan reorganization was completed. 'Everyone',

[10] Febvre, pp. 36 ff., 149 ff., 170 ff.
[11] *ibid.*, pp. 467–8.

Alva wrote to Philip, 'must be made to live in constant fear of the roof breaking down over his head'[12] – a ghoulish maxim which links sixteenth-century absolutism with twentieth-century dictatorship. His next goal was to secure a permanent revenue, free of interference by the Estates, to pay for a standing army of occupation. His newfangled taxes might have the merit of spreading the load to wealthy folk little in the habit of paying, but the 'Tenth Penny' came as a shock to all the trading classes and the workmen they employed. Business was paralysed, and property and patriotism joined hands.

The country's loose-knit structure was now an advantage in some ways: resistance crushed in the south could start up somewhere else. Its best refuge was salt water; 'Sea-beggars' were carrying on what was half guerrilla warfare, half piracy, congenial to many lesser nobles who took part in something like the spirit of the Knights' War in Germany in 1522. But it was the Sea-beggars' intervention during 1572–6 that transformed Holland and Zeeland, hitherto quiescent, into the hearth and home of rebellion. Civic oligarchies, particularly strong and exclusive here, were hardly in a position to prevent this. They were not menaced by angry impoverished masses, with which cooperation would have been as difficult as for the southern patriciates; but they were unpopular with many who disliked their monopoly of power, and could only hope to retain it now by going with the tide, and accepting the leadership of William of Orange. This great lord, half foreign by birth and connexions, had moved gradually, ambiguously, from advocacy of toleration to uncompromising hostility to Spain. None of the other grandees were capable of such an evolution, but in the north they mattered far less.

Alva's patience wore out before his opponents' courage, and in 1573 he left. After as before his reign of blood, the government at Brussels suffered from the vagaries of a distant and dilatory Madrid. Its other weak point was the impossibility of meeting swollen army costs, even with Spanish subsidies. In 1576 another phase of the rebellion began, southern again but this time Catholic; it was provoked by the misbehaviour of the foreign troops, and the 'Spanish Fury' at Antwerp brought about a compact with the north, the 'Pacification of Ghent'. For a while the States-General seemed to be taking over the reins. But it was too cumbrous a body to be able to direct events; and very soon social divisions were breaking out

---

[12] Geyl, *The Revolt,* pp. 102–3.

again. Paradoxically the south was less fit to carry on the struggle because it had more of a democratic or radical tradition than the north to incite and to divide it. In 1579 the four Walloon provinces formed a 'Union of Arras', quickly steered by nervous landowners and city fathers into coming to terms with Spain. All old privileges were confirmed, and the nobles came off particularly well. Flanders soon followed, under the lead of its premier nobleman, the duke of Aerschot.

The six northern provinces had already grouped themselves together in January 1579 in the 'Union of Utrecht'. Outlawed by Philip, William replied with his *Apology*, in which he morally outlawed his enemy, calling on all Philip's subjects, oppressed Castilians as well as Aragonese and Italians, and even the Moriscos of Granada, 'to learn from our example that this tyrant ought not to be endured on the earth'.[13] This philippic helped to prepare northern opinion for the final step, one of 'unparalleled audacity', abjuration in 1581 of the royal authority.[14] Kings, it was asserted then, were made to serve their peoples, not peoples their kings. As a schoolroom adage, Philip and his brother monarchs would have concurred with this, but proclaimed by armed rebels it was truly revolutionary doctrine; and successful revolt might unsettle other Spanish dominions, as Wiliam hoped. Philip would fight to the bitter end to prevent it. His antagonist was murdered in 1584, but the independence movement was solid enough in the north by then to withstand the shock. In the 1590s another round of war between Spain and France relieved pressure. Lengthy negotiations ended in 1609 in a twelve year truce, a *de facto* recognition of the United Provinces.

All this time, power there was being kept and consolidated by the 'Regent' class of patricians, whose interests the slow, protracted warfare suited. For defence against sieges the urban militias disbanded by Alva had to be set on foot again, but they and the guilds were allowed no share in government. William would have liked the lower middle strata they were recruited from, his most ardent supporters, to be enfranchised. But though he became an unshakable patriot he was never a democrat, and in any case a frontal attack on the oligarchy would have meant fatal discord. Thus the masses were getting not much more than a change of masters, sweetened by

[13] Part of the text is given in G. Griffiths, *Representative Government in Western Europe in the Sixteenth Century* (Oxford, 1968), p. 525.
[14] Harrison, pp. 212–13.

a change of religion if they cared for it. Streams of refugees from the south might strengthen them, and were looked at with misgivings by conservatives, as likely firebrands. On the whole the effect seems rather to have been to deprive the popular forces of cohesion.

Religion was another complicating factor. Calvinists, though even with southern additions only a small minority, were the keenest patriots, but their zeal also separated them from the majority, and might even make them intolerant of their Catholic neighbours. Their faith had undergone a lengthy exposure, as nowhere else in Europe, to Anabaptism, and imbibed something of its outlook. 'In the period between 1550 and 1650 a considerable number of Calvinist writers urged that property should be held as much as possible in common.'[15] Not surprisingly, William as well as the Regents was much more sympathetic to the emerging 'Libertinism', nationalist but not in any sectarian way religious. Moreover, like Cavour in nineteenth-century Italy, he regarded foreign aid as essential, and no foreign government would succour a movement socially as well as politically subversive; rebel burghers, even the wealthiest, were bad enough.[16] William even held it necessary to invite a foreign prince to the throne. He had no belief in a republic's survival; his experience of the shufflings of Dutch politicians could not warrant optimism. His candidate was the duke of Anjou, brother of Henry III of France. Relations with France proved as uneasy as Catalonia's were to be, and ended in fiasco. Later on there were similar misunderstandings with England.

By way of constitution there was nothing more, now or later, than the Union of Utrecht, which bound the signatories (joined in 1594 by Groningen) to an indissoluble league, while reserving to each their own rights and customs. A uniform coinage and taxes were to be adopted; joint concerns were to be thrashed out at meetings of representatives, where majority opinions would be binding. But there was never any question of their merging into a single entity; no one was prepared to sacrifice local power, and insistence on local rights also served to keep the mass of the people divided. William soon had to complain that no executive body was being set up, authorized to take military decisions.[17] A disgruntled critic in 1583 accused Regents of dawdling and spinning out the war because of the pickings it gave them, and argued that burghers

[15] Hyma, p. 338.
[16] Wilson, pp. 15, 23.
[17] Text in Rowen, pp. 74 ff.

ought not to meddle with strategy, but leave it to noblemen, who had a natural gift for it.[18]

In 1585, on the English ally's insistence, an executive Council of State was set up, but it was relegated to the background by the States-General, easily enough because its members were hardly more than civil servants, dependent on the politicians for their places and for finance.[19] The States-General itself was a minute body, seldom above a dozen deputies taking part, and the old practice of mandates still an impediment. However, under the spur of necessity conventions were adopted that made for smoother running, and the country's diminutive size and mostly good communications, and the sluggish pace of the war, made the time spent on consultation not too damaging. In addition, Holland was far bigger and richer than any of its partners, and inevitably held the lead; often as the others might chafe, it was difficult for them to combine against it. War was slowly hammering provinces into nation.

Holland itself was far from fully integrated, and issues arose on which an individual town, usually Amsterdam, chose to go its own way. In its Estates many more towns were acquiring seats, but it was only little by little that a share of responsibility could broaden their political vision. Statesmanship was supplied a good deal by incomers from other provinces, or from the south,[20] in the same way that outsiders were to be prominent in the building of Brandenburg-Prussia. Oldenbarnevelt, a native of Utrecht, as Grand Pensionary and Advocate of Holland and its leading figure in the States-General, rose to be a kind of prime minister of the Union, such as the times required whether in republic or in monarchy. He was typical of his class in deeming democracy an evil worse still than tyranny.[21] He worked in partnership with Maurice, the young son of William chosen to succeed him, who held five of the stadholderates. What power these now conferred was ill-defined; but Maurice was content to concentrate on the army, and leave administration to the older man.

Nothing like a Cromwellian army took shape. There was a lack of yeoman material to be forged into Ironsides; and prudent politicians were even more reluctant to mobilize the people than in the

---

[18] Kossman and Mellink, pp. 252–5.
[19] Tex. pp. 130–31.
[20] *ibid.*, p. 31.
[21] *ibid.*, p. 71.

English civil war, which by contrast was to be fought out in a rapid sequence of pitched battles. Their caution spared them any crisis like the Leveller challenge of 1647–9. Like Venice, they fought at sea with their own sailors, on land with foreign professionals. Their army improved with the years, with fewer but more reliable troops, because burgher employers were better than any monarchy at budgeting for regular pay.[22] They might none the less be just as egotistic as their counterparts abroad. Real property was taxed, commercial wealth escaped. War finance rested largely on new indirect taxes, and on borrowing:[23] in other words, the poor had to bear the brunt, while the rich were offered a rewarding investment. They could also farm the excise dues, annually auctioned. In all these fiscal arrangements malpractices abounded, sharpening social resentments which sometimes burst out in rioting.[24] It was one of many ironies of the times that a rebellion, one of whose chief causes was hatred of new taxes, should end by loading the public with them. England was to fare similarly.

Social disharmony underlay the worsening relations after 1609 between the republic's two leading personalities. Oldenbarnevelt harboured suspicions that Maurice was aiming at a crown; Maurice disliked the peace, because war fed his authority. Oldenbarnevelt was equally fond of power, and his methods of engrossing and deploying it were often tortuous, as indeed they had to be since it arose from personal ascendancy more than from his official attributes. The nobility was with Orange: the army was its mainstay, a royal court would advance it. But as a class it was weak; hence Maurice had to turn to the minor provinces jealous of Holland's preponderance, and to a less natural entente with the radical lower middle classes, whose Calvinist fervour might make them welcome renewal of war.

Forces so heterogeneous could find a common platform only in religion. Relations between church and state, left unsettled during the fighting, continued troublesome, as they were in every land where Calvinism took root. The Erastian-minded Regents were determined to keep the upper hand, and were aided by a bitter schism between the stricter Calvinists and the new, milder wing, the Arminians. Holland, with Amsterdam dissenting, lent its coun-

---

[22] Geyl, *The Revolt*, p. 219.
[23] G. Parker, 'The Emergence of Modern Finance in Europe 1500–1730', in Cipolla, pp. 572–3.
[24] Tex, pp. 350–51; J. de Vries, *The Economy of Europe in an Age of Crisis, 1660–1750* (Cambridge, 1976), p. 202; Haley, p. 69.

tenance to the latter, and in 1617, tutored by the firmly anti–clerical
Pensionary, authorized its towns to enlist regular soldiers as a
safeguard against anti–Arminian and Orangist agitation. In August
1618 Maurice persuaded the States-General to override Holland and
order the disbanding of these troops, and then the arrest of Oldenbarnevelt and others. A grave precedent was being set, since it
meant interference by the Union in the affairs of a member-
province.[25]

No social disorder erupted, despite the intense excitement prevailing; between them, theology and politics successfully kept
questions of wealth and poverty out of sight. Oldenbarnevelt was
tried and executed as a public enemy; his henchman Grotius escaped
into exile. The Synod of Dort upheld Calvinist dogma, but did not
release its preachers from official leading-strings. The political
swing did not go nearly as far as might have been expected, even
with war with Spain breaking out afresh in 1621. Decades of struggle
for independence had left the bulk of the public 'thoroughly
republican',[26] and conviction that sovereignty lay with the provinces, not the Union, was impregnable. Maurice died in 1625. His
half-brother Frederick Henry gave the Regents some uneasiness by
his efforts to enlarge his sphere, and by affecting a semi-monarchical
style. But his family connexions abroad and half-foreign court and
army were not much more palatable to the radical elements which
liked to identify their nationalism with the house of Orange. In all
the years to come, whether Regents or Orange were in the saddle,
there was the same 'dictatorship of the upper middle class'.[27]
Orange as a quasi-royal figurehead lent the republic respectability in
Europe; Orange prestige with the people helped to keep their
grudges within bounds.

The cream of the Regent class, those holding office as burgomasters, came of business stock, but by early in the seventeenth
century were evolving into a specialized administrative section,
living on property, perquisites licit or illicit, and investment
income. Any governing body must put a certain distance between
itself and the dominant economic interests, if it is to be able to
regulate relations between them and the rest of the community.
These political managers could even feel some dislike of business-

---

[25] Tex, pp. 643 ff. On Calvinist views of church and state relations, see D.
Nobbs, *Theocracy and Toleration. A Study in the Disputes in Dutch Calvinism from
1600 to 1650* (Cambridge, 1938).
[26] Tex, pp. 661–62.
[27] Renier, pp. 26–7.

men who might outstrip them in wealth and display.[28] Close ties persisted, all the same. Deputies to the States-General might rejoice in their title of 'High Mightinesses', but these patricians could not acquire patents of nobility, as the rich bourgeois of the southern Netherlands were doing. It was an important departure from a prevalent European pattern of behaviour.

There was no model for the United Provinces except the Swiss federation. There was far more external pressure to weld them together, of war or fear of war, and exigencies of foreign trade. They owed much also to a not too long-drawn spell of centralizing rule. Their machinery of government looked clumsily full of over-lapping or divided functions. Yet it may have been little, if at all, more so in reality than Spain's, with its confusion of councils and competing authorities which the crown was never able to straighten out. In the long run survival of so many provincial boundary-lines may have hampered further economic expansion; and national security was repeatedly jeopardized by the 'landward' provinces being preoccupied with the army while those of the seaboard thought only of the navy – a navy whose management was dispersed among five separate admiralties. But all political combinations are more or less artificial and fallible. Here shortcomings could at least be held in check to some extent by an exceptional freedom of criticism and the press.

Heavy urban population made the country uniquely dependent on industry and exports, and the ruling group's close contact with economic life, and undeniable competence in pursuing economic aims, go far to explain its success in keeping power in a country altering in many ways so drastically. Laissez-faire was no part of its philosophy, and it displayed more aptitude for mercantilism than any of the monarchies. It had a hand in the founding in 1609 of the Bank of Amsterdam, followed in 1611 by the Bourse. This was the first public bank of northern Europe, and although until 1683 it was restricted in its operations, its advent cleared out of the way a swarm of dubious private bankers or moneylenders, greatly to the benefit of legitimate business.[29] By mid-century Calvinists formerly cen-sorious of everything savouring of usury were ready to pronounce that a bank under proper civic licence was not disreputable.[30] From

---

[28] Tex, pp. 299 ff. On the town governments cf. Haley, p. 52.

[29] Barker, p. 144. Cf. Haley, p. 40: 'The Dutch were not remarkable for many innovations, but rather for the more effective and intensive use of methods already known elsewhere' (i.e. in finance).

[30] Hyman, p. 333.

the early 1630s a network of new transport canals was being constructed to link the towns and reduce costs. Burton contrasted
Holland's 'neat cities and populous towns, full of most industrious
artificers', with England's decay and poverty.[31]

Many of these artificers were sheltered by craft guilds, whose
continuance paralleled that of the old governing bodies; the two
must have buttressed each other. Both avoided the petrifaction
overtaking similar institutions in most countries, like Cortes and
guild in Spain. But by a tacit bargain the guilds did not press too
perversely for a share in town government, and the authorities left
their framework intact, with its limits on the number of apprentices
taken on and hours of work. Regents could not be immune from the
fear felt by all conservative regimes of the growth of an urban
proletariat. Strikes by cloth workers in Leiden or Amsterdam, talk
of a community of goods, were reminders of the spectre of social
protest, the more so because the towns always had an unruly rabble
of vagrants, beggars, foreigners, unemployed.[32] To keep the populace on the leash there was the burgher militia, an authentic feature
of bourgeois rule which was to reach its acme in the National Guard
of 1789. Its cohesion would be destroyed if the guilds foundered; as
it was, the country had an unusually large, stable middle class.

Marx thought, too sweepingly, of a Holland with more capital
than the rest of Europe put together and a working class more
brutally exploited than any other.[33] Where this picture was most
correct was in Haarlem and Leiden, the two main textile centres,
gorged with refugee labour more easily sweated than most. Inflation, down to 1650, further depressed wages. Some cushioning
was, nevertheless, provided. Burgomasters, here as in some of the
German towns, were not without a streak of paternalism. From a
prudential point of view they could not help being more alive to the
risks of excessive neglect of the urban poor than England's landlord-
rulers. Many erstwhile Catholic properties had been made over to
charity, others to education. Local dues were levied for relief. As in
Scotland, churches collected for the deserving poor.

In the United Provinces the principal towns kept up the old bans
on craft-work outside their walls, while in some countries, with
England in the van, industry was moving into the countryside in
search of cheap labour. But there were newer industries where scale

31 *The Anatomy of Melancholy* (Bohn Library, London, 1923) I, p. 96.
32 Renier, pp. 101–2.
33 *Capital I* chap. 31.

and technology made room for capitalism. Several of them, like paper-making, utilized power from windmills. This and other technical innovations gave Holland a long lead in shipbuilding, and in the carrying trade. Shipping was another sphere conquered by capital. From early in the seventeenth century squadrons of fishing vessels were owned by firms which employed the skippers and crews;[34] in the carrying trade it was the same. An ill-paid, ill-fed race of seamen made up a good part of the labour force, and was often mutinous.[35]

Population may have doubled between 1550 and 1650, going on rising through the early seventeenth century when in many other countries it was declining; and in Holland half of it was urban.[36] This was enough by itself to ensure a qualitative change in life, a transformed mentality. It meant also a heavy demand for food, partly met by imports from the Baltic. Agriculture was being overhauled, and capital, debarred from rural industry, was making its way into the countryside by another route. Extensive new tracts were reclaimed by private enterprise. In western areas, more than in the landward provinces, the seigneurial fabric had collapsed during the war of independence, and small holdings multiplied. But these were soon being bought up by bourgeois investors, who took tenants on short leases and insisted on up-to-date methods.[37] In this defeudalized countryside they were under far less temptation than buyers in France or England to ape the modes of aristocratic forerunners.

Last but not least as an outlet for the entrepreneurial spirit, and one untrammelled by any scruples of policy or morality, was imperialism. Characteristically, jealousies among half a dozen towns eager to break into the East Indies hindered a concerted drive, until Oldenbarnevelt and the government took the initiative in getting speculators together in 1602 to launch the Netherlands East India Company. Before very long it felt entitled to behave like a sovereign state, not surprisingly in a country where each province did the same. Native risings were put down with a savagery that

[34] Vries, *op. cit.*, p. 95.
[35] Boxer, p. 77. Cf. Haley, p. 45: 'As in the case of the sailors who manned the ships, industrial growth was won at the price of terrible conditions for those who laboured.'
[36] K.. Glamann, 'European Trade 1500–1750', in Cipolla, p. 443. J. Dupâquier, 'Population', in NCMH, XIII, p. 94, gives estimates for the population of the United Provinces of 1·2 to 1·3 million in 1550, 1·4 to 1·6 in 1600.
[37] A. de Maddalena, 'Rural Europe 1500–1750', in Cipolla, p. 296.

might have been learned from Alva's reign of terror in the Netherlands.

In the end England was to incubate modern industrialism, while Holland fell out of the race. Lacking coal and steam, its technology marked the highest point attainable by an old-world line of progress, rather than the start of a distinctively modern one[38]. An equal clog may have been the guild; and Holland, like Spain and Portugal, came to depend excessively on colonial tribute. None the less, it was in its time the great path-finder between Europe's past and future. With all its conservative features, its revolutionary deeds could not be forgotten. Louis XIV would be anxious to bury them under the feet of royal armies. Venice too was cradled on the waves, but it lay between the fumes of the Turkish hookah and the Catholic censer; the United Provinces were neighboured by northern France, England, Scandinavia, all that part of Europe which was moving forward, each region helping to push the others on. Politically Holland, and its successor England, demonstrated how the old liberties, in most of Europe drying up, with fresh social and economic currents to animate them could exhibit fresh vitality. By contrast with them, the imposing carriage-way of absolutism was a blind alley, or a divagation, if for a while a needful one, from the true line of European history.

This was fitly illustrated by the destiny of the southern Netherlands. In 1598, between making peace with France and trying to make his last peace with heaven, Philip II was constrained to fall back on the reverse of his initial centralizing plan, and erect the provinces into an autonomous principality under his daughter Isabel and her Austrian husband. An arrangement on these lines for the whole country had often been mooted by his father, much readier to treat his empire as a loose family federation. Isabel and her consort were not simply Spanish puppets, but their position was anomalous, since their state secretary was appointed, their army paid and directed, by Madrid. Government grew more efficient than before, under the guidance of rulers on the spot. Administrative bodies were 'extremely well integrated', and run by 'first-rate secretaries'.[39] Provincial Estates lingered on, and even came to have more to do with spending as well as voting money, and with the running of local affairs.[40] But after 1600, when the government

---

[38] Vries, *op. cit.*, p. 94.
[39] Carter, p. 249.
[40] Parker, *Spain and the Netherlands*, pp. 165–6.

secured an annual money grant, the States–General faded away. After the renewal of war between Spain and the United Provinces in 1621 any shadow of autonomy was lost; 1624 brought reversion to direct Spanish rule.

Economically there was some revival after 1609, as population recovered from a heavy drain. It showed itself chiefly in agriculture, where skill and readiness to experiment were of long standing. Even in industry there was some new enterprise. But convalescence could only be partial. One obstacle was the guild framework, which the conservative government was positively anxious to preserve, instead of merely tolerating. Still more zealously it helped to restore the church, on Counter-Reformation lines, with complete thought-control; the consequent intellectual nullity was the most striking of all disparities between the unfree and the free Netherlands. Physically the country was soon being hamstrung once more by a long series of wars, in the course of which a good deal of territory, including Franche Comté, was lost to France. With all this, in their own way the southern Netherlands were being fashioned into what would ultimately be Belgium; another creation of nation by state, in this case a foreign state, with religion for medium.

Map 3 *France and its borderlands about 1600*

5

France

With great regional diversity, and a national temper – as Frenchmen early began to observe – restless and self-assertive, France was acquiring a form of state whose fits of instability would help to preserve it from Spanish stagnation. Monarchy came out of the Hundred Years War furnished with a small standing army and a permanent tax, the *taille* – the two linked requirements of all governments eager like Lady Macbeth for sovereign sway and masterdom. A century of internal peace, economic expansion, population growth, provided the platform for the Renaissance monarchy of Francis I (1515–47) and his son Henry II (1547–59). Relations between luxurious court and aristocracy were amicable, but the latter remained more high-spirited than could be good for the country, because the regime had been shaped more by resistance to foreign invasion, less by overcoming of baronial conflict, than in Castile or England.

Man may be a political animal, but devising new institutions, or ideas about them, has never come readily to him. Despite all interruptions, there can be found a thread of sameness in many French institutions from middle ages down to Revolution. In the sixteenth century they were changing, but in piecemeal fashion, not on any large modernizing plan. Characteristically, it was in the military sphere that innovation was most continuous.

Alongside the army, officialdom proliferated. At its summit were councils, less clearly defined then in Castile and with fluctuating names and membership. The highest titular body was the *Conseil privé*, reorganized by Henry II and with about thirty participants at the end of his reign, including cardinals, royal princes, and other magnificos. The king was oftener present at the *Conseil des affaires*, whose business was more confidential and crucial. At the apex of the administrative services stood the chancellor; next, as departmental heads, came the royal secretaries, men from the upper burgher or lower noble ranks, who might exercise much influence behind the scenes if talent and propitious circumstances combined. There were four of them by Henry II's time, and he put their offices on a more regular footing. An old-fashioned aspect of the arrangement was that each had charge of a group of provinces and of relations with the foreign countries adjoining. Another was the familiar tendency of son to follow father. One secretary of this epoch, G. de Laubespine, had a son and son-in-law who both reached the same rank after him, as well as numerous other connexions in church and state.[1]

The late Valois court was peripatetic, moving about France as Charles V moved about Europe. Its spacious kingdom had a population approaching 20 million,[2] double that of Spain and four times England's. It might have evolved more properly as two separate countries, northern and southern, like Scotland and England, or like Castile and Aragon. Paris had been the capital of the northern heart-land, and was less well fitted by its situation to be the metropolis of all France and its variegated nationalities. Châteaux in the Loire valley offered a more central, and more tranquil, situation. Various provinces, the *pays d'états*, still had their own Estates, and with them a considerable degree of self-management. They formed two extensive blocks of territory, northwestern and southeastern, partly recent acquisitions; both of them borderlands, where closer central control might be an asset in wartime. By later standards control was very lax everywhere. Appanages went on being created in favour of royal cadets, and there was a scattering of autonomous fiefs, like the viscounty of Turenne which kept its liberties and paid no *taille* well into the eighteenth century. Ordinary seigneurial power, vestigial in the environs of Paris, might remain vigorous in outlying areas. In Britanny, Montaigne remarked, a nobleman could live in state and be scarcely more aware of any king above him than of the Shah of Persia. 'Verily our lawes are very free. . .'[3]

Nobles would not relish the gradually firmer assertion of central authority. One facet of the process was closer supervision of seigneurial by royal justice, which cost it some of its profits. Legal procedure was codified in 1539 by a decree which strengthened the hands of the judge: absolutist tendencies in the political realm thus

---

[1] Sutherland, *Secretaries of State*, pp. 98–9.
[2] Mousnier, *Le Conseil du Roy*, p. 19. R. Mols, 'Population in Europe 1500–1700', in Cipolla, p. 38, estimates the population in 1500 as 16·4 million, in 1600 as 18·5.
[3] *Essays*, Books 1, no. 42.

had a reflection in the judicial. A move towards uniformity was at work, but without much regard for thoroughness or consistency. A tangle of customary law was being codified on a regional, not national, basis,[4] even though its diversities might frustrate royal edicts designed for the whole country; in the same way no standard weights and measures were being adopted. How law worked in practice may be gleaned from the quantity of satire aimed by Rabelais at lawyers, as well as at priests. Judicial functions were habitually mixed up with executive; many centuries of this lay behind the cry for separation of the powers in 1789. They were vested in men loosely called 'magistrates', a word which in French and English was slowly narrowing down from its old sense of 'master'.

It was a chronic impediment that officials at a distance were apt to become unresponsive; out of sight, government was out of mind too, and the pull of local influences was stronger. This had long since happened with the equivalents of the English sheriff – *baillis* in the north and seneschals in the south, men of good family ruling in patriarchal style. A growing cadre of specialized assistants was now keeping them more in line. Above them were governors, whose posts, at first temporary, had become permanent by the sixteenth century and by its end were showing signs of becoming hereditary. They were always aristocrats; their functions were nebulous, and like the new lord-lieutenants in England they often held court posts in addition. Francis I distrusted them, and tried to hobble them, and to restrict them to frontier areas;[5] there they might be useful in organizing defence, like a Medina Sidonia in southern Spain. Reliance was being placed instead on royal commissioners sent out on special duty, men with the old title of master of requests but now endowed with novel and sweeping powers; by 1600 there were a hundred of them, and they were paving the way for the *intendants* of the next century.

Landowners often played a part in the affairs of their neighbourhood, but there was no systematic absorption of the gentry into administration, as was happening in England with its justices of the peace. Lacking steady guidance from above, it was less likely to mature into a coherent class, ready to move with the times. Another

[4] J. R. Major, 'The French Renaissance Monarchy as seen through the Estates General', in Cohn, p. 47; R. Filhol, 'The Codification of Customary Law in France', *ibid.*, pp. 268–9.
[5] Doucet, p. 866.

weakness, and one which went far to cancel out the efforts towards centralization, was the sale of offices, including army commissions. Multiplication of posts, many of them set up only to be sold, weakened the monarchy's hold on its own agents; it made the *officier* or office-holder all the more disposed to think of his place as a benefice, something belonging to him, instead of as a link in a royal chain of command.[6] It made also for much confusion, since he might be in business on his own account as well.

Management by provincial Estates meant the sway of local oligarchies, of which France was in a sense a federation. Urban franchises meant the rule of circles of patricians, who were taking things out of the hands of the *bourgeoisie*, or town–dwellers with citizen status. As narrow cliques they could not withstand pressure from the crown, and needed its good will. The crown showed little desire to level out a bewildering variety of town constitutions; though it intervened increasingly, in its own interests chiefly, and frequently insisted on the choice of its nominee as mayor. Paris was always vigilantly watched. It had a *prévôt des marchands*, elected by sixteen delegates, one from each ward, with four *échevins* or aldermen and a council; but their sphere was mainly commercial. Politically, Paris had far less experience than self-governing London, and would find it much harder to supply national leadership when the throne was in eclipse.

Fiscal machinery creaked badly. Government had only incomplete records of what was being paid, because local expenditure was deducted before the balance was remitted. In the north the *taille*, the main direct tax, was paid by the individual, chiefly by the peasant since the privileged orders and some towns were exempt: in the south it fell on land, including some of the land owned by nobles. Most big towns had gained exemption, in part or wholly. In the *pays d'états* the Estates agreed with the treasury on their quota and made their own arrangements, and the result was that they, like the non-Castilian regions in Spain, paid less. This may have been regarded as helping to ensure the loyalty of the borderlands. Elsewhere officials fixed a quota for each district, and parishioners chosen by their neighbours had the invidious, sometimes dangerous task of deciding and collecting dues. Indirect taxes, loosely known as *aides*, and including the highly unpopular salt gabelle, were growing. They were habitually farmed out to individuals or

---

[6] W. Fischer and C. Lundgreen, 'The Recruitment and Training of Administrative and Technical Personnel', in Tilly, p. 491.

groups, whose operations were on a larger and larger scale.

War being the chief activity of the state, it was above all the swelling military costs that dictated new exchequer methods. There was some reorganization at the centre in Francis I's time, following the disgrace of a minister, Berthelot, whose ill-gotten fortune, transmuted into a ravishing château, still gazes at itself in the river Indre. Responsibility was being concentrated more in a single high officer, the *trésorier de l'épargne*. But receipts continued to fall behind outgoings. There was no way to make the nobility pay anything like its due, though its now rusty liability to army service could be furbished up at times; or the church, though the *décimes* formerly contributed by it on occasion were now being collected as a matter of course. Income from crown lands diminished as these were mortgaged or, especially by Henry II towards the end of the Italian wars, given away. Borrowing had to be resorted to more and more. Sales of *rentes* or annuities fostered a class of rentier investors, as the *juros* did in Spain. They were often arranged through the corporation of Paris or some other city, long accustomed to public borrowing. Loans came from financiers, many of them Italians or other foreigners who made Lyons their headquarters. As the fighting drew to a close, the French government was sinking as rapidly into bankruptcy as the Spanish.

To Machiavelli this disjointed polity, when he compared it with the Turkish, did not appear, any more than to Montaigne, despotic.[7] Absolutist and constitutional ideas could be shuffled together by a writer like Claude de Seyssel, in a manner only possible while France was not yet beset, as it soon would be, by urgent social antagonisms. But constitutional thinking lacked a well-defined place in the scheme of things, because of the failure of the States-General to establish itself. A primary reason for this was the lack of homogeneity of the France over-expanded by the monarchy. Between 1484 and 1560 the States-General never met. Its mode of election, though never in the past standardized, was through successive tiers of gatherings and discussions from parish up to bailiwick, and might seem to give it a broader foundation than the English Parliament had. In reality, grievances which found vent at the bottom lost their way at the later stages, and the peasantry was virtually unrepresented. Of the wealthier sections of the third estate, far more than in England were being incorporated into the official machine, and hence had less need of representation in any

[7] *The Prince*, chap. 4.

body outside it. Deputies were shackled, as in the Netherlands, by mandates, and to settle tax-grants by haggling between government and individual towns, as well as between government and provincial Estates, might be more acceptable to both sides.

That the monarchy was left as the sole national institution was to be a prime cause of the uneven history of the French state, and its periodic relapse into disorder. Another body, it is true, the Parlement of Paris, was flourishing, far more than any comparable organ abroad, while the States-General hung fire; and it was quite ready as the supreme legal corporation to claim a right to speak for the nation. Lawyers had close ties with urban upper strata, landowners, and bureaucracy, and as elsewhere formed a common denominator among them. A number of provincial Parlements were set up by the crown, partly as rivals to the Paris body, partly as concessions to local feeling or for the benefit of litigants far away. They represented also a transplanting of a metropolitan institution to outlying areas, a policy not of centralization but – more practicable and no less advantageous to the government – of uniformity.

The Parlement of Paris had a complex structure, and was not confined to law business. One of its weightiest duties was to oversee the provisioning of the capital, which it could do better than the municipality because its writ ran far beyond the city. Absurdly splendid costume and ceremonial, as of a rival court,[8] advertised its pretensions. It was often at loggerheads with the royal court, particularly under Francis I, but it upheld the state; lawyers could appreciate the distinction in advance of others. It conceived itself as censor or mentor of whoever might be in power, and considered itself entitled to veto royal edicts, a claim perpetually disputed. It did so, very much like the early Stuart Parliaments, in the name of what it deemed the country's ancient constitution or fundamental laws. These laws were hazy; the real bedrock of all such thinking was the existence of corporate rights and privileges which no government could override.

Among these rights, the nobility's were paramount, but it was a very mixed as well as archaic class, and its fortunes too were chequered. Incomes from land might be much or little. Direct farming of estates was a thing of the past, demesnes were let out. Old fixed quit-rents were shrinking as money fell in value, but a range of feudal dues and imposts continued to be lucrative,[9] while

[8] Shennan, *The Parlement*, pp. 229, 244 (illustrations).
[9] There is disagreement as to how much they counted for.

landowners who could dictate short leases and competitive rents were in a happy position to profit by the state of the market. At the other end of the scale were impoverished properties sinking under a load of debt. A brisk turnover of land from owner to owner was taking place.

By degrees the state was supplanting the nobility as the peasantry's chief exploiter. On the other hand, a high proportion of the money collected by state appropriation of the peasant surplus then found its way into noble hands. No less than in Spain, a man of rank in difficulties counted on royal assistance as no more than his due, just as a modern big businessman expects subsidies from his government. To make sure of it he had to be much seen at court, and this was always a gamble: life there, and habits of extravagant display, might cripple him instead. Not all, in any case, could be gratified, and the disappointed would be indignant with a state which ought to exist for their good but might seem to be moving away from them.

Under the spur of need they would divide into factions, and jostle for the best places at the trough. While the old feudal hierarchy had long since crumbled, there was in its place a more tenuous relationship of patron and client, which would sometimes give an ambitious magnate a following among the swarm of gentry, sometimes allow them to push him forward as their figurehead. It was in the south – the reverse of the position in Spain – that the petty nobility was most numerous. Of this mass of stragglers from the past, some families might snap up government posts or berths in the church; but for the larger number whose brains were in their sword-arms, the magnet was war. If it was even more a lottery than court life, an officer as smart as Monluc could plunder not only Italy, but France as well, or its treasury, or in other words the French peasantry. Wars and war taxation represented a quickening transfer of wealth from the masses to the luckiest among their betters, by way of the state.

A primitive democracy of the countryside lingered on in communal ownership of waste or woodland, and in village assemblies, though these might owe their existence (like the *mir* in Russia) to royal officials for whom they were a means of organizing the collection of taxes; and they might be tilted by some peasants being less badly off than others. It showed also in the custom in many regions of equal division among sons. With population growing, this might soon reduce a family to equal poverty. The long-term trend was towards a majority of holdings too small for the cultivator to do more than keep body and soul together on, while the middle grade was squeezed out, and large properties grew larger by absorbing the farms of those who failed. Taxation hastened the descent. After only cautious increases under Francis I, the later stages of the wars left the government no choice but to go to work more roundly. In remote Guienne there was a revolt in 1548 against an attempt to introduce the salt gabelle. A decade later there was insurrection again in the south west, and, much nearer the capital, in Normandy. In 1560 the chancellor, L'Hôpital, lamented that many peasants were having to sell their holdings in order to pay their dues.

Complex interactions were going on between the old order and the moneyed classes which were buying much of the land on sale. Land-buyers, especially away from the neighbourhood of big towns, might soon assimilate themselves to gentry life, and this, invigorated by new blood, could go on intact. But when gentlemen of long pedigree were showing more and more inclination to take up residence in towns, there would be less inducement for townsmen to remove to country estates. Noble status gained by office or purchase might be for life only; in martial France blue blood was far more distinctly a caste than in pacific England. Not all new men would be eager to ape its ways, and commit themselves to the code of feudal prodigality.[10]

Still, very large amounts of capital were steadily being diverted from productive activity into office, land, or *rentes*. No solid bourgeois class was coming together, as a counterbalance to the restless aristocracy. In many parts of France towns were scattered far apart; and to burghers of Bordeaux, those of Rochelle were rivals and opponents. To the overcoming of such particularism the lack of anything like a House of Commons was a serious obstacle. Hence the ascendancy of the monarchy, itself in many ways a divisive factor, was in the longer run the only force capable of drawing these diverse elements out of their blinkered social or local limits. In the meantime, those with a foothold in office could indulge the feeling, however illusory, that they had found a short cut to power, that the state was already theirs.

Cottage industry was spreading quite widely, chiefly in textiles, and industrial capital sprouting, most quickly in northern areas whose development had most in common with the Netherlands

---

[10] R. Mousnier, *Peasant Uprisings in Seventeenth-century France, Russia and China*, trans. B. Pearce (London, 1971), pp. 20–21. Cf. Salmon, *Society in Crisis*, p. 42: 'When the lands of the constable de Bourbon came on the market in the 1530s, 37 out of 40 seigneuries were bought by non-nobles.'

and England. France as a whole lagged well behind those countries. Although guilds were less deeply entrenched than in some parts of Europe, their growing exclusiveness helped to bring a proletariat into being, thus giving capitalism a chance in one way while obstructing it in another. Official policy favoured guilds, as in Spain, and utilized them for purposes of regulation; it discouraged the *confréries* that workmen were struggling to organize on something like trade-union lines. Real wages were falling heavily in the second half of the century, and the government wavered between harsh interventions to keep them down, and efforts at restraining prices. Town workers as well as peasants might erupt, and to add to this menace was in the background the vagrant mass familiar to all western Europe.

A series of bad harvest years starting in 1555 was the prelude to a period of worsening climate and hardship, when food prices, here too, went up faster than others because the number of mouths grew while the yield of agriculture did not. Inflation was at its worst between 1570 and 1600; monetary chaos added to the unsettling effect. No society so ill-knit could undergo such strains without risk of disruption. In 1558 Henry II had to suspend payments on his debt. A meeting was summoned, the first in many years, of the Notables, a nominated substitute for the States-General, with the addition of a bevy of high office-holders. The bureaucracy was being treated as a fourth estate of the realm. This was inadequate, and before long the States-General had to be resurrected. Modern France has turned in emergency to dictators: old France was content to leave things to its king while they were going no worse than usual, but a crisis was felt to call for the nation's collective wisdom. It was in the era now opening that the national assembly took on, though briefly, its most definite and regular shape.

Peace with Spain came at last in April 1559. Symptoms of disorder were spreading, and the government wanted to have its hands free. Henry's death in July, however, left only a brood of degenerate young sons, under the wing of their mother Catherine de Medici. Trouble was now certain. But amid general unrest and longing for change, all classes were fragmented and disoriented, and some potent ideology was required as catalyst. This could only be religion, and religion could meet the need only darkly and confusedly. In 1559 a Calvinist national synod was held in secret. Complaints about the shortcomings of the old church began as usual with the poor, whose discontents might infect the new church. When Monluc was commissioned to suppress the Huguenots in his native

Gascony in 1562 he found it in a condition of social revolt (too luridly depicted it may be in his memoirs), with pastors exhorting their flocks to pay 'neither duty to the gentry nor taxes to the King, but what should be appointed by them'.[11]

But Calvinism with its presbyterian organization understood how to take things out of the hands of the common people, and to win acceptance, of varying shades of sincerity, from many quarters. Its most authentic appeal was to the educated middle classes, but in France it could not enrol anything like a majority of them; the outcome was to polarize them, making a deeper rift than ever before within their ranks. From this point of view the Calvinist entry into the lists may have been untimely, precipitated by a fortuitous crisis, like the Comunero rising in Castile. A radical or revolutionary movement is seldom free to choose the historical moment most favourable to it.

Unable to come forward on its own, unwilling to put itself at the head of the masses, the burgher section of Calvinism had to accept the reinforcement of malcontents from the gentry and nobility. Those readiest to join were, in the main, those most in difficulties, to whom civil as well as foreign war offered opportunity, with the wealth of the church as the most succulent bait. When it came to fighting, the towns could, like the Dutch, raise an effective militia for local protection, but they could not dispense with their feudal allies, who soon came into the lead. Huguenot strength, scattered in patches over mostly poorer areas, was greatest in the south, with its turbulent gentry and its still very imperfect assimilation, political or cultural, to France: southwestward in Poitou and Guienne, southeastward in Languedoc and Provence, and all along the Pyrenees with their little feudatory principalities. As time went on, reform came to be more and more closely linked with defence of regional autonomies and municipal franchises against central encroachment. Calvinism thus played a part here similar to its share in the defence of the Netherlands against Spanish centralism. Conversely the rival cause would appeal to the upper classes of Paris and the nuclear region of the kingdom where, apart from national sentiment, there were powerful official and financial interests in favour of close cohesion.

When Catherine became regent in 1560, her most eligible partner was the middle body of opinion coming to be known as the Politique. Its most tangible basis was the mass of rentiers, office-holders,

[11] Monluc, pp. 206–7, 209.

magistrates, who wanted order and stability but knew that these could not be had without some overhauling of both church and state. Its worthiest spokesman was L'Hôpital, who became chancellor and Catherine's chief adviser in 1560. They had need of backing from public opinion against extremists of both camps, especially against the Guise family, heads of the Catholic faction. If there was to be any effective mobilizing of opinion, it would be through the States-General, and this met at Orleans in December. L'Hôpital recalled in his opening address the antique name 'parliament', still preserved as he said in England and Scotland.

There was firm endorsement of measures which might make the ship of state seaworthy once more, and open the way to reconciliation, and on the lines of the *cahiers* or proposals of the Estates the government drew up a grand reforming ordinance. Unluckily, this proved a dead letter, because of obstruction by vested interests, including the Parlement. Reconstruction could only come by revolution, and there was no true revolutionary force. By the 'contract of Poissy' in 1561 the church was obliged to pay special subsidies; this strengthened the bonds between it and the state, and enabled both of them to go on procrastinating over the reforms demanded of them.

In 1562 the 'massacre of Vassy' ushered in three decades of sporadic civil war. L'Hôpital retired or was dismissed in 1568. Catherine, having failed to reconcile the factions, had to balance between them, not without a degree of success. She felt the importance of restoring to the throne the aura it had been losing, and made grand progresses with the court, during 1564–6 for instance, to display herself to the people. Women rulers had a particular flair, as well as need, for this kind of self-advertisement. Behind the scenes Catherine had to rely on manipulation and finesse, exercised through reliable secretaries. Her workroom in the château at Blois, with its sliding panels and secret cupboards, is a fitting memorial. It was an age, not only in France, of furtive doings, of plot and counterplot, when private codes, coming to be known as 'ciphers', were much in vogue.

Authority was not collapsing altogether. France's limited centralization made it not too hard for officialdom to go on by itself. Provincial governors and civic dignitaries had a not unwelcome chance to recover their freedom of action. Parlements continued their administrative work. Compared with England's not much later, the wars reflected a feebly developed national life; for the most part they were little more than campaigns for booty, with each side ready to look for foreign alliances as well as to hire foreign mercenaries. A popular element was entering the arena, but seldom in other than the crude form of mob outbreaks and massacres.

Among the educated, events provoked fresh thinking about politics. From one side Hotman, in his *Francogallia* in 1573, and Duplessis Mornay, 'the Huguenot pope', elaborated the semi-republican philosophy latent in Calvinism. But it was becoming apparent that Protestants were fated to remain a small minority; hence in a States-General they would always be outnumbered. Their adherents were being forced to remove to their main strongholds, southern towns like Rochelle and Montauban, where a separatist constitutional life could unfold, with its own representative assemblies. This implied renunciation of any hope of winning the country over, and Huguenots could be accused of undermining the state, or 'cantonalizing' France.

It was another symptom of national immaturity that something analogous was taking place in the other camp too, among the popular forces set in motion by religious passion. They acquired an organization in 1576 in the Catholic League, whose aim, however inchoate, was not to go beyond absolute monarchy but to retreat from it to an era of urban autonomy and social harmony; in effect, to turn the country into a collection of 'small Catholic republics'[12]. Strongest in Paris, the League had a generous stiffening of lawyers, who were busy in municipal politics and frequently served as the towns' deputies to the States-General[13]. When this met at Blois in 1576, there was very general invective against abuses like the plethora of useless official jobs. Politically, the League was pushed on by the fact of the heretic Henry of Navarre becoming in 1584 next heir to the throne, and then, on Henry III's murder in 1589, its claimant.

The League manifesto of 1585 was a catch-all, showing conservative chiefs angling for public support: it talked of the rights of the nobility, abolition of new-fangled taxes, regular meetings of the States-General. But in May 1588 power in the capital was seized by League extremists known as 'the Sixteen', a committee with a delegate from each ward. From this sprang a radicalism prepared to

[12] F. Braudel, *The Mediterranean in the Age of Philip II* (2nd ed., trans., London, 1972–3), pp. 1215–16.
[13] H. G. Koenigsberger, *The Hapsburgs and Europe 1516–1660* (Cornell Univ. Press, 1971), pp. 188. On the town governments, cf. Salmon, *Society in Crisis,* p. 247.

denounce all aristocracy as the bloodsucker of the poor. Leadership, however, despite some broadening as time went on, was in modest but respectable middle-class hands, largely of lawyers or minor office-holders, tradesmen, priests.[14] While these men set out to rouse the masses, they did not belong to them, and brought in few reforms, playing on fanaticism instead. On these lines there could be no middle-class revolution. In 1590 the Sixteen were removed, and some of them executed, by the duke of Mayenne, now head of the Guise clan.

Marseilles and other towns emulated Paris, but were only following it into a blind alley. A heavy drop of urban population, especially in Paris, under stress of the wars must have been one cause of this retrogression. Religion as a primitive framework for political parties was soon used up. On the Catholic side its failure was even more signal than on the Protestant. League passion could neither solve social problems nor alter the shape of the state; its outcome instead was to confirm the hold of Catholicism on the towns, and so help to usher in France's belated counter-reformation and with it, in course of time, a monarchy more powerful than ever. Meanwhile, industry was drooping and unemployment rising, food shortages were recurrent. Workmen reacted by trying to band themselves together, but Catholic and Huguenot, drawn as at Lyons from much the same social strata, were as incapable as the middle classes of combining against common foes. In the country-side, less fuddled with theology, it was easier for the people to come out in elemental protest. In 1594–5 formidable armed bands of *Croquants* in the southwest repelled the ravages of troops from both camps. Other areas saw revolts against both tax-demands and feudal exactions; in Britanny from 1590 to 1595 social war between peasant and noble raged.

Clearly the need to bring mutinous countryfolk back under the yoke would be a persuasive inducement to the propertied classes to sink their differences. Men like the feuding lords of Périgord led the way when they joined forces against their rustics. In 1593 Henry IV came to terms with political realities by turning Catholic, and next year he could enter Paris. From then on autocracy was being rebuilt, on a firmer footing then ever. It stands revealed as something that few desired, but nearly all were willing to accept for want of any other solution, any other bond of union for a fragmented nation. It had in its favour the pragmatism of the *Politiques*, divested

---

[14] Salmon, 'The Paris Sixteen', pp. 549–50, 566–7.

now of the constitutional thinking, the aim of broadening political responsibility, which had gone with it at the outset. In 1576 Bodin's treatise on sovereignty pointed the way towards faith in a rejuvenated absolutism. He could still contemplate government as under some restraint, subject to a public right of consent to taxation. As disorder deepened, other theorists dropped any such restrictions, and took up with divine right principles concocted in the first place to counter the League and its claim to make and unmake kings in the name of heaven. Secularism could not yet stand on its own feet.

Henry IV never summoned the States-General. It could not have met without religious and factional grudges being churned up afresh; but equally decisive was his unwillingness to share power with an assembly which had been so ready to assert itself during the troubles. In 1596 he held a meeting of Notables at Rouen, with some elected members among the representatives of the third estate. It claimed a voice in fiscal matters, where a new dispensation was certainly vital to the national welfare; the king was evasive. An obstacle less easy for him to circumvent was the Huguenots' self-government in their own strongholds, sanctioned in 1598 by the Edict of Nantes, which Henry had much ado to get the Parlement to swallow; though its terms were honoured by the government reluctantly and never in full. During 1591–2 Henry annexed to France the autonomous Pyrenean fiefs, his own Navarre among them, as a reassurance – it may be supposed – to both patriotic and Catholic opinion. His political preference was for his new faith, as more in tune with monarchy, and he sought to deprive the Huguenots of their leaders, beginning with the aristocratic sort likeliest to be meddlesome, by making it worth their while to follow his example and turn Catholic. Many did; but the unprincipled self-seeking encouraged by bribery was not conducive to public tranquillity.

Henry's quick and many-sided mind was also an undisciplined one; a vagrant life had made desk-work uncongenial, and endowed him with a gambler's temperament. His mode of transacting official business, as depicted in his great minister's memoirs,[15] looks casual and slipshod, and the amount of money he wasted on frivolities was scandalous. Sully was ideally qualified to make good his chief's deficiencies. He was a one-man ministry in himself, holding an astonishing range of offices and making his mark on them all. Something of his laborious conscientiousness he must have owed to

[15] *Memoirs of the Duke of Sully*, ed. A. Jamieson (London, 1822), e.g. II p. 223.

his lifelong Calvinism. But like the country and the state he was helping to reorganize, he was very much a mixture of epochs and elements. A seigneur by birth, in 1606 he was made a duke; he accumulated estates, lived in feudal splendour; he transferred his post of grand master of artillery to one son, another at the age of eighteen inherited that of *grand voyer* or overseer of roads.

It would have been better for France if the administrative system, to say nothing of the social structure, had been more profoundly shaken by its ordeal, and compelled to reconstruct itself more thoroughly. Henry and Sully, practical men impatient to get the government going again, were satisfied in most fields to work with the machinery they found to hand. A stricter demarcation was made among the principal councils. The large *Conseil d'état et des finances*, diminishingly aristocratic in composition, attended to daily business, while the king decided policy with a much smaller and more informal group of advisers known as the *Conseil secret* or *Conseil de cabinet*. As always governments were keeping an eye on one another's procedures, and Sully seems to have contemplated a set of other boards on the Spanish model.[16] An itinerant government was coming to rest more permanently in Paris. It was desirable to conciliate the tempestuous city, and the central bureaucracy was piling up.

Paris meant also a blossoming court, sure to attract the higher nobility, like Philip III's Madrid. Henry did not altogether welcome this. Whether it was safer, or less unsafe, to keep dukes and marquises scattered about on their estates, or gathered together under their sovereign's eye, was always a moot point. For the more ambitious among them, a place in the royal counsels would make up for the curtailing of their local consequence by royal control of the provinces. This had to be recovered bit by bit, because many of the crown's rights had slipped away from it. Here the elastic use of commissioners on special duty stood it in good stead, and it was now that the practice took on a regular, standardized form. Towns, Paris included, were once more firmly shepherded; supervision was all the more requisite as the nobility dropped into habits of absenteeism and urban residence.

Restored absolutism revived Frenchmen's appetite for government service, with its higher dignity than any other occupation could offer, besides pecuniary advantage. In societies in flux like those of France or England, where multitudes were rising or

---

[16] Buisseret, p. 176.

sinking in the scale, individuals were acutely sensitive to their own and their neighbours' status, and any recognized position was something to clutch at. Much higher prices were being paid for offices, of which Charles Loyseau, jurist and political comment- ator, estimated that fifty thousand were created in the second half of the sixteenth century.[17] In Henry's later years some attempt was made at pruning superfluous posts; on this, public opinion loudly insisted. But in 1604 Sully had confirmed the already familiar practice, by which holders were allowed to hand on their places to successors nominated by themselves, when he instituted an annual payment, the *paulette*, in return. It might help to protect the inde- pendence of the magistrature, especially of the Parlement of Paris which was, in default of a representative assembly, the nation's watchdog against the crown. As a whole, a hereditary though not closed bureaucracy would be a drag on the country, and might at times, as in the Frondes, be a nuisance to the government.

Finance was, as ever, crucial, but the problems it bristled with were intractable because its Augean stables were part and parcel of the mode of existence of the affluent classes, aristocratic or money- making. Some improvement was attainable by a man of Sully's energy and dominance, ready for unrelaxing exertion. From 1602 he was turning the heavy deficits of the 1590s into surpluses. He worked up the rough annual balance-sheet known as the *états du roi* into something rather more like an orderly budget.[18] In this the *taille* had a reduced part. Sully was aware, as L'Hôpital had been, of how cruelly it pressed on the peasantry, and lost no time in for- bidding distraint of farm animals and tools by tax-collectors. Indirect taxes were enhanced instead; the salt gabelle was coming to be the second biggest item of revenue.

Tax-farmers were subjected to some mild checks, but more often irregularities were winked at, partly because some of their illicit profits could be squeezed out of them from time to time when the treasury was hard up. This was a device resorted to everywhere; Hamlet's parable of the ape chewing the sponge sums it up. During the wars there had been further heavy borrowing, largely from the Italian financiers at Lyons, besides sales of crown and church lands; a good part of this floating debt was now repudiated. Sully scrutin-

---

[17] K. W. Swart, *Sale of Offices in the Seventeenth Century* (Hague, 1949), pp. 8, 11. Cf. Salmon, *Society in Crisis*, p. 215: amid political turmoil and commercial instability, office like land gave 'prestige as well as security'; and pp. 161, 223, on the trend towards transferable and heritable office-holding.
[18] Buisseret, p. 85.

ized the *rentes* too, and scaled down the interest payable on them, but they stood on a different footing. They were a 'national debt', and the new dynasty's acceptance of them was also a recognition of the continuity of the state, a principle which royal debts, stretching from generation to generation, did much to cement.

Absolutism was always too likely to drift apart from society, become absorbed in the satisfaction of its own wants. At this stage it had at least some dawning sense of a duty to contribute to national development as well as maintain order; and in France, recovering from disastrous breakdown, a better response might be expected than in Spain. This interlude of peace was too brief for more than beginnings, and the country's natural resilience must have done more to restore prosperity. Still, 'enlightened despotism' was coming into view; and Pombal in eighteenth-century Portugal would look back on Sully as his exemplar.[19]

An agricultural treatise by Olivier de Serres, dedicated to Henry in 1600, is said to have been his favourite reading. Sully was an enthusiast for agriculture, as the healthy foundation of the state. Dutch skill was enlisted to carry out drainage works. Larger units of land, with some use of capital, were one route, if not the only one, to improved cultivation, and *fermage* or farming on capitalist lines by well-to-do owners or tenants was spreading, chiefly in the north. On the other hand, the government had motives for preserving peasant proprietorship. Rural discontent might explode again; Henry had seen more of the villager at close quarters than most crowned heads. Concern for peasant survival was also dislike of seeing the chief taxpayer expropriated by bigger men exempt from taxation or able to evade it. Some protection was extended against encroachments by landowners on village commons and wood-cutting rights, which were a frequent grievance. This helped to keep the small holding in being, and must have been the source of much of Henry's lasting popularity. His memory was evoked in several *cahiers* of 1789 as one honoured all over the countryside;[20] when his tomb was opened during the Revolution a soldier is said to have cut off a lock of his hair to make into a pair of moustaches.

What his measures could really accomplish was limited, nevertheless, in face of compelling social and economic pressures. Lords continued to claim the *triage* or one-third share of the commons, eventually granted by an edict of 1667. They were making the utmost of all their seigneurial rights; archaic feudal dues could be

[19] J. Smith, *Memoirs of the Marquis of Pombal* (London, 1843) I, chap. 2.
[20] P. Burke, *Popular Culture in Early Modern Europe* (London, 1978), p. 151.

brought back to life by lawyers whose speciality they were.[21] This
was to happen again in the next century, and may indeed be called a
chronic impulse of obsolescent feudalism. Share-cropping was on
the increase, and reduced the tenant to such wretchedness that he
might be forced off the land, or obliged to find other work as a
supplement. The bulk of the peasantry was being pushed down into
'a uniform, poverty-stricken mass'.[22] Much of the south was
succumbing to the same decrepitude as most of southern Europe.

Since in industry too France was much less definitely committed
to large-scale enterprise than England or the Netherlands,
businessmen felt more need to turn to the state for assistance.
Montchrétien, an ironmaster who dedicated his book in 1615 to the
next king, had visited those countries, and wanted France to break
their commercial supremacy.[23] Its monarchy was in fact the first of
many to promote borrowings from the pioneer lands of capitalism.
Mercantilist ideas were coming into circulation, and were taken up
in earnest in France earlier than anywhere else on the continent.[24]
They must have done much to draw crown and bourgeoisie closer.
Henry set up a trade commission with spokesmen of commerce
from all over the country. He and Sully were willing to subsidize
and shelter manufactures like Lyons silk. Such policies were not
new; they went back to Louis XI, but they were being given a fresh
and more vigorous start, accompanied by a spate of grants of
industrial patents.[25] Part of their purpose was to absorb idle labour-
power which otherwise might be mischievous. Lyons, for instance,
was situated in an infertile region whose poverty made labour for
industry plentiful. A parallel motive can be recognized in a series of
pronouncements which lifted the ban, often reasserted during the
later sixteenth century, on participation by nobles in trade or
industry.[26] Room was thus made for the aristocratic entrepreneur,
by now a far from unknown species in Europe. A government

---

[21] B. H. Slicher van Bath, 'Agriculture in the Vital Revolution', in CEHE, p. 108;
J. de Vries, *The Economy of Europe in an Age of Crisis 1600–1750* (Cambridge, 1976),
p. 65.
[22] P. Croot and D. Parker, 'Agrarian Class Structure and Economic Development',
Past and Present, no. 78 (1978), p. 44.
[23] Lublinskaya, chap. 3.
[24] H., Kellenbenz, 'The Organization of Industrial Production', in CEHE, p. 480.
[25] Nef. p. 84.
[26] B. Supple, 'The Nature of Enterprise', in CEHE, p. 448. P. Anderson, *Lineages of
the Absolutist State* (London, 1974), p. 127, n. 16, points out that strict rules of
derogation had only come in quite late; while the *noblesse de l'épée* remained
homogeneous, they were unnecessary.

might well consider, like Dr. Johnson, that a man is never more innocently employed than when he is making money. But events soon demonstrated that few French nobles or their progeny were prepared as yet to turn their hands to anything so usefully mundane.

Sully's work on roads, bridges, canal projects, river navigation, achieved little at the time but pointed the way to benefits for the economy as well as for administration and army. Against it must be set the internal customs barriers and the tangle of feudal tolls, eloquent testimony down through the centuries of the short-comings of monarchical power or will. Moreover, in manufactures as in agriculture the government had reasons for favouring small-scale units.[27] In centres like Lyons collisions between capital and labour were breaking out; against such disturbances the guild structure could be looked on as an insurance. A flood of industrial regulations poured out, largely – as one must suspect in all such cases – to give official quill-drivers something to do, but incorporating some provisions to make guilds less exclusive and give the artisan more chance of rising to be a master. Here too revenue was a consideration: guilds would pay to have their privileges confirmed. All this would delay the rise of capitalist industry; but the biggest obstacle must have been a scarcity of entrepreneurs, men of industry-building instinct. Too many alternatives attracted money away. Huguenots were a special case, because hardening exclusion from public life left them to fix their endeavours on business. By comparison with England, industrial and commercial life remained regional rather than national.[28]

It was only for short intervals that any monarchy could be content to apply itself to constructive work. A soldier most of his life, Henry may have felt that without fresh victories abroad he could not impose himself for long on France, that is to say on its restless nobility. Sully held to the conventional maxim that the way to keep the nation in health was to have a foreign war every now and then, to drain off evil humours; the army would be the remedy for feudal distempers, like manufactures for plebeian. He too was an old campaigner, and Sainte-Beuve's essay on him underlines the warlike side of his nature. 'Il y a du Louvois en lui, ce qui n'était pas dans Colbert.'

[27] D. Bien, 'The Ancient Regime in France', in N. F. Cantor (ed.), *Perspectives on the European Past* (New York, 1971), part 2, pp. 12–13.
[28] Nef, p. 11; cf. E. Le Roy Ladurie, 'A Long Agrarian Cycle: Languedoc 1500–1700', in Earle, p. 145: 'The rentier mentality prevailed over the spirit of enterprise.'

Henry's murder in 1610 cut short his nefarious schemes. It was very much a lesser evil, since at the price of some minor disturbances it kept France for some years longer out of a senseless European war. Louis XIII was a boy, and squabbling grandees were soon at their old games. It was still tacitly taken for granted that men of their rank were above the law, not amenable to punishment, all the more if they were connected with the reigning family. Disaffection among princes, and among their swarm of bastards, showed how royalty was still embedded in aristocracy and shared its mentality; also how old dynastic inclination to view the throne as a collective family asset lingered on.

Disorder was more superficial now because its authors were seldom identifiable with any ideology, and could enlist little public support, though ties of clientage still honeycombed upper-class life. Magnates like Condé resorted to foreign backing, or the threat of it, to blackmail the government into buying them off. They had to cloak this with some sort of demagogy; it was an era, as in other western countries, of burgeoning public opinion, to which a deluge of pamphlets bore witness. Political ideas were outrunning institutions, but the rebellion of Condé and his cronies in 1614 was followed later that year by the calling of a States-General. Its sessions, prolonged to March 1615, resulted in a programme of administrative, fiscal, and judicial reforms, with meetings of the assembly to be held every ten years. Many of these points were embodied in an ordinance of 1618; but the Parlement was allowed to block it, and the States-General was never called again. Whatever its weaknesses and dissensions, it had displayed all too much firmness and competence to please a government not remarkable for either.[29]

Once again, instead of a concept of 'king in parliament' winning acceptance, there was a return to the old pattern of autocracy. From 1621, when Luynes came to power, and more forcefully after Richelieu elbowed his way into office in 1624, the trend was towards order and renewed centralization. This constant formula of European absolutism carried no guarantee of success, which depended on the environment. Richelieu was a man of the same stamp as Olivares, pursuing similar aims by similar methods, but he passed into history as a distinguished statesman instead of a discredited charlatan, because France was a different country from Spain. It has been noted, for instance, that sale of office went further

[29] Hayden, pp. 5, 217.

in France, but did less harm.[30] A bureaucracy is conditioned by the society around it, and affected by intangibles like the Jansenist leanings of many *parlementaires*.

Once more, there was no question of getting rid of a useless and troublesome nobility. Richelieu himself belonged to this class which was perpetually having to be saved from itself, except that as an ecclesiastic he stood somewhat apart, like sundry other French ministers down to much later times. Their employment served also as a curb on the tendency of high office to become hereditary, and a new aristocratic grip on government. Richelieu was a southerner like Olivares, originating from near Chinon in Poitou, long the capital of France and in the religious wars a Catholic stronghold. He acquired the historic castle there and removed part of its stonework for the building of his new château, a proceeding which might be said to typify the very narrow breach he was making in the citadel of birth and rank. In his *Testament* he could write of the nobility as entitled to sympathy, victim of an overbearing bureaucracy which was shoving it aside, though he added that it must be restrained from high-handed treatment of the common people.[31] His mission in fact was another chapter in the monarchy's long-drawn task of pushing and prodding noblemen into a new era.

Richelieu, like Olivares, started with a show of interest in improvements and progress; he was angling for businessmen's approval when he took the high-sounding title of superintendent of commerce and navigation. His economic projects have sometimes been taken too much at their face value.[32] An ambitious and aggressive politician would turn automatically before long to war, to make him indispensable and cut through his domestic difficulties. One attraction was to furnish a pretext for attacking the Huguenots and depriving them of their political franchises. His propagandists accused them of trying to erect a Dutch-style republic within the country.[33] More or less unreal enemies had to be sought, as heretics were in Spain, because the country's real enemy, blue blood, was immune from attack. France might be an ill-assorted agglomeration, but it faced no such problem as Spain did with Aragon and Catalonia. Since Henry IV's death most Huguenots had shifted towards royalism and divine right; at the same time they were growing socially more conservative, repudiating any radical

[30] J. Vicens Vives, 'The Administrative Structure of the State', in Cohn, p. 86.
[31] Richelieu, pp. 20–21.
[32] See e.g. Hauser.
[33] Lublinskaya, p. 69.

ideas.[34] Their lower classes were embittered, and at Rochelle were strong enough to force some democratic changes on the municipality. When Richelieu's offensive came in 1627, the Huguenot camp was divided.

As always, war had every political recommendation and every financial drawback. By 1626, when Richelieu called an assembly of Notables, instead of a States-General, and submitted a budget statement and plan, there was a dismal deficit. Though the *taille* stood at 19 million *livres*, twice as much as in Henry IV's time, only 6 million reached the central treasury, whose total income of 16 million was less than half its outgoings.[35] Richelieu fell back on loans. More and more he had to fall back on the peasantry too, and add to its tax burden at a rate that only the state's growing armed strength kept from being reckless. Frequent resistance had to be put down, at the cost of some of the extra revenue brought in. It was fiercest in some backward, poverty-stricken western provinces, and discontent was more definitely directed now against official extortioners, rather than against landlords. Often peasants were not alone, but rioted or revolted along with or in the wake of other classes. It was a feature of plebeian risings in all countries that they liked neighbours of higher status to take the lead, or appear to be in the lead; they could be buffers against reprisals, and a district might feel a solidarity of its own against the outside world.

There were urban outbreaks too, of which taxation was one cause: at Rouen, for example, in 1639. On its side the government had an irresistible weapon in what was now a large standing army, still composed in good part of foreign mercenaries. Its authority over the provinces was being strengthened by the setting up of *intendants*, reliable officials from the *noblesse de la robe*. They were disliked not only by high-born governors but by the Parlements, whose sphere too they trenched on. How far they were able to cut through the dead wood of the old local officialdom, and bear down obstruction, is not clear.[36] Their other and more vital duty was to make sure of more money being screwed out of the taxpayers. By 1642 they were the government's principal fiscal agents, and the area each was responsible for was one of the twenty or thirty

[34] D. Parker, 'The Huguenots in seventeenth-century France', in A. C. Hepburn (ed.), *Minorities in History* (London, 1978), pp. 16–17. Cf. Anderson, *op. cit.,* p. 92, on the inability of a Huguenot movement dominated in the countryside by nobles to appeal to the peasantry.

[35] Lublinskaya, p. 298.

[36] Fischer and Lundgreen, *op. cit.,* p. 502.

généralités, or revenue-collecting areas, into which the country was divided. As usual the monarchy was showing itself more resolute against the masses than against the classes.

All this helped to bring it about that by the 1630s the economic recovery initiated by Henry IV and Sully was petering out. By 1648, when the Thirty Years War but not the war with Spain ended, the government was bankrupt, and interest on its debts had to be scaled down. This and bad harvests helped to precipitate the disorders of the Frondes, or 'slings', a name that well expresses their failure to rise above the level of skirmishing. Underlying them was deep-seated unrest, but this could find no effective outlet.[37] By contrast with the revolution in England, against far smaller grievances, these disturbances were an index of the country's scanty political progress under the monarchy. Paris, not any breakaway province, was the focus, but it was quite unequal to the role of London.

For France and for Europe the penalty was the restoration of absolutism under Louis XIV, starting with a fresh phase of economic recovery steered by Colbert, which was fated to slow down in its turn with the resumption of aggression abroad and crippingly expensive attempts at conquest. Absolutism was revolving in its old vicious circle. A belated way out of it was being prepared by economic and social development, spasmodic as this might be. Loyseau's portrayal of French society as a jumble of disparate categories or corporations[38] was commencing to be out of date, as contemporary images of any society are likely to be. A threefold divison, nationwide instead of local, into aristocracy, bourgeoisie, and labouring mass, was taking shape. Louis XIV represented an equilibrium of the first two, with him as arbiter and director, at the expense of the third. France was the hybrid nation of Europe, partaking of both the conservatism of Spain, together with its religion, and the mental and technical vitality of the northwest.

[37] E. Le Roy Ladurie, 'History and Climate', in Burke, pp. 151, 154.
[38] Mousnier, *Les institutions*, pp. 14–15.

6

England

English society in the sixteenth century was moving from a feudal to a modern or capitalist stage more quickly than any other country except the Netherlands; but the old order was disintegrating faster than a new one could take its place. Government was suspended over a confusion of competing elements, social and economic. It had the countervailing advantage of being based on an unusually compact territory, comprising London, the southeast, and the Midlands, the area economically and culturally in advance as well as politically; a region as antipodean to the north as Falstaff to Hotspur. It was an integrating factor, for instance, that the two universities lay within fifty miles or so of the capital, while the Inns of Court, virtually a third, were in London itelf.

Incomparably the biggest and richest city, London was the unquestionable centre of power. Its population may have reached 200,000 by 1600, and doubled again in the next half-century:[1] very rapid growth, as well as size, helps to explain its weight in early Stuart politics. Some incomers were drawn from decaying provincial towns, another example of the displacement of activity from area to area so prominent in Spain and the Netherlands, but here the process was reinforcing instead of weakening the area previously in the lead. Others, refugees or workmen and merchants seeking opportunity, flocked to London and southeast England from the continent, bringing with them their special skills.[2] London's eccentric location in a corner of the country closest to Europe, and

[1] E. A. Wrigley, 'London's Importance in Changing English Society and Economy 1650–1750', in P. Abrams and E. A. Wrigley (eds), *Towns in Societies* (Cambridge, 1978), p. 215.
[2] V. G. Kiernan, 'Britons Old and New', in C. Holmes (ed.), *Immigrants and Minorities in British Society* (London, 1978), pp. 35ff.

its abnormal growth, went together: far more than any other metropolis it was always a European as well as a national city.

Edward IV, Richard III, Henry VII might be called collective founders of a new monarchy; but little as the battle of Bosworth in 1485 may have meant by itself, the advent of the first Tudor marked a sharper dynastic break than any other throne underwent. Outside Muscovy, scarcely any new chapter opened with so stormy a train of conspiracies, revolts, executions. Having neither secure legal title nor much armed force, the Tudors had to resort to arbitrary measures against any individuals who aroused their suspicions. Yet their authority in terms of an apparatus of government remained so exiguous that to call them 'absolute' rulers may seem more a misnomer than in any other case. In order to survive they had the most compelling motive for enlisting the broadest support among the propertied classes, and even up to a point among the masses. First and foremost, Tudor power rested on the more substantial gentry, or landowners of the middle grade of wealth. They were facing changing times and perplexing problems, and the monarchy could give them the leadership they stood in need of, filling the place left partially vacant by the nobility. Financial and other backing from the citizenry saved the crown from excessive dependence on a single class. There were numerous ties, however, between these two categories, and they had a meeting-ground in the House of Commons.

Between Henry VIII's rupture with Rome and marriage with Anne Boleyn in 1533, and the accession of her daughter Elizabeth in 1558, monarchy and country went through a quarter-century of renewed turmoil. This was complicated by European entanglements, and strife with both Scotland and France; it was further compounded by the Reformation. The downfall of the old church was a resounding shock, which would reverberate in the minds of ordinary people whether they welcomed it or not, and familiarize the idea of innovation, of the mortality of things hitherto immutable. The spectacle of church plunder going far less to the crown or the public than to grasping individuals was one to inflame the social discontents rampant in those years of storm and stress.

Poorer townsfolk were suffering from inflation of food prices since early in the century, hastened now by currency debasement. Pressure on the peasantry was worsening, and in 1548–9 provoked widespread risings, most threatening in East Anglia and the West Country. They were too dissimilar to make common cause. Kett in East Anglia was a leader of substantial cultivators, forward-looking and Protestant, whereas in the traditionalist southwest the protest was conservative and Catholic. Still, there was enough to strike consternation into a landowning class growing unwarlike, and less capable of self-help than continental nobilities in the same predicament. It was the state that had to come to the rescue and suppress the revolts, with the aid of hastily collected German and Italian mercenaries.

Peril drew the landed classes together and rallied them round the throne. Under stress of the long period of uncertainty, the machinery of state was expanding, especially during the ten years after the fall of Wolsey when another plebeian, Thomas Cromwell, was at the helm.[3] One aspect was the strengthening of control over the borderlands. An act of 1536 clipped the wings of the Palatine courts of Chester, Lancaster, and the most powerful of all, Durham. The Council of the North, set up in 1537 after the Pilgrimage of Grace, was overhauled after the disturbances of 1548–9. 'Acts of Union' of 1536 and 1543 incorporated the Welsh Marches into the Principality; the lordships were superseded by the Council in the Marches, and all Wales was brought under English common law. For its inhabitants Henry professed in the act of 1536 'singular zeal, love and favour': he was showing it by trying to turn them into Englishmen. English law and education made Wales more orderly, but it was the better off who reaped the rewards, while free peasants sank to the condition of a humble tenantry. Their language was preserved by a Welsh Bible, but the strength of the assimilating forces at work can be seen in the way Cornish, very unlike neighbouring Breton, was drifting towards extinction. Beyond the Irish Sea the Pale or medieval colony still had its parliament at Dublin, but Tudor policy aimed at a firmer grip, and this would lead on to a programme of conquest of all Ireland.

'Household government' can be said to have been left behind in England long since, yet policies and decisions continued to be made in a highly personal fashion (as in foreign affairs they continued to be down to 1914). 'Bureaucratic' government was scarcely yet in existence; office-holders were few, and a great deal of public work was done by private employees of statesmen. A modern civil service could only develop along with a clearer conception of the state, which was dawning, if still cloudily, as values and ties of an older day dissolved. Thinkers and poets gave it currency; it rested at

---

[3] See Williams *et al.*, in *Past and Present*, on G. R. Elton's thesis of a sweeping administrative reorganization inspired by Cromwell.

bottom on the interests of the well-fed classes, and denoted primarily their deepening sense of vital collective concerns.

If there was a tyranny in Tudor times, Pollard wrote, it was belief in the all-importance of the state and its right to demand sacrifices.[4] 'State-sanctions, deep, or bottomless', as Herrick was to call them,[5] had the final word. Monarchy would remain potent while it could identify itself with this towering new shape. But as yet the state was equally bound up with the monarch, and when he was removed from the scene, as when Henry was succeeded in 1547 by his young son, no respect for it stood in the way of a massive plundering of crown lands and resources by the same men who had worked under Henry to fortify royal power, and were using it now against recalcitrant peasants. In turn Somerset as Lord Protector, and then Northumberland, amassed prodigious loot, some of it portioned out to a clamorous train of followers. These magnates were displaying the same irresponsibility that all aristocracies gave way to when not firmly bridled.

Elizabeth's long reign, from 1558 to 1603, allowed the idea of the state to plant itself more firmly, even if there was always a wide discrepancy between the awe-inspiring idea and the officialdom that was its outward manifestation. It fell heir to more of the majesty of the old church than did the sovereign who was Supreme Governor of the new one; it was indeed only in countries where the Catholic church was dismantled that modern political thinking could take wing. The state owed much also to a patriotism fed by foreign conflicts with more national significance than any earlier ones, and with a strongly religious tinge as well.

For Shakespeare, however important the occupant of a throne as embodiment of authority, a republican state like Venice or ancient Rome was also a high and mighty thing, invested with a mystique of its own. What this meant to the literate and the possessors, a crowned head could be to the commonalty, left by the crumbling of its old world in want of a new allegiance, a new image. A young woman with whom monarchy and dynasty were renewing themselves, Elizabeth could fill an emotional as well as practical want. She had known danger during her sister's reign, and told a foreigner now that she owed her throne to her people, not to the nobility.[6] With only a fledgeling church, she had to do her own advertising, to

---

[4] A. F. Pollard, *Factors in Modern History* (new edn, London, 1926), p. 77.
[5] 'To the Earl of Dorset' (p. 182 in *World's Classics* edn).
[6] Neale, *Elizabeth*, p. 58.

play the part of queen of the English as much as that of queen of England. Self-display and courting of applause may have come more naturally to her, as to Catherine de Medici, than to masculine rulers. It was a novel style, the antithesis of that of her grim former brother-in-law in the Escorial, who doubtless thought it highly undignified.

Behind the glamour of royal progresses and triumphal arches lay anxious calculations of how to distribute a limited supply of honours, posts, rewards among influential claimants, so as to enlist maximum attachment and give minimum offence.[7] For statesmanship of a higher order Elizabeth's reputation has declined, perhaps unduly: she was at least as remarkable as all but a very few of the – mostly very unremarkable – rulers of that century or the next. She is taxed with hesitant, jejune foreign policies,[8] with procrastination and neglect of basic problems,[9] with having no long-range strategy, only a dexterity of the moment.[10] But shuffling difficulties off till tomorrow was part of the mentality of all absolutism (if not of all government). If there was something of after-me-the-deluge in her philosophy, her position was an exceptionally vulnerable one, and her survival for so long a feat by itself. She has been accorded praise as at any rate 'a supremely good judge of men', and even if she often jangled with her ablest ministers, or disliked some of their opinions like Walsingham's advanced Protestantism, she did not drop them.[11]

Internal equilibrium was the grand aim, and this, and European distractions, disinclined both Elizabeth and her chief adviser William Cecil, or Lord Burghley, to administrative experiments. After her early years no major changes were undertaken at the centre. There the mainspring was the Privy Council. An initial move was to halve its membership, which had swollen to forty or more; the implication was that no one could claim a place simply on the strength of birth or wealth. High office, on the other hand,

---

[7] See W. T. MacCaffrey, 'Place and Patronage in Elizabethan Politics', in Bindoff *et al.*

[8] C. Wilson, *Queen Elizabeth and the Revolt of the Netherlands* (London, 1970), p. 123, has no doubt that she kept foreign policy decisions in her own hands. He draws a similar picture of Burghley as a fumbling, bumbling mismanager of foreign affairs.

[9] See e.g. Kenyon, p. 13.

[10] See e.g. G. Donaldson, *Scotland: The Making of the Kingdom, James V – James VII* (Edinburgh, 1965), pp. 5–7, 114–15.

[11] Brooks, p. 14.

entitled an indeterminate number of men, including the secretaries of state, to a seat. The Privy Council was learning to make use of committees, though it frittered away too much time on trivial odds and ends, and attendance was irregular. It had its own president, a Tudor creation; Elizabeth was rarely present, and made a habit of drawing out her councillors separately and informally.[12] Faction divided them,[13] and very likely this pleased her as much as rifts within his councils pleased Philip. As at Madrid too, the more blue-blooded resented the ascendancy of upstarts like Burghley and his group. This inner circle, even if it found the queen often hard to manage, had a common purpose and determination, steeled by Protestant convictions, a sense of closeness to God,[14] which lent it in critical junctures something of the temper of a Committee of Public Safety.

Ministers had ill-defined duties, and how much they counted depended on their abilities: the three outstanding principal secretaries were, in turn, Burghley, Walsingham, and the former's younger son, Robert Cecil. Burghley gave up the post in 1572 to become lord treasurer, but went on concerning himself with business in general. He was taking over from a veteran who died in harness at the age of 87, a pointer to the conservative tone of administration; though it must be said that improved methods of accounting and central auditing were part of the Tudor achievement,[15] dictated by impecuniosity. Burghley was fond of grumbling, and declared that what he got as treasurer was not enough to run his stable; earlier on he complained that his Scottish mission in 1560 left him 'oppressed with debt' and unrewarded, but in fact he was more than reimbursed before long by being given the Court of Wards, one of the most lucrative appointments, and land.[16] Walsingham took less good care of himself, and was beggared by single-minded devotion to duty. Lower down was an officialdom small but for the most part functional, if the many posts attached to the royal household, showy and wasteful as everywhere else, are left out. Emoluments were as imprecise as other aspects of place-holding. Few incumbents drew a good regular salary; what they were entitled to make by way of fees from the public was

[12] Neale, *Elizabeth*, p. 72.
[13] *ibid.*, p. 181.
[14] See e.g. Read, *Cecil*, p. 444.
[15] R. Braun, 'Taxation, Sociopolitical Structures, and State-Building: Great Britain and Brandenburg-Prussia', in Tilly, pp. 260–61.
[16] Brooks, p. 220, citing Froude; Read, *Cecil*, pp. 191–2.

unclear, but their philosophy was to charge what they could get the public to pay. Many had other sources of income, such as law.

Their financial imbroglios epitomized those of the government, faced with mounting calls on out-of-date and inadequate revenues. Elizabeth kept afloat by strict economy in most directions: in this virtue she and Gustav Vasa, the parvenu king of Sweden, stood alone, and she may be said to have personified the English amalgam of feudal and bourgeois habits. Crown land had been reduced by alienations and long leases, although a fair amount was left and sales were resorted to periodically. Customs receipts were buoyant, and there were always close relations between Tudor rulers and the City moneybags who accommodated them with credit – not without misgivings at times. 'The loan of £150,000 makes many of our citizens shrink and pull in their horns', John Chamberlain wrote to a correspondent in December 1598.[17]

In all countries a point came when taxes granted by Estates, originally for emergencies, turned into standard revenue; this point was being reached now in England.[18] Wars aggravated Elizabeth's needs, despite the fact that they were frugally conducted, with much use of conscripts and privateers. Money was asked for, and granted, in every parliamentary session of the reign, though her loving Commons were less profuse with money than with loyal effusions. Taxes went on being voted in the archaic form of 'Tenths', paid on urban property, and 'Fifteenths', on rural; by 1603 these were worth no more than a beggarly £30,000.[19] 'Subsidies', payable on both land and moveables, were a more recent addition, and an act of 1534 endeavoured to ensure that they would tap wealth more fully. It is a gauge of the relation between crown and property that the effort was soon given up, and their yield slipped during Elizabeth's reign from about £100,000 to £80,000, while the value of money also fell. In 1563 the taxes voted brought in altogether £180,000; a subsidy from the clergy was worth another £42,000.[20] With sums like these may be compared the fortune squandered by the queen's favourite, and later lord chancellor, Christopher Hatton, on building himself a mansion in Northamptonshire; he left debts in 1591 of over £40,000, half of them owing to the crown.[21]

[17] *Chamberlain Letters*, p. 10.
[18] See G. R. Elton, 'Taxation for War and Peace in Early Tudor England', in J. M. Winter (ed.), *War and Economic Development* (Cambridge, 1975).
[19] Tanner, *Documents*, pp. 598 ff.
[20] Read, *Cecil*, p. 302.
[21] Brooks, chap. 16, and pp. 359–60.

Assessment and collection had to be left mostly to local agents, themselves taxpayers with more concern for their own pockets than for the exchequer. English landowners had not secured the exemptions enjoyed by their order abroad (though noblemen were separately and very indulgently assessed for the subsidy[22]), but they found other ways and means of not paying over-much. Tax-evasion could be practised by individuals as well as classes. Very poor cultivators got off scot-free, being left out of the 'subsidy book' or tax roll; but this was seldom if ever revised, and it was frequently alleged that too much of the burden was being shuffled off on to the yeomanry.[23] On the other hand, Sir Thomas Smith, the senior public servant whose glowing description of the English realm was published in 1583, may have had ground for saying that the gentleman paid more than his share of other contributions, national or local, 'to save and keepe his honour and reputation'.[24]

Altogether the monarchy's most deep-seated weakness, which would prevent it from indefinitely cumbering the scene like the Spanish or French, was its lack of adequate sources of income, and with them a standing army. Conversely, this was the greatest asset of Parliament, an already well-established institution for which England was a country of convenient size. A province like Navarre or Dauphiné was too small for its Estates to rise above parochial concerns. France or Castile were too big and heterogeneous for any assembly to take a comprehensive view of. England came somewhere between.

Numerous but mostly very small, the towns had always been part of the nation, and a freedom from excessive localism showed in the absence of those mandates which cramped deputies in so many representative bodies. During the sixteenth century the House of Commons, already large, expanded from 296 to 462 seats (and further in the next two reigns); not mainly because of the crown wishing to pack the chamber, but at the prompting of county magnates, themselves prodded by country gentlemen eager to gain entry. This clearly raised their standing, even though a borough seat conferred much less prestige than being chosen as one of the two

---

[22] Kenyon, p. 38.
[23] See e.g. Campbell, p. 137 (relating to 1626); Braun, *op. cit.*, p. 266. Opening Parliament in 1593, the Lord Keeper voiced the government's dissatisfaction with the assessment system, 'abused generally through the realm in the taxation of men of wealth that should have given most. . .'. Read, *Burghley*, p. 487.
[24] Sir Thomas Smith, p. 41.

members for each shire.

When Sir Thomas Smith described Parliament as 'the most high and absolute power of the realme of Englande',[25] he may be supposed to have had in mind its functioning under the sage guidance of royal servants like himself. Henry VIII in like vein had talked of himself and Parliament as 'knit together in the body politic'.[26] Experienced privy councillors always had a place and provided tactful but firm tuition. The government would wish to associate the nation with its policies in contentious matters like the setting up of the new church, or the possible choice by Elizabeth of a husband – an issue which gave Burghley occasion to tell his Scottish correspondents that 'all that the Queen's Majesty intendeth to do must be ruled and directed by her laws and by consent of her three Estates.'[27] Ordinarily the chief motive for holding elections was money, and ministers would prefer to hold them as rarely as they could. In Elizabeth's forty-four years there were ten parliaments, with thirteen sessions in all, a respectable but not very impressive total. Even before her reign the Commons had shown themselves no mere camp-followers, and as time went on there were signs of impatience with the government's leading-strings. Business was being conducted on more sophisticated lines; committees sprouted, the committee of the whole house was in the offing. Towards the end, while a fair proportion of dutiful votes could still be counted on, something like an opposition party was looming up, with 'those remarkable pioneers in political tactics', the Puritans.[28] An era was at hand when faction, based on personal followings and patronage,[29] would give way to authentic political alignments.

In 1569 the 'Rebellion of the Northern Earls' marked a last flicker of feudal resistance, with Catholic encouragement. Even in the distant north, where until lately there had been a flourishing 'lineage culture' presided over by great families like the Percies, feudal ties

---

[25] *ibid.*, p. 48.

[26] C. H. McIlwain, *The High Court of Parliament and its Supremacy* (New Haven, 1910), p. 338. Cf. Pollard, pp. 262 ff., on the 'general harmony between King and Parliament'.

[27] Read, *Cecil*, p. 311. G. W. O. Woodward points out that the Parliament of 1529 passed 70 statutes on economic and social regulation, besides those concerned with religion, and that to keep abreast of matters of this sort the government would have to go on making use of Parliament. 'The Role of Parliament and the Henrician Reformation', in Cohn, p. 117.

[28] Neale, *House of Commons*, pp. 241, 296; cf. Read, *Burghley*, chaps 16, 24.

[29] See Ives.

were enfeebled by the spread of a newer outlook;[30] they were dwindling to the kind of clientage between greater and lesser land-owners that could be found anywhere. Some hundreds of poor folk were executed,[31] but what mattered more was that the old turbulent baronage of the Wars of the Roses was now a thing of the past. In place of it, a more modern set of magnates was growing up, enriched with monastic land and crown favours. Its fostering by the crown was in a way a retrograde policy, but one in line with the instinct of monarchy everywhere, mistrustful of all over-mighty subjects but isolated and uneasy without them. If they could not do without it when in a tight corner, as at the time of the 1548–9 risings, the need was reciprocal. All through the sixteenth century, when force was required to maintain order, or in an emergency like 1588, the government relied quite heavily on levies raised by big landowners.[32] Only after army and bureaucracy were fully-fledged would kings feel able to reduce grandees to merely ritual duties, like handing Louis XIV his shirt of a morning.

It was from among the new magnates that lord lieutenants were likely to be drawn. Their office, largely superseding the old one of sheriff, was initiated late in Henry VIII's reign as a temporary commission to a man of high standing in some area when disorder threatened it. In the course of Elizabeth's war with Spain, though there was not yet a lieutenant for each county, it became a perm-ancy. Often the incumbent held office in the capital too, and had to delegate his lieutenancy duties to deputies belonging to the local gentry. In any case he was a pillar of the landed classes as well as of the government, and might behave as a sort of umpire between them. All peers set great store by pre-eminence in their own districts, and the post of lieutenant was its best confirmation. They advertised their rank also by housing themselves splendidly. In an age when all classes with money, down to the yeoman, were rebuilding or enlarging their dwellings, the rich were erecting palaces like the Hatfield House on which Burghley's son spent

---

[30] M. E. James, 'Concept of Order', p. 53; cf. *English Politics and the Concept of Honour*, pp. 70–71, 79–80.

[31] Punishments, like taxes, regularly fell most heavily on the poor. Bacon remarks that with gentlemen Henry VII was content to make an example of a few individuals, 'but for rascal people, they were to be cut off every man', and all the low-born followers of Perkin Warbeck whom he captured were hanged. *History of Henry VII*, in *Works* (New York edn. 1878) II, p. 237. Bacon fully approved of this treatment of the 'scum'.

[32] S. E. Finer, 'State- and Nation-Building in Europe', in Tilly, p. 119.

£30,000. Stately houses and spacious parks, in a land-hungry country, flaunted their owners' dignity and set them apart from the rude
world.

In their earlier years it seems to have been deliberate Tudor policy
to strengthen the lesser landowners, as against the insubordinate
magnates.[33] This promoted the development of the already vener-
able and peculiarly English system by which local government was
left for the most part to the gentry, or its upper layers, in the guise of
justices of the peace, under the supervision of the Council. Political
reliability continued to be an essential criterion. In 1569 every
justice was called on to declare his acceptance of the Act of
Uniformity.[34] To the importance of their ordinary work
Lambard's book on the JPs in 1581, one of several, was a tribute. A
universal craving for assured status in an age of change was enough
to keep their number swelling. To be 'in the Commission' was a
distinction, to be 'of the Quorum' a superior badge. Parvenu land-
buyers may have been all the more covetous of them.

For a man of means willing to exert himself they could pave the
way to higher things. One such was John Petre, owner of large and
well-run estates in Essex. Assiduous at quarter-sessions and assizes,
he also took to spending part of each year at court; he was knighted
in 1576, served as MP in 1584–7, and in 1603 attained the peerage.
An average JP was content to be cock on his own dunghill. He
might have a clerk assisting in his official work as well as in running
his estate: here as well as higher up, the line between public and
private was still hazy. Only a few were anxious to wrestle with the
complicated county business of the quarter-sessions. For this there
was growing reliance on the clerk of the peace, a functionary with
legal training and a staff of assistants who kept the session records.[35]
There was much the same intermingling of judicial and administrative as in France, and a good many squires had some smattering
at least of law. In terms of efficiency this amateur management may
have performed no worse than the sort of professionalism then
available on the continent.[36]

There, two distinct structures, seigneurial and bureaucratic,
stood side by side; in England there was an intertwining, and the

---

[33] Stone, *The Causes*, p. 63.
[34] Read, *Cecil*, p. 453.
[35] See Barnes.
[36] W. Fischer and P. Lundgreen, 'The Recruitment and Training of Administrative and Technical Personnel', in Tilly, pp. 460, 478.

state was more an outgrowth from society than something imposed on it. A JP was a government appointee, but he was also a seigneur in other costume; his official authority made up for the weakening of the manorial court, and the principle of landownership carrying with it power was preserved. Very often too the squire chose his own parson; he possessed indeed, as was to be objected to his descendants three centuries later, 'a variety of rights and prerogatives, which, in the aggregate, amount to little short of patriarchal sovereignty'.[37] As Sir Thomas Smith said, the grand purpose of government was that common people should be 'kept alwaies as it were in a bridle of good order', and it was in England that he believed them to be bridled most effectively.[38] Power must often have been misused. When justices were in charge of raising levies for foreign service – a task largely taken over in Elizabeth's later years by the lord lieutenants – they would impress twice as many men as were called for, in order to make money by selling discharges.[39] No doubt their clerks took a hand in the game. Central tutelage was a restraint, and infused a modicum of regard for public interests, while it also helped to weld the squirearchy into a class with a common outlook and capacity for collective action. Among a small élite of this class, Puritanism could foster both a higher public spirit and a firmer corporate consciousness.

Towns similarly were left to the rule of their own magistrates, under observation from above. They were nearly as oligarchical as the countryside: almost everywhere 'closed corporations' were to be found, and there was bad blood between them and the excluded. London was exceptional in having a relatively democratic as well as elaborate constitution, with its lord mayor, its Court of Aldermen, and a Common Council elected since 1467 by the livery companies or guilds. These in many ways directed civic policies, and chose the four MPs, who unlike those of most petty boroughs were always citizens. As a political model, London was something that no other country possessed. But ordinarily the men at the top, like those in the minor towns, were natural clients of the crown which sheltered them, and far removed from their humbler fellows. A London preacher in 1603 asserted that artisans were being saddled with most of the tax burden: 'every year I have heard an exceeding outcry of

---

[37] G. C. Brodrick, 'The Law and Custom of Primogeniture', in J. W. Probyn (ed.), *Systems of Land Tenure in Various Countries* (revised edn, London, 1881), pp. 120–21.
[38] Sir Thomas Smith, p. 89.
[39] Cruickshank, pp. 15–16.

the poor that they are much oppressed.'[40] That patriotic Londoner John Stow maintained on the contrary that men of means 'for their countenance and credit sake' often paid more than their due,[41] which may be about as true as what Smith said of the shires. Tax rolls are evidence of the very uneven distribution of property in towns.[42]

A very rapid turnover of landed property, the reverse of the situation in Spain, was the most visible hallmark of a society in flux. The strikingly free market in land, to which the Reformation lent an immense speculative impetus, went with freedom of owners to dispose of their acres, most unfettered between roughly 1450 and 1650.[43] Many of the gentry were using it to protect their lineage by adopting from the nobility the practice of primogeniture.[44] But mutability of family fortunes was a stock theme of Elizabethan and Jacobean writers. At the close of the sixteenth century only one old family was still afloat in the Ripon district of Yorkshire.[45] Heralds' visitations uncovered a similar state of affairs far and wide.[46] The outcome was contradictory: as a class, landowners were firmly based and flourishing, as individuals they were highly insecure. The distinction between the whole and its parts has not always been kept in view in latter-day controversy over whether the gentry were 'rising' or 'sinking'. It was not patent to conservatives at the time, accustomed to think in personalities; for them social reality was disturbingly at variance with the time-honoured notion of the 'great chain of being', which sanctified the hierarchical arrangement of society.

Their misgivings were not altogether misplaced. A dominant landed class was still there, but it was altering, from their point of view, for the worse. Individuals who kept going were the shrewder or more grasping sort, and competition for survival was tempering

[40] G. B. Harrison, *A Last Elizabethan Journal* (London 1933), p. 321.
[41] Stow, II, p. 213.
[42] J. F. Pound, 'The Social and Trade Structure of Norwich 1525–1575', *Past and Present*, no. 34 (1966), pp. 50–51.
[43] Cf. Brodrick, *op. cit.,* p. 98: 'It is impossible not to connect the rapid growth and singular independence of the English gentry under the Tudors and Stuarts with the limitation of entails and freedom of alienation which characterised this remarkable period.'
[44] J. Thirsk, 'The European Debate on Customs of Inheritance 1500–1700', in Goody, pp. 183, 191.
[45] Ripon Civic Society, *Ripon: Some Aspects of its History* (Clapham, Yorks, 1972), pp. 77–8.
[46] Campbell, p. 37.

them and altering their view of many things. This process of adaptation was hastened by new entrants. A seventeenth-century writer perturbed by the decay of old families spoke of London as 'a cradle of nobility'.[47] A convection current was carrying new-made wealth out into the countryside, where it would often continue to cherish its connexions with the City, or the law-courts. Anywhere within range of the bigger towns, London most of all, it was unlikely that land-buyers would be sucked too deeply into old-world rusticity. More than in France, land-ownership was partially bourgeoisified. It was indeed largely because the gentry class was being thus renovated that it could be a reasonably responsive instrument of Elizabethan rule.

Since population was growing fairly rapidly, agriculture was called on to produce more food, and succeeded in doing so better than in most countries, though at the cost of grave strains and dislocations in rural life. Technical improvements as well as use of new land made a contribution, though it is not clear how quickly they were being taken up; they included fodder crops, for instance, as part of longer rotation cycles, and irrigated meadows.[48] It is a notable fact that London's food supply, unlike that of most big European cities, could be left to the free play of the economy, and its demands may have accelerated agricultural change.[49] As a great magnet attracting food from quite distant as well as nearby areas, the London market may also have hastened the advent of capitalism in the countryside. It was towards agrarian capitalism on a nation-wide scale that England was moving, the sole country ever to do so; it took the hybrid form represented by the trio of landlord, farmer, and labourer, with the power of the squirearchy to fortify it.

Between 1560 and the 1590s the rise of food prices slowed down appreciably, a fact to which Elizabeth must have owed much of her popularity; all royal reputations hung a great deal on such fortuities. But over a far longer period food prices were rising briskly, while the real wages of farm labourers declined. To take advantage of this happy combination, an estate had to be unencumbered by too many tenant rights, and a long-drawn attack on these was under way. Intricacies of a still feudal law and custom of tenure lent themselves

[47] Sharp, p. 45.
[48] P. Croot and D. Parker, 'Agrarian Class Structure and Economic Development', *Past and Present*, no. 78 (1978), pp. 38–9; A. de Maddalena, 'Rural Europe 1500–1750', in Cipolla, p. 319.
[49] M. J. Daunton, 'Towns and Economic Growth in Eighteenth-century England', in Abrams and Wrigley, *op. cit.*, p. 258.

to manipulation. As Le Roy Ladurie has said, agrarian capitalism in England can be seen springing directly from feudalism.[50] 'Fines' levied on non-freeholders for renewal of leases could be as profitable as rack-renting. Even if, as some have argued, such 'seigneurial action' was not the principal factor in agrarian change,[51] it remains the case that rents were rising more quickly than prices, especially, it would seem, after about 1590.[52] The landowners' share in the national income was improving.

Blows such as higher fines fell on cultivators one by one, at odd times, not on the community collectively or at regular seasons; this made them less likely to kindle protest than a tax, or enclosure of a village common. Also, landlord exactions together with a widening market economy, with all its uncertainties and pitfalls, accentuated a sorting out of the peasantry into luckier and unluckier. Yeomen or 'husbandmen', owning their farms, were well placed to share in the windfall gains: they often traded in addition in cloth, lent money, and were accused of hoarding and profiteering.[53] These early kulaks were among the keenest of land-buyers. Yet there was enough solidarity left to allow discontent to break out not only in local protests but in widespread disturbances such as the Midlands revolt in 1607 and the Western rising as late as 1628–30. Enclosures were still going on, like the nibbling at village commons by French and Castilian lords; legal obstacles to them were removed by Parliament in 1621 and 1624. Smallholders survived in numbers until the later seventeenth and early eighteenth centuries. But well before then the transformation coming over the countryside was very apparent, with effects morally as well as socially degrading to many. Tudor writers contrasted the bold English rustic with the spiritless, cringing French peasant; in mid-seventeenth century a 'Digger' pictured the servile tenant coming before the tyrannous landlord 'in as slavish a posture as may be; namely with Cap in hand, and bended knee,

---

[50] E. Le Roy Ladurie, 'Peasants', in NCMH XIII, pp. 119, 134.

[51] Croot and Parker, *op. cit.*, pp. 40–41. Maddalena (*op. cit.*, pp. 301–2) argues that about 65 per cent of cultivators had some legal protection, and that until about 1650 more land was being sold to them than expropriated from them.

[52] Stone, *Causes*, p. 68, dates this from 1600; J. P. Cooper from 1560: 'In Search of Agrarian Capitalism', *Past and Present*, no. 80 (1978), p. 49. See also G. Batho, 'Noblemen, Gentlemen, and Yeomen', in Thirsk.

[53] Campbell, pp. 35, 72–3, 190. Cf. C. Howell, 'Peasant Inheritance Customs in the Midlands 1280–1700', in Goody, pp. 151–2: by the sixteenth century, testators were leaving portions to younger children in cash, an indication of 'the growing prosperity of yeomen and husbandmen during the inflationary years'.

crouching and creeping. . . '.[54]

In industry too capital was making itself felt. Moneyed men were buying land, but the slight growth of bureaucracy meant that not many of them were being drawn off into government service, as in France and Spain. Conversely, less officialdom was required than in France or Spain to brace the country together because it was merging into a national market, an economic counterpart to the administrative unification in progress. Roads might be, as one of several ineffective highway acts complained in 1555, 'very noisome and tedious to travel and dangerous'[55], but they were free of the tolls that choked so much traffic on the continent. Some newer industries had need of novel technology and substantial investment, and were capitalistic from the outset. Mining, chiefly of coal, was making strides. It gave landowners another source of income, and they and the yeomen were participating in manufactures in a variety of ways. Even if it is well to recall that industry still made only 'a minuscule contribution towards the gross national product',[56] it was a dynamic force. By 1600 England was beginning to possess 'a robust and highly diversified industrial structure', ahead of any other country except Holland.[57] Another resemblance to Holland was the large sector whose livelihood came from the sea,[58] and which lay therefore outside the boundaries of the feudal-agrarian life in which most of Europe was embedded.

Early in Elizabeth's reign the debased currency was reformed, by an operation beneficial to both government and public.[59] It was an indication of how England was moving that the Privy Council had a financial adviser as modern-minded as Gresham, and that it issued a pamphlet to enlighten the public on the reasons for its action. Like other governments, but more seriously than most, it took for granted a duty to regulate economic as well as political life. Weak in coercive force, and coping with a rapidly changing society, it was constrained to do more thinking than others about social policies. It had some paternalistic sense of an obligation to protect the weak; it could not wish to goad the poor into rebellion. It shared with

---

[54] J. C. Davis, 'Gerard Winstanley and the Restoration of True Magistracy', *Past and Present*, no. 70 (1976), p. 82.
[55] Tanner, *Documents*, p. 498.
[56] Kenyon, p. 15.
[57] D. Sella, 'European Industries 1500–1700', in Cipolla, p. 415.
[58] At least half the population, C. V. Wedgwood thinks – surely an over-statement. *The King's Peace 1637–1641* (1955, London edn 1966), p. 23.
[59] Read, *Cecil*, chap. 9.

law-abiding householders a somewhat exaggerated fear of the menace of vagabonds, who were often only workmen moving about in quest of jobs;[60] a fear 'closely allied with the concern over rebellions, rumors, false reports, and sedition'.[61] Public anxiety could help the government by making the country readier to accept firm rule. But its sources of information were unreliable, and so were its means of getting its wishes carried out. It was a complaint of the Norfolk rebels of 1549 that JPs had kept them in the dark for years about what the laws said.[62]

In that troublous year a directive was sent to the Council of the North to restrain rack-renting.[63] Dismissal of farm workers before their term was out was forbidden; some curb was put on landlord freedom to enclose and eject. A statute near the end of Elizabeth's reign, 'for the maintenance of husbandry and tillage', reasoned that 'extreme poverty' ought to be prevented, and the wealth of the realm 'dispersed and distributed in many hands'.[64] Attempts were made to regulate food prices, and there was more readiness than in France to think of adjusting wages to the cost of living.[65] The Statute of Apprentices of 1563 made work compulsory, but also pointed out that wages as fixed when prices were lower could not be enforced now 'without the great grief and burden of the poor labourer and hired man'. A system of poor relief was being built up, more persistently than in any other country, and was capped by the Poor Law of 1601. It was an urgent need because in England the riches of the old church, partly destined to charity, had been so thoroughly dissipated. But it could not be got into working order quickly, and Elizabeth's enactments could make little impression on the problem of poverty: 'this legacy she passed to the Stuarts' – along with many others.[66]

Burghley thought textile workers 'of worse condition to be quietly governed than the husbandmen'.[67] Whether the government's preoccupation with social peace and order made it averse to industrial growth, with the recurrent spells of depression and

---

[60] Beier, p. 64.
[61] Kelly, p. 69. His Apendix I gives a chronology of riots and revolts from 1536 to 1641.
[62] Tawney, *Agrarian Problem*, p. 385.
[63] Tanner, *Documents*, p. 326.
[64] Prothero, pp. 95–6..
[65] J. U. Nef, *Industry and Government in France and England 1540–1640* (1960, New York edn 1957), p. 132.
[66] Kelly, p. 132.
[67] Supple, p. 235.

unemployment it brought with it, has been much debated, especially with reference to the act of 1563. In reality the argument is very inconclusive, because the bill was extensively modified during passage through the Commons, and its industrial provisions were never firmly enforced. Grants of monopoly patents did put some obstacles in the way of enterprise. They were acceptable as a means of getting new branches of production started, but they were too apt to be bestowed by a hard-up government as rewards for services. A recipient acquired the right, usually farmed to someone else for a lump sum, to levy tolls on all engaged in the business in question.[68] It was a sign of the times, and of the distance now between Parliament and any representative assembly in any other kingdom, when in 1601 on its insistence monopolies were prohibited.

The old feeling of identity between queen and nation had evaporated. A critical mood was astir, with European events to fan it. It was highly unsettling that Elizabeth felt compelled to support revolutionary causes abroad, and to cut off the head of a deposed sovereign who was besides mother of the heir presumptive. A series of three famine years in the mid-1950s pinched the poor; and the demand for men for the army, over five thousand annually in the last eighteen years of the reign, was an astonishingly severe drain on the country's manpower.[69] The government had no legal title to send militiamen overseas, but never hesitated to do so;[70] constitutional rights were for men of property, not labourers. All classes were wearying of the war effort, and the prolonged fighting in Ireland was crippling the government's finances. Forced loans were frequent, and later ones remained unpaid; wealth too was being subjected to conscription.

The advent of a new king from Edinburgh in 1603, by very remote hereditary right, passed off with no more disturbance than a Guy Fawkes plot. Here was a sharp contrast with the long ordeal of dynastic change in France, and proof of the consolidation of the state. England's civil wars would be fought over the rights of the throne, not any trivial question of rights to the throne. In the meantime James VI and I seemed in some respects a not ill-qualified successor. Unlike any of the Tudors except their founder, he had plenty of hard-won experience before coming to the English

[68] See Brooks, pp. 221–2.
[69] Cruickshank, p. 134.
[70] *ibid.*, p. 8.

throne. His book on what he called 'free monarchies', given to the
world in 1603, included in its title 'the Reciprock and Mutuall Dutie
betwixt a Free King and his Naturall Subjects', and he was more
accommodating in practice than he sometimes sounded in declamation[71] – if only from indolence. He did, however, expect a freer
hand than had been vouchsafed to him in Scotland, and soon had
cause to feel that he was only exchanging feudal turbulence for
more sophisticated obstruction.

He had no fondness for going among his people and inviting their
acclaim, like Elizabeth, though he was only too ready to address
them in print, but at the start he seemed not indisposed to work
with Parliament; the first of his reign had five sessions between 1604
and 1610. Relations very quickly soured. One sore point was the
Commons meddling with foreign policy, a jealously guarded royal
preserve. To James any questioning of his prerogative was
anathema, naturally enough because, as Hume was to say in his
History, it rested on traditional acceptance, not force. There was a
shrill note of personal vanity too in his homily to Parliament in
1610. 'The state of monarchy is the supremest thing upon earth . . .
government is my craft. . . I am now an old king . . . I must not be
taught my office.'[72] This implied an unrealistic conception of
kingship in the abstract, unaffected by place or circumstance. Its
pretensions were ballooning while the country's need of it
contracted. Things went even worse in 1614, with the 'Addled
Parliament'. There was not yet a clear-cut demarcation between
government and opposition, but indignation was aroused by
official efforts to get reliable candidates elected.[73] When the House
met there was a dearth of experienced men on the government side
to guide it as in Elizabeth's day; Sir Ralph Winwood, the newly
made secretary of state, had never sat there before. An impasse was
soon reached: it can be said to have marked the breakdown of the
Tudor constitutional balance.[74]

When not soaring on wings of divine right, James was too often
playing truant, indulging in his recreations of hunting and the
bottle. A minister of adequate stature to fill the gap was urgently
needed, as in other countries, but none came forward after the death
of Burghley's son Robert Cecil, earl of Salisbury, in 1612. Instead,
favourites came to the front, tactics were improvised. Ugly court

[71] As Kenyon, p. 69, reminds us.
[72] Prothero, pp. 293–5.
[73] Moir, pp. 52–4.
[74] *ibid.*, p. 169.

scandals cast discredit on the government. Monarchy stood at the apex of two distinct hierarchies, administrative and aristocratic, and the second of these was tainting the first with its odour of decay. As abroad, its instinct when in difficulties was to turn to the sovereign. To give lavishly to those about him was an intrinsic part of a ruler's style of living, and every royal household practised conspicuous waste as it were on principle. Elizabeth had been aware of the danger in this, and gave away chiefly smiles: she 'seldom gave boons', Thomas Fuller wrote, 'and never forgave due debts'.[75] James after his long Caledonian penury relished carefree prodigality, and scattered sinecures, pensions, lands. Court and nation were drifting apart, a tendency which can be traced on many levels. Realism in the public theatre, make-believe in the court masque, diverged into separate arts.

Nothing had come of negotiations for a reconstruction of the out of date fiscal system, to assure the government of solvency, and at the end of 1614, with the failure to obtain a parliamentary grant, its coffers were empty. They were replenished to some extent by Lionel Cranfield, an able financier from the City, promoted in 1622 to Treasurer. But the budget could be only very precariously balanced. More crown lands were having to be parted with, and offices sold more liberally. They were a risky speculation; only a few made fortunes out of them, but others could always hope. Titles too were up for sale. On the commercial and industrial side there were confusing cross-currents. Both the old financial oligarchy of London and some of the younger groups just finding their feet had some reasons for satisfaction. But there was resentment at attempts to smuggle monopoly patents back, in spite of repeated bans. They were designed now to raise money for the exchequer, but did it little good; they amounted to 'inefficient taxes on enterprise', most of whose yield failed to reach it.[76]

Several convergent factors were bringing about a prolonged depression in cloth exports, a vital sector of the economy. Certain business and other opposition circles were clamorous for a turnabout in foreign policy, to allow them to break into the colonial field. Readers were being regaled with books of travel and exploration, encomiums on English merchants and seafarers, breathing the nascent spirit of imperialism;[77] Holland was showing the way.

[75] Cited by Brooks, p. 351.
[76] Supple, p. 227.
[77] Wright, chap. 14.

James was going in the teeth of all this by moving from a sensible peace with Spain to an ill-judged entente with Spain. Envious esteem for the stablest of monarchies, the rock of order, must have helped to draw him on. Opponents could play on anti-Spanish and anti-Catholic sentiment, with all the more relish because it could be made use of to divert the discontent of the urban poor away from the rich and against the government.

In his final years a senile James was being supplanted by his son Charles and their joint confidant Buckingham. Parliament had to be allowed to return to life after a gap of seven years, more self-assertive than ever. Seats in the Commons were being contested now less for the sake of personal standing, more from public or party motives.[78] There was eagerness to canvass voters, the printing-press was busy with propaganda. A modern political vocabulary was entering the language.[79] Those qualified to vote may have been more numerous than formerly, though still a minority. James's third parliament in 1621–2 impeached his chancellor, Bacon, and Sir Giles Monpesson as a monopolist; his fourth, in 1624, impeached Cranfield, now earl of Middlesex. In 1626 Charles I's second parliament impeached Buckingham. The idea of ministerial responsibility was dawning.[80]

Parliament had an ally, always unlike its intermittent self in the field, in the common-law courts, whose practitioners formed a link, social as well as political, between landowners and businessmen. Invoking legal and constitutional principle against royal prerogative, they were acting much like the Parlement of Paris when it refused to register royal edicts, but with broader public backing. It was a portent when Sir Edward Coke, previously a zealous servant of government, had to be removed in 1616 from his place as chief justice. Talk like his of defending Magna Carta and ancient rights against newfangled innovation contained much bad history, as similar talk in France did, but also a more meaningful core, the possibility of medieval 'liberties' being widened into something nearer resembling modern 'liberty'. As in the Netherlands, continuity and revolutionary change would go together. For the

[78] See J. H. Plumb, 'The Growth of the Electorate in England from 1600 to 1715', *Past and Present*, no. 45 (1969).

[79] 'Politician', 'parliamentary', 'disorder', etc. had appeared in the sixteenth century, and many more such terms were being coined now. 'Cabinet council' seems to date from 1625. See L. P. Smith, *The English Language* (London, 1912), pp. 204, 218–19.

[80] Tanner, *Constitutional Conflicts*, p. 65.

government, the church was as prompt an ally as the law for Parliament. Preaching a long series of sermons against miscreants like Guy Fawkes, Bishop Andrewes equated kingship with the social bond itself. 'They be enemies of mankind, in being enemies to them by whom order and peace is kept in mankind.'[81] James made his views clear at the outset when he dismissed Puritan pleadings with the trenchant maxim: 'No bishop, no king.'

Between 1621 and 1629 political friction turned into crisis: Parliament 'moved with remarkable speed to change the constitutional balance',[82] while its leaders warned the country of how representative bodies had been snuffed out by monarchy abroad.[83] Both sides were viewing their differences in the – sometimes distorting – mirror of events on the continent. Charles's quarrels with his three early parliaments ended with the dissolution of March 1629 and a lengthy *Declaration,* clearly intended to impress the public even though it began by emphasizing that 'princes are not bound to give account of their actions, but to God alone'. It raked up all the opposition's misdemeanours, including (perennial complaint of governments) their 'not well distinguishing between well-ordered liberty and licentiousness'.[84] It was a royal Grand Remonstrance, and the prelude to eleven years of non-parliamentary rule.

In those years monarchy in England was essaying the transition to a more unhampered, 'absolute' authority, towards which France and Austria were forging ahead. It could not stand still, but must either advance or allow itself to be pushed aside. It sought, as rulers or ministers in other countries sporadically did, to make administration more rational, uniform, efficient, to turn it into enlightened despotism, dictating to all classes, the prisoner of none. One facet of its philosophy was an awareness of pressing social perils, which only a firm and impartial hand could moderate. It felt the urgency of finding work for multitudes suffering from the cloth depression, especially after 1628 in East Anglia, and of implementing the Poor Law.[85] In the same spirit it tried to prevent wages from being pushed down, and to restrain enclosures.

Such measures might conduce to the welfare of landowners collectively, by cushioning class relations, but could not be welcome to them individually. They were further antagonized by

---

[81] Andrews. p. 23 (1607).
[82] Stone,
[83] Kenyon, p. 40.
[84] Gardiner, pp. 83 ff.
[85] Supple, pp. 244–5.

taxation which fell largely on them, a reversal as it were of the order
of nature. It would take a long time to find workmanlike means of
tapping urban wealth, and the peasantry which bore the brunt of
taxation in France was ceasing to be equal to it in England.
Modernized administration had to be got going with the help of
archaic revenues disinterred by crown lawyers from musty
archives, very much as lawyers in France were ferreting out
obsolete feudal dues, or as Olivares was reviving obligations of
military tenure in Castile. Distraint of knighthood, or payments
enforced in lieu of the expensive and unwanted honour of being
knighted, was one such device; its success encouraged more daring
ventures, imposition of Ship Money on inland counties the most
controversial of all.[86] Methods of collection might be as unpalatable
as the sums paid. An indignant speaker in the Short Parliament in
1640 declared that sheriffs raising Ship Money 'send out men in
favour or mallice and are as grievous as the task masters of Egipt.'[87]
All this is a reminder of how little royal government had done all
this time, here as abroad, to overhaul its essential structures. Yet its
old ways were as well entitled as anything else to claim the sanction
of the grand old constitution that opponents were always harping
on. Charles was marching backward with his gaze on the future, the
opposition striding forward with its eye on the past.

English landlords were tightening feudal screws on their tenants,
but were none the less exasperated by the government doing the
same to them. At the same time, as JPs they were being chivied by
the Privy Council into greater activity, often for the carrying out of
policies they disliked; the government was treating them as if they
were the cadre of paid officials which it needed but could not yet
afford. Star Chamber, hitherto a reputable Tudor creation dis-
pensing quicker and cheaper justice than the common-law courts,
was discredited by being used to reinforce its programme. Excessive
use was made of the church. Most of Charles's top men were at best
mediocre, when men of first-class calibre were required; an example
of how a leaky ship of state will attract a bad crew. It was Archbishop
Laud who, not unmindful it may be supposed of the precedent of
Cardinal Richelieu across the Channel, became the leading minister.
A bishop, Juxon, was made treasurer, others were seated in the
Council.

---

[86] See H. H. Leonard.
[87] E. S. Cope and W. H. Coates (eds.), *Proceedings of the Short Parliament of 1640*
(London, 1977), p. 143.

This again was archaizing. The ecclesiastical machinery Laud was cranking up, with much strained use of the Tudor court of High Commission, belonged properly to a feudal, agrarian society, such as most of Catholic Europe still was, and could not work smoothly in a more complex one. The Anglican church had been hastily knocked together like a Noah's Ark, even if its timbers gained some seasoning from passage of time. Its benefices could not yet attract men of rank, though they were sufficiently restored in worth and respectability to beckon to humbler talent. Laud was the son of a Reading clothier, and never shed his uncourtly manner. Samuel Harshnett, made archbishop of York in 1628, was the son of a Colchester pastrycook. In its nominations the crown was recapitulating the preference of all early absolutism for assistants of modest station. A vein of anti-aristocratic feeling is discernible in the attitude of some of the prelates, while as plebeian upstarts they were the more obnoxious to the gentry.

The eleven years were not without their achievements, but these were meagre. Protection of the poor was too ineffective to earn gratitude from the masses, while powerful interests were only too successfully irritated; and despite all expedients, finance was falling into hopeless disorder. Still, it might have been possible to keep going. However disgruntled, the landed classes were not likely to break out and rebel on their own, and without Parliament they had no rallying-point. Opportunity came to the keener opposition groups, action was rendered unavoidable for the rest, by way of an extraneous event. In 1638 Scotland rose against Charles's encroachment on its autonomy, as Catalonia was about to rise against Olivares. Crisis exposed the brittleness of the regime; the psychological props of any such self-isolating autocracy grow frail as time goes on. England possessed a voting system adequate to give expression to a swing of national feeling, as the two elections in 1640, of the Short and Long Parliaments, demonstrated. Next year another external happening supervened – rebellion in Ireland. Tudor and Stuart colonialism was rebounding against its authors. England by itself might just be manageable, the British Isles were not. There ensued another electoral victory for the opposition, in London, where again the existence of political organs responsive to public opinion (as in a lesser degree in Barcelona) was important.

Opposition had been held together a good deal, as in all such cases, by detestation of individuals. The higher classes wanted to get rid of some institutions irksome to them, like Star Chamber and High Commission, as well as men like Laud and Wentworth. What to put in their place was far less easy to agree on. Meanwhile Charles had no option but to drift towards a league with the more conservative groups and regions, the same that the monarchy in earlier days had subdued in partnership with what were now its enemies. This realignment was never clear-cut, and throughout the civil wars tangled emotions and aspirations compelled each side to turn to religion for warrant. It remains impossible to say with any precision what the wars were fought for. If any straightforward answer could be given, it would have stared the men of the time in the face, or been unearthed by now by generations of laborious research. Most of the lawyers, officials, landowners, MPs in the two camps were recruited from the same strata, even from the same families. In each, only an élite minority was militantly resolute; but this can be said of all grand historical conflicts. And while it may be admitted that 'the class war theory of the Marxists has only limited applicability to the seventeenth century',[88] *class* is altogether a complex, composite phenomenon, never so much a reality as a concept, but not a meaningless one; and many strands of class struggle were very obviously present in Elizabethan and early Stuart England.

The decisive thing pushing England into what can be called a civil war within the upper classes, as well as within the nation, may have been a third force extraneous to them, like the Scots and Irish risings, the irruption of the masses on to the scene. It was the hatred of common people for all the privileged – for Shakespeare's 'nobility and tranquillity', profiteers whose saint, the commonwealth, they do not pray to 'but prey on her, for they ride up and down on her'.[89] England had long been the arena of a general scramble to attain wealth or avoid penury: men would do and risk anything and everything, Burton wrote in *The Anatomy of Melancholy*, 'rather than endure this insufferable yoke of Poverty, which doth so tyrannize, crucify, and generally depress us.'[90] This yoke the masses had suffered most gallingly. In the army debates in 1647 Colonel Rich the radical was to estimate that if any property qualification at all was retained, five sixths of the people would be excluded from the franchise.[91]

The disinherited were looking, confusedly but passionately, for

---

[88] Stone, *Causes*, p. 54. Cf. 71–2, where it is argued that to define the alignment of parties in 1642 in terms of class is impossible.
[89] *Henry IV* Part 1, Act 2, Sc. 1.
[90] I, p. 399 (Bohn Library, London, 1923).
[91] *Clarke Papers* I, pp. 315.

some alleviation of their lot. Tumult in London in 1640 was as loud as in Paris in 1789, and as in France then there were widespread disorders in the provinces, enclosure riots among them: 'the whole economy and social order seemed on the point of breakdown'.[92] In June 1642 Charles warned Parliament that continued opposition would open the way for a rising of the masses which would subvert 'all rights and properties', and reduce everything to anarchy or mob rule by leaders like Jack Cade or Wat Tyler.[93] To suppose that such warnings, uttered by both sides, were merely devised to make the other side's flesh creep,[94] is unconvincing. On the contrary, the grand line of division may well have been disagreement about how to deal with the popular excitement, whether by trying to damp it down or by giving it a controlled outlet.

As in the revolt of the Netherlands, the diffusion of literacy brought by Reformation allowed radical ideas to reach all sections of the middling classes, and in the towns many lower down. But there was the ever-present and fateful gap between them and the rural poor, whose concern was with immediate economic and social grievances, with hunger, not political reform, and who were not easily accessible to the religious watchwords that meant so much to the literate. Alienated from the body politic, they could not feel that either side was their side. When they had risen in the past it was for the most part alone, as was the case with peasant risings all over Europe and Asia. This might well hasten their defeat, but it was more in accord with their instincts to come together on their own than to fit into any wider combination. Now they sank into inertia.

By the time Charles was defeated and a new order had to be framed, it was unmistakably clear at least that underlying all else were questions of property. Before long it was equally clear that whoever had won, it was not the common man. 'He hath fought to enslave himself', Colonel Rainborough sombrely declared, 'to give power to men of riches, men of estates, to make him a perpetual slave.'[95] Progress is a very complex thing. The revolution, climax of a century of change and ferment, was the thunderstorm which finally dispelled medieval twilight and inducted England into

---

[92] Kenyon, p. 141.

[93] C.Hill, 'From Lollards to Levellers', in M. Cornforth (ed.), *Rebels and their Causes* (London, 1978), p. 51.

[94] Stone, *Causes*, p. 77. For an opposite thesis see Manning: 'the conflict was precipitated by popular risings against sections of the nobility and gentry. . . ' (preface).

[95] *Clarke Papers* I, pp. 325–6.

modernity. It came because the old framework of institutions and ideas was too wormeaten to survive; a new one, not in all respects better, was taking its place.

7

Scotland

Scotland defended its independence heroically in the middle ages, but was too backward and poor to make much of it, to develop as a stable feudal kingdom; it was then equally unable, by itself, to evolve into a viable modern state. Its core consisted of little more than the Forth-Clyde valley, about the size of Catalonia, with some appendages, chiefly Aberdeenshire to the northeast and Ayrshire to the southwest; not enough to ballast so big, scattered, and mountainous a country. Only exchange of grain for cattle provided some peaceful tie with the Highlands, and in the eyes of Lowland burghers Highlanders were not fellow-Scots, but barbarians, as they were to be still in the days of Baillie Jarvie. With the continent, however, especially the Baltic lands, the east coast had many links. All towns of any note were on or close to the sea. Traders and adventurers moved far afield in quest of opportunities wanting at home; Scotland formed one of the links between western and northern Europe, and owed to this much of its vitality and receptivity.

James IV's death at Flodden in 1513 inaugurated another in a long chain of Stuart minorities. James V grew up to resume the Sisyphus-like task of political building. He inherited from the earl of Arran's regency a small band of men whose loyalty was to the government rather than to the individual in power:[1] to the state, that is, an entity coming to birth more belatedly than in England. He enforced order by methods brutal but telling, and in 1540 sailed trimphantly round the north and reannexed the Western Isles to the crown. But in 1542 he too succumbed to an old, besetting temptation of Scottish rulers by blundering into war with England; defeated at Solway Moss, he died, aged thirty, leaving – worse legacy than his father's – only an infant daughter.

[1] C. Bingham, p. 79.

Scotland had a hereditary monarchy, a recognizable capital in Edinburgh, though the court was more peripatetic than the English, a Privy Council, and a Parliament, far less well developed than England's, besides a less formal 'Convention of Estates' which might meet for more circumscribed purposes. Clergy, nobles, and royal burghs made up the three Estates. The gentry, known as 'small barons' or 'barons of the shire', were not represented till the end of the century. Nor did they acquire till much later the taste of English squires for seeking urban seats; burgh representatives were therefore more genuinely civic than in England.[2] There were thirty or forty 'royal burghs' in mid-century, towns directly under the crown like those of the *realengo* in Castile, as distinct from the mostly lilliputian 'burghs of barony' on the lords' domains.

Royal burghs themselves were small enough: even Edinburgh had only about 30,000 inhabitants. Minor ones only sent representatives intermittently. They might take more interest in the meetings of the Convention of Royal Burghs, which started in the earlier sixteenth century and was an annual institution from 1578. Total attendance in Parliament might be no more than sixty. It was coming to be presided over by the chancellor, not by a Speaker of its own, and it was overshadowed also by a committee of its members known as the 'Lords of the Articles', although these might comprise half the total attendance, with the same number from each order. They usurped all the parent body's functions, and only submitted their proposals to a vote at the end. Laws so passed had little more weight than 'Acts' of the Privy Council.

The Estates could be spirited enough when it came to refusing 'aids', all the more because, as in England, nobility was not exempt from taxpaying; also because, by contrast with either England or Castile, only the towns entitled to representation paid the third estate's contribution, set at one sixth of the total. Tax-collecting was farmed out to the sheriffs, local magnates like provincial governors on the continent, who had made their posts hereditary.[3] Revenue was derisorily small, and the crown lands, formerly swollen by confiscations, were dwindling. Exceptionally heavy recourse was had consequently to the church, whose moral decay and isolation left it in no shape to resist. In the first half of the sixteenth century its traditional share of taxation, two fifths, was being increased to half.[4]

---

[2] Terry, pp. 62–3.
[3] Lee, *James Stewart*, p. 8.
[4] Donaldson, *James V – James VII*, p. 132.

Much of the country was far less under the authority of the crown than under that of nobles, often fortified by 'charters of regality' which made them petty sovereigns in all but name. In Galloway an earl of Cassilis, 'thinking him self gritter than any king in thear quarteris', had no scruple about roasting a titular abbot in front of a fire, to induce him to make over his title to the property.[5] Rebellions were frequent; they might, it is true, amount to no more than 'bloodless demonstrations',[6] but fighting and feuding could plunge districts into chaos; it was some relief, like bleeding to a fevered patient, that mercenary service abroad drew off swarms of swordsmen. As a last resort the government would empower one noble, by 'letters of fire and sword', to take punitive action against another. There was no more unruly baronage in Europe than this, 'selfish, false, bloodthirsty, desperate, almost beyond parallel'.[7] There is a peculiar note of hysteria in the annals of its violence, as of a class left behind by history, doomed to self-destruction. Round every great family clustered its cadet branches, so that Crichtons, Ramsays, or Ogilvies were very much like clans.[8] Lowland feudalism, particularly in the Borders and other outskirts, had something of a tribal quality; conversely in the Highlands the chief's power and ownership of the clan lands had a markedly feudal cast, derived from outside.

Lords were having to find other means, besides armed robbery, to keep their incomes up to their expenses. One was 'wadset', by which part of an estate was virtually mortgaged and lost in return for a loan. During this and the next century the older and strictly military form of tenure, wardholding, was giving way to the feu, or feu-ferme, free of explicit feudal obligations though still, in such a state of social life, carrying with it much of the relationship of lord and vassal.[9] There was too little guarantee of life or property for any man to be safe on his own. To the lord a feu brought a sum of ready money, the 'grassum' paid on entry by the tenant and his successors; apart from this only a fixed quit-rent, of declining real value, was payable. Feuing greatly enlarged the number of lairds, or gentry. Although less independent of the nobility than in England, they were growing more conscious of themselves as a corporate body.

---

[5] Fyfe, p. 24.
[6] Donaldson, *Mary*, p. 84.
[7] Lang, II, p. 212. Cf. Carlyle's 'hungry sanguinary pack of Earls'. *Historical Sketches*, ed. A. Carlyle (4th edn, London, 1902), p. 3.
[8] Grant, p. 51.
[9] Smout, pp. 126–7.

Some of them tried in 1560 to secure parliamentary representation; in fact the first shire 'commissioners' did not take their seats until 1594, and it was longer before all shires were regularly represented.[10] Connexions with the merchantry were another fillip: they inter-married with it, their younger sons went into trade, they shared with educated townsmen the profession of law. Many of the lawyers who staffed the central administration – exiguous enough, to be sure – were drawn from the gentry of counties close to Edinburgh: Fife, where lairds abounded, and the Lothians.

Formal serfdom had gone out long before, and was not reviving now on the land; there was no need of it, for with growing popu-lation and competition for farms the cultivators could be effectively squeezed as tenants on short leases, or tenants at will with even less security, and subject to a variety of customary dues in kind or in services. Many tenants were too poor to work farms by themselves; hence the several forms of 'run-rig', by which groups of families took land as collective tenants, and might work a farm made up of scattered strips, crudely and quarrelsomely, with a primitive eight-ox plough and at times some hired help.[11] It was a survival from communal agrarian habits of very early date; something like it could be found in Celtic western Ireland down to the nineteenth century.

Tenurial conditions for the humbler sort were worsening. With the spread of feu-farming, the more favourable position of those known as 'kindly tenants', on whom custom conferred a degree of occupancy right, was being eroded. Extortionate grassums were demanded for renewal of leases, like fines in England. Rents, largely paid in kind, were being screwed up, and might amount to a third of the gross yield of the land,[12] a yield so slender that any smaller share of it would have been too small to sustain a locust-army of idle consumers battening on a population of between half a million and a million. Landless labourers were many, and their condition bleak. They were likely to be paid not in cash but with food and sometimes a patch of land.

With all this, Scotland was one of the few countries to experience no peasant revolt of any magnitude. One reason must have been that the upper classes were well armed, in a society far more military than Tudor England and less in need of a strong state to apply

[10] Donaldson , *James V – James VII*, p. 5.
[11] J. G. Leyburn, *The Scotch-Irish* (Chapel Hill, 1962), pp. 16–23; Smout, pp. 112–13.
[12] Smout, p. 129.

coercion. Cultivators were of very mixed sorts, scarcely capable of combining. Moreover the entanglements of clan or kinship, lingering in this corner of Europe as in so many parts of Asia, hindered class feeling. Along with the poor man's habit of shaking off his troubles by removing, often abroad, they could make for a rough, plainspoken demeanour, out of key with his real servitude, which struck many foreign visitors. It did the lords no harm, and they were left free of any compulsion to close their ranks and stop squabbling. Their feuds, by involving their dependants, divided and weakened the plebeian mass still further.

Towns were themselves landowners, a fact still recalled on the Borders by an annual 'riding of the marches'. An inscription at Selkirk commemorates the town's first provost, murdered in 1541 on his way to Edinburgh to uphold its claim on some lands in the vicinity. Provosts might be nominated by the crown; in Edinburgh they were so habitually, the capital thus being closer in status to Paris than to London. Some towns were always under the thumb of a neighbouring landowner. Internally they were going the same way as most others in Europe, and more easily because since 1469 free election of burgh magistrates had yielded to self-perpetuating oligarchies, the Gild Merchants. Their members were all the more firmly in the saddle because of their connexions with the gentry round about. There were doubtless conscientious men among them, like the Alexander Peter, treasurer of Arbroath, lauded in his epitaph in 1630 for his zeal in all 'common work'. 'He devised our school and he hung our bell', it concludes.[13] But the run of town records testify to 'general inefficiency' and 'considerable corruption'.[14]

There was constant sparring between the city fathers and the middling strata, organized in the craft guilds which had appeared late on the scene in Scotland. A riotous dispute at Edinburgh in 1582 led to government intervention and to the artisans being accorded eight places out of the eighteen in the council; they could not hold office, but would have some say in elections. This arrangement was adopted by several other towns. It was as much as the craftsmen could get, since there was no alliance between them and the unorganized mass of journeymen and casual labourers, whose grievances over wages broke out from time to time in tumults. If the rural poor were more submissive than in England, the urban

---

[13] R. L. Brown, *A Book of Epitaphs* (Newton Abbot, 1969), p. 100.
[14] Grant, p. 105.

poor were apt to be less so; for one reason because English industry was migrating from provincial towns to the countryside, whereas towns in Scotland, like those in the Netherlands, clung to their monopoly of trade and industry. Economic privilege kept the guild-masters, the aristocracy of labour, less rebellious than they might otherwise have been, but at the cost of leaving production technically unprogressive.

James V inflated the royal patronage by gaining formal concession in 1535 from Rome of a right of appointment to all prelacies. Unable to trust his nobles, he made much use of churchmen in administration. This did nothing to arrest the moral decay of his partner the church, which laid it open to attacks like Sir David Lindsay's satire of 1540, *The Thrie Estaites* – 'by far the most brilliantly-written drama of the period' anywhere in Britain.[15] At the same time the wealth that furnished so much to the royal exchequer was on the ebb. Well before the Reformation a great part of it passed, by way of *commendams*, long feu leases, and other devices, into lay hands, chiefly aristocratic. This was proceeding so smoothly that it has been questioned whether the nobility had any reason to seek the church's overthrow for the sake of its spoils.[16] In the long run in any case, Protestantism in its intransigent Calvinist form would be taken up most wholeheartedly in the towns, where its organization could be fitted into the civic framework. But at the outset its fortunes depended more on what backing it could get from the lairds, which varied markedly from region to region. Protestantism was strongest at first in Fife, with the town of Dundee; it was distinctly weak in Edinburgh.[17] Capital cities – Paris is a salient case – were likely to be too closely attached to the old regime, clerical as well as secular, to change faith readily. Size and independence made London exceptional. Among the poor, as in all countries, Reformation gave new expression to stirrings of discontent.

In the fighting leading up to the establishment of Protestantism most of Scotland was apathetic, though an unwonted public opinion was beginning to be aroused by the rival appeals and manifestos; and the active participants were more concerned with politics than with theology. James V's widow, Mary of Guise, was regent from 1554 to 1560, and her French troops and assistants enabled the reformers to stand forward as the party of national

---

[15] A. M. Kinghorn, *Medieval Drama* (London, 1968), p. 134.
[16] Donaldson, *James V – James VII*, p. 137; Cowan, p. 5.
[17] Cowan, pp. 20, 26–8.

defence, as a few years later in the Netherlands, and to bespeak aid from England. What was decisive was the preference of most of the nobility, gaining ground ever since the lesson of Flodden, for an English entente;[18] the Auld Alliance was crumbling. Leaders were found in Lord James Stuart, the later earl of Moray, an illegitimate son of the late king, and William Maitland of Lethington, one of the race of lairds in state service, who was to rise to secretary of state. In 1560 French forces had to be withdrawn, and the Protestant faith was proclaimed by Parliament.

Next year James's daughter Mary, widow of the young French king Francis II, returned. Her brief reign demonstrated that politics was a harder game for a woman to shine at in Scotland than in England, and all the harder if she embroiled herself in matrimonial and amorous vagaries. Mary was far less a Catholic bigot, a Scottish Mary Tudor, than her Kirk critics suspected. But she came back from France, full of the ideas of continental absolutism';[19] and she was very much a foreigner. Yet she was not a complete failure, and had more support in the country than has usually been reckoned.[20] There may well have been substance in the allegation of one adherent that many nobles were determined to get rid of her before her twenty-fifth birthday, when a Scottish sovereign had a pre-sciptive right to revoke grants of crown lands made during his or her minority.[21] At any rate, in 1567 her opponents compelled her to abdicate in favour of her infant son James, and next year she sought refuge and found captivity in England.

Parliament had been showing signs of greater animation, but it was too imperfect a body to grasp the opportunity of another long minority. Instead there was a fresh series of regencies, which might almost be called the normal government of Scotland, as of Tibet. Moray ruled not unsuccessfully in the three years allotted him. He, like Maitland, was as deep a calculator as the times required, and as Sir Walter Scott was to portray him.[22] He understood that a ruler of Scotland could not sit at ease, but must stir about and see his orders carried out. He was at Linlithgow when he was murdered in 1570 by the Hamilton faction. In England by this time faction-fighting was being transmuted into court intrigue, in Scotland it still relied on rougher arguments. Three years of strife followed, until in 1573

[18] Donaldson, *James V – James VII*, p. 137.
[19] Russell, p. 137.
[20] Donaldson, *Mary*, pp. 124–5, 136–7.
[21] Donaldson, *First Trial*, pp. 131–2.
[22] *The Abbot*, chap. 18.

the ruggedly Protestant earl of Morton, of the great Lowland clan of Douglas, defeated a party which wanted Mary restored. This now included Maitland and the majority of magnates; Morton had English backing, but his triumph owed most to support from lairds and burgesses,[23] strengthened politically by the Reformation as it was strengthened by them. Morton 'held the contre under great obedience', a contemporary wrote, but grew too 'proud and disdanfull' of his fellow-nobles[24] – the mentality of the feudalist at the top of the heap, with clan rancour to inflame it. He was also busy feathering his nest, while the public smarted under a depreciation of the currency.

When Morton's turn came to be overthrown and executed in 1581 there was a government in being, if a rudimentary one, for James to take over. Only fifteen at this date, he was soon exhibiting 'very remarkable political ability and sagacity'.[25] From 1584 he had as secretary an able administrator in Lethington's brother, John Maitland of Thirlestane, who in 1587 was made chancellor. He was the first man in that century, neither peer nor prelate, to hold the lofty post, and his promotion gave umbrage to the aristocracy. It was men of his middle rank that James preferred to employ. Like many other rulers, he tried to surround himself with loyal faces by creating a bevy of new nobles, mostly endowed with old church lands they had got hold of. Some of them were or had been in government service, and they could in some degree counterbalance the military nobility; though in so feudal an environment they would be apt to assimilate themselves to it before long – a familiar European experience.

Poverty and consequent lack of force handicapped all efforts to reduce the country to order. In place of a regular army there was only a mixture of feudal array and militia. From time to time a 'weapon-showing' was announced; in 1587 all Edinburgh men were summoned to appear in Greyfriars kirkyard with specified accoutrements.[26] But only too many of those with arms would have been better without them. An act of 1585 forbidding 'bands', or confederacies, a right or custom cherished as warmly by the feudalists as by the anarchic Polish nobility, could not amount to much more than a sermon. The Borders were as lawless as ever, and

[23] Donaldson, *James V – James VII*, pp. 166–7.
[24] Sir James Melville, in Fyfe, p. 50.
[25] Donaldson, *James V – James VII*, pp. 214–15.
[26] Cf. the description of a 'weapon-showing' in Walter Scott's *Old Mortality*, chap. 2.

in Ayrshire between 1597 and 1601, near the end of James's sojourn in Scotland, there raged a bloody vendetta between two branches of the Kennedies.[27] He could do little but play off one set of ruffians against another, a complex game at which he became proficient. In the western Highlands the formidable Campbell clan, which had turned protestant, was gravitating towards the crown, in pursuit of its own aggrandizement, and in an irregular fashion could be used by the government as its policeman.

On the towns James could not lean with much confidence; Edinburgh at times was one of his nuisances. Hence he was the less disposed to build up Parliament as an ally; it was too likely to be utilized by restless grandees. For other reasons he mistrusted the Kirk, whose genius might seem more republican than monarchical. An Anglican was to make it his boast that English churchmen 'never were known to *beard their Sovereigns* – a thing as natural to the Scottish Presbytery as eating and drinking to other men'.[28] James's court had no Habsburg ceremonial to screen it from a rude world. His former tutor, George Buchanan, maintained in *De Jure Regni apud Scotos*, in 1579, that his countrymen had always possessed and often exercised the right to punish or remove bad rulers. Such doctrine, whether expounded by Calvinists in Scotland or France, or by a Jesuit like Mariana in Spain, was less novel than medieval, a refusal to move with the absolutist times. But James could not wish to be reminded that he was only on the throne because his mother had been ejected from it.

Calvinism was less easily kept on a leash than in Holland, where it was only one of several Protestant movements. With the gradual melting away of the hostile majority in the country, at least passively Catholic but leaderless,[29] the Kirk could pose as an authentic national institution, more representative than Parliament had ever been. From its beginnings in gatherings held in 1560 and 1561 the General Assembly, combining ministers and laymen, developed into an annual event; as subsidiaries it had provincial synods and, from 1580, district presbyteries. In hours of disturbance it could exert an influence on behalf of order, but it was sometimes inevitably drawn into the maze of faction. James looked on its leading spirits as unruly demagogues. He won a round in 1584 when Andrew Melville, one

[27] Fergusson, pp. 67 ff.
[28] Dr Thomas Pierce, cited in J. Nichols, *Calvinism and Arminianism* (London, 1824), p. 218.
[29] See J. R. Elder, *Spanish Influences in Scottish History* (Glasgow, 1920), pp. v–vi, on Spanish efforts to exploit Catholic feeling.

of the most outspoken, was forced to betake himself to England; his flight was followed by the 'Black Acts', promulgating royal supremacy and episcopalian principles. James always hankered for a bench of well-schooled bishops; but many reverses and disappointments were in store for him.

There was some room for collaboration; poor relief was one field. James was unlucky with his weather, for in spite of some economic growth it was an era of bad harvests and abnormal food scarcities. Between 1571 and 1601 prices almost tripled, partly because of the bad state of the currency. An act of 1579 made it the responsibility of each burgh and parish to provide for the needy by a local impost. This was surprisingly early; fear of social disorder must have been a motive, but there was also the Kirk's conscience, and its collections and fines usefully eked out the irregularly paid rates. It could sympathize with the sufferers the more readily because itself for long poverty-stricken. It had a chronic grievance over not receiving even the paltry allowance promised it in 1562, of a share (roughly a moiety) with the crown of one third of the former ecclesiastical revenues. These jeremiads were often coupled with the contention that property once devoted to charity should again be applied to 'sustentation of the poor'.[30] Down to the mid-1590s the Assembly could be heard denouncing with old Testament thunders the 'cruell oppression of the poore tennents', 'extreme thraldome in services', 'universall neglect of justice'.[31] Little by little such protests were muffled, as radical ministers came to be overshadowed by respectable lairds and burghers. Moreover, clerical incomes were slowly bettering, and by the end of the century were sufficient to attract younger sons of lairds, who tended to supplant the educated townsmen previously in the van. During the seventeenth century, 'to a very large extent the ministry was upper-middle-class.'[32]

James, like some of Europe's other shaky sovereigns, had to have recourse to the arts of propaganda, and in 1600 he made the foiling of the mysterious Gowrie conspiracy the occasion for a display of them. A concourse welcomed him into the capital and escorted him to the mercat cross or city centre: there his chaplain gave a statement of what had happened, which 'the King himselff secoundit and confirmit, to move the people to dewtie and thankfulness.'[33] This

---

[30] Peterkin, p. 29; cf. W. Notestein, *The Scot in History* (London, 1946), pp. 133–4.

[31] Peterkin, pp. 434–5.

[32] Donaldson, *James V – James VII*, pp. 151–2.

[33] Fyfe, p. 116.

enabled him to get the better of the recalcitrant Edinburgh ministers, and reaffirm his episcopalian programme. But no ruler wanted to depend on common people more than he was obliged to: the instinct of all was to repose inside their palaces as soon as they safely could. Like so many a later Scot, James never saw a finer prospect than the highroad that led him in 1603 to England.

He had been meditating a new designation to cover both kingdoms;[34] he now announced that the two of them constituted 'Great Britain', and set up a joint commission to plan full union. This was bold innovation, by contrast with the prevailing type of relationship between two or more countries with a single monarch, the one established not long since, for example, between Castile and Portugal. There was a precedent in the closer federation of Poland and Lithuania in 1569, which may well have impressed James. His wife was Danish, and Poland like other countries round the Baltic was thronged with Scots. He must have hoped that union would strengthen his hand in both kingdoms, and would tranquillize Scotland by assimilating it into the more orderly English scheme. Each hung back, however. Englishmen had no fancy for Scotsmen sharing in all their trade. Scots were apprehensive of what the proposal would mean in practice, as their awareness of things on the continent might well make them. Their Parliament professed itself willing, but only on terms of 'a trewe and friendlie Unioun' which would not degrade Scotland into 'a conquered and slavishe province' like those governed by Spanish viceroys.[35]

Great Britain thus became another of Europe's binary states. Edinburgh is further from London than Madrid from Lisbon, twice as far as Saragossa. Yet monarchy could sometimes work less badly by remote control than on the spot. No Scottish factions could usurp control of a court far away in the south; and it had much ampler means of rewarding those who earned its approval. There was some self-deception in James's boast of sitting in London and governing Scotland with his pen, but he really had some cause to congratulate himself. He had no viceroy, but the Privy Council, or a small inner group, mostly reliable officials, managed affairs under his direction. As for the Parliament, he found means to nominate the Lords of the Articles, though a form of election was preserved. A copy of English local government through justices of the peace,

[34] D. Hay, 'The Use of the Term "Great Britain" in the Middle Ages', *Proceedings of the Society of Antiquaries of Scotland* (1955–6), pp. 64–5.
[35] Wedgwood, p. 34.

which James had taken an interest in while still in Scotland, was installed in 1609.

He took a different step, which was to lead towards both his own partial success in ruling Scotland at long range, and his son's total failure, with an Act in 1606, holding up religion and justice as the two perennial pillars of authority and order, and making known that episcopacy was at last to be fully restored. Sessions of the Assembly in that year, and in 1610 and 1616, were packed, and some obstructive individuals prosecuted and banished. It would seem that the moderate majority of ministers were able to reconcile themselves to the changes; and the Assembly continued to meet and do its work. By the end of the reign there were two archbishops and eleven bishops, in the enjoyment of comfortable incomes; not aristocrats, but from families of lairds, some of burghers.[36] But James would have done well to ponder the result of Philip II's plan to bridle the Netherlands with a posse of Bishops. He went foolishly far with his 'Five Articles of Perth' in 1618, 'a serious tactical error' attributable to age and long absence from the Scottish scene.[37] He had come north and made a progress in the previous year, but it was his sole visit.

Invigorating currents both intellectual and economic were at work to keep Scotland from drying up, like Aragon or Sicily, when deserted by its king. Prices were levelling off, bad harvest years happened to be fewer. There was some official encouragement of manufactures, and foreign craftsmen were being invited to settle. To the government one recommendation of commercial activity was its adding wealth and weight to the burgher class and its gentry relatives, the best-behaved social elements. But the economy was more subject than the English to feudal warping. Landowners dabbling in industrial enterprises could use their power to depress wages.[38] Some had mines on their estates, and coal was an important product. To make sure of a labour supply an act of 1606, confirmed in 1641, tied colliers to the mines as serfs, if not slaves.[39] The same fate was befalling the salt-pan workers; it was a glaring exception to Scotland's general freedom from serfdom. For some of the landowning class and their dependants further opportunity was provided by the colonization, jointly with England, of Ulster, first-fruit of Anglo-Scottish partnership and prophetic of much imperial expan-

[36] Lang, III, p. 13; Donaldson, *James V – James VII*, pp. 221–2.
[37] Donaldson, *James V – James VII*, p. 209.
[38] Johnson, pp. 58 ff.
[39] R. P. Arnot, *A History of the Scottish Miners* (London, 1955), pp. 3–4.

sion to come.[40] A sign of progress was the decay now setting in of the patriarchal power of the Border chiefs.[41] Shorter work was being made of plebeian evil-doers in those parts. It is recorded in his memorial in Dunbar parish church that Sir George Horne, of the reorganized Border Commission, made earl of Dunbar in 1605, 'condemned and caused hang 140 of the humblest thieves'. In the less barbarous regions the old strongholds of the nobility were giving place to a new, more urbane and comfortable style of 'Scottish baronial' architecture.

In James's final years there was some deterioration, with a recrudescence of trouble on the Borders and in the Highlands. An absentee ruler needed competent deputies, and the Privy Council was running short of them. Charles treated it merely as his mouthpiece – it contained half a dozen prelates – and his English councillors were consulted equally little on Scottish affairs. Scotland was his private appanage; perhaps he had in mind at times his uncle King Christian of Denmark, licking Norway into shape. But Christian was in Norway very often. It was always rash to try to govern on absolutist lines from a distance; and Charles had no regular army, and Scotland unlike Norway had till very recently been a kingdom standing on its own feet. A threatened resumption of old crown lands alarmed the nobility on the threshold of the reign. Later on Laud's meddlesome ambition to bring Scotland into uniformity with Anglicanism allowed a united front of classes to be forged, under the banner of the National Covenant. There was then no one to carry out the stream of orders from London for firm action. Charles was beating the air.

Open rebellion when it came in 1638 was remarkably well planned and effective by comparison with those of the same period on the continent. Unlike Catalonia or Portugal, Scotland or at any rate the Scottish leadership was not trying to break away and return to independence; its goal was rather integration with England on new bases.[42] But the country had not yet matured far enough to produce a party which could combine with the more progressive forces in England. Instead, it ended by becoming a drag on the English revolution for which it had given the signal, and helped to restore the monarchy it had been the first to defy.

---

[40] Other Scots were pushing into the Shetlands and setting up as lairds there; see B. Smith, introduction to reprint of Thomas Gifford's *Historical Description of the Zetland Islands* (Sandwick, 1976).

[41] See on this Walter Scott's letter to Lord Dalkeith, 23 Nov. 1806.

[42] This fact emerges clearly from Stevenson's account.

Map 4   *The Baltic lands in the later sixteenth century*

8

Scandinavia

Scandinavia entered the sixteenth century as the Kalmar Union, a federation set up in 1397; it sprawled from Iceland to Finland, with a population which may have reached one and a half million in 1500, less than two and a half a century later.[1] In the 1520's a more democratic Sweden broke away from the hegemony of a heavily feudalized Denmark which, however, retained possession of its southern region. It was the first of only two nations to win independence during the century. More akin to Sweden in social composition, but still more sparsely peopled, Norway remained attached to Denmark. Scandinavia had one face turned westward, but two of the capitals were on the Baltic, and the third, Oslo, at its entrance; all three lay on the eastern rim of their countries. Far smaller than the Mediterranean, the northward-running inland sea brought the nations round it into sharper contact and collision. Thanks partly to the embitterment stirred up between them by their separation, Denmark and Sweden developed an intense preoccupation with external aims and problems, and to this their state history owed much.

From various points of view Scandinavia was an extension of northern Germany. Nearly all Reformation ideas came to it from Lutheran Germany. Economically in medieval times a German colony, in the sixteenth century it had to shake off this sway, but it benefited at the same time from German commercial and technical expertise, in mining for instance, as many other countries did. Militarily, it was the same story: the German mercenary, that *vade*

---

[1] R. Mols, 'Population in Europe 1500–1700', in Cipolla, p. 38. Sweden's population about 1600 is estimated by Oakley, p. 83, at 750,000; by Stomberg, p. 323, at a million, including Finland; Andersson, p. 164, gives 850,000, and 350,000 for Finland, a generation later.

mecum of sixteenth-century governments, as ubiquitous as the Peruvian silver that often set him in motion, played a considerable part in both Denmark and Sweden. Without him state-building in the north would have been a good deal more difficult.

Denmark, its ruling family linked with the German principality of Holstein, belonged as much to Germany as to Scandinavia, and to a sector of it bordering on the more feudal northeast. Court, nobility, towns, administration were all Germanized, the peasantry and fisherfolk alone truly Danish. Over flatlands well suited, like the plains of north Germany or Poland, for armoured cavalry to ride down mutinous villagers, the countryfolk in spite of tenacious resistance were being reduced to servitude. Nobles whose greed was whetted by rising grain prices were expanding their share of the land from a quarter to more than two fifths, and enforcing heavier labour services;[2] they did well also from the export of cattle which was a mainstay of the economy. Judicial powers in the landowners' hands helped to keep peasants in their place. The *Rigsraad* or council was an aristocratic citadel; in the *Rigsdag* or Estates the burghers, spokesmen of a class very small and still semi-foreign, could only squeak while nobles roared or brayed.

Hemmed in by the nobility, the crown made spasmodic efforts to emancipate itself, and to prevent landowners from engrossing so much of the surplus that there was nothing left for it to tax. Christian II (1513–23) was clearly conscious of how absolutism was building itself up in the west when he angled for middle- and lower-class support against the aristocracy. But the burgher class could not help much, and though Christian devised laws with some promise of protection for the peasants, he did not – no anointed king could – ally himself with them to resist their masters. On its domains the crown was always tempted to resort to the same modes of exploitation. Christian was true to his royal trade in turning too much of his energy to external enterprise, the scheme of a Baltic commercial empire with Sweden brought back under Danish supremacy. Success in this would no doubt have assisted him at home. Instead it was an expensive failure, and in 1523 the nobles deposed their king, reaffirmed the elective character of the throne, and put on it his uncle Frederick. Deposition of a monarch, scarcely thinkable in France or Spain, was to be seen again in Europe's northern marches, in Scotland and Sweden.

[2] J. de Vries, *The Economy of Europe in an Age of Crisis 1600–1750* (Cambridge, 1976), p. 58.

In 1534 social conflict broke out, entangled with religious issues. Copenhagen favoured Lutheranism, while the nobility opposed it; but when it came in the end, with reinforcement from outside, confiscated church lands fattened nobles as well as king. With this added wealth, they were growing sated, torpid, disinclined to foreign adventure. To spirited rulers, on the other hand, Denmark might well seem the prison it was to Hamlet, and they would go in for exploits abroad as Christian II had done. Shortage of money often clogged them, but they had a special revenue in the Sound tolls on shipping entering and leaving the Baltic, and in fishery dues. Naval, military and colonial activities gave scope for a not insignificant apparatus of government to be put together.

In the 'Northern Seven Years War' of 1563–70 with Sweden, Frederick II of Denmark was the more headstrong aggressor. It was typical of both belligerents to be able to enlist seamen of their own, but to depend largely on German soldiery. There were few gains and heavy costs, and in his later years Frederick, very much a man of the late-flowering northern Renaissance, betook himself to achievements of another kind, in the realms of science and culture. His thick-witted nobles were contemptuous of the experiments he sponsored in agriculture and manufactures;[3] but he was also setting the pace in an aristocratically costly style of living. His hunting-seat of Frederiksborg, rebuilt by his son, was the most elegant of a cluster of châteaux near the capital.

Christian IV, who came to the throne as a boy in 1588 and reigned for sixty years, was a good epitome of his era. Well educated, a huge hearty man, strongly paternalistic, he was always travelling over the county, acting not seldom as judge, accessible to all his subjects and popular with them. In his early years he showed some signs of a disposition to loosen the landowners' grip, with the backing of the townsmen.[4] Such an alliance was not really practical politics. Chafe as he might at his nobles' obstructiveness and egotism, he was after all one of them, a partaker in their tastes for enormous drinking and carefree spending. Where he did try to coerce them was in the military sphere. His army's backbone still consisted of German cavalry and Scottish or other foot, but he was in his way very Danish, and wanted to add a native element in the form of recruits to be provided by landlords and holders of royal fiefs.

[3] Toyne, p. 114.
[4] Gade, p. 79.

He had a passion for the sea, and gave charters to companies intended to open trade with the East and West Indies. Sea air kept Denmark mentally alive; the contrast between its serf-worked countryside and ocean-ranging commerce was as striking a one as any country could exhibit. But Christian's obsession was with building a navy, and using it to confront the old enemy Sweden. His 'Kalmar War' of 1611–12, pointless and destructive, saw him fighting – unlike most kings by this time – at the head of his forces, and closed with Sweden having to pay a swingeing indemnity. This emboldened him to plunge in 1625–6 into the Thirty Years War, against the advice of sober counsellors. It was on a scale far beyond Denmark's resources, and before long a Habsburg army was entering the country. Nemesis came in 1643 with a Swedish invasion, and the treaty of Brömsebro in 1645 meant loss of part of the Danish-held territory in southern Sweden, and of Sound tolls on Swedish shipping; it set the seal on the decay of Danish power.

Royal ambitions were forced inward; meanwhile economic growth fostered by the government was nourishing the merchant class, which found a partner in the clergy. As everywhere, Reformation transformed a church aristocratical at the top, rustical at the bottom, into a mainly middle-class body, whose corporate sense was stiffened in Denmark by its having a place in the Estates. With their backing, in 1660 a monarchical coup inaugurated full hereditary power, ratified ten years later by the absolutist *Lex Regia*. This brought no fundamental change. Administration was re-organized, but there was no attack on the position of the aristo-cracy, no revolution from above, and from 1660 the *Rigsdag* never met again before the nineteenth century. Royal power and central-ism had become ends in themselves; it was only much later that they began to be used to reshape the country.

Commercialism showed at its worst in the treatment accorded to Iceland, still not forgotten there. Strong-arm competition between English and Hanseatic traders was ended in 1547 by the island being leased to the city council of Copenhagen for an annual payment. In 1602 a full trading monopoly was created for a company of merchants drawn from the Danish towns, who scandalously abused their rights: the result was 'a century and a half of inhuman economic oppression and almost constant misery'.[5] European imperialism made its first essays inside Europe, and Denmark was guilty of a form of it which Castile, less mercantile than some of its

---

[5] Magnússon, pp. 107, 115.

dependencies, was under less temptation to indulge in.

Norway fared very much better, although it too, in theory still a distinct kingdom, in reality had far more the status of a colony. Its poor level of development put it at a disadvantage; the overlaying of vernacular speech by literary Danish was an expression of this in cultural terms. In the Baltic arena Norwegian timber, shipping and seamen gave Denmark a harmful illusion of being more powerful than it really was. Norway was dragged into disputes of little concern to it; but its peacetime burdens were not crushing, and taxation was lighter than in Denmark.[6] Even here the Reformation, bringing humanism with it instead of following on it as in Germany, struck some sparks. Among a few there was a birth of interest in the national past, and a feeling about the national present, less anti-Danish than anti-German because chiefly confined to Bergen with its colony of Hanseatic merchants.[7]

Administratively the trend was towards direct rule through Danish officials, on whom fiefs were bestowed. Here in fact some features of the centralized autocracy ultimately achieved in Denmark could be tried out in advance. In 1572 a new department was set up to coordinate business. Reformation benefited the crown more than in most countries, because there was no strong nobility to demand the lion's share of the spoils. It emerged as by far the biggest landowner, with an increased proportion also of the tithes and fuller authority over the clergy. When in 1591, however, a first regular meeting of Estates was held at Oslo by Christian IV, who made thirty visits to Norway, one of the four chambers was reserved for the clergy. Another represented the peasantry. Society all the same was growing less egalitarian during the sixteenth century, as money economy spread. Small freeholders were declining to the level of tenant farmers; lumbering fell into the hands of bigger men; fishermen were trapped by debts to merchants into a primitive capitalist dependence. Yet Norway, like Sweden, was to prove a reservoir of the democracy so rare in Europe. After about 1650 the deterioration of peasant conditions was halted and reversed.

In Sweden, never subjected to serfdom, peasant proprietors formed more than half the population, and were reckoned to own a little more than half the land. (Finland, already a Swedish possession, was even more a country of peasants.) The gentry had few pretensions to gentility, and were scarcely more than prosperous yeomen.

[6] Larsen, pp. 262–3.
[7] *ibid.*, pp. 273–4.

Primogeniture was not practised, so that estates were liable to frequent division, and mostly consisted of aggregates of scattered farms. A small aristocracy had ruled the roost within the Kalmar Union; it did not much relish the break, and was not enamoured of its upstart king, founder of a 'new monarchy' in a more literal sense than any of the others. Gustav Vasa, who led Sweden to freedom, was not a man of the highest rank. His strongest support came from the province of Dalarna, well to the north of Stockholm, where there were few nobles, and where in the Bergslag area small-scale ironworking was carried on.

Local institutions and customary law provided the infrastructure for a state still to be built, which would turn out very unlike most of its contemporaries. Village affairs were debated at meetings open to all inhabitants. Towns were very small, yet each elected a burgomaster and council, with a general assembly as final arbiter. There were district gatherings in which all taxpaying peasants could take part, and provincial bodies whose assent was required to new taxes or laws. In these latter the bigger landowners could assert themselves; and the *Rad* or royal council belonged, as in Denmark, more to them than to the monarchy. Gustav made frequent use of the *Riksdag* or Estates, whose lower houses could be marshalled against the nobles. Its composition and functions were ill-defined, but the four chambers included one for the peasantry, though only for taxpaying freeholders, and with representatives nominated rather than elected.

A new ruler, of a nation starting life afresh, would be readier than most to look for novel methods. Gustav could not be content to leave things as he found them; he could maintain his position only by systematic building up of power. One of his earliest and boldest strokes was to smuggle Reformation into a country where few as yet desired it. This could only be accomplished through the *Riksdag*. He disguised his intentions when he summoned a meeting in 1527 at Våsterås, a township inland from Stockholm often chosen for the purpose. Here he complained feelingly of his straitened means and his people's ingratitude, and threatened to abdicate. A parvenu sovereign could indulge in demagogy that one born in the purple could not well stoop to. It was agreed that the accumulated wealth of the church should be taken over: everyone preferred this to more taxation, and the nobles counted on getting a good slice. Thanks to his popular backing, Gustav was able to fob them off with very little, and land in the possession of the crown swelled to more than a quarter of the total, considerably more than the nobility owned.[8] Sweden was the one country where revenue from the royal demesne was of growing importance. Gustav was always a landowner first and foremost. What he could get from taxes was meagre and uncertain: his main revenue was the rent of his farms. It was paid mostly in kind, so that he had large stocks of commodities for sale and no scruples of dignity about driving a hard bargain.[9] He set himself, moreover, to improve the land, by clearing forests and draining marshes. All this might be still within the framework of medieval life and thinking, yet force of circumstances was making it the prelude to a new epoch. Gustav saw the need for some industrial growth, and brought in Germans to improve iron production, while craft guilds in the towns were revitalized. A national market economy was being inaugurated, like the state, largely from above.

Having relieved the old church of its wealth, Gustav set himself to make good use of its successor. In Protestant lands the lower clergy were becoming as indispensable in administrative routine as prelates in the higher walks of government in Catholic countries. In addition Gustav expected his clergy to preach loyalty and docility. Much of this was unpalatable to the more idealistic Lutherans headed by Olaus Petri, and disagreements were sometimes lively. Parishes were tenacious of an old right to choose their pastors, who presided over village meetings and would often take their stand with the parishioners when there were grievances. They came as a rule from among the substantial farmers, since there was only the scantiest urban middle class to furnish candidates.

Religious friction was symptomatic of a gap opening between Sweden's rustic democracy and a youthful monarchy impatient to put itself on a level with its compeers abroad. Gustav obtained a foreign bride of princely stock, and went in for a regal style of living, refitting several castles as palaces. A peasantry can be deeply royalist, but it becomes so through long conditioning, chiefly by oppression which invests a king with the halo of an imaginary protector. Free Swiss peasants had no hankering for one, Swedes did not take kindly to a king who wanted to be more than a figurehead. A peasant democracy has no comprehension of any state machinery being necessary; its ideal is to be left alone. Dalarna was quickly disgruntled with its champion, and after rebellion in the early 1530s was subjected to stricter control.

To draw the realm closer together was an essential aim of Gustav,

[8] Heckscher, p. 67.   [9] *ibid.*, p. 66.

and the Riksdag was valuable to him because, among other things, it represented all Sweden, otherwise not much more than a loose bundle of provinces.[10] In local administration the royal bailiffs who managed the crown properties were taking a bigger hand. Others supervised the towns. For such duties men from the gentry were adequate, and, their own means being so modest, they were easily attracted into state service. Above this level there were few state-building elements in Sweden's sparse population. Gustav was soon resorting to German bureaucrats; as his resources expanded he could employ more of them at Stockholm, where government business was coming to be concentrated, though the court still went its rounds and the *Riksdag* had no fixed meeting-place.

All foreigners are more or less obnoxious, and particularly when they bring new-fangled devices for getting money out of the tax-payer. A German chancellor appointed in 1534 added fuel to dis-content, and in 1542 revolt broke out in another province, Småland in the south, with a peasant named Nils Dacke in the lead. With watchwords partly religious, it bore some resemblance to the Pilgrimage of Grace six years earlier in England. One grievance, significantly, was the wearing of foreign costume by the upper classes, which was to be so repugnant to Peter the Great's subjects in Russia. German mercenaries were employed to put the rebellion down. Gustav all the same never entirely forgot that he too had been a popular leader, and that it would be dangerous to quarrel with his people too much. He made amends by getting rid of some of his Germans and their innovations, while he strengthened the throne by getting the *Riksdag* to recognize it as hereditary, instead of elective. A native military organization was brought into being: a small force, half standing army, half militia, whose recruits in peace-time would spend most of their year at home, or on plots of land assigned to them. It was meant to be voluntary, but soon came to be based on an obligation of each group of peasant families to contribute one man. This might be more burdensome than taxes to pay professionals; and free peasant recruits proved awkwardly hard to discipline.

In one of the manifestos he was fond of issuing, Gustav sought to impress on his people their need of a government strong enough to shelter them from invasion or piracy.[11] It amounted to an apologia for the state which he was building. He did indeed give Sweden an

---

[10] Roberts, *Early Vasas*, pp. 39, 43.
[11] Andersson, p. 135.

orderly, undisturbed time on the whole, and this must explain most of the mild prosperity it seems to have been blessed with. This in turn must have done more than anything else to get his policies generally if grumblingly accepted. But if Sweden had to be equipped with the paraphernalia of a state for the sake of survival in the era now opening, state and nation were only very gradually fused. This disjointedness, or combination of artificial and organic, had an analogy in the Vasa temperament, that of a dynasty highly gifted but morbidly mistrustful, often erratic, sometimes mad.

It was in keeping with the alien quality of the regime that in 1580 a Frenchman, Pontus de la Gardie, was given command of the army, a post normally held in all countries by a native aristocrat. Gustav, and his descendants after him, were habitually at logger-heads with their aristocracy, except when they joined forces in adventures abroad, sometimes even then. Yet no monarchy could do without a nobility, even if the two were as often at cross purposes as man and wife. After Gustav there was a more frequent promotion of new men, to balance the older families. Exotic titles of count or baron were bestowed on many, and those honoured were often themselves foreign. All nationalism is riddled with contradictions, but it was an odd phenomenon that Sweden should be continuing its march to nationhood under the direction of a band of Dugald Dalgetties from far away.

An astonishing number of Scots founded noble houses, like the Andrew Keith, illegitimate son of a man of rank, who entered Swedish service in 1568 and was made a baron.[12] Foreigners settling down in the country like this would become Swedish in course of time, more quickly than the Danish nobility ceased to be Germanic, and the same was happening in urban life. Formerly trade was in the hands of outsiders, mostly Germans, who came and went. Now there was an intermediate stage when foreign traders and craftsmen were urged to come and settle, and had to obey Swedish regulations. When the port of Gothenburg was founded in 1607 on Sweden's scrap of west coast, it was peopled at first chiefly by Netherlanders, along with another good seasoning of Scots. Much of the history of the Scottish people was being made far away from Scotland.

Gustav Vasa pursued cautious external policies, which mitigated the less good consequences of the nation's rise, but before long it was being dragged into aggressive designs calculated to benefit the

---

[12] Berg and Lagercrantz, p. 12. Cf. J. N. M. Maclean, *The Macleans of Sweden* (Edinburgh, 1971).

few at the expense of the many. These ambitions were hastened by Gustav's extraordinary decision to create appanage duchies for the three sons of his second marriage. This semi-partition of the country, after his lifelong efforts to unify it, can scarcely be explained rationally, unless perhaps he despaired of his eldest son's capacity to carry on his work. Interludes of fraternal strife were inevitable, and presented the aristocratic faction with opportunities to regain ground.

Gustav's domestic troubles had been mostly with the people: those of his son Eric (1560–69) were with the bigger nobles, still resentful of the Vasas as nobodies. He was initiating what they were to object to for generations as 'the rule of secretaries', confidential royal advisers like Jören Persson, son of a clergyman and educated abroad. However, Eric was going out of his mind, and his brothers joined the aristocratic opposition which in 1568 dethroned him. Transfer of the throne to John III was approved by the *Riksdag*, which thus had a fresh occasion to come forward in national politics; a long period of anxiety at least kept the government from sinking into a rut.

John's appanage had been Finland, very apt to lure him into the maelstrom of eastern Baltic politics; as king he pushed on with expansionist schemes across the sea, starting a tradition of imperialism which haunted Sweden for a century and a half. A further momentous complication was his marriage with a Polish princess; tortuous manoeuverings led to his son Sigismund, brought up a Catholic, being elected in 1586 to the vacant Polish throne. Meanwhile defence and administration of the Baltic acquisitions contributed to the growth of the state apparatus. At the same time colonial fiefs obtained by Swedes infected them with the Germanic appetite for serfs to exploit that Denmark suffered from. At home the brunt of the war costs fell on the common people, in taxes and conscription. On Finland it fell heaviest of all. In 1596 revolt broke out there, a peasant rising against high-handed officials and disorderly troops.

Eric's fall was a carnival for the nobles, who could extort wide concessions from his brother. Among these were exemptions for the peasantry on their estates from taxes or army service; one of many illustrations of how lords might in their own interests shield cultivators from the rapacity of the state. John like Eric was bent on personal rule, through bureaucrats he could rely on. But his commitments abroad hampered him, and the nobles, who always felt entitled to the chief government offices, were acquiring more political experience and finesse. A party was forming with Eric Sparre for leader, the *Rad* for bastion, and a theory, appealing to medieval precedent, of constitutional government. Its theory was quite similar to that of the opposition in England a generation later: its aim was the narrower one of replacing monarchy with oligarchy.

When John died in 1592 and Sigismund fell heir, the Sparre faction welcomed the prospect of an absentee foreign ruler who would, they mistakenly thought, be content to leave things in their hands, as much as or more than the Kalmar Union had done. Sigismund in fact wanted real power, and to cement it a restoration of Catholicism. He was challenged by his uncle Charles, another of Gustav's younger sons, who was obliged to appeal to popular feeling as expressed through the Estates and the national church. Sweden went through a brief second war of independence; Sigismund and his adherents were beaten; in 1600 Sparre and others were executed, and the party of oligarchy was relegated for a while to the background. Charles became regent, with the assent of the Estates, and then from 1604 reigned as Charles IX. He had to continue to lean for support on national sentiment and on the *Riksdag*, now able to establish itself as, more than ever before, a regular component of the political system.[13] The defeated nobility was biding its time, and was only kept at bay by repressive measures. Conflict with Poland and Russia, and attack in 1611 by Denmark, imperilled the country and overloaded the exchequer. Crown lands were having to be sold, usually to noble buyers for want of others, which strengthened them as much as it weakened the government.

In 1611 the Vasa state seemed at the mercy of its enemies, within and without. The noble faction was renewing its hold on the Rad, and finding a fresh chief in Oxenstierna. Its first prize was the charter which Charles's youthful son, Gustavus Adolphus, was compelled to sign in 1612. All higher posts were to be reserved for men of rank; foreign policy as well as legislation would be subject to the approval of the Council. These terms were much like what Sparre had sought. But the setting was different. A point was being reached in the evolution of the state, as happened wherever it was successfully established, when nobles wanted not to dismantle it but to build it up further for their own purposes. Exigencies of war hastened this. The aristocracy was now a very mixed body, moreover, not all of which could vegetate comfortably at the expense of

[13] Oakley, pp. 90–91.

the cultivator, and it was the military wing, not the drones, who called the tune. Men with an eye on army promotions, colonial posts and lands, would insist on the government, whoever headed it, being efficiently run; and they would lionize anyone who could lead them to victory, as Gustavus soon showed he could do. Forced to look abroad for a stage which would give him freedom of action, he would concentrate on war. Oxenstierna, chancellor from 1612, was left in command at home; but he speedily learned that only in partnership with the king could he and his friends expect to prosper.

Rule by royal secretaries was supplanted by an officialdom of blue blood; it too had to learn that it could only run the country on condition of changing its own habits and ideas drastically. For backwoodsmen, as in all such contexts, the great stumbling-block or *pons asinorum* was the necessity of submitting to education, with its implied admission that a pedigree was not sufficient by itself. Schools were being opened for sons of good families, but not confined to them; Uppsala university received handsome endowments from the king; emulous young gentlemen finished their preparations abroad. In 1626 'Statutes of the nobility' defined its composition and grades, but did not close it to newcomers. Talent and energy were at a premium, competition ensured their getting a chance. Long archaic, the traditional great offices of state were reviving as focal points of new *collegia* or departments. These owed much to Dutch procedures; they were put together by stages, but two ordinances framed in 1612 to regulate exchequer and chancellery laid the foundations. Under the chancellor's eye there was taking shape an executive which could operate even during the king's repeated absences. Before long, boards were evolving into ministries,each headed by a responsible individual with a seat in the *Rad*, and this was taking on something of the character of a cabinet.

Law-courts too were being renovated. Not much of Roman law, with its authoritarian principles, was adopted, and Sweden like England was a country where the jury, that expression of the medieval representative idea in the field of justice, lived on. Ordinary townsmen's right to express their feelings through representative bodies was confirmed; the continuing wish to entice settlers from abroad may have helped towards this. Administrative areas called *lan* were replacing the unwieldy provinces. Their governors were men of rank, but had exacting responsibilities and a regular secretariat. Centralizing aims showed also in Gustavus's dislike of the old appanage system, now being terminated. Closer supervision was applied to Finland, hitherto as a grand duchy not much meddled with by Stockholm; though it was accompanied by the setting up of Estates, as in Danish Norway.

Newer possessions won on the other side of the Baltic were carved into *län*; by the end of the reign the majority of these units lay outside Sweden. They could not be so effectively managed, because administrative cadres were being over-stretched, and social conditions were unpropitious. In Esthonia the peasants were wretched serfs, the lords German, controlling the Diet and not caring who was their ruler so long as they were left a free hand with their underlings. Formerly compelled to fight for their masters, since the later fifteenth century the bondsmen had been disarmed, and taxed instead to pay for mercenaries.[14] Gustavus could not tackle the lords directly, if only because his wars left him no leisure. He hoped to use the church as a civilizing instrument, as it was in Scandinavia. In 1627 a commission led by the church leader Rudbeckius went to Esthonia, but not much was accomplished.[15] None the less, the epoch of Swedish rule was to be looked back on gratefully in later days by the common people; whereas the lords welcomed and connived at Esthonia's passing under Russian rule, which showed much more respect for their privileges.

Monarchy and aristocracy in Sweden were winding up their long-drawn feud on the only possible basis, a joint programme of war and expansion. From some points of view it was a national programme as well, or could be made to appear so. Hostilities continued to stimulate the economy on some lines. Mining was a field where the government had a stake in many European countries, and could grow by taking on economic functions. With ambitions far outrunning its actual strength, Sweden was a pioneer in the harnessing of natural wealth to war. Its copper, of which more reserves had been discovered in the 1570s, was joining iron as a rewarding export, and being manipulated as a tool of foreign policy. After 1627, when the Calvinist émigré from the southern Netherlands, Louis de Geer, moved to Sweden with a force of craftsmen from Liege, iron-smelting was greatly improved. The prince-bishopric was a credit to the church militant as one of Europe's armament centres, and the arms industry was a pacemaker of technology. 'Swedes still displayed an outstanding inability to undertake entrepreneurial tasks.'[16] In Denmark other foreign

[14] E. Uustalu, *The History of Estonian People* (London, 1952), pp. 61–2.
[15] Roberts, *Gustavus,* pp. 419 ff.
[16] B. Supple, 'The Nature of Enterprise', in CEHE p. 458.

Calvinists were being employed to handle timber exports, contracts, and loans.[17] Large areas of Europe were under foreign
economic ascendancy, as others were of political, and it might look
as if Scandinavia was becoming one of them, as it had been in
Hanseatic days. But here too, first as state and then as nation,
Sweden was to show an exceptional faculty of assimilation, which
must have owed much to the free, open elements in its social life.

Popular support for government and army was indispensable,
and the national assembly, which might have faded at this point as
in so many other countries, displayed fresh vitality. In 1617 a
definite organization and functions were given the *Riksdag* for the
first time. Its four houses were to meet separately and conduct
orderly discussions on 'propositions' laid before them by the
government. They had no right of initiative, and clearly the
government intended to keep them well in hand. Part of its object
was to do away with the old time-consuming process by which
Riksdag decisions had to be confirmed by the regional assemblies.
Gustavus summoned the assembly oftenest in his early, difficult
years, seldomer later on, and then with the fourth Estate at times
left out. None the less, it was of incalculable moment for Sweden's
future that its parliament was still in being.

It mattered greatly too that the church, firmly planted like the
Kirk in Scotland as a national institution, and fortified by the
confrontation with Catholic Poland, could defend its autonomy,
more robustly at this date than the *Riksdag*. Gustavus and
Oxenstierna wanted to integrate it, along with everything else, into
their system. It was quite ready for partnership, but it jibbed when
they tried in 1623 to fetter it as German princes did their Lutheran
clergy. Its standard-bearer was the doughty Rudbeckius, a
champion both of the church and of the common people. The
people had need of whatever aid or comfort they could get, for war
burdens were heavy. Sweden was one of the first nations to adopt a
modern version of conscription, everywhere a galling load.
Disturbances in those old hotbeds of unrest, Dalarna in 1614 and
Småland in 1617, were in part protests against it. All through the
1620s there were local outbreaks, and with Gustavus's intervention
in the Thirty Years War in 1630 things worsened. When he was
killed in Germany in 1632, leaving only a young daughter, oligarchy
once more seemed on the point of attaining its goal. In 1634

[17] H. R. Trevor-Roper, 'Religion, the Reformation, and Social Change',
Historical Studies IV (1963), pp. 21 ff.

Oxenstierna got the *Riksdag* to underwrite a highly exclusive 'Form of Government'. Meanwhile more and more land was passing to the nobility, and the condition of the peasantry deteriorating towards a level not far from serfdom. Winning empire abroad and losing freedom at home have often gone together.

Oxenstierna had overreached himself however by his eagerness to engross power for himself and his kindred, even more than for his class. From 1617 to 1640 three of the five highest offices were held by Oxenstiernas.[18] This was standing the pyramid on its point. Besides, now more than ever the dominant class was one habituated to state service, as well as to making the state serve it and its wants. Its lower grades were as much a bureaucracy and officer-corps as a gentry. To keep government and country going without the *Riksdag* was impossible, and in the following years its business grew. When war ended at last in 1648 it was ready to make a stand against the big landowners, and fear of a general uprising of the peasants – many of them accustomed to arms – lent gravity and urgency to the threat. In 1650 the three non-noble houses, in a very long-drawn session, voiced the nation's grievances against the profiteers; in 1655 these were compelled to disgorge some of their gains.

There was a sequel a generation later in the *Reduktion* of 1680, which deprived big landlords of a great many crown domains they had come by, and broke their supremacy. They were being treated very much as the church had been a century and a half before when its property was requisitioned to meet the country's needs. At this time the political trend was towards absolutism, as in Denmark, but with the old alliance of throne and nobility more thoroughly disrupted. A monarchy for which foreign adventure had become an addiction[19] was incapable of settling down to reconstruct its power on a more pacific footing. Instead it ran amuck in Europe. When this reached its inevitable close, Sweden turned to parliamentarism.

---

[18] S. H. Steinberg, *The Thirty Years War* (London, 1966), p. 19.
[19] Cf. P. Anderson's dictum that Sweden's rulers 'consistently applied force with consummate skill to misconceived targets'. *Lineages of the Absolutist State* (London, 1974), pp. 189–90.

9

Germany

Germany may have embarked on the sixteenth century with a population of a dozen million,[1] swelling as time went on especially in the crowded southwest. Straddling the continental middle, between Baltic and Alps, Rhineland and Poland, it reached into disparate environments and shaded into other nationalities; more than any other country it was a hectic mixture of opposites, benighted feudalism side by side with bustling towns, inventions, progress. It was too heterogeneous to be governed from one centre, rather than too large. In area it did not vastly exceed France; Russia was far bigger, but far more uniform. Capitalism was making its entry, with landowners as well as businessmen taking part in mining, metal-working and other activities. It had its usual stimulating but dislocating effects. To many it seemed that only usurers and monopolists were flourishing. This interacted with the price rise, highest here too in the food market because production failed to keep pace with population. A crescendo of jarring interests, common to most of Europe, was more disturbing because of the absence of a central authority competent either to moderate class strife or to quell outbreaks expeditiously. Each restless force was left to seek its own way out of its difficulties, as the lesser nobility of western Germany did in the 'Knights' War' of 1522.

Together with the Reformation, the Peasants' War of 1525, culmination of decades of smouldering strife, was the sole great national event in centuries of German history. Even so it engulfed only parts of the country, the politically fragmented centre and southwest. But from its starting-point in the countryside it blazed up into a rebellion of all the discontented, including miners, towns

[1] R. Mols, 'Population in Europe 1500–1700', in Cipolla, p. 38. Some estimates are considerably higher.

at odds with their overlords, poorer townsmen at odds with their patricians, and it found leaders from very diverse social strata. Hence it has been possible to view it as an early attempt at a national or 'bourgeois' revolution.[2] It can at any rate be called a convulsive effort, on a grand scale, to break rusty fetters, open the door to a new life. As such it may be compared with the revolts a few years earlier in Spain.

Agrarian relations varied widely. Outside the northeast and some parts of the southeast, serfdom harnessed to demesne production was rare, and *Leibeigenschaft* or personal bondage implied status rather than function. It was hateful because of exactions like heriot or death–duty at a rate that might reduce an inheritance by a third.[3] Feudal dues and obligations of many kinds were manifold, and to make the most of them lords were endeavouring to repair the seigneurial fabric which in western and middle Germany, as in France, had in later medieval times been crumbling. Protracted local struggles against this, and against encroachments on common lands of the sort so widespread in Europe, threw up 'an impressive network of institutions' for defence of rights enshrined in 'countless village charters'.[4] Now rebel bands raised the flag of village self-rule, and appealed to old custom and tradition.[5] All Europe's rebels, down to the Long Parliament, invoked good old days, a better world of the past, as in later ages Europe's conservatives were to do.

In the 'Twelve Articles', the most prominent of many manifestos, the insurgents demanded an end to bondage: one human being should not be the property of another. Other clauses show that no black and white line marked off freedom from unfreedom; labour services were wrong when excessive, but were not rejected altogether. This reflected the more moderate wing of a rising everywhere broadly divided into two, with men like Thomas Münzer to represent a much more radical trend. Heterogeneous social elements were hard to combine; and the lack of a unified state which allowed rebellion to spread so far (like the temporary absence of monarchy in Spain in 1520) also meant a weakness of anything transcending local consciousness. Once enough professional troops were collected, defeat came quickly, and on its heels ferocious

---

[2] See the discussion of Engels and his endorsement of this view in *Journal of Peasant Studies* III (1975), pp. 89 ff.
[3] D. Sabean, 'Family and Land Tenure', in Scribner and Benecke, p. 184.
[4] R. Brenner, 'Agrarian Class Structure', *Past and Present*, no. 70, pp. 56–7.
[5] H. Buszello, 'The Common Man's View of the State', in Scribner and Benecke, p. 110.

repression, one of the first and worst white terrors of modern Europe.

In some ways the lords' triumph was illusory. Peasant resistance was not permanently broken, but went on obstinately at the grass roots, in a fashion harder to deal with than armed defiance. There was no halting the drift towards peasant agriculture, small holdings inherited, partitioned, sold by occupants, subject to payment of rents and customary dues. These were not in most districts being increased, because landowners did not want to cripple their culti- vators;[6] they must have feared too that over-much provocation might set off another explosion. Over a great part of western Germany peasant proprietorship was looked on with favour by princes, as providing them with their best basis for taxation, very much as in British India the *ryotwari* policy was sometimes preferred to the *zemindari*, and revenue collected directly from the peasantry without landlord intermediaries. A petty ruler might have less sympathy with his nobles because he had less need of them, and, himself only a glorified landowner, wanted to set a distance between his government and them.

In spite of this, the outcome of 1525 did in much of Germany signify a permanent banishment or alienation of the peasants from the national life. Previously their struggles had given them a modest place in it, and made them a 'political estate' in many southwestern territories;[7] they had weapons, of a simple type, and shared in maintenance of local order. Now they were disarmed; they might even be deliberately cut off from education, and thereby from any chance of rising in the social scale.[8] In his chronicle of the events of 1525 Sebastian Franck, a humanist of liberal views, dwelt on the poverty and sufferings of the masses and the savagery with which they were put down, yet condemned them as a wild, barbarous race. It was the attitude of the upper classes everywhere to the children of the soil, as an alien species, or a brute beast only half broken to the yoke, like Caliban by Prospero's torments. Luther's furious repudiation of the rising was in much the same key. His preaching had been its catalyst, and an alliance seemed to be forming between two movements each in its own way revolu- tionary. There was an abrupt end to any chance of this, and from now on Lutheranism would be a substitute for practical progress,

[6] J. Bücking, 'The Peasant War in the Habsburg Lands', *ibid.*, p. 173.
[7] P. Blickle, 'The "Peasant War" as the Revolution of the Common Man', *ibid.*, p. 20.
[8] Bücking, *op. cit.*, p. 173.

instead of a stimulus to it.

In 1525 many men of the town trained-bands, most of them artisans and plebeians, joined the peasant forces, while the rich free cities of the southwest like Augsburg and Strasburg sent contingents to aid the princes instead.[9] Sixty or more 'imperial' towns had full autonomy, and from near the end of the fifteenth century constituted an estate in the Reichstag; though from having too few objects in common they played a weaker part than their collective weight entitled them to, as compared with the first chamber, that of the seven Electors, and the second, likewise a combination of lay and clerical, of the other princes. By contrast with northern Italy, the other breeding-ground of urban independence, they had not extended their control over the surrounding countryside. As a result they were not brought into conflict with one another, as Italian cities were; they did not swallow one another up, and they remained more truly urban than towns often were, though there were some, like Metz, where holders of neighbouring lordships formed the ruling circle.[10] Proximity to the Baltic allowed a number to cooperate in the Hanseatic League, but mostly they were kept apart by intervening territories. They were at very uneven stages of development, strewn about as it were in time as well as in space; most of them were quite small. They were numerous in the west, as were ecclesiastical principalities and 'imperial knights' owing allegiance to the emperor alone. It was the more sluggish east, where disintegration had gone much less far, that was destined to take the lead.

In principle all *Bürger* were invested with the civic rights which others, like the settlers in suburbs outside the walls, lacked; in practice what counted were the classes and class enmities which crystallized more sharply in the small world of a town than in the national theatre. Holders of municipal office were turning into a hereditary patriciate and intermarrying with the older aristocracy. They were on bad terms with the middling sort, entrenched in craft guilds; and these, grown exclusive and rigid, were embroiled with their journeymen, who strove to organize against their masters. Capitalism had a basis in the 'putting-out' system, most in evidence in towns producing for distant markets; they were to be found chiefly in the south, like Nuremberg.[11] From early in the century

[9] S. Hoyer, 'Arms and Military Organization', in Scribner and Benecke, p. 105.
[10] K. Brandi, *The Emperor Charles V*, p. 616.
[11] Friedrichs, pp. 32, 45.

there were angry clashes between rich and poor.

Reformation in the towns, unlike the principalities, almost always came about through pressure from below.[12] It might be accepted by city fathers as a means of averting social strife, but sometimes helped to loosen their monopoly of power. It was then the urban intelligentsia that did most to spread Protestant ideas. But this meant a widening schism between the thinking of Luther, adapted to the princely domains and the bucolic east, and that of Zwingli, Bucer, and then Calvin, rooted in the more advanced southwest and in an urban and humanist environment. Germany's chances depended very much on this more dynamic force.

How far it could go depended in turn very much on whether the German cities could be reinforced by those of neighbouring Switzerland, led by Zürich, where Zwingli's leadership rested on the guild masters and artisans.[13] The Swiss confederation of a dozen cantons and their associates, with merely consultative meetings of a Diet at Zürich from time to time, was very loose; it might be called the negation of a state. Its members still nominally belonged to the Holy Roman Empire, and nothing hindered them from affiliation with German towns outside their own borders. Zwingli dreamed of a federal republic of Swiss and south German cities, which might have anticipated Holland as a European focus of innovation.

These cities had more ready money than most princes for paying troops, and Switzerland and over-populous southwest Germany were the recruiting-grounds of the best professional fighting-men in Europe. But Switzerland had too little cohesion to serve as nucleus of a wider combination. Its Alpine cantons and their free peasantry, the most democratic communities in Europe, remained Catholic, for want of social divisons to push them towards change. In a civil war in 1531 Zwingli was killed. Within the urban cantons too, headway was lost. Oligarchy became more uncompromising in the later half of the sixteenth century, with each town under the thumb of a few hundred families. Zürich was one of the few where craft guilds retained a voice in municipal affairs. All towns sucked wealth out of the countryside round about, which they, far more than the German cities, held in subjection, and which was cumbered with feudal lordships as well. Any league of popular forces urban and rural was ruled out. Peasant uprisings sometimes had more success in bringing together Protestant and Catholic.[14] The

12 Moeller, p. 61.
13 Birnbaum, p. 42.
14 Oechsli, p. 213.

crushing of the last of them, in 1652–3, left patrician and landowner supreme.

Germany's political dispersion did not preclude, and among the literate positively fostered, national consciousness of a kind. It brought the nation, the people, into the foreground, more than in France or Spain where collective sentiment gathered round the throne. Even princes would sometimes talk about their 'beloved fatherland of the German nation'.[15] Patriotic declamation was often stridently aggressive and bombastic, to make up for Germany's real nullity.[16] Imperial authority was more than a ghost, and even a ghost can make itself felt if people believe in it. Down to much later times ordinary men supposed that the emperor really was the all-highest;[17] it was an indication of how little their actual rulers meant to them. But efforts in the first half of the sixteenth century to overhaul the Holy Roman Empire and breathe fresh life into it came to little or nothing. The best that could have been hoped, and it might well have been better than any of the absolutist regimes, was a federation firmly enough welded to defend the frontiers and keep the peace inside them. But if this was too much for Switzerland to accomplish, it was far too much for Germany. Most of the bigger princes felt able to stand on their own feet, and it was they who predominated in the Reichstag.

There was something like a move towards federation in 1500 when the empire was divided into ten 'Circles', to facilitate regional collaboration. The only one to show much life was the one known as the Suabian League: its members must have had presentiments of the 1525 revolt, which it took the lead in suppressing. National unity was not an aspiration of 1525,[18] but it might seem for a while as if the advent of Protestantism could give Germany a new bond. The Schmalkaldic League founded in 1531 adopted a constitution next year and was subsequently joined by nearly all Lutheran states. Meanwhile Charles V's position was contradictory. Unlike his Habsburg ancestors, semi-hereditary emperors since 1438, he had large dominions outside the empire, but these took up most of his attention, and the foreign resources which gave him material strength sapped his moral authority. So also did the fact that he adhered immovably to the old church when most of Germany was abandoning it.

[15] Clasen, p. 5.
[16] H. Kohn, *The Idea of Nationalism* (New York, 1945), pp. 130 ff.
[17] *ibid.*, p. 335.
[18] Buszello, *op. cit.*, p. 117.

His opportunity came in 1546–7, through rifts among his opponents, whose ardour must have been damped too by another social revolt a dozen years before, the Anabaptist eruption at Münster. In the 'Schmalkaldic war' the princes gave only a shuffling leadership. Many cities took part, at heavy cost in tax levies. Machiavelli had paid tribute to their reputation of being always well prepared for action, with their walls, moats, artillery, and stocks of provisions.[19] It was not easy for them, however, to act outside their defences. Many were bottled up, like Augsburg and Cologne, both encircled by ecclesiastical territory. It was on the rebellious cities that Charles's hand fell heaviest. Nuremberg, exceptional in having retained a purely aristocratic constitution, stood loyal to him, and he interfered in Augsburg and more than twenty other towns to restore oligarchy and sweep away the share of the guilds in government – very much as in Ghent in 1540 after the crushing of its revolt.

Against the princes he could, for the time being, plan only limited moves. They on their part showed no sign of being able to recover by any efforts of their own. Just as foreign resources had enabled him to launch his coup, it was a foreign enemy, France, whose intervention halted Charles and rescued Protestantism and princely autonomy, with German support but on the whole in too facile a manner for the country's good. In 1955 the Peace of Augsburg terminated the contest, giving each ruler freedom of choice between Catholicism and Lutheranism. Exclusion of the Zwinglian and Calvinist creeds sealed the failure of the cities to assert themselves, and their supersession by the principalities, whose capitals were outstripping them in magnitude and importance.

Political stalemate was followed, partly as cause and effect, by economic. Prosperity in the southern cities took the same downward curve as in some though not all of the Hanseatic towns a century earlier. Large-scale industry failed to advance beyond a certain point. Glass-making in middle Germany is one example of production receding in the seventeenth century from a capitalistic to a petty craft structure.[20] Some degree of economic falling off, relative if not absolute, was overtaking Germany as a whole by 1600, while pressure of numbers intensified social tensions. Decline was rendered irreversible for long to come by the Thirty Years War.

Charles's abdication left his brother Ferdinand, to whom he had early transferred the original Habsburg patrimony of Austria, and

---

[19] *The Prince*, chap. 10.
[20] Ludloff, pp. 68–9.

who was his deputy in German affairs, to negotiate the compromise. A long lull followed. To gain the imperial title Ferdinand had to canvass princely assent, Protestant included. He and his son Maximilian needed all the help they could get from Germany against the Turks. In this quiet interval, when all other political or social forces seemed to have shot their bolt, the princes were left to consolidate their position. It was still equivocal. They were not royalties, even if Roman law, making its way in and blending with customary law, helped to impart a fresh gloss to all constituted authority. They were mostly small fry, and the modern state required a certain magnitude in order to command respect, an air of grandeur and remoteness. Many had no fixed headquarters, and jogged about from one to another of their not always contiguous domains. There was a patent streak of fantasy in Luther's veneration of kings, in a Germany with scarcely any worth the name, and he himself was aware at times of what unpromising material he had to make do with.

Another foible of these rulers was that they often partitioned their possessions among their offspring, revealing how much they thought of themselves as big landowners rather than small sovereigns. Philip of Hesse, that Lutheran stalwart, left his territories to four sons; in Hanover the reigning family did not adopt primogeniture until it received the electoral dignity at the end of the seventeenth century. Multiplication of petty courts must have been welcome to the flocks of courtiers and officials because it multiplied places for them. On the other hand, partitions might give rise to troublesome quarrels and disorders, and sometimes the Estates took upon themselves to put a stop to the practice.

Not many princes had the stimulus of foreign contact and competition to rouse emulation, and to give their subjects a sense of common purpose with them. Austria enjoyed this dubious advantage, and Brandenburg with its long frontier with Poland; the Palatinate lay close to France. Hesse was surrounded by other German lands, and so, except where it abutted on Bohemia, was Saxony. Those destined to distinction derived much of their temper from involvement in European politics. Within Germany the imperial framework could be a safeguard for weaker rulers against being swallowed up by stronger; it thus had the drawback of making for worse and worse fragmentation. Stirrings of national feeling fostered a public opinion, hallowed by the Reformation, against internecine warfare. Fear of new mass revolts must have made princes deem it prudent to respect one another's rights.

Despite religious schism, the country was entering on a long era of quiet inter-state relations which ought to have made it a model for Europe.

These princelings were little plagued by the military preoccupations which beggared more splendid monarchs. If they were careful they could scrutinize and husband their incomes more successfully than a king of France or Spain could ever do with his millions. There was a Jewish poll-tax, a revenue the pious western countries had sacrificed by expelling their Jews; and some, like Saxony and Austria, drew tolls from mines. All the same, most rulers were habitually hard up. Inflation and court extravagance were enough to run them into arrears. Their family estates might have to be sold or mortgaged for ready cash, and rights of regality alienated to landowners. Church lands impounded at the Reformation usually went the same way, or were given to courtiers, those sturdy beggars of all Europe. Application was necessary therefore to *Landtags* or Estates, and they, more tenaciously than parliaments of bigger nations, clung to the old-fashioned principle that their grants were for special occasions only. In addition they might keep the management of the sums voted in their own hands. This was one of the routes by which committees came to overshadow their parent bodies.

Attempts to curtail or take over a prince's powers had been quite frequent. On this petty stage constitutional habits might take hold more readily than in large kingdoms. Frequently committees of Estates undertook administrative as well as financial tasks, like the Spanish or French provincial assemblies, and might perform reasonably well. In them, as in the more serious-minded rulers and city fathers, a sense of responsibility could be freshened by the religious winds blowing over Germany. To evolve further the Estates would have to broaden their public base, and this could not be easy when so many of the towns stood outside the principalities, and the peasantry had a place only in a handful of local diets. There was in fact very little concept of further constitutional progress. In the more extensive principalities each region might have its own body, interested only in local affairs. It was the stronger princes who were pressing, by the sixteenth century, for combined assemblies such as came into being in Brandenburg, to represent their whole territory. Clearly they, like the rulers of the Netherlands, expected to find it simpler to deal with these gatherings than with a bevy of small, obstinate bodies such as the one which drove a governor of Jamaica to protest that 'arguing with Assemblys is like philosophising with a Mule.'[21]

Princes of active disposition were building up more of a formal structure of government. Officialdom was expanding, with what came to be the special German characteristic, an after-effect of the great religious clash and its frustrated idealism, of a fussy and minute conscientiousness. Sale of offices did not become usual until the seventeenth century;[22] one reason must have been scarcity of purchasers. Salaries could be frugal, for Germany abounded in university men, as well as soldiers, seeking employment. They carried ideas up and down, and administrators could learn from one another's experiences, and from methods pioneered by the free cities. In this roundabout fashion the cities were making part of their contribution to the nation.

Transfer of responsibilities like education and charity from the ecclesiastical to the secular sphere quickened the growth of the state, on its better side.[23] A ruler's authority was fortified by his becoming head of his own miniature church. Pastors might as in England be chosen by local landowners, but there were bishops appointed by the ruler to shepherd them; Reformation bred a more literate and respectable clergy, who could be entrusted with a range of minor civil service duties. In addition they expounded Luther's doctrine of the duty of passive obedience, sowing the seeds of the irreproachable political naïveté and docility that Treitschke found in Saxony three centuries later.[24] Civic magistrates too could quote Lutheran scripture: at Hamburg in 1602 they dwelt comfortably on the subject's duty of submission even to tyranny.[25] In daily life there was a parallel emphasis on the duty of the poor to submit to the rich. Luther's table-talk shows him in his later years still conscious that Germany society was unjust and oppressive, but also deeply pessimistic about the little success of his movement in regenerating human nature, and driven to think the common man sinful enough to deserve his fate.

Most of the bigger states lay eastward, and were deficient in

---

[21] R. S. Dunn, *Sugar and Slaves* (London, 1973), p. 159. Later on local assemblies could be made use of by princes strong enough to manage them. After the Landtag of Brandenburg faded out in the seventeenth century 'the local "county" estates or *Kreistage* became the basic bureaucratic unit in the countryside'. P. Anderson, *Lineages of the Absolutist State* (London, 1974), p. 263.

[22] K. W. Swart, *Sale of Offices in the Seventeenth Century* (Hague, 1949), p. 90.

[23] Cohn, *Government in Reformation Europe*, Introduction, p. 11.

[24] *History of Germany*, ed. G. A. Craig (Chicago, 1975), p. 155.

[25] Moeller, p. 115.

urban life and in circulation of ideas as well as goods. On the other hand, they were more unifiable than most of western Germany, because more amorphous, with few free cities or other intrusive elements. Saxony might seem a likely candidate for leadership, but that its reigning family and territory were divided. What was now Electoral Saxony was in a fairly flourishing condition under August 1 (1553–86) and his consort Anne. They were content with a simple household, attention was paid to the economy, crown estates were run on model lines. Leipzig was doing well; burghers made themselves heard in the local *Landtags*; mining, especially of silver, lent animation to commercial life as well as revenue to the government. Here and elsewhere in Germany landlords continued to take part in mining and metallurgy, which required capital; in the more ambitious enterprises shares were often held also by monasteries, municipalities, traders. This provided a link among the better-off classes, and even the men who did the work got something. At the festivities for a christening in his family in 1591, the Elector joined in the miners' procession, and there were songs by them and animal shows.[26]

Such jollities fostered amicable relations, while Protestantism could inculcate careful stewardship of the good things provided by Heaven, and a paternalistic sense of accountability for the spiritual and general well-being of the people. Lutheranism harmonized with such impulses in agrarian society much as Calvinism did in urban life. Some church property was diverted to education, and a university was opened at Leipzig. A university was a feather in a prince's cap, and a nursery of clerks and clergy for his service, and of teachers. Schools meant much to Lutheran Germany, partly because adults seemed so unresponsive to the Gospel, partly because governments of petty states with limited physical force depended on the pedagogue as well as the preacher to instil habits of obedience. Inspection was meticulous, bulky reports were compiled.[27]

A like spirit was at work in Württemberg, in south-central Germany, under Duke Christopher (1550–68), a sincere Lutheran with a passion for drawing up rules and ordinances. Here town life was active, and the tradition of municipal regulation can be seen transfusing itself into wider administrative routine, with the Estates as a channel. They were to preserve their vigour as late in German

[26] *Fugger News-Letters*, First Series (1568–1605), ed. V. von Klarwill (London, 1924), pp. 183–4.
[27] Strauss, 'Success and Failure', p. 43, etc.

history as any, and with burghers instead of nobles in the lead. Paternalism wore a less amiable guise in Lippe, a small backwater under Calvinist sway in the northwest, most of whose inhabitants were serfs. Invigilation over them combined close scrutiny of morals and faith with detailed ordering of wages and registering of feudal services.[28] More generally in northwest Germany government policy, as well as their own dogged if undramatic struggle against landlordism, favoured the consolidation of a rural middle class of substantial tenants with hereditary leases, who took a busy part in the grain trade – farmers in the same category as English yeoman or Catalan *payeses*.

All the expanse eastward from the Elbe and northward from Saxony and Bohemia to the Baltic formed a large bulge, made up of extensive principalities with a torpid existence of their own. Brandenburg stood out as an Electorate, but it was landlocked, while all the coast as far as Poland was occupied by the very retarded duchies, more Slav than German, of Mecklenburg and Pomerania. Most of the towns in all the region had long been decaying, and instead of trying to restore them rulers took advantage of their debility to gain a firmer grip on them, with the prime motive of extracting more money, which enfeebled them still further. Compared with the true-blue western monarchs, with a degree of detachment from the interplay of classes, these understudies were more heavily embedded in the nobility, and shared its anti-burgher as well as anti-peasant attitudes. They were aided by the familiar internal discord between leading merchants and craft guilds. There might be friction of another sort between towns like Stralsund and the neighbouring villages which they lorded it over.[29] When a government interposed, it was in favour of the rich, who by becoming dependent on it would be the more tractable and their towns the more easily fleeced.

While state burdens rested a good deal on the towns, the weightier task of supporting the nobility fell to a peasantry tied more and more closely to the land. This shackling might be designed to keep labourers' wages down, and leasing of land for money rents never disappeared,[30] but extension of compulsory labour services was the salient fact. It was facilitated by the already inferior standing of the Slav or Balt rural element, and by the landowners engrossing

---

[28] Benecke, pp. 355–6.
[29] Carsten, *Prussia*, p. 162.
[30] M. Malowist, 'Le commerce de la Baltique', in *La Pologne au Xe Congrès International* (Warsaw, 1955), p. 136; Rosenberg, pp. 228–9.

judicial powers. Roman law, couched in terms of slavery, could do more harm here than in western Germany. In Brandenburg during the second half of the sixteenth century the number of days weekly that a ploughman might have to work for his lord, in place of old customary money payments, was being added to, until by early in the next century it was practically unlimited. In Pomerania and Prussia things were much the same. There were some peasant risings, as there had been on a minor scale in Prussia though not in most other areas in 1525,[31] but on the whole enserfment was being submitted to with far less resistance than southwestern Germany had offered to lesser evils. A primary reason for the difference must have been the scarcity in the northeast of common lands and the habits of village cooperation, self- management, and solidarity that went with them.[32] There were few regular forces at the disposal of the landlord. But the stiffening of the labour code was a long-drawn process. Lutheran indoctrination fostered passivity. For the bolder spirits there was the alternative of flight; it was restricted by the fewness of the towns, where not many malcontents could find refuge.

Western European demand for grain and other primary products hastened the onset of 'feudal capitalism', that hybrid between two economic ages, production organized by means of serf labour. It was one more of the many expedients by which nobles all over Europe, especially their struggling lower ranks, a nuisance to themselves and to everyone else, were trying to extricate themselves from their difficulties. Aristocracy was less likely to feel a snobbish aversion to trade when there was no active bourgeois class to be feared and despised. As master of serfs, moreover, the gentleman saved his honour – like the robber-baron of the Rhineland in another way – because his mode of living still rested on force, on the sword. Both through local dealings like sale of his own gin in his own tavern, and through direct bargaining with foreign merchants, he undercut and further injured the towns.

Administration was more in the hands of the nobility than of a middle-class officialdom. It was tenuous enough, yet the land-owners' competence at it showed them, like the English squire-archy on other lines, as a commercializing class, picking up businesslike habits. They could adjust their collective affairs

[31] H. Wunder, 'Peasant Organization and Class Conflict in East and West Germany', *Past and Present*, no. 78 (1978), pp. 51–2, and 'The Samland Peasant Rebellion of 1525', in Scribner and Benecke; Brenner, *op. cit.*, p. 58.
[32] Brenner, *op. cit.*, p. 57.

through their organ, the Estates. More than anywhere else in Germany these assemblies were not merely persisting but gaining in stature, though representing only a privileged minority and its simple requirements. Instead of a clerical first chamber, they were coming to have two for the landlords, greater and lesser; the third estate was insignificant. So constituted, these gatherings could not rise to a level worthy to be termed 'national'. Nation and nobility were one and the same, and a polity too exclusively the preserve of a single class cannot amount to an authentic state. So far as this can be said to have existed, it was running down. These landowners had no need of elaborate government at home, and could shut their eyes to any need of external defences. It was only spasmodically that princes tried to make themselves felt; when they did, they were apt to call in foreign advisers, whom they could better rely on. By helping to demoralize the towns they were undermining their own best prop. Often hard up, they were obliged to sell or mortgage crown lands, or apply to the *Landtag*, that is to the nobles.

In Prussia when the lands of the Teutonic Knights were secularized in 1525 the Grand Master, Albert of Hohenzollern, got himself accepted as duke by giving the knights positions at court or as *Ämter*, district officials.[33] But the old well-knit organization, with the general chapter of the knights at its summit, bequeathed to the new state a republican spirit hard to exorcize. Finance was as usual the crux; a revenue chamber was the chief component of the Council, whose members' duties were laid down in household ordinances on the pattern adopted in many German principalities. All high posts had to be held by Prussian nobles, and the nobility as well as burghers were opposed to the spirited foreign policy Albert wanted to indulge in, because of its costs. Hence much friction between him and the Estates, whose first house here was the prelates and district representatives of the officials; in the third, that of the towns, only Königsberg counted.

Albert's relatives in Brandenburg seemed for a while to be faring better. Management of crown lands could set standards for bureaucratic running of the state,[34] as it did in Sweden. Competent officials with legal training improved the finances.[35] An old direct tax was restored; even beer, despite remonstrances, was taxed. Progress was interrupted after Joachim I's death in 1535 by extravagances,

---

[33] W. Hubatsch, 'Albert of Brandenburg-Ansbach', in Cohn, p. 169.
[34] Marriott and Robertson, p. 92.
[35] R. Braun, 'Taxation, Sociopolitical Structure, and State-Building: Great Britain and Brandenburg-Prussia', in Tilly, p. 256.

including war, which along with rising prices piled up debts, and enabled the Estates to strengthen their position. Joachim II (1535–71) fell foul of them every now and then, and sank to being little more than their pensioner. In 1604 another of his line, Joachim Frederick, set up a privy council of men in his own confidence, evidently as an offset to the overweening nobility; his successor had to give way and allow this body too to be taken over by it.[36]

Transformation would begin with a change of scale, enlargement of the ruling family's dominions. This might allow it to baffle the vigilance of the Estates against foreign policies calculated to entail risk and expense, a mentality so oddly at variance with that of the fighting ancestors or descendants of the Junkers. In 1610 the Hohenzollerns inherited part of Cleves-Jülich in northeast Germany; in 1618 ducal East Prussia fell in to the main branch of the dynasty, whose possessions thus suddenly stretched across northern Germany in three discontinuous blocks. It was this purely dynastic, irrational coincidence that gave the Electors their real start, by immersing them and their subjects in German and European affairs, opening with the Thirty Years War. A random group of provinces began to harden into a state, while Mecklenburg, lacking any such momentum, remained a feudal backwater. Everywhere the state was partly artificial, or only very roughly congruent with the society it overlaid; in smaller, more malleable realms this might be all the more the case. With that remarkable entity, the Hohenzollern military state, the degree of artificiality was to be exceptionally high. Not unrelated to this is the fact that it ended by committing suicide.

Many Junkers were very petty landowners, whose needs would outstrip sooner or later their means. They or their sons would be willing, like so many Swedish nobles, to attach their fortunes to those of an expanding state. After the Thirty Years War and its handsome gains, Frederick William, the Great Elector, was able to enter on a contest with the *Landtag* and subdue it. An agreement in 1653 recognized his political authority, but left the landowners with full powers over their serfs. It was a logical formulation of an understanding implicit in much of the history of absolutism, outside western Europe at least. Thereafter only local Estates were summoned.

Further south, two principalities had struck out earlier on a similar path. Bavaria was under Catholic rule, the Palatinate under Calvinist, but they belonged to rival branches of the same

---

[36] Carsten , *Prussia*, pp. 177–8.

Wittelsbach family. In a small way the second of them was one more of Europe's political doublets, since it combined the Rhenish Palatinate, whose capital Heidelberg lay close to France, and the Upper Palatinate, well to the eastward on the borders of Bavaria and Bohemia, with Amberg for centre. This foothold in two distinct areas, each exposed to the tides of European politics, was something to inspire vaulting ambition.

At each end of the religious scale events might be set in motion by outside influences. John Casimir of the Palatinate (1583–92) surrounded himself with Calvinist mentors from abroad. Refugees were coming, as they were to Geneva, fertilizing both manufactures and culture. Calvinism here might be regarded as heir to the Zwinglian movement, but it could not rekindle the old fervour, because allied with autocracy instead of civic democracy. For an experiment in absolutism the principality was in some ways well adapted. In the fifteenth century Estates had met fairly often, but had failed to gain an established place. There was a robust nobility, of some six hundred families, endowed with many privileges and most of the higher posts;[37] but in the Council, reorganized by ordinances of 1554 and 1557, it had a competitor in the legal and clerical contingent.[38] Towns were being stripped of some of their self-governing rights, and there was pressure from above towards uniform constitutions.

As against this, pursuit of external aims brought their usual accompaniment – financial embarrassment. Much of the territory had been acquired in parcels by conquest, and in the early sixteenth century debt made the rulers depend on supplies from their subjects.[39] Yet in the absence of functioning Estates, this might in the long run work to their advantage. In the two decades before 1618 a flow of money was raised by means of a complex arrangement of loans from towns and wealthy individuals, many of them nobles. In 1603 a commission of their representatives was set up to supervize the debt, the moneyed classes becoming in this way associates in their rulers' programme. It was another illustration of a truth of modern history which Barnave was to point out before his death in the French Revolution, that no class is more disposed to uphold any regime than its creditors.[40] They had cause for repentance when the

---

[37] Cohn, *Government of the Rhine Palatinate*, pp. 152, 215.
[38] Clasen, pp. 12–13.
[39] Cohn, *Government in Reformation Europe*, pp. 79, 113.
[40] A. J. M. Barnave, *Power, Property and History (1556–1579)*, ed. E. Chill (New York, 1971), p. 146.

Thirty Years War opened with the Elector trying to seat himself on the throne of Bohemia, and coming to grief.

Bavaria, in the southeast, had some affinities with the northeast, among them a subjugated peasantry and a nobility fortified by Estates. In 1514 these laid it down to their debt-pestered ruler, who was making arbitrary demands for money, that constitutional rules must be observed, and government carried on by agreement with a council. Such maxims were commonplaces of the late-medieval 'Estates-monarchy'. Protestantism, in so many ways a common denominator of Germany at its actual stage of development, gained entrance quickly, and was soon hand in glove with the noble and burgher opposition. Luther might preach submission, but his upper-class adherents preferred to leave this duty to the unprivileged, and they could find a pretext for their own insubordination in defence of the true religion.

In Bavaria before long they encountered a drive towards monarchical power. Early in the sixteenth century the partitioned family possessions were reunited and primogeniture prescribed. They were extensive enough to fire a prince's ambitions, and there was a second incentive in the danger of being swallowed up by the Habsburg octopus which hemmed Bavaria in on three sides. The two neighbours were natural rivals. Both were composites of hill and plain; both lay closer than most of Germany to the Mediterranean world. Albert V of Bavaria (1550–79) was encumbered at the start by his liabilities, but from 1563 he was taking the offensive against his obstructive nobles, and getting the upper hand by winning over some of their leaders.

At first from calculation, later from conviction, the dynasty remained faithful to Rome, and was well rewarded, with control over its own church as thorough-going as any Lutheran prince's, and ecclesiastical principalities outside for its relatives.[41] Clerical support was indispensable; conversely, political backing was necessary to the Counter-Reformation because in Germany religious reaction went against the grain of national evolution. Catholicism was being resuscitated by foreigners like the well-born Dutchman Peter Kanijs (St Peter Canisius), and Jesuits were called in as early as 1549 to begin licking the university at Ingolstadt into shape. In Canisius's *Sum of Christian Doctrine*, which has been called the most influential writing of the Counter-Reformation,[42] a vein of

---

[41] Steinberg, p. 25.
[42] J. Brodrick, *The Progress of the Jesuits 1556–1579* (London, 1946), p. 158.

Christian socialism is apparent. He as much as Luther insisted on obedience to command, but he denounced oppression of the poor, and 'defrauding the labouring man's hire', as sins no less heinous than murder or sodomy.[43] Most of this could of course be safely forgotten once prince and prelate were firmly in the saddle.

Success came rapidly. An administrative nucleus had developed before 1500, in the shape of a Council similar to those of Württemberg, Saxony, and many others. Its procedures owed something to the imperial *Hofrat* at Vienna, but for the most part it was a native growth. From it a collegiate array of financial and other boards stemmed; as in a bigger monarchy like Spain it led to the ruler keeping personal control through secretaries or a small cabinet. Collision with the Estates resulted as usual from the government catching the fever of expansion, with its calls on men and money. Here it proved a simple matter, once the bull was taken by the horns, to tame the Estates by excluding Protestants; neither nobles nor urban upper classes were prepared to rouse the common people.

Before long there was no need to summon the Estates, only a small committee which could be bullied into voting taxes. Power was consolidated, during a very long reign from 1597 to 1651, by Maximilian I, who also acquired the Upper Palatinate and Electoral rank. Heavy-handed with heretics and witches, he had the paternalist spirit of the better Lutheran rulers, and improved hospitals and schools. But his schemes abroad were costly, like those of the Palatinate, and it was the villager who had to pay the cost, and at times mutinied. Under the code of 1618 customary tenants lost their rights unless they could produce legal titles;[44] landowners were thus compensated for the political curbs they had to accept. State service, in addition, was more and more attractive to the less well off among them or their sons.[45] Reaction was triumphing the more easily because the towns were not strong, and it then further undermined them. Bavaria was approaching the Counter-Reformation norm of a neo-feudal society with court and landlord, priest and peasant as its chief constituents.

[43] English edn, St Omer, 1622, pp. 50, 260, 263–4.
[44] G. Renard and G. Weulersse, *Life and Work in Modern Europe (Fifteenth to Eighteenth Centuries)* (London, 1926), p. 294.
[45] Demeter, pp. 273–4.

Map 5   *The Austrian Habsburg lands and northern Italy in the later sixteenth century*

10

The Habsburg Lands

The archduchy of Austria handed over by Charles V to his brother Ferdinand was the old southeastern March of the Germans, a narrow wedge thrust out along the Danube valley among Slav peoples. A polyglot destiny was foreshadowed very early when the Alpine duchies of Styria and Carniola, and then Carinthia, came to be attached to it, and their mostly Slovene peasantry fell under German lords. Tirol, added in 1363, was a long westward tentacle across Germany's mountainous south. Altogether the Habsburg dominions belonged more to the uplands than any other important state in Europe, and the uplands were a storehouse of valuable minerals. Copper was a leading item. Silver contributed to the revenues and helped to mould the designs of the Austrian Habsburgs as well as their Spanish cousins.

Minting of silver and debasement of coinage brought early inflation, from which landlords, lay and clerical, suffered because they had leased out most of their land at fixed rents. As in Germany, they sought compensation by stiffening old feudal dues or exacting new ones, and this was resented all the more because serfdom had been waning, and most peasants had hereditary tenure.[1] They joined in the revolt of 1525, with most determination and some success furthest from Vienna and highest up in the mountains, in Tirol where Gaismair, a follower of Zwingli, drew up a constitution for 'a people's republic dominated by peasants and miners'.[2]

After this stormy interlude Ferdinand's dominions might seem to have a fair prospect of evolving into a national state. Its Slav admixture would not make it more heterogeneous than England's

[1] J. Bücking, 'The Peasant War in the Habsburg Lands', in B. Scribner and G. Benecke (eds), *The German Peasant War of 1525: New Viewpoints* (London, 1979), pp. 161–2.
[2] H. Buszello, 'The Common Man's View of the State', *ibid.*, p. 136.

or Scotland's Celtic fringes made them, and could mark it off from the common run of German principalities. But the rulers were involved in the politics of the empire, and with aspirations heightened by the imperial title borne by their family since 1438 they were always on the prowl for more possessions, however un-Germanic. In 1521 Ferdinand married the sister of Louis, elective king of Bohemia and Hungary, while his own sister married Louis. Five years later Hungary was overwhelmed by the Turks at Mohacs, and Louis was killed. He ought to have known better than to tempt Providence by marrying among the Habsburgs, Europe's grand matrimonialists. Ferdinand laid claim to both thrones. His claim was feeble, but there was no ready alternative, and in 1527 he managed to get himself crowned king of Bohemia.

This kingdom, embedded in Germany, had always been linked with the empire, although fully autonomous. Hungary was far more alien, but it was in immediate peril of extinction, from which Ferdinand and his brother might rescue it. But Transylvania in the northeast broke away; from 1541 the Turks were in Buda; all that was left was the western strip nearest to Vienna, with Croatia as a southward appendage. Like Castile in the western Mediterranean, Austria was becoming in some sort the bastion of central Europe against the onslaught of Asia, and as such had, as Engels saw, a historical mission, however bunglingly discharged.[3] The rustic daubs with which Slovene bee-keepers adorned their hives were of a later day, but their themes of battle with the turbaned Turk recorded grim memories. For common people Turkish rule might in fact be less unbearable than that of their own, often not much less foreign lords; the worst fate was to be fought over by trampling armies, each as brutal as the other. Fynes Moryson learned something about the Habsburg forces when he was at Ancona and watched fifty brigands and murderers, pardoned on condition of serving in Hungary, paying their vows to a miraculous image of the Virgin. At Vienna he found it dangerous to walk the streets at night, partly because of the proximity of the army, supposed to be defending Hungary but 'governed by no strict discipline'.[4]

In a Habsburg sphere so vastly enlarged, diminutive Austria could not be an equivalent of England in the British Isles, or Castile in Iberia. Only by riveting a centralized authority on its new

[3] In an article of 1887–8, cited by H. B. Davis, *Nationalism and Socialism* (New York, 1967), p. 35.
[4] *Itinerary* (London, 1617), Part 1, Bk. 2, chap. 1; Part 1, Bk. 1, chap. 5.

acquisitions could the dynasty hope to assert itself. Infidel without and heretic within were warnings against any loitering; it set promptly about the task of welding a miscellany of provinces into an empire. They were all at least contiguous, unlike those of the Spanish crown, and there were German minorities in both Bohemia and Hungary, though it was only in course of time that these would become Habsburg auxiliaries. The outcome, visible by early in the seventeenth century, was a fairly compact block, contrasting with such earlier, laxer unions as that of Bohemia and Hungary before 1526.[5] These belonged to the true east-European or agglutinative type of combination, whose units – countries where only the nobility counted – could be shuffled about at random, unlike the more intricately constructed western nations.

This was the only big monarchy which underwent no change of dynasty within the epoch of absolutism, but there was an anomalous exception to its centralizing programme in the ruling family's fidelity to the appanage system. Charles was following this when he parted with Austria; Ferdinand in turn made a will portioning out his lands among his three sons, with the eldest, Maximilian II (1564–76), getting the lion's share: Austria, Bohemia and Hungary. For the management of the Alpine fiefs a family confederacy had some merits; but acceptance of undivided inheritance and responsibility in the next century would be one mark of a more mature absolutism.

Ferdinand came on the scene, young as he was, already imbued with authoritarian views by his upbringing in Spain: he must have been disagreeably impressed by the Comunero outbreak there. He came to Vienna with a posse of Spanish assistants, as his brother entered Spain with an entourage of Netherlanders, and the officials he established in the Austrian towns had a resemblance to *corregidores*. Other ideas he soon commenced putting into effect had been fumbled with by his grandfather Maximilian I, guided perhaps by the Burgundian methods known to him through his matrimonial windfall of the Netherlands. Absolutism was an institution of European growth, whatever its national variations. An ordinance of 1527 created a series of central organs, and an orderly routine of business was soon being worked out. It was complicated by intermingling of Austrian and imperial affairs. The *Hofrat* or privy council, focal point of government as in western capitals, was

---

[5] S. Verosta, in appendix to S. von Herberstein, *Description of Moscow and Muscovy 1559*, ed. B. Picard (London, 1969), p. 104.

for long concerned primarily with Germany; so, very often, was the imperial chancellery, and it was not until 1620 that a separate Austrian chancellery came into being.[6]

A war council set up in 1556 was important from the first in bringing the Habsburg possessions under unified control. It was to a great extent round its military organization that this state was growing up, even though shortage of means delayed the establishment of a standing army until well on in the seventeenth century. Still more than any of the western armies, the forces employed were a cosmopolitan lot. It would seem that the lesser nobles, in France or Castile so eager to join the colours, showed much less alacrity here. They had more of a backwoods mentality, which made them slow also to seek careers in the bureaucracy. Educated middle-class men, whom they looked down on as loftily as on ploughmen, had the better opportunity to win official posts, and might climb to noble rank and grants of land.[7] Lacking these alternative occupations, the old nobility was the more constrained to squeeze its tenantry.

Habsburg strength might be a protection, but it was a painfully expensive one. The treasury, as organized in 1527, administered at first chiefly the crown's own sources of income. Money for the wars had to come mostly out of grants from the Estates. Each of the old provinces had its assembly, in Upper and Lower Austria and Styria with the same fourfold structure as in Aragon, and a similar standing committee between sessions. Deputies were always prepared to haggle and obstruct, and often wanted to supervise the spending of what they grudgingly voted. Like some Estates in Germany, they took a hand in local administration; in fact the tug of war between them and the monarchy was something like a contest between rival governments.

Religion lent unction to opposition. Lutheranism flowed into this region as naturally as into nearly all Germany, among all classes and among Slavs as well as Germans. Until late in the sixteenth century a modified religious freedom was one badge of Austria's still partially belonging to east-central Europe, with its diluted or decentralized authority. Upper Austria was the stronghold of Protestantism, here strongly tinged with Calvinism, which attracted the gentry. In this hilly area most landed properties were of moderate size, and the gentry counted for more than the magnates. Minor nobles often felt most attachment to representative bodies, local

---

[6] Schwartz, pp. vii, 19.
[7] Bücking, *op. cit.*, p. 165.

rather than national. Centralism carried to any point attainable in that age could not deprive the master of a large estate of importance in the life of his district; smaller men had more need of a collective forum.

With some paternalistic feeling, but also with a self-regarding concern for the flow of tax-money and of army recruits, the government might take an interest in conditions in the village. An edict of 1597 restricted labour services in Upper Austria to two weeks annually.[8] Yet the state, whose mounting costs fell as everywhere to a great extent on the peasantry, might come to be felt as a worse oppressor than the landlord. Ploughman and noble might share the same creed, though any combination between them against the government would be fragile, and any revolt by the peasants united government and landlord against them, as happened in 1525. By and large Austria may be said to present the spectacle of a regime not much wanted by any class in particular. Instead of growing out of internal relations and requirements, this state was being built up, more disproportionately than any other except Prussia later on, by external necessities or ambitions. Only when it reached a certain point in this ascent would the nobility fall into place round it.

An index of this was its excessive reliance on a church which most of its subjects were deserting. Nascent absolutism faced a harder task in post-Reformation conditions than in western Europe where its foundations were laid with the help of an undivided church. Now a revitalized Catholicism, which could be depended on both for monarchist ideology and as part of the machinery of state, had to be conjured up by arduous effort. The government led the way, inspecting and prodding and subsidizing. When the breezes of Counter-Reformation began to blow, the sails were ready to catch them. In 1552 the first Jesuits were installed, in 1556 a college was founded for them at Vienna. In 1572 they set to work at the Styrian capital, Graz.

'Bohemia is one of the richest, civilest and strongest nations of Europe', an English visitor reported.[9] It had at any rate more taxable wealth than any other Habsburg land, and was called on to contribute twice as much to the wars as Austria. Its many weakening rifts invited this penalty. Like all the old kingdoms, it was a conglomerate. Upper and Lower Silesia and the two Lusatias, all

[8] B. H. Slicher van Bath, 'Agriculture in the Vital Revolution', in CEHE, p. 117.
[9] See J. V. Polisenský, *Britain and Czechoslovakia* (2nd edn, Prague, 1968), p. 32.

mainly German, and Moravia were linked to Bohemia proper by a crown whose significance was symbolic, even mystic, rather than practical. Each had its own assembly, and on occasion a 'General Diet' met, somewhat as the Aragonese provinces might hold a combined Cortes. This Diet as regulated in 1446 had three chambers, for the nobles, gentry, and burghers; only the first two had voting rights. In both Bohemia and Moravia it was the magnates who laid down the law.

A German influx was continuing, and the advent of Lutheranism favoured the spread of German speech and culture. This was disliked by many descendants of the Hussites; but the religious scene was as much fragmented as the territorial. Class divisions were deepest of all, and were aggravated by the drift of the economy. In some respects there was deterioration. As in Austria, silver-mining began to find it hard to compete with America.[10] On the other side of the ledger there was a decided growth of manorial industry, in iron-working, glass-making, and other branches, as well as of demesne farming. Here the advantage lay with richer landowners, who had their own woodlands to furnish fuel and an adequate command of labour.[11] For most of this period there was no resident court at Prague, and hence no lifeline of royal favours for the aristocracy, which had therefore more incentive to exploit its material assets.

By so doing it lifted itself higher above the gentry, and subjected the business class to unequal competition. It inflicted still more injury on the peasants, who in the Hussite national resistance had done a great deal of the fighting while the nobility came off with most of the gains. In 1497 they were declared bound to the soil, in accordance with the prevailing trend in east-central Europe. Exactions might take the form of labour dues, but in Bohemia with its comparatively advanced economy there was often an incongruous linkage of compulsory labour with money wages and money rents.[12] Food prices in all this part of central Europe rose sharply in the second half of the sixteenth century, while wages fell behind. In Bohemia landowners reaped the benefit by taking a

---

[10] J. V. Polisenský, 'The Thirty Years War', *Past and Present*, no. 6 (1954), p. 40; S. Hoszowski, 'Central Europe and the Sixteenth- and Seventeenth-century Price Revolution', in Burke, p. 97. Evans, p. 38, gives a more favourable picture of prosperity at least among the nobles and citizens of royal boroughs.
[11] See Myska..
[12] Polisenský, *'Thirty Years War'*, cit. supra, p. 38; I. Wallerstein, *The Modern World-System* (New York, 1974), p. 307.

bigger hand in the grain trade, buying up the peasants' crops and forbidding them to sell in town markets.[13] In one way and another feudal bonds were being drawn tighter, and the cultivators' rights whittled away.

In 1547 when Charles was launching his blow in Germany, the Estates came together unsummoned at Prague, reaffirmed the elective basis of the monarchy, proclaimed religious freedom, and set up a steering committee with four members from each order. But as in Germany defiance was hollow, because of disunity. Charles lent his brother some Spanish and Walloon troops, the Estates climbed down, and Ferdinand entered Prague unopposed, while the nobles made haste to desert their urban allies. He struck hardest at the Bohemian Brethren, as the most recalcitrant of the reformed sects, and, like Charles in Germany, at the towns.

His wings were quickly clipped by the imperial defeat, and in his remaining years he had to be satisfied with nursing a party of adherents. This could only be the Catholic camp, even more needful as a prop in Bohemia, where the Habsburgs were interlopers, than in their own Austria. In 1556 the country had its first Jesuit inoculation. Maximilian had to practise conciliation. He wanted to get his son Rudolph accepted in advance as successor, as in Hungary too, and his theology fluctuated with his political circumstances. He could even be suspected of Protestant sympathies, and there was no doubt that he detested his Spanish relatives cordially. Catholicism was still dwindling, until by the late years of the century it may have kept the allegiance of no more than a tenth of the nation.[14]

Rudolph made a fresh start by transferring his court to Prague, well away from the Turks, leaving a governmental nucleus at Vienna to cope with Austria and Hungary. His highly polished but morbid mind, a denizen of a twilight age, hovered between culture and the occult; but he or his ministers were taking up afresh the task of breathing life into Catholicism and attaching it intimately to the dynasty. Rebellion in the Netherlands was a warning against neglect of danger; it could also, it is true, be viewed as a warning against indiscreet haste. Catholics might be few, but among them were some of the magnates, who in all the eastward realms were apt to be less staunchly rooted in national feeling than the gentry, and more adaptable to a system like the Habsburg. Rudolph's very cosmopolitan court at Prague was a beacon for them. And by the

[13] Hoszowski, *op. cit.*, pp. 89–99.
[14] Evans, p. 35.

end of the century many impoverished lesser nobles were sinking
into dependence on them.[15]

On the Alföld, the marshy Hungarian plain, lived under Magyar
ascendancy a mixed population, with urban settlers from Germany,
very gradually assimilated, and Slav and Rumanian communities
whose higher strata were largely replaced by or transformed into
Magyars. Only the Magyar nobility and its congeners of other
stocks formed the 'nation', all the rest outside the towns being mere
hewers of wood and drawers of water, known expressively as the
misera plebs contribuens. Magyars, like Poles, were much addicted to
Latin, as a badge of civilized status; and rank in east–central Europe
had a flavouring of racial superiority as well as class.

Starting as early as in the west, though with less success,
monarchy had striven to make head against the feudalists; Matthias
Corvinus (1458–90) buttressed his power with plebeian officials and
foreign soldiers. Little came of these efforts, and it was partly as a
consequence of their failure that the same period saw the peasantry
being pressed down. Revolts culminated in the great rising of 1514,
crushed by the landowners with the aid of foreign mercenaries
whom they too knew how to make use of. It was in this condition
that the country had to face the Turks when its small cavalry army
was overwhelmed in 1526 at Mohacs.

Tempted by rising prices and promising markets, in what
remained of Hungary the lords, like those in Bohemia, were
moving into the business of agriculture, at the expense of the
peasants from whom they had hitherto been content to receive
rents. Produce could be sold abroad as well as at home; Austria
would buy, and Hungary like Poland supplied food to many towns
in central Europe. An antiquated claim to a noble monopoly of
wine-sales was being revived. Cattle, some of it bought from the
Turkish part of the country, was a principal export item. It was
another trade of which nobles in various countries tried to secure a
monopoly. Being less at the mercy of weather, cattle-rearing
brought in more stable returns than grain, and salesmen of rank
knew how to evade toll-payments.[16] They were dealing in wheat as
well, bought from the peasants or obtained from them, like wine, as
part of their dues. All this stimulated a trend towards demesne
farming, and with it a steady extension of serf labour, in the early

[15] Polisenský, '*Thirty Years War*', *cit. supra*, p. 39.
[16] Z. P. Pach, 'Sixteenth-century Hungary: Commercial Activity and Market
Production by the Nobles', in Burke, pp. 114–17; K. Glamann, 'European Trade
1500–1750', in Cipolla, pp. 469, 473.

part of the century employed only on a lesser scale;[17] as in Bohemia it might be combined with compulsory paid work. A law of 1548 was a landmark in its spread. Anywhere from England eastward, seigneurial authority might promote some form of commercialized agriculture, larger-scale market production, even if in a country like Hungary this was developing on very different social lines from England's, as a variant of 'feudal capitalism'.

In the half-century after Mohacs it often seemed that the strip of western or 'imperial' Hungary would be swallowed up with the rest by the Turks. In one of many pleas for relief, Ferdinand wrote to his brother in 1552: 'les affaires vont tousiours de mal en pis' . . . 'le danger nest petit de totalle perdition.'[18] There were moments when he could glimpse the fact that social injustice was opening the door wider to the invaders, and urge a relaxation of serfdom.[19] His grandfather Ferdinand had enforced concessions in Catalonia; but in Hungary the peasants were no longer in a condition to fight, and a Habsburg was too much an outsider to play umpire in class conflict. As to the Magyars, any concept of an authentic state was beyond their ken; it implied a broader social basis than a single class, a nobility however numerous, can supply. Like their Polish cousins again, the nobility could feel an ardent sense of nationality, but this was not, as it was coming to be in the west, bound up with loyalty to a political authority; the two things had to evolve separately.

Break-up of the national territory did not prevent the social structure from persisting with extraordinary tenacity. County administration was the stronghold of the middle gentry, and enabled them to hold their own against the big nobles and foreign rulers as well as against the masses. Its office-bearers, including from 1548 the sheriff or *vice-comes*, were elected by them. Meanwhile Habsburg strategy was to gain as much footing as possible in central affairs. An old royal council was being superseded by new arrangements, including the Habsburgs' own chancellery with members responsible for Hungarian business, and a new treasury. Magyars were little consulted; the office of *Nador* or 'Palatine', deputy of an absent king and custodian of national rights, was left unfilled from 1562 to 1608, while the armed forces which ought to have been under his direction were brought under that of the Habsburg commanders. Rudolph lost no time in trying to centralize power further

[17] Pach,. *op. cit.*, pp. 118–19, 122.
[18] *Correspondenz des Kaisers Karl V*, ed. K. Lanz, III (Frankfurt on Main, 1966), p. 389.
[19] Jaszi, p. 43.

through his military council at Vienna; there were loud complaints from the Diet in 1583.

This institution was taking shape under stress of the changed situation: mass meetings of nobles were crystallizing into an assembly at Pressburg (Pozsony), which outwardly looked much like Parliament in England. There was an upper house for magnates and prelates, a lower one for the gentry, with two representatives after 1608 from each county, and the burghers. The Diet was a bulwark against Habsburg encroachments as much as a rallying-point against the Turks. Distrust of the rulers was partly expressed and strongly buoyed up by the Calvinism widely adopted among the nobles, while the towns turned to Lutheranism. Here too the best prospect of support for the monarchy was from the magnates. Hereditary titles, a novelty in eastern Europe, were distributed among them. But Vienna's agents were rarely distinguished by tact, and friction was chronic. To the end of the century nearly all the aristocrats remained Protestant, and they regarded themselves as allies of Vienna rather than vassals, who if displeased could balance between it and Stamboul.[20]

Hungary's satellite or colony, Croatia, had a degree of autonomy, with a *Sabor* or assembly at Zagreb; but social oppression here was intensified by being national oppression also. Many of the superior lords were Magyar or German, and far the greater part of the land belonged to magnates and the church. In such an exposed frontier region the position of the smaller gentry, mostly native Slavs, was precarious. Peasants frequently absconded, fleeing from Turkish incursions if not swept off by them, or taking refuge with the Turks as the lesser evil. It was all the more desirable to tie them to the land, and during the sixteenth century labour services were being extended. Repeated risings led to the peasant revolt of 1573, which spread to the Slovene population of the Alpine duchies. It was one of the most formidable outbreaks of social conflict anywhere in the European countryside. War burdens were one cause, as in many other cases; and Croatia resembled the Polish Ukraine and southeastern Russia, where the biggest upheavals of all took place, in lying in the agitated borderlands between Europe and the Muslim world.

Once authority rallied its forces, German professionals with cavalry and fire-power among them, the rebels were expeditiously suppressed.[21] Few towns were of any size, and none entered the

---

[20] Marczali, p. 129, n. 1.
[21] See Bromlei.

fray. There was nothing to lift the peasants' ideas above an elementary level. Although they suffered from war-taxes and from being conscripted to build forts or perform other services for the army, as well as from landlord rapacity, they showed some naïve faith in the goodwill of their distant ruler Maximilian, and sent deputations to him; he responded by sending troops to help in putting them down. They then had some notion of making their leader Matthew Gubets king of a free Croatia. These Slavs had for centuries had no native ruler, yet belief in kingship still haunted them. It is no wonder that simple Spaniards or Russians put so much misplaced trust in their sovereigns.

Despite its failure the revolt left long memories. Slovene partisans in the Second World War sang one of its songs when they attacked a landowner's mansion:

> The castle is burning,
> The count is running,
> The wine is flowing —
> Blood must flow too.[22]

The weakness of the feudal lords in the crisis and their need of government aid were not lost on Vienna, which saw an opportunity to tighten its hold on the province. Before 1573 was out a new *Ban* or governor was appointed without reference to the *Sabor*, whose functions were soon being cut down. More Germans or other newcomers were given estates. All along the frontier with Turkey, adventurers from anywhere and everywhere were being installed in small fiefs, to form military colonies. These tactics were clumsy, irritating, and not very effective for defence, but they were safer than reliance on the local gentry, or entrusting arms to the rebellious masses. Introduction of foreign ingredients was an essential and permanent feature of Habsburg methods everywhere.

While Croatia was subjugated, Transylvania sturdily went its own way. In Vienna's eyes it was a subversive example to imperial Hungary, whose northern sector marched with it. It was however not so much a rump Hungarian state as a federation, somewhat like the Swiss but drawn closer by pressure from outside, of the 'three nations', as they called themselves: Magyar, Szekely (a mixture of Magyar and Rumanian), and Saxon. In the first two of these the

---

[22] I owe this to Dr Bozhena Ravnihar, of Ljubljana, who was a medical worker with the Partisans. In 1974 a striking statuary group of peasants with clubs and scythes was erected outside the old fort at Ljubljana, in memory of five centuries of Slovene peasant revolts.

leading groups were landowners, in the third burghers, originally from Germany. In 1542 they agreed on a constitution: there was to be an elected prince, ruling with a council drawn from all three communities and with the assent of the Estates. It was a 'social contract' from which all but nobles and wealthier townsmen were excluded. Some rulers enjoyed considerable power, profiting by the far from complete harmony among the partners. Bethlen Gabor astonished and intrigued Europe from 1613 to 1629 scarcely less than Gustavus, the Lion of the North, whom he resembled both in Protestant fervour and expansionist ambition and in trying to develop the economic resources of his little country.

In the opening years of the seventeenth century the Habsburg state underwent a crucial transformation into a more thorough-going absolutism. This was preceded by crisis within the reigning family, a disarray as deep as the Valois dynasty's towards its end. Not only were the three branches stemming from Ferdinand still in being, but there were dissensions among Maximilian's sons, fiercest betwen Rudolph and the third, Matthias. Monarchy and madness were often near allied, and Rudolph's cleverness drew closer and closer to the brink, while Matthias seemed more and more clearly the man who could give the leadership now becoming indispensable. International complications were crucial. Among them was the 'Thirteen Years War' with the Turks, which broke out in 1593, and marked a favourable turn of the tide in the long eastern contest. On the other side, Spanish influence was reasserting itself in German and Austrian affairs, as it had sundry means of doing. An English emissary at the imperial court, then at Augsburg, reported in 1581 that most of its members were in debt and dependent on Spanish pensions.[23]

Both Spanish and Catholic interests demanded a more active exercise of the imperial power in Germany. This was being called in question by the more mettlesome Protestant princes, with Christian of Anhalt as their tactician, and one of his devices was to foment Protestant intransigence in the Habsburg lands. For a Habsburg party the ecclesiastical rulers, headed by the three Electoral arch-bishops, were obvious candidates. Most of them drawn from princely or aristocratic families, they had the usual difficulties, including refractory Estates, to wrestle with. In addition, their anachronistic principalities ran the risk of being taken over by Protestants and secularized. Imperial authority was exerted to prevent this;

[23] I. D. Colvin, *The Germans in England 1066–1598* (London, 1915), p. 210.

it was also brought to bear against the free cities, more vulnerable than the heretic princes.

Meanwhile Counter-Reformation zeal was finding no more congenial field than the multifarious Habsburg empire. As its momentum increased it might drag so inorganic a creation further than real Habsburg interests warranted. Religious reaction was set in train with least difficulty in the Alpine duchies with their mixed and divided population. Charles of Styria was an active persecutor. He exhibited the greater readiness of both Austrian and Spanish Habsburgs than of any other dynasty to put members of their own families into the church, as well as to bring ecclesiastics into administration; four of his fifteen offspring entered the church. His young son Ferdinand, from the first a diehard upholder of both Catholicism and autocracy, continued his work with a more brutal determination. A Fugger report of October 1599 spoke of intense persecution in Graz, and the death under torture of the secretary of the Council in Carinthia.[24] Little by little resistance was worn down, and although each province was allowed to keep its Estates, it was typical of the outcome that henceforth Styrian towns were allowed only a single representative.[25]

At Vienna Ferdinand's counterpart was the truculent cleric Melchior Khlesl, in charge of church reform from 1590, later president of the Privy Council, and in 1616 cardinal. As son of a burgher (and convert) he, like Charles's middle-class bishops in England, may have relished making life uncomfortable for upper-class malcontents. His task was an uphill one, all the same. While in northern Germany under Protestant rule the new religion had grown conservative and quiescent, in the southeast it could still be a restless force, both political and socially. Under its banner the Estates and their backers could pose as defenders of their countries' rights against arbitrary, and especially foreign, government.

With many individuals this stand, and their religion, were quite sincere; with the classes they belonged to, both served as cloak for selfish interests. In the late 1590s there was peasant revolt, most resolute in Upper Austria where feudal exactions were being screwed up. Religious and social grievances were intertwined, and landowners could sympathize with the first, but not the second. Towns here were as feeble as in Bavaria; this did much to facilitate

---

[24] *Fugger News-Letters*, First series (1568–1605), ed. V. von Klarwill (London, 1924), pp. 245–7.
[25] E. Wangemann, *From Joseph II to the Jacobin Trials* (London, 1959), pp. 66–7.

the advance of the Counter-Reformation. In Europe generally, in fact, peasants were further and further isolated from any possible allies, except, as at times in France, on a very local stage. Fighting alone, the Austrian peasants were doomed to defeat, though their struggle smouldered for several years. Troops from Slav areas were brought in to put an end to it. To utilize one nationality against another was a Habsburg trait. But the nobility was cutting itself off finally from the common people, without whose support it would before long find itself just as helpless.

In Hungary religious meddling gave all disgruntled factions a common cause, and went a long way to counteract whatever credit the Habsburgs might claim as defenders against the Turks, in matters of worship so much more tolerant. As the Turkish war dragged on, moreover, the Diet was driven to expostulate in 1602 that the foreign soldiery was doing more harm than the enemy. There was disaffection among the great landowners, whom Vienna's German, Italian, or other non-Magyar agents were pushing into the background. At the same time pretexts were found to confiscate estates and use them to reward these intruders. To infiltrate an alien element into the higher aristocracy was equivalent to the creation by western monarchies, and by the Habsburg in Austria, of a new nobility to neutralize the old one. It was to be a prime tool for riveting their dominions together, but practised in Hungary at this stage it was liable to rebound.

What brought discontents to the boil was a rash attempt to occupy Transylvania, where the regime set up by the Italian general in charge quickly incurred so much odium that the Habsburg forces were swept back and Austria itself was threatened. This was the emergency that brought Matthias to the front in 1606, when a conclave of archdukes recognized him, instead of Rudolph, as head of their house. He abandoned Transylvania, and late in that year negotiated peace with Turkey. This set him free to interfere in Bohemia, where Spanish and clerical diplomacy was hard at work to promote the Catholic party.[26] It was by siding with the opposition in 1608 that he compelled Rudolph to hand over to him all his other territories. To secure recognition by the Estates of Austria and Hungary, Matthias had to give far-reaching pledges to both. Hungary was promised religious freedom, that is freedom for the dominant groups in each area to choose what creed to enforce, and the office of Palatine was to be restored; the Diet insisted that the

---

[26] Chudoba, p. 186.

throne was still elective. It was almost an anticipation of the *Ausgleich* and the Dual Monarchy of two and a half centuries later.

Naturally the Bohemians were all the more bent on similar concessions, and they were displaying vigorous if rather empty activity. A committee of thirty was appointed; Silesia gave its adhesion; and there was a brief closing of ranks between the chief offshoots of the Hussite tradition, the conservative Utraquists and the radical Bohemian Brethren. In July 1609 Rudolph had to sign the *Majestätsbrief* or 'letter of majesty' which authorized the Protestants to appoint 'Defenders' as watchdogs of their rights. Its authors may be supposed to have borrowed some hints from the Edict of Nantes of eleven years before. In 1611 dynastic dissension reached its most acute and damaging stage, and Matthias entered Bohemia and got the Estates to compel his brother's abdication in his favour. In return he had to agree to their demand for the crown to be again elective, and cede sweeping powers to them. Virtually, Bohemia was turning itself into a republic; but its leaders shrank from the final step. To set up a republic was an enterprise which only the most advanced and most revolutionary nations had courage for; the Dutch only half succeeded, the English only momentarily. Its time would come in the end far away from Europe, beyond the Atlantic.

In 1614 Matthias tried the novel experiment of a convocation at Linz of delegates from the Estates of all the Habsburg lands, in the hope of inveigling them into a fresh Turkish war through which he could regain the initiative. This came to nothing, and in Bohemia he fell back on his predecessor's game of nursing the Catholic faction and trying to pack the government with it. To make sure of the future, he had to arrange the succession. He was one of five brothers without legitimate offspring, and this opened the way to a re-concentration of authority. It was their first cousin, Ferdinand of Styria, who stood out as the strong man needed by the dynasty at this critical juncture in its fortunes and in European politics. Matthias took pains to get him adopted as heir, a manoeuvre regularly made use of to circumvent the elective principle.

It was folly in the Bohemian leaders to fall in with it, and to suppose that he or any Habsburg would be content with the role of constitutional monarch. By March 1618 they were sufficiently undeceived to call a general assembly in protest at the way things were going. Many nobles attended, few townsmen: pressure was put on the towns by royal officials, but their lukewarmness was one more sign of how feudal reaction and class division had enfeebled

the nation. The nobles went ahead, and advertised their resolve in
May by the suitably melodramatic gesture of 'defenestrating' the
two most overbearing aristocrats in the royal council, Slavata and
Martinic. A kind of provisional government was set up by the
Estates, and Count Thurn – who unlike the two scapegoats belonged
to the German minority – was charged with enrolling an army. No
one seems to have been particularly charged with raising money to
pay for it; after all the whole record of these Estates was one of
objecting to taxation. Bohemia and Moravia, which set up a direc-
tory of its own, were not fully at one. Yet union between the
provinces was all the more urgent when classes were so little able to
combine.

Matthias died in March 1619. Ferdinand carried off an unopposed
election as emperor, Protestant Germany being as usual at sixes and
sevens. A family compact with Madrid had already been rigged up,
and the imposing support he was getting from many quarters was a
tribute also to the coordinating skill of the Counter-Reformation
and its chiefs. Ferdinand's opponents accused him of planning to
turn the empire into a hereditary monarchy. His aims may not have
stretched so far; his first concern in any case must be to make himself
master in his own house. In July the Estates of Lower Austria, or
their Protestant membership, refused to recognize him, and next
month they made a compact with the Bohemians and with Upper
Austria. Their manifesto denounced the 'Spanish severity' of the
government.[27] A concerted and almost successful attack was made
on Vienna, which was also menaced in 1620 by Bethlen Gabor.

But in political terms all this presaged a reversion to the old
east-European style of loose confederations among nobilities,
instead of an advance towards something higher. Having formally
deposed Ferdinand, the Bohemians were looking round abroad for
a figurehead, both because they were still not bold enough to
proclaim a republic, in the face of conservative Europe and of their
own discontented masses, and because they hoped for potent
foreign succours. These the adopted Calvinist candidate, the Elector
Frederick of the Palatinate, failed to produce. A meeting of delegates of Hungary, Bohemia and Transylvania at Pressburg sent a
joint deputation to Stamboul to bespeak Turkish aid, likewise not
forthcoming. This looking to outsiders instead of to the people was
reminiscent of the German princes' reliance on France seventy years
earlier to save them from Charles V.

[27] Schwartz, pp. 80–81.

Lower Austria was quickly subdued, with the aid of a savage band of Cossacks from Poland. Upper Austria showed the same unpreparedness when assaulted by Ferdinand's kinsman and ally, the Bavarian ruler and his general Tilly, in July 1620. Warned by defeat, the able and realistic Austrian leader, Baron Tschernembl, called on the Bohemian landlords to rally patriotic enthusiasm by emancipating their serfs; but he called in vain, as progressives in the Polish national movement of the nineteenth century were to do. It would not indeed have been easy to make effective forces overnight out of plebeian volunteers, but the peasant revolts of that epoch indicate that they could have been at least doughty auxiliaries.

Frederick brought some German and Hungarian mercenaries, so ill-paid and disorderly as to provoke villagers into reprisals – a reduction to absurdity of a war of patriotic defence. At this game the polyglot Habsburg state, now establishing itself conclusively, would be hard to beat; it owed more than any other to a cosmopolitan swarm of mercenaries, and to foreign subsidies for their pay. What was wanted to meet this machine was a nation, and the nation that fought through the Hussite wars no longer existed. At the battle of the White Mountain in November 1620 – skirmish and hill equally diminutive – most of the infantry on the Bohemian side was German, much of the cavalry Hungarian; the bulk of the invading forces hailed from the Spanish Netherlands and Italy. Frederick was summarily routed, and fled.

Ferdinand II was in a position now to do all and more than Ferdinand I had hoped to do in 1547. As the progeny of international forces, owing its legitimacy to conquest, the Habsburg government could behave in a more revolutionary fashion than any regime resting on native foundations. Twenty-seven executions in Prague in June 1621 formed the swelling prologue to confiscation in a series of stages of half the soil of the country. Once at least, a century before, after expelling a duke of Württemberg, the Habsburgs multiplied smallholdings in order to enlist peasant attachment. There was no thought of such a strategy now, any more than the beaten party had thought of restoring the ploughman's freedom. Nor could Ferdinand contemplate turning all these estates into crown land; he must form at once a body of vested interests pledged to the new order. Properties were given away to reward loyal adherents and, very extensively, to endow a new nobility of aliens in Habsburg service, from as far away as Ireland, who could be counted on for loyalty because they would owe everything to their employers.

A remodelled Bohemian administration was inaugurated in 1621, the chancellery was removed to Vienna, and in 1627 an organic law made the crown fully hereditary and vested all legislative power in it, as well as the prerogative of appointment to all offices. The Estates survived, but with no right of initiative, no purpose except to assent to tax demands; a chamber for the clergy was added by way of ballast. Towns lost all autonomy. In the same year Protestants were ordered to leave within twelve months. It was only two decades since the final expulsion of the Moriscos; the impulse to purge the commonwealth by mass conversion or banishment, so much an obsession of Counter-Reformation psychology, emanated from Spain. Catholic Germans were brought in to fill gaps in the towns, and as officials; division within the country was thus worsened, to the government's advantage.

In Austria too there was harsh persecution, and the opposition of the nobles and burghers was broken at last. The political downfall of the old nobility was typical of the fortunes of this class in eastern Europe, where absolutism did not grow 'naturally' as in the west, but was imposed by external force, as in Bohemia (and, much later, in Poland), or by an autochthonous government with foreign backing, as in the old Habsburg lands. These eastern landowners had successfully defied their own former rulers, and subjugated their peasantry, but their naïve egotism made them too short-sighted to recognize the strength of the newer forces arrayed against them, an irresistible combination of military and ideological.

It was left to the peasantry, as in various parts of Europe, to fight a rearguard action. In 1625–6 it was once more in revolt in Upper Austria, with the same embitterments as before against exploiters and priests. Striking at both landlord and official, it could help to heal the breach between them. The Estates were at the end of their long period of political animation. Their base in society was too narrow for any real chance of an evolution to constitutional monarchy, cutting short the stage of absolutism that all western countries found unavoidable in moving out of the middle ages. Yet Austrian as well as Spanish Habsburgs could feel a conservative respect for time-honoured institutions; Ferdinand showed this when he made Tirol an appanage for a brother. Besides, finance was a troublesome business which they were not sorry to share with others. Much complicated work over the assessing and collecting of taxes was still left to the Estates or their committees. They and the government long continued to work together in this fashion; but from now on the government had the upper hand.

Central administration was being more systematically organized Its nucleus was the Privy Council, growing in size, whose deliberations Ferdinand unlike his two predecessors regularly attended.[28] Another change was the one often to be observed at this point in the flowering of monarchy, from a council with a strong gentry and middle-class element to a more aristocratic one. On the other hand members were not drawn from the old nobility, but were almost all new men, who rose by state service and built their fortunes on its pickings.[29] This difference from seventeenth-century Spain with its aristocratic leadership was not unconnected with the fact that Austria was a rising, Spain a sinking power.

Vienna from now on was the permanent focus, and was blossoming into a truly royal, not merely provincial capital. This helped to clothe the regime with a national character, and Austrians could find solace for lost liberties in the feeling, flattering if irrational, of belonging to the metropolis of empire. There were mundane as well as sentimental advantages in the presence of a wealthy court. With its social limelight and cosmopolitan culture, as well as the high posts and dignities in its gift, the court would attract the higher nobility of all the Habsburg lands. A typical family drawn to it was that of Kobenzl, which like so many others had risen by state service, from the late sixteenth century when Johannes became proprietor of the cavern-castle of Predjama in Slovenia and climbed the official ladder to the governorship of Carniola. Just as kings quarrelled with their nobles but could not do without them, grandees as they came under the spell of culture had need of a collective atmosphere of refined luxury which nothing but court life could supply; rugged independence was left to feudal lords in backlands like eastern Poland.

Even in restive Hungary this lure was at work. Khlesl's hectoring, before he fell from office in 1618, stirred resentments there afresh, and they broke out dangerously in the stormy opening of Ferdinand's reign. Immersed in problems further west, he was obliged to come to terms and confirm Hungary's privileged status. Its grievances were compounded by prolonged economic depression in the early decades of the century, which must have had something to do with sagging food prices in the markets Magyar landlords looked to, while cessation of war with the Turks allowed production to thrive. Catholic missionizing went on, but along with it

[28] *ibid.*, pp. 114, 131.
[29] *ibid.*, pp. 397–400.

more care was being taken to humour the magnates. All classes in Europe were ambivalent in their attitudes to the state, the highest pre-eminently. Up to a certain stage in the state's ascent, aristocracy was everywhere a centrifugal force; but more often than not it was also at odds with the swarm of minor gentry, stiffened in many lands by the Reformation. Now in Hungary it was feeling the pull of the monarchy, and simultaneously seeing the light from Rome, whereas a solid phalanx of the Magyar squirearchy held fast to Calvinism and self-rule. To the *misera plebs* was left the comfort of a cult of the outlaw, the defier of an unjust society; it was shared with the common folk in Croatia and Bohemia, and flourished more in eastern Europe in general than in the west.[30]

The slow-dragging Thirty Years War tested and strengthened the machinery of government and its military driving-wheel. At its close imperial sway in Germany was a shadow, but authority within the Habsburg dominions was firmly consolidated. Instead of the league of gentry-corporations that dissidents had envisaged, the empire was evolving into something more like a union of great landowners, with a reinforcement of new men brought in by a state fit by now to exert a formative influence on the upper classes. At the same time, the old aristocracy could absorb the newer, as well as being leavened by it. This process would be smoothed by a well-endowed Catholicism, most of whose plums would always go to distinguished old families. Lower down was a cosmopolitan cadre, civil and military, whose descendants Engels would speak of as 'a race of their own; their fathers have been in the service of the Kaiser, and so will their sons be. . .'.[31]

Protestant defeat left the state too closely tied to a church militant and triumphant, but destined before long to grow rigid and lifeless. Lack of a true national basis would make it harder for the Habsburgs to shake themselves free of the incubus. They were as yet far from having arrived at the more constructive or enlightened phase of absolutism represented by Henry IV and Sully, though there was a sort of archaic substitute in the flow of charities quickened by religious revival. Much in the transformation of the Habsburg empire so far was only tentative, and the later stages it was to go through were many.

---

[30] P. Burke, *Popular Culture in Early Modern Europe* (London, 1978), p. 165.
[31] *Germany: Revolution and Counter-Revolution* (1851), chap. 4.

11

Poland

Eastern like western Europe combined marked contrasts with underlying similarities. All the eastern economies suffered from drawbacks of soil or climate, lack of fertility or water or sunshine; the west's richer physical as well as historical endowment put it in the lead. Reduction of the cultivator to serfdom was an attempt to make up by more intense exploitation of labour for the inhospitality of nature and the scantier population that went with it. This as well as distance from the sea made for sluggish urban and commercial development, and towns were thinly scattered even by comparison with most of Germany. Poland and Hungary, neighbours separated by the Carpathians, were the typical polities of the east-central European belt. Like medieval Spain they were societies of 'Asiatic' cast in superimposing peoples like classes, instead of simply gathering them under one government as France or Britain did. Their towns often started as foreign settlements, while peasants of many stocks lived under Magyar or Polish lords. Beyond lay Russia, more remote from the western countries in cultural ancestry, more akin to them in having a fairly homogeneous mass of population over which a strong national state could be reared.

Poland like Hungary developed political forms which suited its nobility well enough, and took on a fixity hard to change when they grew manifestly obsolete. Its ancient capital, Cracow, lay in the southwestern corner of the country as it came to be, in close touch with central Europe; from there the Poles were sucked out into a broad no-man's-land eastward. Their advance across open, half-empty plains ('Poland' means *plain*) had little need of central direction, and resulted in no compact feudal hierarchy such as in western Europe was the forerunner of the centralized state. Instead, there was an undisciplined horde of warriors, or nobles, linked together by ties of clan. Family was all-important, genealogical ramifications were traced far and wide.[1] The poorest could pride himself on equality with the greatest. Hereditary titles never came in, though official titles were prized as a substitute.

When the Piast dynasty died out in 1370 the Jagellons, grand dukes of Lithuania, became through a marriage alliance, dictated by common needs of defence against the Teutonic Knights, kings of Poland as well. Lithuania was a backward, shapeless agglomeration of lands in the frontierless eastern marches. Its upper classes were soon adopting Polish speech and manners, and moving further away from the mass of their subjects. Class could evolve into nationality, just as nationality might constitute class. As a result the connexion proved enduring, unlike many others in the annals of this part of Europe, but not permanent, because ordinary Lithuanians would ultimately want to set up on their own. Poland-Lithuania as a dual entity was larger than the Holy Roman Empire, and had not very much more in the way of government. Its two centres, Cracow and Vilna, were four hundred miles apart, and much further in terms of history and associations. External trials brought moves towards closer affiliation, instead of accession of strength to the government. A long-drawn conflict with Russia on the Baltic coast, ending in 1562, was followed by the last of these, the Union of Lublin of 1569 which joined kingdom and grand duchy into the 'Polish Republic' or commonwealth.

Pressure had to be put on the Lithuanian magnates to accept this: it led to successive transfers of their loosely held southeastern territories to the Polish sphere, much as Naples and Sicily passed from Aragon to Castile. Fusion was still not complete. The two Diets met as one body at Warsaw, close to the boundary between their countries. Each of these retained its own laws, officers of state, treasury and armed forces. None the less, a truncated Lithuania would sink from now to a Polish province. For Poland the risk was of becoming as amorphous as Lithuania had been. As to the eastern borderlands, they were subjected now to a far more aggressive domination than they had known before, fired by greed for land and serf labour and before long by the zealotry of the Counter-Reformation. Polonizing of the upper classes, an influx of Polish landlords with Jewish traders in their train, turned the Ukraine into a colony, and at last into the graveyard of Polish power.

Lithuania had been a breeding-ground of very large estates, ruled at their own whim by their proprietors who also lorded it in the

[1] Lednicki, p. 125.

pany-rada or council. Below them was a lesser nobility envious of the superior position of the *szlachta*, the similar class in Poland, and well disposed to union as a means of achieving the same status. Poland too had its magnates (*pan*), especially 'Little Poland', its southeastern extension towards the Ukraine, but under its less supine government oligarchy had been held in check, and it was the middle gentry who were coming forward from the later fifteenth century. A tenth of the whole population was 'noble', and the majority of estates covered no more than a single village. As in Hungary, a swarm of poor gentry scarcely differed from free peasants.

Cracow's merchant patricians had a dignified place, and the richer traders and some urban crafts were prospering. But many minor townships were subject to feudal lords, and in general the towns were too thin-sown and multifarious to constitute an estate of the realm. In 'Royal' or Polish western Prussia, Danzig and others successfully upheld their franchises, now and then by resort to armed force; but they were German. Many others were partially German in origin, and the 'Magdeburg law' or self-governing rights they had been granted had the effect of detaching them from the national life. It was only in western Europe that cities were free and strong enough to assert themselves, but sufficiently enmeshed in national affairs to have a radicalizing influence on them. Townsmen were forbidden to acquire estates, so that a free land market, with all it implied, was cut off. Their leading circles were at odds with the ordinary burghers, as they were all over Europe. Another divisive factor was the large Jewish section, constituted by a decree of 1551 into a self-governing, self-contained community.[2] For Polish Jewry the sixteenth century was a golden age, and its numbers may have risen from about 50,000 to 500,000 between 1500 and 1650.[3] But many of its professions, of moneylender, tax-farmer, estate-manager, were not such as to endear it to the common man, any more than in old Spain; while, as there, its presence hindered the rise of a native middle class.

In the tight-packed western countries international conflict accelerated political growth; Poland's frontier wars were many but touched its life more superficially. Cracow was sheltered by its geographical position, unlike Paris or London or Vienna. There were few models for state-builders to copy; for long the Habsburgs

[2] I. Friedlaender, *The Jews of Russia and Poland* (New York, 1915), pp. 105, 162.
[3] C. Roth, *A Short History of the Jewish People* (London, 1936), pp. 289–90.

were floundering, France was paralysed, Sweden was too different. Internally, there was little open struggle between classes or within the dominant landed groups to require a powerful regulator. Taxation fell primarily on the cultivators; the nobility however did not want the state to take too much of the fleece, and this endemic contradiction was being solved in a way far less favourable to the government than in France. Alienation of crown lands to magnates by the needy monarchy further diminished its resources. From the later fifteenth century most prelates were appointed by it, but this did not make the wealthy church eager to contribute more than a pittance to its expenses, even under the shadow of Reformation.

Polish gentlemen were even less inclined than their Austrian compeers to enter state service, whose appeal indeed dwindled steadily across the continent from west to east, as far as Russia where a service-nobility was being reared artificially. Royal officials (*starostas*) superseded the feudal governors of provinces (*voivodes*), but this meant less than parallel changes in other countries, because the nobility was virtually withdrawing itself from their authority. In 1518 the crown renounced jurisdiction over peasants on noble or ecclesiastical properties. From some years before this date regional assemblies of nobles, or 'dietines', were choosing delegates to attend the national Diet or *Seym*. This was a right that the Lithuanian gentry too gained in 1566, by an annexe to the 'Lithuanian Statute', or charter of noble rights, of 1529. Representative assemblies were a novelty so far east, and only took shape, belatedly and imperfectly, when in most western lands they were faltering, and could not set a heartening example. In the *Seym* the upper house or Senate was not a House of Lords, but an enlargement of the old royal council, made up of prelates and lay dignitaries chosen by the king but then irremovable. Deputies of the lesser nobility formed a disorderly lower house. They were bound by instructions from the dietines, which received notice beforehand of proposals to be laid before the Diet; the gentry was far more reluctant than in England to delegate power to a national institution. As to the burgher class, Cracow alone was represented.

The last three Jagellon reigns, from 1501 to 1572, formed an epoch in Polish history, when the outlines of a state constitutional in a feudal sense were emerging. Initiative lay with the gentry rather than the aristocracy, and there was a recurrent tug of war between the two houses of the *Seym*. A persistent aim of the gentry was to compel the magnates to bear the cost of government by restoring lost crown lands. Restoration was in fact ordered in 1562–3, but could not be fully enforced. An alliance between minor nobles and crown would have been logical, but the former, too confident in their local bases, were blind to their need of royal leadership, and equally to the king's need of concessions from them to strengthen his hand. The court was nearly as obtuse, and in any case to marshal a straggling multitude of squires and squireens was an arduous undertaking, only feasible in England for very specific reasons.

It was more tempting to look for short cuts. Sigismund I (1506–48) in his later years was trying to bring to the front a batch of aristocratic families of his own creation, a proceeding likely to antagonize both tiers of the nobility. Sigismund II (1548–72) commenced by seeking an understanding with the Habsburgs, highly obnoxious to the gentry in whose eyes they always stood for monarchy avid for untrammelled power. It was in the foreign sphere that rulers shackled at home must try to assert themselves; but this confronted them with the need for troops, which meant money, and plans for reconstructing both revenue and army hung in the air. All nobles with enough land to be comfortable on wanted to be rid of their obligation to perform military service, while they refused to pay taxes to equip a fighting force more useful in the new conditions of warfare, for which the mass of impoverished gentry could supply recruits.

In 1493 and 1496 the Polish peasantry was formally bound to the soil. Anyone defiant enough to leave lost whatever he could call his own; in Castile the peasant's right to go away with his belongings had just been recognized. A Polish humanist in his work *De Republica Emendanda*, published abroad, advocated fair treatment for all classes, including the cultivators;[4] but he went unheeded, like other lone voices with the same message. As often happened, it may have been the smaller landowners who were in most haste to tie their few ploughmen down and squeeze all that could be got out of them; gentry power would be harmful to peasantry as well as government. Subjugation of peasant peoples of other stocks could not but have a deleterious effect on all agrarian relations; the quelling of peasant rebellion in Hungary and Germany must have inspirited landlords in Poland.

One day weekly of labour for the lord, the minimum fixed in 1520, was soon turning into two or three, and then more. Abundant labour being thus ensured, the other half of the process was the adding of more land to the lord's demesne, by termination of leases

[4] Kot, p. 8.

or by pilfering from village commons. There were no more than sporadic outbursts of resistance. Things were getting worse by degrees, and not at the same rate in all districts. Malcontents might succeed in absconding. Some could find work in towns; others joined an outflow from the western and central provinces, more populous than the rest, and managed to reach the Ukraine, where they were accorded some years to settle down before being called on to pay taxes. Even the less fortunate were not as a rule being deprived of their own holdings – the fate overtaking the rustic in England – even if their ownership was becoming as illusory as the English labourer's freedom. A class of comfortably-off cultivators remained, if in diminishing numbers; they might have to perform no more than carting or similar services, or might pay money rents: those close to town markets would be best able to earn the necessary cash. Stratification of the peasantry may have been the decisive obstacle to large-scale resistance.

Prices were rising, more sharply in the second half of the century. There were frequent complaints of the cost of living by pamphleteers and orators in the Diet.[5] Money prices had indeed only a restricted relevance to what was still primarily a natural economy, like so much of Europe. Wages were paid as a rule in kind; barter was common. Living at home and consuming most of a growing surplus with family and dependants, the bulk of the lesser nobility was relapsing, as in northeast Germany, into rustic torpor. All landowners, however, would want to sell some portion of the contents of their granaries, in order to buy things not produced on their estates. For this purpose the bigger landowners with more working hands and output were the best placed; especially those with access to the river network which was the principal medium of transport, with the Vistula as the grand highway.

Given these assets, subsistence agriculture could flower into 'feudal capitalism', or commodity production by serf labour. It had markets abroad as well as at home. Grain was the foremost export, but timber, flax and hemp, hides and wool, were also high on the list. They moved by way of Danzig, at the mouth of the Vistula, and other Baltic ports, or overland into Germany. Grain found buyers in deficit western areas; the quantities changing hands were marginal to the European economy, and not enough to explain by

[5] S. Hoszowski, 'Central Europe and the Sixteenth- and Seventeenth-century Price Revolution', in Burke, pp. 98–9.

themselves the enserfment of the Polish peasantry,[6] but quite enough to have a bearing on social trends. In the long run these were in the direction of enriching a minority of bigger or luckier land-owners; exports would also stimulate greed for more land and labour in the Ukraine.

How serfdom affected total production is hard to gauge. Agri-culture made a not inconsiderable advance in the later fifteenth century and the sixteenth century; the cultivated area grew; three-crop rotation and cattle-rearing spread.[7] But too much progress consisted in some eating more because others ate less. Cultivation based on serfdom could be run by stewards trained in management and marketing, but it did not make labour zealous or efficient. As time went on this might lead to diminishing returns, and the output of the peasants' holdings seems to have dropped because they were left too little time to work them. In Poland and most of eastern Europe, from these as well as natural causes grain yields during the century and a half after 1600 were exceptionally low, lower even than in southern Europe.[8]

There were symptoms of economic recession towards 1600, although it was another fifty years before the towns felt the full impact of shifts in the rural economy. They stood to benefit by the wealth extracted from the peasantry and partly disposed of to them. On the other hand, urban industry, while taking some steps towards larger-scale undertakings in novel branches like paper- or glass-making, felt competition from the bigger estates, where forms of manorial industry like those in Bohemia and other lands, drawing on local materials and serf muscles, were developing. There was expansion in mining, in which all the propertied classes could join hands, as in Germany. Lead mines were being drained and exploited by a company in which citizens of Cracow and of the mining towns, noblemen, and the crown all held shares.[9]

---

[6] Malowist, 'Le commerce de la Baltique', p. 129; cf. Kula, p. 99, and B. H. Slicher van Bath, 'Agriculture in the Vital Revolution', in CEHE, p. 119. K. Glamann estimates Baltic grain received by western and southern Europe in the first half of the seventeenth century as meeting the consumption of no more than 750,000 people. 'European Trade 1500–1750', in Cipolla, pp. 465–7. The loss to producers in eastern Europe, chiefly Poland, was greater than the gain to foreign consumers.

[7] *Cambridge History*, p. 44; Gieysztor, p. 177; Hoszowski, 'Central Europe', *cit. supra*, p. 118.

[8] Slicher van Bath, *op. cit.*, pp. 80–81, 121.

[9] H. Kellenbenz, 'Technology in the Age of the Scientific Revolution 1500–1700', in Cipolla, p. 202; cf. p. 209.

Polish industry had to face competition from foreign goods too, cloth heading the list. Commercially, towns suffered through land-owners being able to deal with foreign traders, and to dodge pay-ment of custom duties. How little a nobleman thought of mer-chants as a useful part of the nation was made plain by a law of 1565 barring Poles from export and import trade altogether, even if such a ban could not really be enforced. No Polish maritime activity developed; even that of Danzig declined, for most of the Baltic business was handled by Dutch shippers, a colony of resident Scots, and other outsiders. Just as Spain's coastal provinces were mainly not Castilian, nearly all of Poland's seaboard was occupied by the dependent but autonomous fiefs, non-Polish and Lutheran, of West Prussia, Courland and Livonia. Landowners exporting produce in return for luxuries were concerned for Poland's hold on routes and outlets; in other words, parasitic interests compelled the country to squander energy on holding alien lands washed by an alien sea. Smaller landlords yawning their lives away on their acres would take little notice of any matters of state, so long as they were left in peace. Meanwhile royal revenue shrank as demesne farming ex-panded, since only peasant land paid tax. Yet the crown had no thought of trying to shield the cultivator; instead it tried, ineffec-tively, to ingratiate itself with the nobility at his expense.

In 1572 the Jagellon line came to an end. Like those of Bohemia, the political classes in Poland had no real relish for monarchy but were unequal to the effort of forging a republic. Any new king would have to be elected, whereas in the west stricter hereditary principles ensured that a defunct dynasty – Valois, Tudor, Spanish Habsburg – would always leave some legitimate successor, how-ever remote. No Pole could be chosen without too many heart-burnings being stirred up, and in the next fifteen years three elections brought to the throne a Frenchman, a Transylvanian and a Swede. Three interregna exemplified a besetting ailment of elective monarchy, as hereditary crowns suffered from royal minorities.

They opened the way to full establishment of a 'gentry demo-cracy', a serf-owners' Utopia of liberty, equality and fraternity. Its standard-bearer was John Zamoyski. A man of humanist edu-cation, he found his ideal in the aristocratic Roman republic, whose ghost still walked here and there, as it did in Shakespeare's *Julius Caesar*. There was always a dash of make-believe in gentry demo-cracy, and much scope for demagogy on the part of the magnates, such as Zamoyski himself soon rose to be. Its tendency was to dissolve the country into a loose association, for a scattered squirearchy was little better able than a peasantry to throw up a regular national leadership or any but a negative programme.

One expression of incoherence and unrealism was the Reformation movement, most widespread in the 1550s and 1560s, which had the virtue of tolerance and the drawback of superficiality. In 1573 the 'Confederation of Warsaw', a reaction to the Massacre of St Bartholomew in France, proclaimed freedom of religious choice for all the privileged. But no creed could bring together burghers and landowners, as Calvinism did in France or Britain. Townsmen inclined to Lutheranism; Calvinism drew adherents from such categories as the gentry of Little Poland and the Lithuanian magnates. Others joined the Bohemian Brethren; a minor sect of Polish Brethren, with Unitarian leanings, was unique in having some Anabaptist tinge also, and sympathy with the worsening lot of the masses. A right to form confederacies was always claimed by Polish (as well as Scottish) nobles, and their sects might be called an extrapolation of it from secular life into spiritual.

At the time of the first royal election, in 1573, Zamoyski raised the alarm over the Habsburg candidature, and secured the adoption by the *Seym* of the principle that all of blue blood, high or low, were entitled to a vote. His party was determined to tether the crown more closely. Henry of Anjou, brother of Charles IX, was chosen, perhaps because distant, strife-torn France might be expected to meddle least. But he had to sign pledges to respect all noble privileges, and to summon the Diet every two years; and these 'Henrician articles' were included from then on in the *pacta conventa* imposed on all rulers. Poland was giving itself a written constitution long before most countries, but a very circumscribed and inelastic one. Henry quickly disappeared to his homeland in search of a more comfortable throne. In the next contest the Senate, mouthpiece of the magnates, voted for a Habsburg, as a curb on the obstreperous gentry, thousands of whom gathered tumultuously at Warsaw. Led by Zamoyski, they wanted a Polish sovereign, a scion of the long-departed Piast dynasty, but the only one worth considering was a woman; they fell back on a plan of giving the crown to Stephen Bathory, prince of Transylvania, and marrying him to her.

To the magnates, Stephen was always an unwelcome upstart.[10] They smarted even more under the ascendancy of that other nobody, Zamoyski, who as chancellor put on airs and speedily accumulated a fortune. He held several governorships, offices

---

[10] *Étienne Báthory*, pp. 155–6.

which gave little strength to the crown but could bring wealth to the notables who secured them. Bathory had to seek prestige by eye-catching activity on the frontiers, including a war with Russia. This condemned him to much tedious haggling with Diet and dietines, which might admire a dashing campaign but had no desire to foot the bill. The old army array, a *levée en masse* of the gentry, had helped to bring this class forward politically, but militarily it was obsolete: this, and their growing unwillingness to serve, were not unconnected with the political decline that was to overtake the gentry before long. Bathory wanted money, to build an up-to-date army, with gunnery and a reliable infantry to supplement the knightly cavalry. He enlisted Cossacks from the borderlands, and foreign mercenaries, German and Hungarian, but could not afford many. A Habsburg-type force composed of such materials could be serviceable to the government at home as well as abroad; in the gentry it would start the same suspicions as English landowners felt of any standing army for so many years after the Commonwealth.

In addition, Bathory, always a staunch Catholic, was aligning himself closely with his church. It could figure as the sole national institution, offering Poland a badge of unity, as divided Protestantism could not, against enemies of other faiths, and disguising the fundamental disunity of the Polish people. In the course of the penetration of the Ukraine, the church gathered fresh ardour, and also much of the best land there to add to its impressive holdings in all the eastern provinces. These resources gave it ampler means of gratifying needy or aspiring members of gentry families, who could be given managerial posts in its service, as well as benefices. The gentry lacked the motive of their Magyar cousins for clinging to Protestantism against unpopular foreign rule. For the aristocracy, who as elsewhere were leading the return to the fold, the courtly Italianate culture associated with the Counter-Reformation had a charm, and Jesuit schooling was a passport to it.

Bathory died in 1586 without a son to follow him, and next year Sigismund Vasa was chosen. He was a nephew of the last Jagellon, brought up a Catholic by his scheming father, King John of Sweden. Zamoyski and the gentry party favoured him because Sweden might be a useful friend in the Baltic, and because the rival faction wanted Maximilian of Austria. The latter's candidature was predictable. To the Habsburgs the spectacle of the rise of the gentry in Poland was bound to be a warning, a spur to their efforts to make sure of their power at home. To their own nobility it was an incitement to thwart them, and by winning the Polish throne they might be able to put a damper on it, besides gaining a loftier position in Europe. There was a brief civil war, a calamity Poland was safeguarded from at most times by its looseness of texture. But the logic of Sigismund's position pushed him into courses close to those the Habsburgs were pursuing. He lived indeed through the epoch in which Habsburg autocracy was firmly established, and looked to it as his exemplar. Still more than Bathory, he counted on the church; too hopefully, for the Counter-Reformation could not be a substitute for missing keystones, though it could cement them where they existed.

In 1605 Zamoyski died, and history was beginning to leave his followers behind. Next year Sigismund asked the *Seym* for a regular annual revenue and a permanent army. The surly gentry insisted instead on fresh clogs on the government, and the imbroglio resulted in the 'Sandomierz rebellion', which invoked the right, maintained on occasion in Hungary too, of insurrection against unconstitutional rule. Sigismund suppressed it with the help of Zolkiewski, who was making his mark as the most distinguished Polish commander of the time. Its collapse was in one aspect a milestone in the retreat of Protestantism, but was not equally a triumph for the crown. In 1609 the Diet served notice that the constitution was unalterable.

Sigismund like Bathory had to pin his hopes on achievements abroad, and he was tempted to gamble too often and deeply. His obstinacy in pushing his title to the Swedish throne landed Poland in a protracted conflict. In 1610 he invaded a Russia at war with itself, with the aim of regaining border territory and even of mounting the Russian throne and converting the country to Catholicism. Led by Zolkiewski, his army reached Moscow, but the glorious daydream quickly faded, and such exploits could do nothing to pull the nation together. In 1613 Sigismund entered into a secret compact with the Habsburgs, but it was not a moment when they were in any shape to render effectual aid.

Of the aristocracy, which Sigismund wanted to attach to his star, he could only depend on those who were making their careers at court; and compared with newly ennobled Habsburg councillors, they were really making use of the government much more than they were working for it. They became ministers for life, and entrenched themselves in the Senate, which increasingly overshadowed the lower house. Economic fluctuations were subjecting all the higher classes to a process of reshuffling, and it was a partly renovated species of magnates, a blend of feudal and plutocratic, that was coming to the top. Most powerful of all were the masters of huge estates, virtual principalities, in the eastern regions. They could aspire to as much autonomy as German princelings had, and were already indulging in private wars among themselves, besides embroiling Poland in adventures from which the nation could not gain.

In the anarchic Ukraine only such potentates could establish settlers, including land-hungry members of the gentry, and protect them. Apart from Tartar raiders, there was a sturdy frontier population, swelled by fugitives from serfdom or their descendants, and readier to take up arms than the broken-spirited masses in the old provinces. Among them, the Zaparozhe Cossacks were the most formidable. Free men and freebooters, they were a rude republic organized on military lines, with elected chiefs.[11] Democracy, wilting over nearly all Europe, could still have a brief flowering in this no-man's-land. These Cossacks were making common cause with the oppressed peasantry of the Ukraine, in the name both of a simple patriotic or regional feeling and of defence of the Orthodox faith against Catholic intrusion. There was a Cossack revolt in 1590, a peasant revolt in 1596, and thereafter an increasing convergence of the two movements. Poland's strength was being worn down.

Sigismund's son, Vladislav VII (1632–48), in his later years toyed with thoughts of using a Cossack army to coerce the *Seym,* much like Strafford, it has been remarked, meditating the use of an Irish army against Parliament.[12] A similar resemblance can be seen between the Irish rebellion of 1641 and the great Ukrainian insurrection headed by the Cossacks under Khmelnitsky. In May 1648 the Polish army was cut to pieces, and a jacquerie swept the province. A devastating Swedish invasion of Poland followed; the Polish people was paying the penalty for the reckless expansionist ideas of its ruling class. Popular anger at the calamities was diverted away from the upper classes against the Jews, long hated as their factotums.[13] Many communities were destroyed, and the epoch of Jewish prosperity was at an end.

So, by this time, was Poland's. Sigismund's removal of the capital in 1590 to Warsaw did little but accelerate the decay of Cracow; this citadel of the old-world merchants had been injured by the shift from the westward trading routes to the Baltic. Poland's

[11] Hrushevsky, pp. 221 ff.
[12] Allen, p. 105.
[13] N. Bentwich, *The Jews in Our Time* (Harmondsworth, 1960), pp. 36–7.

lack of a vigorous metropolis must be reckoned one cause of its political failure. More general decline was coming later than in Hungary, but in the second half of the seventeenth century was catastrophic. Smaller towns were running down. Because during 1550–1650 what a peasant could buy in exchange for what he sold fell heavily, while for landowners, especially the bigger ones, the position was the opposite, these towns were finding too few customers in the surrounding countryside, and artisans found it paid them better to leave and work on estates.[14] Conversely, urban shrinkage deprived small rural producers of their market,[15] and the twofold process was spiralling. An embryo national market was relapsing into a local barter economy, and again economic and political dissolution accentuated each other. Literate Poles were racking their brains for the causes of this decadence:[16] as in Spain, Minerva's owl was flying after dark.

Gentry-democracy too was flagging. It saved Poland from many of the banes of absolutism, but too much at the cost of the Polish people for any true republic to arise from it. The gentry itself, whatever its illusions about 'golden liberty', could not in the long run escape one horn or the other of its dilemma – monarchy or oligarchy. Having brought about a withering away of the state, it was sinking into subservience to the magnates. One handicap was that minor landowners went on portioning out their properties among their sons, whereas from the late sixteenth century the great men were entailing their estates in western fashion and so keeping them intact.[17] They might besides have lands here and there across the country, and so were not ruined by disasters affecting one province or another.[18] Idle unwarlike squires bred too fast, small patrimonies were weighed down by debt. All this compelled more and more of the lesser fry to look for patrons.

Their loss of independence ironically echoed the peasantry's. In turn it was to be succeeded by loss of national independence, a recapitulation of the fate of Bohemia and Hungary. At bottom, the breakdown of the Polish realm can be traced to the inordinate number of nobles. Substantial landowners can afford (if so inclined) to cover state costs out of their own or their tenants' superfluity;

[14] Kula, pp. 94–5, 107.
[15] Malowist, 'Le commerce de la Baltique', pp. 141–3.
[16] Hoszowski, 'Central Europe', *cit. supra*, p. 123.
[17] J. P. Cooper, 'Patterns of Inheritance and Settlement', in Goody, pp. 198–9.
[18] Kula, p. 110–11..

impoverished squireens cannot. Blue blood was left to console itself with its indefeasible superiority to the ploughmen whom it looked down on as an inferior race, descended from Ham as one of Mickiewicz's characters recalls, instead of like itself from Shem.[19]

---

[19] English edition of *Pan Tadeusz* by G. R. Noyes (London, 1930), pp. 100.

12

Russia

By mid-sixteenth century most of the Russian lands were gathered together under the hegemony of Muscovy, whose capital occupied a central position at a junction of routes and waterways. Its rulers were claiming all Russian territory as their patrimony, an idea in part dynastic but implying some national sense, however hazy. Unification met with far fewer impediments than in countries further west, because the various principalities were hardly more than loose bundles of princely or noble estates. Tartar domination had left Russia in many ways a tabula rasa. Union's less beneficial side, which Germany avoided, was that it brought into being a country too big and unwieldy to be ruled by any normal, reasonable methods; and this was worsened for centuries to come by the scarcity of population that Catherine the Great was to deplore, a manpower capable only under cruel compulsion of the immense exertions demanded of it. In 1600 there may have been under sixteen million people.[1]

All round the Muslim perimeter of Europe, war against the Crescent helped to generate expansionism within Christendom as well, a fact of which Venetian history was the smallest illustration and Muscovite the largest. Conflict with Asia was the chief rationale of this clumsily powerful state, and gave it an affinity with the Habsburg. But it meant that while Russia was seeking closer contact with Europe, it was at the same time still being enmeshed with some of Asia's most benighted regions. In 1552 the khanate of Kazan was conquered, more than four hundred miles east of Moscow, itself four hundred miles further east than Stamboul; and in 1556 Astrakhan, at the mouth of the Volga. Like Spain, Russia was expanding in Europe and winning a colonial empire simultaneously, but its colonies were contiguous with it instead of oceans away, and bound up with its own political development. Asian

[1] R. Mols, 'Population in Europe 1500–1700', in Cipolla, p. 38.

levies or auxiliaries were part and parcel of Russian armies; Tartar or half-Tartar families were plentiful in the aristocracy. There was an oriental flavour in the long-continued practice (shared by Spain) of uprooting and transplanting masses of people, an instance of how this Muscovite state might have a more direct, sweeping impact on the life of its people than any further west except Spain. Serfdom, however, which was to do more than anything to barbarize the country for ages, was a novel phenomenon there, and not Asiatic but European.

'The manner of their government is much after the Turkish fashion', wrote Fletcher, English envoy to Russia, expressing a common European view; he thought it 'plaine tyrannicall'.[2] It was, in fact, a more highly centralized form of state-feudalism than western monarchy presided over, more closely akin to Muslim Asia than to Europe. Barbaric features of Moscow life struck Herberstein, the Habsburg diplomat who was there twice in the earlier sixteenth century. Slaves were many, among them broken men who voluntarily surrendered themselves to a patron, and might receive offices of trust from him. This resembled the *commendatio* of the western Dark Ages, and Russia's dark ages were not yet left behind. Even the highest men at court were called, and called themselves, the monarch's slaves. It is interesting to find a man of Herberstein's day asking himself the question 'whether such a people must have such oppressive rulers or whether the oppressive rulers have made the people so stupid.'[3]

Other observers surmised that ignorance and superstition were deliberately fostered by the church.[4] Ages of strife with the infidel had infected Holy Russia with a fanaticism as limitless as Spain's. Church wealth, especially monastic, was considerable, even if only a few monasteries singly possessed a great amount of land. As in the Latin church, monks came largely from the upper classes, so that when these bequeathed property to monasteries they were endowing themselves. Because parish priests could marry, the celibate prelates often began as monks. Towards the government the church's attitude was ambivalent. It was highly tenacious of its privileges, and persisted in engrossing more land in spite of royal disapproval. On the other hand, it stood in need of a central authority's countenance against all who might molest it, including the peasantry. It was willing therefore to give unstinted moral,

[2] Fletcher, p. 20.
[3] Herberstein, pp. 43–4.
[4] M. S. Anderson, *Britain's Discovery of Russia 1553–1815* (London, 1958), p. 25.

though not financial, support to the monarchy, and invest it, as sole paladin of the one true church, with a brighter halo than any in the west could pretend to. 'One and all agree that their lord's will is the will of God', Herberstein reported.[5] In a more practical way prelates were also royal councillors, and ecclesiastical schools turned out educated men for the growing bureaucracy. There was no such European thing as a university.

Russia could pose as successor to the defunct Byzantine empire, and Ivan III's Byzantine wife Sophia was a fit consort to elevate the throne. Besides the Constantinopolitan title of Autocrat, he and his son sometimes used that of 'tsar', or Caesar, with which the next ruler, Ivan IV – 'the Terrible' – was crowned in 1547. Their family claimed kinship with the Roman empire of the west as well as the east; it traced its descent from a brother of Augustus named Prus,[6] a genealogy emblematic of the freakish or abnormal quality of the whole regime. The Kremlin was still a fortified complex of old Slav type, but its architecture was of partly Italian design; its hybrid features might be said to reflect an old-style 'patrimonial monarchy' taking on a more modern spirit. Territorial growth by itself compelled a shift; administrative tasks were outgrowing the framework of the royal household.[7] Earlier and later notions jostled for very long, and to the end tsarism could not shed its original instincts with any completeness. This dynasty never entirely abandoned the appanage system traditional in all the Russian principalities.

At the top of Russian society was a landed nobility with many peculiarities, which, even more than most, could not be led, only dragooned. Ethnically, the boyars were a very mixed lot, with Finnish, German, Lithuanian, Greek ingredients as well as Tartar. This made it harder for them to combine into a coherent class or party, while their alien blood must have inflamed the hatred of them revealed in times of social upheaval. Merging of the principalities brought together former princely families, and their nobles, in obedience to Moscow, and with them inextinguishable jealousies enshrined in the complicated *mestnichestvo* or table of precedence. This was an aristocracy harnessed, far more fully than in the western countries with their richer supply of suitable men, to the work of administration. Through government service new men could join their ranks; entrances and exits to and from the boyar grade were always taking place.

[5] Herberstein, p. 43.
[6] Wipper, p. 18.
[7] R. C. Howes, pp. 80 ff.

Newcomers received grants of land, on terms of continued obligation to serve, whereas the *votchina* or estate of an old family was hereditary. But it was likely to be diminished by partition among heirs, the custom at all levels of property-holding in Russia, with the royal appanages at its apex. In the long run all estates would gravitate towards a common condition and liability to state duties. A 'Boyar Duma', in its inception a feudal grand council, was in process of turning into a functional part of the administration, not unlike the Polish senate except in being less independent of the sovereign. About 1550 it had some fifty members, who might on momentous occasions be joined by the Metropolitan and other prelates. Some of its members were present as senior officials, heads of the *prikazi* or departments. It held daily sessions, often presided over by the tsar. Its business was miscellaneous, as with all government in that age, legislative and judicial as well as executive.

Departments started with a clerk or two under some functionary; they proliferated by the end of the century to thirty or more. Their duties were not always clearly demarcated, and some, like the bureau of military affairs, were much more important than others. Officialdom was coming to be graded into a hierarchy of ranks, or *chin*, a bureaucratized version of the table of precedence. Ranks corresponded in some measure with social strata further west, though with an artificiality marking a country where the state came before and moulded society rather than growing out of it. By nationality they were as much a jumble as the boyars. In one list of families at the higher level, only about a third were Russians, the rest Lithuanians, Tartars, or immigrant westerners.[8] Everywhere foreigners had a share in building the modern state, and the more backward a people the more there was for them to do. Their ubiquity in modern Russian history was another facet of the contrast between an emergent nation and the state clamped on to it.

We have a picture from a foreign resident, Heinrich von Staden, of the graft and extortion practised by leading officials in the capital.[9] Away from Moscow they had still more of a free hand. Provision was made for *voivods* or local governors by what was known as *kormlenie*, or 'feeding', which meant that various imposts were earmarked for their upkeep; they took as much more as they could. Most of the real work of policing, road-mending, and so on, was assigned to the *starosty*, district elders chosen by the peasants and petty gentry, and acting without remuneration. Thus the com-

[8] Kluchevsky, II, p. 110.
[9] Staden, p. 9.

pulsory principle was applied to all, but with many compensations for the high, none for the low. Land – or the peasants on it, which might come to much the same thing – paid taxes, at differential rates; monastic estates were exempt before 1584. Thanks to sweeping conquests and recurrent confiscations, the crown itself owned vast tracts of land, a source of strength unrivalled in any other country.

For regular soldiers, foreign mercenaries were employed as everywhere, but Russia found them costly and unreliable, and they wanted pay in cash, which was not abundant. There was no host of small landowners to provide a fighting force; instead there took place a gradual creation of such a class by the state. The *pomeshchiks* began as horsemen, each granted a small fief (*pomestye*) for his maintenance. They were recruited at the outset from the flotsam and jetsam of society, even slaves, but son was soon beginning to succeed father. It may be supposed that the most aspiring were the cadets of noble families, 'sons of boyars' as the whole corps came to be honorifically termed. They were not a standing army, though they might be called up at any time; they had no proper training, they were an anachronism when they began, and they were to prove on the whole (which is saying a good deal) the worst army on the continent.

They were not 'landowners' in any strict sense; they might be compared with the *jagirdars* of the Mughal empire, officers paid by a temporary assignment of the revenue of a specified area. But in agrarian society where possession of land, or rather licence to rob its tillers, was the highest felicity, these men were certain to want to turn their fiefs little by little into properties of their own, which they could continue to live on in old age. Their successful efforts, in the century between 1550 and 1650, were profoundly to influence Russia's evolution. Their number, about 25,000,[10] may seem disproportionately small, but far more must have passed through their ranks; there were always some who were dropping out or getting killed. They had much to do with the crystallizing of classes out of the loose floating mass of the Russian people.[11] They were pace-makers in the intensifying exploitation of the peasantry. Most of their grants were trifling, only a few hundred acres, and, given the primitiveness of Russian agriculture, the ploughmen would have to be squeezed hard indeed to produce a living for the master. Supplementary grants of cash from the government, when it had

[10] Hellie, p. 24.
[11] Kluchevsky, III, p. 162.

any, were meagre and irregular.[12] Army growth all over Europe, if
geared to external aims had a secondary purpose in the quelling of
internal unrest, which its own costliness did a great deal to fan. In
Russia the interplay was particularly close.

Russia had no peasant proprietors. Land belonged to state,
church, or lord: from about 1550 merchants were being debarred
from purchase, not, however, too rigorously. Here was a situation
without parallel in Europe, the outcome of long insecurity and of
superabundance of land, where cultivators could roam from district
to district on condition of paying toll to the proprietor of the soil
they raised a crop on. Paradoxically, they would only turn into
peasant owners, or gain the sensation of ownership, through being
fettered to the land. Elements of serfdom had always existed, and
were now multiplying, in spite of – or because of – the fact that the
economy was making appreciable progress, in some ways on the
same lines as the Polish. On large estates a three-field system was
spreading by 1500, and population was on the increase. Unlike
Poland, Russia exported to the west only items such as hemp and
furs, but there was an incipient internal market in grain; and even if
exchange was still far more through barter than by money, foreign
trade was bringing in enough extra currency to give even Russia a
taste of the omnipresent price-rise.[13] Landlords wanted to farm
more acres themselves, and therefore to compel peasants to
perform more unpaid labour for them, two or three days weekly in
the season, or even more, instead of the eight days or so a year
formerly customary. Rent payments in cash or in kind (*obrok*) were,
all the same, more widespread than labour duties or *barshchina*.[14]

Peasants were less well able to resist because they often had no
local roots or attachments, and might live in minute, isolated
hamlets in forest clearings. Where there were compact villages, the
peasant commune could give some protection, more on crown
lands than on seigneurial estates. Frequently the ploughman's
remedy was to remove to some other estate where he could get
better terms. The pushing back of the eastern and southern frontiers
opened up new soil, and there was a steady exodus from the old
central provinces, an escape to the borderlands parallel with the
western drift from countryside to towns. As a counter-measure it
was being made the rule, more precisely in a revised code of 1550,
that the peasant could move only at one time in the year, after the

[12] Blum, pp. 200–201.
[13] Mousnier, p. 170.
[14] Blum, pp. 204, 207, 225.

harvest. Even this right was soon being curtailed. It might be clogged by debt: many cultivators had to borrow from their land-lord, at high interest, and he might also be the collector of their tax–dues.

Moscow was swelling into a good-sized city, imbued with the mentality of a metropolis, and attracting an exotic throng of merchants from east and west. Most towns were poor things, growing only sluggishly. They were still semi-rural, while much craft-work was carried on in the countryside.[15] This hampered any urban specialization, or rise of craft guilds. There was none of the civic or political ethos that animated towns in the west, except some lately annexed ones on the western borders like Novgorod or Pskov, formerly autonomous, where embers of a republican spirit smouldered. Such as they were, Russia's towns were at any rate Russian, not half-foreign like so many in eastern Europe.

Townsmen fell into fixed categories, with corporations of wealthy merchants at the top. They too had obligatory duties to perform; these might be lucrative, and were recompensed by tax-exemptions and other favours. In many ways a healthily plebeian nation, Russia knew no aristocratic disdain for trade: monasteries were large traders, and the ruler's own estates produced surpluses for the market, as they did in Sweden. Commerce between Europe and Asia was reserved to the government and added significantly to its revenues. Merchants aided officials in its management. At times of political dissension, these activities drew them into politics, where they behaved not as a solid bourgeoisie but as an erratic satellite gravitating to one side or another according to their financial interests of the moment.

Ivan IV was born in 1530 (his subjects dated events from the creation of the world), and succeeded his father Vasily three years later. His mother made a competent regent: in Russia as in so many other lands women had a hand in state-building. She died in 1538, perhaps by poison, and brutal faction-fighting broke out, chiefly between groups of the court nobility at Moscow. It was not a question of a 'boyar party' wanting to throw off state control, but only of rivalry for the levers of power. At such junctures a ruling class showed its features more plainly, and the boyars were a class still imperfectly fused, which could arrive at a sense of collective interest only under firm royal tutelage. Ivan – 'that merciless and truculent *Moscovite*', as Evelyn was to call him, [16] or in Hume's

15 Lyashchenko, p. 210.
16 John Evelyn, *Numismata* (London, 1697), p. 305.

words, 'John Basilides, a furious tyrant'[17] – grew up under the shadow of of disorder, like Louis XIV a century later, and like him reacted with a determination to make the throne unshakable.

Talented advisers gathered round the young ruler, and formed an inner ring within the Duma. The 1550s were a time of reconstruction, accompanied by a fresh influx of methods and men, among them Russia's first printers, from Germany and other countries. While the new reign was being launched, the church was a useful standby: the metropolitan, Makarii, sponsored the group round Ivan, which included two who had been the tsar's tutors, Adashev and the churchman Sylvester. In return, the church could expect the government to turn a blind eye to some of its shortcomings. Russia went through no Reformation, but here too it was an age of religious controversy and criticism. In 1551 the government summoned an ecclesiastical conference, and plans to remedy abuses were canvassed. Scarcely anything came of them; the official classes cared much less about complaints of the clergy's drunkenness and immorality than about their own grievance, its getting hold of too much land. It was ordered that grants to the church must obtain official sanction; this proved difficult to enforce, but its properties were to bear heavier taxes.

Direct taxation of the masses was a fundamental of the tsarist state, and it was rising faster than any seigneurial dues.[18] A somewhat more equitable system of assessment and payment was devised now, though the principle of joint responsibility formed part of it. So it did in the sphere of crime and punishment, which was regulated by a new *sudebnik* or law-code in 1550. Harsh as this was, it showed at least a bureaucratic attention to 'carefully regulated legality', which the government would soon be flouting.[19] As a concession to public impatience with official corruption and misconduct, it ordered severe penalties for these misdemeanours, and closer supervision of local administrators. Decrees of 1555–6 began a process by which *kormlenie* was abolished, along with many of those whose livelihood it was. Their elimination would enable the central government to appropriate more revenue for its own requirements, swollen by war. More police work was assigned to the *starosty*, and an elected local body, the *zemstvo*, would have collection of taxes as its prime responsibility. Reorganization did not mean local self-government,

---

[17] David Hume, *History of England*, appendix to chapter 44.
[18] Blum, pp. 228.
[19] H. W. Dewey, 'The 1550 *Sudebnik* as an Instrument of Reform', in Cohn, p. 307.

but an extension of the state machinery with fresh burdens thrown on unpaid and unwilling assistants.

Insatiable state appetites left few unscathed. An edict of 1556 insisted on an obligation of military service by all landowners, or armed men furnished by them, not only by holders of fiefs. These were being more systematically classified, and gaining thereby in corporate consciousness. It was indeed in this reign that the servicemen grew into a recognizable 'gentry'. Their coming of age was marked by admission of their representatives to a national assembly, the *Zemsky Sobor*. A gathering in 1549–50 may or may not have been the authentic first meeting of this body, destined never to take on a definite institutional shape. Joint sessions of Duma and Holy Synod had often been held, and always formed part of a *Zemsky Sobor*. In 1549–50 spokesmen of the service gentry in the Moscow region were added. Next time, in 1566, officials, merchants of the higher grade, and the gentry at large, who supplied 204 of the total of 374 members, found a place.[20] But membership remained variable and ill-defined, and rested on nomination rather than election. In structure the *Sobor* with its two component parts had a resemblance to the Polish *Seym*, the model most familiar to Russians and not one to make their rulers desirous of going very far with the experiment. In such a society an assembly could have no real autonomy, no life of its own; a genuine parliament was an impossibility.

Conquest of Kazan was followed in 1558 by the opening of a long-drawn attempt to occupy Livonia and its Baltic coast, far to the west. Like nearly all wars of the absolute monarchies, this had very questionable motives. Baltic harbours meant nothing to the Russian people, which wanted protection instead against Turk and Tartar, who in 1571 burned Moscow; the church's conservatism always made it uneasy about western contacts and contagions. The state had its own impulses or obsessions. Its growing strength drove it to claim a place in Europe, which would also raise the tsar still higher at home. Control of foreign trade and the income derived from it gave it a significance for him out of all proportion to its national value. Officialdom shared its master's interest in expansion; so did the big merchants, with eyes on far-flung trade routes; also the more enterprising of the army men, or their sons. Somewhat as in contemporary Ottoman campaigning, manpower coming forward stimulated conquest, and conquest provided new

[20] Vernadsky, pp. 113–14.

lands to endow new men.

At first things went well, but reverses soon followed. Russia's ill-trained cavalry were encountering in Poles, Swedes, Danes, more formidable antagonists than nomad Asians; the infantry, the town-based militia of *strieltsi* or musketeers, now at Moscow being put on a permanent footing as the first nucleus of a regular army, was no better. Some of Ivan's intimates seem to have disliked the adventure, and Prince Kurbsky's defection inflamed his suspicious nature. Sylvester had to retire in 1560, Adashev fell into disgrace. Several other boyars deserted to the enemy, in spite of aristocratic families having to stand surety for their relatives' conduct: collective responsibility prevailed at the top of society as well as the bottom.

Ivan sought to isolate his opponents by the melodramatic manoeuvre of quitting Moscow in 1565 and threatening to abdicate – in imitation, it may be guessed, of Gustav Vasa. Moscow had not forgotten the anarchy of his boyhood, and public feeling there, which had weight, brought about his triumphant return on his own terms. In 1566 he called the first fully-fledged meeting of the *Zemsky Sobor*, which gave him and his war something like a vote of confidence. But this was its last meeting in his reign. Ivan was revealing his true bent, and that of the regime as a whole, when he resorted to very different tactics, the creation in 1565 of the ill-famed *oprichnina* – one day to be the subject of Tchaikovsky's opera on tyranny and revolt. Its name was an old term denoting an appanage estate or dower. What it meant for Ivan was a state within the state, a group of territories, eventually covering half the country, where he would set himself to realize his dream of total and unrestricted power. A streak of madness always clung to the Russia of the tsars, compounded from the semi-theocratic isolation of the throne, the nation's uncertain footing between Europe and Asia, the misery of the masses. Ivan's mind, as unveiled above all in his diatribes against Kurbsky,[21] inhabited a strange world, a hotch-potch of violent reality and of abstractions, a fantastic jumble of theology, classical history, Old Testament. Royal authority was of God, it must be absolute for the country's safety, to disobey it was sin. While Ivan invoked Heaven he let the church feel the weight of his fist; it was time to demand subservience from it, not mere benevolence. When the metropolitan Philip, who came of aristocratic descent, criticized Ivan in a sermon, he was arrested, and made away with in prison. It was more drastic treatment than

[21] See Fennell, *Correspondence.*

Philip II's of his archbishop about the same time.

Ivan's godlike moods alternated with others, of morbid anxiety, such as induced him to sound Queen Elizabeth about asylum at a pinch in England. He shut himself up with his guards and confidants in a fortified wolf's lair in the forests, and directed a reign of terror. It was not in any symmetrical fashion a class war, of the service gentry, his most reliable tools, against the aristocracy: all classes furnished victims, and there were boyars among his lieutenants. But some of old princely stock were executed and their lands turned into fiefs for the ever-hungry gentry. Others were removed to estates far away from the capital: the practice too of uprooting and removal could be applied to élite as well as commoners. It all marked a stage in the rise of the fief-holders and the subversion of the older aristocracy, parallel with the rise of the gentry in Poland except that in Russia they were coming forward as the retinue of the crown. They were virtually recognized as landowners by being authorized to collect their own rents and impose labour dues. Politically, this cemented their loyalty, professionally it would diminish their willingness to be called up from their properties; but such contradictions were an incurable weakness of an anachronistic system.

The climax was the wholesale killing and pillaging at Novgorod in 1570, directed by the tsar in person, in revenge for suspected plots.[22] A time came when Ivan began to understand that indiscriminate brutality was overreaching itself, and the chiefs of the *oprichnina* were executed in their turn. By 1572 it was being wound up, though arbitrary rule went on in other guise. 'How long such a government can continue', the hardened soldier of fortune, Staden, was moved to reflect, 'only the Almighty God knows.'[23] Chaos in central Muscovy, on top of war taxation and droughts, accelerated the flight of peasants, and brought on agrarian crisis. By the 1580s grain prices were rising faster than others.[24] Small fiefs fared worse than the bigger estates, because conditions on them were worse and made the cultivators more eager to get away. Fief-holders fell into debt to monasteries or merchants: some took French leave, like the peasants, and joined the Cossacks of the southern borderlands, others took to banditry, which was rampant. Fletcher passed numbers of abandoned villages on his way to Moscow, and saw an 'almost infinite' multitude of vagrants, many of them desperate and

[22] Staden, pp. 26 ff.
[23] *ibid.*, p. 56.
[24] R. Hilton and R. E. F. Smith, Introduction to R. E. F. Smith, *The Enserfment of the Russian Peasantry* (Cambridge, 1968), p. 22.

dangerous.[25]

Ivan himself was worn out; in 1583 he had to conclude the war, and all the blood and treasure it had cost were thrown away. Next year he died, as unregretted as Louis XIV. Having killed his heir in a fit of ill-humour, he was followed by his younger son. Fedor was a cipher, but unlike his father in boyhood he had round him a group of councillors sufficiently able and experienced to prevent a relapse into feudal broils. They were the more willing to cooperate because there was good reason to fear more serious, social disturbances if order broke down. There were jealousies none the less between the older nobility, led by the Shuisky family, and the less distinguished figures brought to the front by government service. These were headed by Boris Godunov, who had won his spurs in the *oprichnina*, and whose sister was married to the tsar.

Godunov made an efficient enough minister. The agricultural crisis was brought under control, in the sense that landowners found themselves well off again, but at the cost of harsher subjection of the peasantry. It is a vital feature of Russian history that the subjugation of the peasants, instead of being effected by the landowners as in middle or east-central Europe, was an intrinsic part of the rise of monarchical power. It was the petty fief-holders who were most clamorous for it, and they were the ones it was most necessary for the government to appease. It suited wealthier landlords to have some degree of freedom of movement left to the peasants; they could offer loans or concessions to attract them to their estates. Service men were often away on campaign, and unlike the Polish *szlachta* or east-German Junkers, they were strangers without any time-honoured name in their districts. More restrictions had been imposed on peasant mobility; Godunov virtually annulled it, and in 1597 he fixed a term of five years within which runaway serfs could be recovered, a task in which again petty owners had most need of state help. By the end of the century the rural masses were declining towards a condition hardly distinguishable from slavery. Men could be sold from one master to another apart from the land.

Fedor died in 1598, and the ancient dynasty of the Ruriks was at an end. As always, this was an ordeal calculated to bring all disruptive forces into the open. Russia was still very much alone, and to import a sovereign from abroad would go against the grain. Godunov had the best practical though not genealogical claim (he

[25] Fletcher, pp. 47, 116.

was of Tartar ancestry), and he had been preparing the ground carefully; he was earning the gratitude of the gentry, and he had elevated the archbishopric of Moscow to the rank of patriarchate, installing an adherent of his own. The *Zemsky Sobor*, summoned again after its long inanition, with little hesitation elected him tsar. Theocracy had some drawbacks; it had to be made to appear, much as in a papal election, that the choice was really God's, the assembly merely acknowledging it. This fiction was good enough for the governing circles, but to the masses a man-made tsar was a strange anomaly, and Boris never lost the air of a usurper.[26]

He cultivated divine right all the more assiduously, instead of relying on the *Sobor*, whose support in any case would only have been worth having if it were broadened into a more genuinely representative assembly. But there was only an inchoate middle class, while there could be no conciliation of the masses without the whole system collapsing. Hence Boris's dilemma was really insoluble, and hurried him into a tyranny like Macbeth's. Once on the fatal throne, he seems to have fallen a prey to the same morbid distrust of everyone round him as his old master Ivan. The aristocracy, which hated and feared him, he could intimidate; what was about to shake the monolithic state was popular revolt. Riotous protest in the countryside made itself felt in the 1580s and 1590s; it was inflamed by the pressing down of the better-off and worse-off peasant strata into one undifferentiated mass. A craving among the poor for marvels and miracles, in the Time of Troubles now at hand,[27] was one expression of their wretchedness; some of them were ready to attempt the miracle of overthrowing oppression. Providence gave its usual signal at last with bad weather and harvests. Where agriculture was so feeble as to give at best two- or three-fold yields,[28] hunger was always present and famine never distant. During 1601–3 cannibalism was heard of.

There was no progressive section of the propertied classes for the pauper multitudes, rural or urban, to rally behind. By themselves they could hit on no better idea than a new tsar – a triumph indeed of hope over experience – and could find one only in a pretender masquerading as a scion of the old line. Their Perkin Warbeck, the 'False Dmitry', seems to have been first set in motion by dissident boyars. It was a complication for movements of revolt in every country that foreign meddling was almost a certainty, and Dmitry

[26] Kluchevsky, III, p. 51; Mousnier, p. 155.
[27] Avrich, p. 18, etc.
[28] Lyashchenko, p. 181.

soon had the covert backing of Sigismund III. It was at the head of a motley host of Polish gentry-adventurers as well as rebel peasants and Cossacks that he marched towards Moscow. Thus challenged, the regime speedily displayed its frailties. Boris's best guards were his German mercenaries (Scots and English soldiers also figured in these broils[29]), but they were expensive and too few. Most of his other followers deserted him before he died in 1605, and Dmitry entered Moscow amid plaudits.

There were too many conflicting demands to allow him to choose any consistent line, or satisfy any class. Polish behaviour soon provoked a rising in the capital, and he was killed. For conservatives the danger now was of popular excitement getting out of hand, and they made haste to install Vasily Shuisky as tsar. He was acceptable to the rich merchants, with whom he and many other landowners had links, but unlike Boris he sought no confirmation from the *Sobor*, preferring to parade his connexions with the Ruriks. His fellow-nobles insisted on pledges for their own future security. At this point they were in a position to regain some of the ground they as a class had been losing to royal centralism. But like all other social forces, aristocratic reaction was divided. The less wealthy were more closely tied to official place and, with mass discontent seething, the others too had need of the state as their buckler. Their problem was to strengthen it against the people, while weakening it against themselves – a problem nearly as hard as squaring the circle.

Russia's growth, over long ages, was a history of the people running away from the state and the state coming in pursuit of them. Resistance was liveliest in outlying areas where runaways were threatened with reduction to serfdom in their new-found homes. Among these the Cossacks, free frontiersmen of the southeast like those of the Ukraine, were the most spirited, and Ivan Bolotnikov, ex-serf turned Cossack, proved the ablest popular leader whom the times threw up. His manifestos called on the poor to rise against the rich, and he can, conjecturally, be deemed a true social revolutionary: he has been credited with the ideal of a democracy of small peasant proprietors.[30] But for the Russian peasantry, so much of it footloose and rootless, any social ideology or programme was peculiarly difficult to conceive, and the forces of revolt were too mixed for any leader to weld together. Mordva and Chuvash and other border tribesmen were joining in; Russia's

[29] Anderson, *op. cit.*, p. 10.
[30] Mousnier, p. 187.

many-sided crisis was in one aspect its first great colonial revolt. Among the Cossacks a wealthier stratum could join hands with disgruntled sections of the poorer southern gentry. The heterogeneous levies with which Bolotnikov laid siege to Moscow in 1606 fell apart; those still with him were routed next year, and he perished.

Savage reprisals followed against peasants in rebel areas, but unrest was spreading to Moscow and other towns, and in the western trading city of Pskov there was an uprising of craftsmen, shopkeepers, *strieltsi*, against the hated merchant patricians. Scattered urban outbreaks could not combine, and were each put down. Russia's great size – like China's – meant that social revolt was always restricted to one or more localities, and could never attain nationwide dimensions. A new pretender, a second Dmitry, marked political retrogression from the level reached with Bolotnikov.

Nevertheless, the menace of social upheaval, and Polish invasion, convinced the aristocracy that it was time to ditch Shuisky and seek a radically new arrangement. Negotiations with the Polish commander, Zolkiewski, led to an agreement that Sigismund's young son Vladislav should be tsar, on carefully specified conditions. These have been called the highest point reached by Russian political thinking in the entire period, because they made it incumbent on the monarch to rule in conjunction with the national assembly, and gave guarantees of private rights also, for instance trial before punishment.[31] The boyars' intention was to transform autocracy into oligarchy, for their own behoof, but there is also discernible the outlook of a maturing bureaucracy, its belief in the rule of regulation, if not of law, and security of rights for those who had any. Considering how Russia was to fare in the next three centuries, any alternative whatever must have been less bad; and this solution would have admitted a breath of western, somewhat less heavily tainted, air.

History seldom allows logical choices. Vladislav would have to adopt the Orthodox faith, and his father refused to hear of it: he was in fact determined to be tsar himself; this, even if feasible, could not be welcome to Zolkiewski as a pillar of the Polish gentry, since it might make Sigismund too powerful at home, just as possession of Bohemia made the Habsburgs too powerful in Austria. Polish troops in Moscow once more antagonized the populace, and religious indignation was fanned by the patriarch Hermogen.

[31] Kluchevsky, III, pp. 38–42.

Armed bands sprang up, merchants donated money for a regular
force under respectable command. In October 1612 the patriots
fought their way into Moscow, whose primacy in the national life
had grown more evident during the Troubles. Immediately the
movement, like its forerunners, split into its discordant elements. A
meeting of the *Sobor* held out the only prospect of a consensus: in
the prevalent anarchy it was a life-line to be held on to. It met early
in 1613, and on a broader basis than ever before, with delegates
from provincial towns and even from some sections of the peasantry.

For the throne, several foreign names were mooted, the favourite
being a Swedish prince: his backing was aristocratic and official, but
he might have been the best alternative. Clergy, southern gentry,
most burghers, wanted a native sovereign. So doubtless did the vast
majority of Russians, the peasants; hence a native candidate would
be better able to keep them quiet, a fact which smaller, vulnerable
landowners would appreciate more keenly than great men. The
choice fell on Michael Romanov, who was of an eminent family and
was too young to be feared, for some time to come at least, by his
fellow-nobles. No restrictions were placed on his sceptre, as they
had been on Shuisky's; it would have taken too long to hammer
them out, and the needs of the hour were pressing. Agents were
sent round to the towns, in a perfunctory show of consulting public
opinion; what was really being done was to associate the new tsar as
much as possible with hereditary right and the old dynasty; his
utility for overawing the masses would depend very much on the
mystic aura of monarchy being restored.

Tsarist Russia had revealed its more than Habsburg artificiality.
Once the steel framework of state power failed, a society riddled
with contradictions which the state itself deepened fell into
disorder, and the only escape was back into the sheltering prison of
despotism. English observers noticed that, after all the late calamities, Ivan the Terrible's memory was respected, even venerated.[32]
Deliverance from the Poles in 1612 resembled that of Russia from
the French in 1812, or Spain in 1814; the poor joined in resistance to
an invader and then, out of weariness and illusion, submitted
passively again to their home-made chains. 'The rainbow of
heavenly peace' could now shine out, that enthusiast for autocracy,
Karamzin, was to write.[33] There was at least economic recovery.
Government, landlords, monasteries, vied in settling cultivators on

[32] Anderson, *op. cit.*, p. 143.
[33] *Karamzin's Memoir*, p. 118.

fields that had gone out of use. Demands on them were soon stiffening once more, and land-tax fell more heavily on the individual as the commune, on private estates, disintegrated.[34] But for a generation the chaos and flight from the land of recent years enfeebled the peasant's will to resist.

The man who put the new government on its feet, after his return from Polish captivity in 1619, was the tsar's father, Filaret. He had been forced into the church, as a rival, by Boris Godunov, and now became patriarch. Collaboration between church and state could not be closer, and it basked in the Orthodox zeal revived by the Troubles and the collision with Poland. This allowed Filaret to put some check on a noble orgy of self-enrichment. There was the fact, too, that the boyar class was altering. Its older ranks had been thinned by the *oprichnina*, and then by the wars; they were injured too by the lavish feudal style of living which often, as in other lands, failed to reckon with changing conditions. Many families dropped out, and although newcomers were as eager as the new dynasty to ape their predecessors, the aristocracy was growing more amenable to firm state guidance.

Like other tiros, the Romanovs indulged in more pomp and made themselves more unapproachable than the rulers before them; but foreigners discovered that all the talk at this haughty court was of prices of hemp, flax, or potash.[35] Foreign trade continued to link it with the merchants; as in Asia, it was through collaboration, or collusion, of bureaucracy with commercial capital that the grandest fortunes were to be made. Merchants and gentry were the two classes which counted in the lower chamber of the *Sobor*, and the government leaned on this a good deal. The assembly's session of 1613 was prolonged to 1615, and ten in all were held during the reign. As abroad, financial difficulties made opportunities for it, and these were very acute; the treasury at the outset was empty, loans and special taxes had to be resorted to; there was monetary, and as always fiscal, confusion. But to take advantage of the situation, and secure a permanent foothold, the assembly would have to widen its public platform. Instead, this was contracting, for no peasant spokesmen were included after 1613.

What the assembly really accomplished was to press the selfish claims of the gentry more insistently. Too crude and traditionless,

---

[34] Blum, p. 234.
[35] Pokrovsky, I, p. 84. He drew exaggerated conclusions about the dominant role of merchant capital, with the tsars as its tools; see on this G. M. Enteen, *The Soviet Scholar-Bureaucrat* (Pennsylvania State Univ. Press, 1978), pp. 3–4, 38.

as a class, to produce any outstanding leader like Zamoyski in Poland, or any ideas of its own, the gentry could not do without the monarchy as a shield against those above it as well as below. Late events had shown how dangerous neglect and discontent could make it. Filaret promptly inaugurated a distribution of state lands to provide more fiefs, and ordinarily these were reserved for sons of the gentry. As grants turned into private estates, they suffered like others from partition among heirs. By mid-seventeenth century there were nearly forty thousand of them, averaging a very few peasant households each.[36] Meanwhile their occupiers grew less and less useful for their ostensible function. They dodged military duty, or sent serfs as substitutes, or deserted as soon as they got a chance. If Russia wanted to play the game of war again, it would have to bear the burden of two armies, one of feudal malingerers, the other of regular troops.

No sooner was there some recovery from exhaustion than Filaret was panting for another round with the Poles. War came in 1632, and ended in 1634 without the recapture of Smolensk which would have been a feather in the Romanov cap. The *Sobor* had to be asked for extra funds, and taxes rose; the army was swallowing up nearly half of all revenue. Filaret died in 1633, and there was another fiesta of land-looting by the big men about the court. This behaviour was not confined to Russia, and was another manifestation of how all aristocracies looked upon the resources of the crown as their own. Public anger was simmering, and was given loud vent in the assembly of 1642; the classes represented there were less well sheltered than in most countries from taxation and official high-handedness. When the insignificant Michael died in 1645, he was succeeded without demur by his son Alexis; political Russia was now grown-up enough to quarrel over government policies rather than over who should be tsar. Alexis was only sixteen, and once more the men in power, led this time by Morozov, feathered their own nests, while novel taxes were imposed on the country, some of them borrowed from abroad. Governments picked up one another's bad habits more readily than their better ones, if only because the former were much more numerous.

Rich merchants shared the odium, because many of them were tax-farmers as well. Class hatreds in the bigger cities were intense, and exploded there now rather than in the countryside; the middling strata of craftsmen and taxpayers were the most vigorous in

[36] Hellie, p. 214; cf. p. 24.

protest. In Moscow, with a population of perhaps 150,000, the first of a long train of disorders broke out in 1648. In western Russia next year there was a wilder, fiercer rising in Pskov; Novgorod followed. By this date twenty thousand *strieltsi* were stationed in Moscow, and as many in the provincial towns, even in peacetime. In the capital their command, Zolkiewsky had noted, was as important a post as that of the janissaries at Stamboul, and was entrusted only to a ruler's close relative or trusted lieutenant.[37] But this gendarmerie too had its grumbles, and was proving unreliable.

Grievances were manifold, but too contradictory to combine in a single movement. It was the nobles and merchants in the opposition who came to the front, and got the detested Morozov banished and the *Sobor* called for what was to be its last significant meeting. Their purpose was not to win any concessions for the masses, but on the contrary to unite the propertied classes, and consolidate the social order, at the people's expense. The *ulozhenie* or law-code of 1649 was this assembly's monument.[38] It marked a stage of development (in a country where, for better or worse, lawyers played a far smaller part than in the west) at which it was time for systematic legislation to replace odds and ends of enactment and custom. The gentry's right to hand on properties to heirs was confirmed. Chapter XI of the code, dealing with the peasantry, abolished any time limit on recovery of absconders. No legal status or rights were conferred on the peasant on seigneurial land, who was left still worse off by comparison with those on state land; this inequality must have been an impediment to large-scale risings. Townsmen were being similarly tethered: they were forbidden to leave their places of residence, as many were doing in order to extricate themselves from collective tax-obligations. State power, instead of forging a nation, was breaking up the Russian people into something like a medley of sealed-off castes.

Riots and disorders persisted; monarchy had not regained the superstitious reverence paid to it of old. In the countryside individuals or groups went on taking to flight, sometimes after burning crops and houses, even killing their masters. But it was characteristic of Russia's invertebrate society, so unlike the rigid carapace of the state, that the next great upheaval – the rebellion headed by Stepan Razin in 1667 – started like Bolotnikov's earlier and Pugachev's later in the Cossack fringe of the southeast. Its eventual defeat gave clinching proof to all the higher classes than in submitting to tsarism

[37] H. S. Zólkiewski, *Expedition to Moscow*, ed. J. Giertych (London, 1959), p. 103.
[38] Text in Smith, pp. 141 ff.

they had put themselves in safe hands.

State-building went on, with European example to urge it: in the west absolutism was nearing its zenith, while Poland was a warning of the consequences of weakness. Still at a formative stage, Russia could adopt methods and equipment from abroad more freely than Poland had done. There were now some fifty departments; they were still very haphazardly put together, and in much need of overhauling, but at the summit the Duma's collective custodianship was giving way to that of individuals, forerunners of the ministers of later days. Similarly, provincial governors were being given a more undivided responsibility, with a chain of officials below them.

Under the patriarch Nikon there was a similar tightening up of ecclesiastical authority over parish priests, hitherto chosen by their parishioners and too apt to share their feelings. This and other innovations led to schism, an obscure symptom of inarticulate discontents, and persecution of the 'old believers'. With mutineers of its own to deal with, the church was all the readier to turn its spiritual artillery against enemies of the state like rebel peasants. But when it showed signs of wanting to play first fiddle instead of second, the government's reaction was drastic. In 1666 it deposed the presumptuous Nikon, and reduced the patriarchate to complete subordination. It was in the nature of such a regime that the clergy should be brigaded with the civil and military personnel and taught to render the same unfaltering obedience; and the church had too little support among the people to be able to resist.

In the analogous sphere of secret police, initiated by Ivan IV, Russia had no paragon except the Inquisition. It made up for deficiencies of administration which tsarism by its nature was incapable of ever remedying. It was a feature also of the state's elevation above, or partial emancipation from, the sections of society on which it rested. A nineteenth-century Russian radical was to declare that, though the tsarist state favoured certain classes, it did not correspond with the real needs of any.[39] No state can ever do so perfectly; but this detachment, which did not mean any neutrality between rich and poor, but rather self-absorption, the state's preoccupation with its own well-being, had been implicit from the outset in a polity artificially built from above, with so many aliens among its builders. Its repeated efforts at reorganizing the armed forces point the same way. By mid-century what was to become the standard pattern was taking shape: an infantry army

[39] Cited by A. Besançon, *Les origines intellectuelles du Léninisme* (Paris, 1977), p. 162.

supplied by selective long-term conscription, and drilled on foreign lines into an array of automata, serviceable at home or abroad. As always, the state was creating an army in its own image. In 1682 the old cavalry was at last disbanded.

The *Sobor* accompanied it into oblivion. Meanwhile, the two landowning classes were coalescing. Razin's rebellion went far to unite them. A single category of landownership was the outcome, invested with judicial and police powers. Henceforth there would only be distinctions of wealth and culture, the richer adopting outlandish fashions, the poorer satisfied with old bucolic ways. Small squires might be on terms of rough familiarity with their serfs. 'The same knout hung over both. . .' Belinsky was to write, 'the same corn brandy cheered the hearts of both.'[40] Western influences were coming in, but under such evil auspices as to darken instead of alleviating Russia's worse attributes, by helping to rivet serfdom and militarism on the nation. Everything foreign, good or bad, was made hateful to ordinary Russians. Foreigners were repelled by the spectacle of what they did much to bring about. Herberstein had seen 'a pitiable people, their lives and property the prey of the nobles'.[41] Milton, for many years a diligent collector of information about Russia, came to the conclusion that the poor there were more wretched than in any other land.[42]

---

[40] V. G. Belinsky, *Selected Philosophical Works* (Moscow, 1948), pp. 112–13.
[41] Herberstein, p. 39.
[42] 'A Brief History of Moscovia', in *Prose Works*, ed. J. A. St John (London, 1848) V, pp. 160–61.

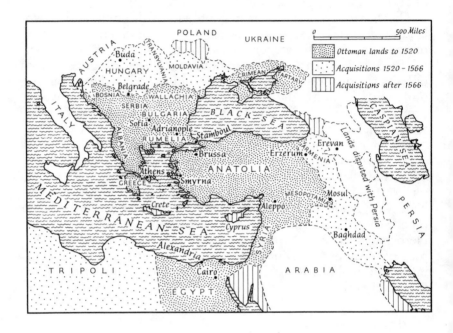

Map 6   *Expansion of the Ottoman Empire*

13

The Ottoman Empire

One of many puzzles of sixteenth-century Europe is whether Turkey was part of it or not. Its empire sprawled over three continents, and most of it lay outside Europe. Yet it included nearly all the Balkan peninsula, whose population was still mostly Christian. Its capital from 1453 was one of Europe's most famous and ancient cities. Much of the élite of its army and governing class was European by race, its rulers had scarcely any Turkish blood in their veins. To some extent Turkey made one of the European 'family of nations', chiefly by virtue of involvement in its quarrels. Its first trade agreement, with France in 1536, was partly a cover for a political entente, sought by France after the Spanish victory of 1525; during 1543 Toulon was a Turkish naval base. From 1583 there was an English envoy at Stamboul, trying to make trouble for Spain. French ambassadors were among the earliest foreigners to write descriptions of the empire, and may have been biased in its favour. But it won admiration from many westerners, the army for orderly discipline, the government for its rational, non-feudal structure, as China's was to be admired in the eighteenth century. Busbecq, who as an Imperial envoy had no reason for partiality, attributed Turkish success to the fact that promotion went by talent, instead of as in Europe by birth.[1]

Turkey diverged radically from the western countries in other ways, less likely to win their esteem. Its European affinities were closest with Russia, which as a model it may have influenced; each of the two was in its own fashion the successor to Byzantium. But Turkey was fundamentally non-national. 'Turk' had no more than a linguistic meaning, and the realm was 'Ottoman', or *Osmanli*, from the name of its founder Osman, rather as another empire took

---

[1] See extract in Merriman, pp. 177–9. Lamouche, p. 190, credits the Ottoman régime with 'a regularity and concentration of powers far more complete than anywhere else'. It is an odd sidelight on the European element in Turkey that Roland and St George were admired as Turkish heroes. P. Burke, *Popular Culture in Early Modern Europe* (London, 1978), p. 149.

its name from the Habsburgs. Far more than in any western land the
state arose here primarily to serve external aims; it was a conquest-
state, organized for war. Its government was a species of absolute
monarchy which western rulers may at times have envied; but
writers as different as Machiavelli and Shakespeare[2] were conscious
of an alien quality, of what came to be called 'Oriental despotism';
it represented the purest type of dominance of state over individual,
impossible, because of its complete artificiality, for any western
polity to match.

It was set up on the ruins of the Byzantine empire, reproducing
some of its features and some of those of the earlier Muslim
kingdom in Anatolia of the Seljuq Turks.[3] When this broke up the
Ottoman principality began as one of its western fragments, on the
Byzantine border; a marcher state, like Austria or Prussia, where
religion and plunder – so often in history twin motives of conquest –
could attract stalwarts from all over Asia Minor. Expansion was
directed eastward too, against Muslim contenders, but it was the
assault on Christendom that lent moral strength, while material
strength owed much to what was learned from European inventive-
ness, in gunnery above all.

Outlying *begs* or warlords always strained at the leash. To combat
this, the rulers had to enlarge their personal following; they did so
on a stereotyped plan originating in central Asia, and carried by
Turkish conquerors into India too. An ever-growing number of
men were enrolled in the sultan's own service, receiving salaries
from the treasury. They were 'slaves', like a tsar's entourage, but
the term was a loose one, denoting dependants with a total and
exclusive loyalty; collectively they formed the ruler's 'family'. The
institution can be traced back to the retinues of nomadic tribal
leaders; its vast extension as framework for empires suddenly
towering up in the recurrent political vacuum of western Asia and
northern India was not evolution, but a substitute for it.

Devotion and *esprit de corps* were ensured by the individual being
cut off from all previous connexions. This was more easily effected
with newcomers to the country and its faith. A born Muslim could
not be enslaved: hence no native-born subject of the sultan could be
a member of his household. A high proportion of its personnel
entered it as men or boys captured in the Balkan campaigns, or
carried off from Poland or the Ukraine for sale at Stamboul by the

[2] *The Prince*, chap. 4; *Henry IV* Part 2, Act 5, Sc. 2.
[3] On the Seljuq organization see *The Book of Government* (*Siyasat-Nama*) of one of
its ministers, Nizam al-Mulk, trans. H. Darke (London, 1960).

vassal Tartars of the Crimea. They were slaves who if left at home might well have been serfs. As it was, they went through a careful training in the palace schools,[4] a more methodical preparation than government servants anywhere else received, and were assigned to civil or military tasks in accordance with their capabilities. Those who displayed proficiency had opportunities denied to most aspirants in Europe. Acceptance of Islam was coming to be obligatory in the first half of the sixteenth century; it is possible to suspect that professions of faith were sometimes less than genuine,[5] like those of the *conversos* in Spain.

Ottoman practice might be called an extravagant version of the preference of European rulers for officials from the middle walks of life instead of the aristocracy, and produced, in its bizarre way, a very monolithic governing class. A sultan could have declared more accurately than Louis XIV that he, or he with his household, was the state. This class was supplemented by an influx of renegados, mostly from Mediterranean lands, who shook the dust of their stepmotherly countries off their feet and often turned Muslim, or Jews expelled from Spain. To the army they contributed master-gunners, to the administration experts particularly in finance. In a great measure this un-European empire was being built by Europeans, as the new Spain was built with the help of Jewish converts, the new Russia with the help of westerners.

In a regime where everyone else was a *novus homo*, making his way by his own exertions, the ruler alone inherited his place; though even he might be said to rise from the ranks of the royal offspring. As in other Islamic kingdoms, none of these were any more legitimate than the rest, and there was no fixed rule of succession; the best or luckiest prince won, his brethren were got rid of. This kept them from being nuisances after a new reign began, and Frenchmen may have sighed for a like deliverance from their superfluous Bourbons. But it made clashes very probable towards the end of a reign; and social discontent could take advantage of dynastic contests to show its face. Princes might be dealt with unceremoniously, but the dynasty had to go on. Still more fixedly than in Europe, continuity of royal blood was identified with the survival of society, a conception deriving from a primitive past to

[4] Lybyer, pp. 71 ff. Cf. p. 196: 'The results were well-nigh incredible; they constitute a wonderful demonstration of how little the human spirit is limited by the ignorance or the restricted and humble life of ancestors.' He concludes that the Ottoman empire is 'still thus capable of imparting valuable ideas', p. 198.
[5] Merriman, p. 154.

which Turks stood close. Any individual descendant of Osman was essentially a transmitter of his race; and it followed in a sense that if in one way monarch and state were the same, in another the ruler was only the first servant of the state. It may go with this that the tombs of even the mightiest sultans at Stamboul are plain and modest, dwarfed by their gigantic mosques.

Mehemet II, 'the Conqueror' (1451–81), was raised by his capture of Constantinople, that Troy of ten centuries, to a higher pinnacle of sovereignty than his ancestors. The city was to be the permanent Ottoman capital, as unchanging as the dynasty, by contrast with the movable headquarters of other Muslim lands. In so cosmopolitan a centre the rulers might feel more free and secure, as well as strategically well placed, than anywhere on the Anatolian plateau where the bulk of their Turkish-speaking subjects lived. Mehemet and his greatest successor, Sulaiman I (1520–66) – the Magnificent, as foreigners, not his own people, called him – renovated and embellished the long-decayed city, with the same desire as Christian kings for an imposing and well-affected capital. A Fugger agent's letter gave a long account of festivities in 1582 to celebrate a prince's circumcision, with entertainments by tightrope dancers and many others, and distribution of food; another in 1587 chronicled a public parade of Christian prisoners.[6] Byzantine pomp was taken over and magnified to oriental proportions; 'the revenues of a province were unhesitatingly squandered on an Imperial pageant.'[7] Stamboul was growing as rapidly as the empire, and by Sulaiman's accession may have housed 400,000 people.[8] It lived at the empire's expense, consuming much and giving little in return, its provisioning watched over by 'a meticulous, authoritarian and *dirigiste* government'.[9] All capital cities were parasitic more or less, this one perhaps more than any other.

In earlier times high office was often, as in feudal Europe, vested in a great family. Enthroned in Stamboul, Mehemet was able to dismiss his aristocratic chief minister, and from then on to promote scarcely any but men of his household. His *Qanun-name* or administrative code 'established the final form of the institutions of the state'.[10] There were few obstacles here to symmetry, such as

[6] *Fugger News-Letters*, First Series (1568–1605), ed. V. von Klarwill (London, 1942), pp. 70 ff., 116–18.
[7] Sir C. Eliot, *Turkey in Europe* (new edn, New York, 1908), p. 55.
[8] F. Braudel, *The Mediterranean and the Mediterranean World in the Age of Philip II*, 2nd edn, trans. S. Reynolds (London, 1972–73), pp. 347–8.
[9] *ibid.*, p. 351.
[10] H. Inalcik, 'The Rise of the Ottoman Empire', in Cook, p. 47.

western governments ran into when they tried to rationalize their long slow accumulation of odds and ends of machinery. Sulaiman, known as *Qanuni*, the law-giver, issued a mass of decrees on duties of administration, and on more general matters like land-holding. Yet here as in Christendom, laws were more easily made than executed, and if carried out might do more harm than good. Sulaiman was too remote from his subjects to know how his enactments would really affect their lives.[11] They were audible only when they rioted; in the west there were at least some channels for more orderly expression of feeling.

Mehemet was in effect his own prime minister. It was in Sulaiman's reign, though this was always looked back on later as the Ottoman apogee, much as Philip II's was in Spain, that the ruler began to withdraw from minute attention to detail.[12] Business must have become too voluminous for any one man to keep in touch with, and ministers might be better able to delegate portions of it, and so keep abreast. It was now that the grand vizir came to the front, over-topping the other ministers, and several had unusually long terms of office. Sulaiman broke with tradition at the outset by appointing not a seasoned man of affairs but his youthful favourite, Ibrahim, son of a Greek seaman, whose phenomenal rise made him also a governor-general, and later husband of one of the sultan's sisters. Intoxicated with power, he ended by arousing his master's suspic-ions, and was executed or murdered in 1536. Of the other vizirs, one had charge of law: he by exception was a Muslim born, since law was largely Islamic; the *Defterdar* was responsible for finance, the *Nishanji* for administration, but he was sinking to a keeper of seals and being supplanted by his head clerk, the *Reis Effendi*, who specialized in the always crucial field of foreign policy. ('Effendi' was one of a good many Turkish borrowings from Greek.)

These and various departmental heads made up the Divan or Council, whose elaborately regulated sessions tok place four times weekly.[13] Much of its time, as with similar bodies everywhere, was

[11] Lybyer, p. 160. Shaw commends Sulaiman and his grand vizir Lüfti Pasha for careful attention to justice, p. 87, and to fiscal arrangements. 'The entire financial organization of the state . . . was systematized and institutionalized', p. 101. As with similar meticulous planning in Mughal India, one may wonder whether it had as much existence in reality as on paper.

[12] Sari Mehmet Pasha, introduction by W. L. Wright, pp. 21, 29. Shaw goes so far as to say that in practice a sultan had 'very limited power', and was rather a symbol of central authority than its real wielder, p. 165. Over-centralization always brought with it its own negation.

[13] For detail see N. M. Penzer, *The Harem* (1936, new edn, London, 1965), pp. 100 ff.

taken up with judicial cases. Sulaiman did not attend, but left the grand vizir to preside, though he let it be thought that he might at any moment be listening through a grating. Though the Divan had onerous functions and a regular institutional form, it was a collection of individuals with separate responsibilities rather than a 'board' in the western style. Each dignitary had his own slave-household, a smaller replica of the sultan's. The grand vizir in particular was assisted by a secretariat of his own, educated men with good prospects; but this too was a household organization, not a department of state with continuity of experience. Governors similarly had their own staffs. In sum there was an army of quill-drivers, but not a true civil service such as western countries were groping towards. High officials piled up fortunes, not seldom forfeited when they fell from grace. A revenue minister condemned to death in 1535 left six thousand slaves to be taken into the sultan's service; one of them, a young Serb captive, rose to be his last grand vizir, Sokolli.[14] Such expropriations were a form of death duty in a very literal style. Even the property of those who died in good odour paid a ten per cent levy to the exchequer.

Each central organ was duplicated on a descending scale in each province and district, where every official had 'virtually unlimited authority' in his own sphere.[15] Above the *sanjak-beys* or governors were *begler-begs*, governor-generals, of whom there were ten in Sulaiman's time, headed by those of Rumelia ('Rome'), or the Balkans, and Anatolia. Both these two normally resided in Stamboul, an arrangement more convenient for keeping them under the sultan's eye than for allowing them to keep their subordinates under their own eyes. Provincial assignments frequently went to members of the royal household, as a means of concentrating authority and checking the fatal tendency of governors to drift out of control, as was always likelier to happen in Asia's vast conglomerations than in small European kingdoms. In Rumelia governorships were often given to tributary chiefs from Asia Minor whom it was deemed politic to keep away from their own peoples.[16] Cash salaries could only be paid at the centre; other posts had fiefs attached to them, for the support of the incumbent and of a body of troops at his disposal, land-grants to be held only during tenure of office.

Like its European compeers, the Ottoman government took a

[14] Finlay, p. 54.
[15] Sari Mehmet Pasha, pp. 22, 37.
[16] Alderson, p. 20.

rough and ready view of local administration, and was satisfied to harvest its dues and quell resistance, with small regard for uniformity or perfection of detail. In Serbia things were managed more loosely than in the neighbourhood of Stamboul; districts were often left to be run by men elected with the pasha's approval, and the democratic village commune persisted.[17] In some areas, chiefly in Bosnia, feudal landlords had turned Muslim and been allowed to keep their estates. In occupied Hungary many of the gentry retained both their land and their religion, and their county assemblies went on side by side with the Turkish administration. Sweeping confiscations, however, were the general rule in conquered territory, and the land was cut up into fiefs, like those of governors on a more modest scale. Western governments too were always ambitious of conquest, but this was seldom now with the intention of dispossessing landholders, as in earlier times, except in so backward and alien a region as Ireland. Their soldiers wanted wages in cash, not land; there was besides a respect for ownership, for property as the social keystone, just as there was a feeling that states, or provinces once independent, were permanent entities, not to be obliterated from the map. Such notions had little meaning for the Orient, and although among the Turks a category of privately owned land was recognized, this was on the whole foreign to their way of thinking.

A fief was, more exactly, an assignment of the revenue from a certain area, the larger ones known as *ziamat*, the smaller, much commoner, as *timar*. A fief-holder had to serve when called on, bringing other horsemen with him if his income was sufficient to support them, and providing equipment. In principle a grant was temporary; in reality the system was semi-hereditary: the son of a *sipahi* or fief-holder could normally expect to receive a grant in his turn. Altogether the lesser men, or *timariots*, bore a marked resemblance to the Russian *pomeshchiks*, with the difference that they were still further separated from the peasantry by race and creed; those higher up might be compared with the *encomenderos* of Spanish America. Legally a *sipahi* was only entitled to specified dues from the cultivators, in cash or kind. The Balkans had been easily overrun because they were suffering from acute social enmities, with landlords trampling on peasants, so that the Turks could be in a way liberators; and while the empire was still expanding prosperously, its demands on the peasantry could remain fairly moderate.

[17] Temperley, pp. 119–20.

Fief-holders lived as a rule in fortified villages or towns, rather than on the land, but it was part of their function to be an army of occupation, and not all were called up at the same time for campaigns beyond the frontiers. That the Ottoman centre of gravity was for long on the European side of the Straits is indicated by the fact that the *timariot* forces of Anatolia were less formidable and reliable, while for a long time the Muslim population there was more rebellious than the Christian population of the Balkans. Asia Minor had little reason to thank the sultans for subjugating it, whereas the *sipahis* of Rumelia owed everything to Ottoman conquest. But such an organization was very hard to keep in trim, and flaws were soon creeping in. After 1530, as a precaution against irregularities, bestowal of nearly all fiefs was removed from provincial to central handling. Registers showing the income of each and the number of armed men to be supported by it were compiled. This too would require a very trustworthy staff to maintain it properly.

Sipahi zeal and devotion waned as time went on. Wars were bringing more hard knocks than rewards. More and more fief-holders in each polygamous generation were sons of members of the *kullar*, the Sultan's 'family', resentful of exclusion from the official world in which their fathers had moved. Their dissatisfaction seems to have had a share in the sedition of the prince Mustafa, executed in 1553. Rising prices, that universal European phenomenon, impelled them to screw up their takings. No doubt they had always found ways to squeeze something more than their due out of the peasantry, and knew how to evade edicts of Sulaiman designed to protect cultivators. Luther remarked shrewdly enough that if the sultan announced freedom from taxation for three years in any new lands occupied, 'the common folk would joyfully yield to him', but would soon be disillusioned.[18] Before the end of the reign many peasants were said to be abandoning the soil.

Once enthroned in Stamboul, Mehemet II added to his titles that of *Kaisar-i-Rum*, or Roman emperor. A good part of the old administrative framework was taken over, much as Muslim rulers in India borrowed many of the methods of their Hindu predecessors. At the same time the sultans assumed the patronage and regulation of the Orthodox church which had been a prerogative of the Byzantine rulers. Patriarchs continued to be chosen and inaugurated, with all

---

[18] *Table Talk*, ed. W. Hazlitt (London, 1857), p. 356. Luther considered the Turks barbarous, though militarily formidable, e.g. p. 354.

the old ceremonial, by the government.[19] They and their clergy had no more scruple about praying for the sultan than the Russian clergy in former times for the Tartar Khan. Mostly Greeks, they like many of their literate fellow-countrymen were perfectly at home in the Ottoman empire. It conferred on them spiritual supremacy over all Orthodox Christians, in return for which the Greek hierarchy 'served as an instrument of Othoman police'.[20] A regular under-imperialism was at work, as has often happened.

Tutored by its priests, the Christian population had a degree of autonomy, or rights of self-management under its own laws, within the *milat* system, an extension of the Byzantine custom of giving self-governing privileges to colonies of foreign traders. Ottoman thinking ran in terms not of nationalities but of religious communities, which might have a national flavour. The principal *milat* included all Muslims, whether Turkish or not; there was no distinct place for the Arabs. The Armenian *milat* corresponded with an Armenian people, deciding all questions of its own under the guidance of its priests. Their head, as well as the Greek patriarch and the chief rabbi, had to reside in the capital. Highly centralized in so many ways, the empire thus had its own equivalent of the provincial and urban franchises which tempered governmental centralism in Europe. Turkish skill at dividing and ruling was often commented on, and the *milat* system, by letting each community keep to itself, may be called a specimen of it. Non-Muslims paid a special tax, which seems to have brought in a considerable proportion of total revenue, but rather because non-Muslims were so numerous than because of the level of the tax, evidently not high enough to make many think of changing their faith. In religious toleration Ottoman rule stood far above anything to be found in Europe. Pleading for freedom of conscience in the Netherlands, William of Orange pointed out that there was no interference with it by the Turks.[21]

None the less, this was incontrovertibly an Islamic empire, deriving its only coherence from the dominant faith. Islam has no 'church', yet problems could arise which were very like those of church and state in Christendom. Religion was represented officially by the *'uluma*, jurists versed in the sacred law, and more popularly by the dervishes or sufis, more resembling friars; often suspected of heterodoxy, these formed a link with the naïve cults of

---

[19] See Luke, pp. 14 ff.
[20] Finlay, p. 46.
[21] F. Harrison, *William the Silent* (London, 1931), p. 163.

the common folk, here as in Christendom semi-pagan. 'Through
them heresies spread, uprisings were concocted, mobs were
gathered, and holy war was preached.'[22] Their appeal was strongest
in the old Muslim lands, where they were implicated in various
anti-Ottoman movements.[23] This made the government all the
more disposed to favour the regular clergy. Sulaiman gave
unstinted donations for mosque-building and other pious purposes.
To a degree quite exceptional in Islamic history many of the *'uluma*
were incorporated into the state apparatus, much as churchmen and
university men were helping to rear the bureaucratic state in
Europe. They graduated from higher or lower colleges under state
supervison, and entered a complex hierarchy where they might
look forward to promotion from post to post.[24] Many served as
cadis or judges; Rumelia and Anatolia each had a *kaziasker* or chief
justice.

No other subject of the sultan had so exalted a station as the
Sheikh-ul-Islam, supreme expounder of the *shari'at* or sacred law.
His assent was required to decisions of peace and war, or to a
sultan's deposition, and his life was sacrosanct. There were difficulties about reconciling the *shari'at* with the secular laws (*qanun*,
another Greek loan-word) which sultans claimed the right to
promulgate. As the sixteenth century went on the *'uluma* were
asserting more and more vigorously a right to act as censors, whose
approval – like that of the Paris Parlement – was required for all
novel legislation. They were less easily brought to heel than the
priesthood in Russia. Strong rulers could keep them in their place,
weaker ones gave way to their encroachments. A turning-point
came with the end of expansion; with the empire thrown on to the
defensive, its confident spirit gave way to an inward-turned
mentality, accompanied by a bigotry and preoccupation with
minute observances which fortified clerical ascendancy.

An area where interests converged was the *waqf*, or pious bene-
faction, known in all Muslim countries. Mosques and their ancillary
schools or hospitals were often founded by the government, but
other endowments came from individuals, with the dual aim of
earning merit and making provision for heirs. Absence of fixed title
to land, and arbitrary rule, meant insecurity of ownership and

[22] Lybyer, p. 207.
[23] See B. G. Martin, 'A Short History of the Khalwati Order of Dervishes', in
Keddie, e.g. pp. 281, 284.
[24] R. Repp, 'Some Observations on the Development of the Ottoman Learned
Hierarchy', *ibid.*, pp. 19–22. Cf. Shaw, pp. 135 ff.

inheritance; *waqf* property was inviolable. A benefactor assigned resources to some deserving purpose, and his descendants were named as trustees, and lived on the surplus income. Many found-ations were of public works, such as bridges, markets, fountains, which the government seldom considered its responsibility. It did register private funds devoted to them, and supervized their guardianship;[25] but only sleepless vigilance could prevent here-ditary custodians from appropriating too much of the revenue entrusted to them.

Islam everywhere was an urban culture. Towns flourished in the Balkans, and new ones, starting as garrison posts, were planted. As in all Asia, a town was first and foremost a seat of local government, destitute of any political existence of its own; here was one deep gulf between Ottoman and European. It might none the less shelter a sturdy populace, organized in guilds or fraternities – as in Catholic countries, with religious trappings, usually supplied by the most popular and least doctrinaire of the dervish orders, the Bektashi. Whether or not they owed anything to Europe, guilds must have owed much to the currents of migration within the empire, especi-ally the flow of population to Stamboul when it was being re-peopled. Settlers would look for forms of association to help them find their feet; so would the multitudes of emancipated slaves, for servitude in Islam, unlike the European colonies, was not perpetual. Economic life benefited. There was 'a most impressive range of traditional industrial crafts', which could be turned to military account as well: through the fraternities artisans were enrolled to accompany the army on campaign.[26] They would be far more useful than most of the campfollowers who cluttered up western armies; and the practice would help to infuse into the urban popu-lation a concern for the empire's fortunes. Associations were kept under official scrutiny; they could be troublesome when grievances rankled. Townsmen as well as *sipahis* in 1561 may have inclined to Bayazid, another of Sulaiman's rebel sons, the more so because it was a year of widespread food shortages.[27] In the longer run guilds were likely to have the same constricting effect on technical progress as in Europe.

Mercantile enterprise was plentiful, but was being left increas-

---

[25] Lybyer, p. 147; Inalcik, *op. cit.*, p. 52.
[26] A. N. Kurat and J. S. Bromley, 'The Retreat of the Turks, 1683–1730', in Cook, pp. 182, 184. Guilds had 'all kinds of social functions', and sometimes brought together members of different religions. Shaw, pp. 156–8.
[27] Braudel, *op. cit.*, pp. 989–90.

ingly to non-Muslim minorities, Greek, Armenian, Jewish, whereas earlier on there had been a stirring class of Turkish traders. Some continued active, and an English commentator plausibly suggested that 'natural Turks' were going in for pursuits like commerce because they were excluded from office.[28] An English visitor, however, reported that Turks practised trade only 'carelessly and coldly', and were very anxious to avoid being thought rich.[29] Muslims paid only two and a half per cent import or export duties, non-Muslims five per cent; this could have the topsy-turvy effect of diverting official preference to the unbelievers, because they brought in more revenue.[30] In any case the tariff margin was too narrow to outweigh the greater perseverance and the foreign connexions which Jewish or Greek merchants often had, besides being probably more adept than Turks at concealing their wealth. The prevailing martial spirit was enough, as in Spain, to cast a damp on humdrum counting-house business. The consequent absence of a native Turkish bourgeoisie, and with it of anything like mercantilist ideas at Stamboul, made it easy for foreigners to acquire commercial concessions or 'capitulations', and opened to them a spacious market.

Anatolian villagers down to this century spoke of their sovereign habitually by the title of *Kunkiar*, 'Spiller of Blood'; in their eyes killing was 'the primary, natural and obvious function of the head of a military state'.[31] Sulaiman's armies were at their best only when he himself was there to lead them.[32] When his successors ceased to command in person, they dwindled to ciphers; whereas western monarchs could retire from the camp, about the same time, with less harmful results. Frequently the grand vizir also took the field. Clearly an exceptionally firm administration was necessary to enable the two to be absent for long spells on distant campaigns.

The bulk of the Ottoman armies consisted of the fief-holding cavalrymen and a mass of irregular horse, wild Tartars from the steppes. But their forte was in two more fully professional branches, one very European, the other very Asiatic. The first was

---

[28] R. Knollys, 1603, cited by Lybyer, p. 44. Cf. P. Anderson: 'the level of the Ottoman economy never achieved a degree of advance commensurate with the Ottoman polity.' *Lineages of the Absolutist State* (London, 1974), p. 376.
[29] Fynes Moryson, *Itinerary* (London, 1617), Part 3, Bk 3, chap. 1, 'Turkey Described', p. 126.
[30] Finlay, pp. 27–8.
[31] Luke, pp. 199–200. He led thirteen major campaigns, and spent ten years in the field. Shaw, p. 87.
[32] G. R. Elton, *Reformation Europe 1517–1559* (London, 1963), p. 145.

heavy artillery, for sieges but also used on the battlefield. It must have helped to deter governors or feudatories in outlying provinces, as it did in Europe, from seeking too much independence. At Mohacs in 1526 it was largely by superior gunnery that the Hungarian army was overwhelmed. More generally, it was by able leadership and careful preparation, rather than superior numbers, that Ottoman triumphs were won.

The second decisive arm was the regular soldiery of the imperial household, a cavalry corps and the celebrated janissary foot. When Magyars and janissaries met, Europeanized Asiatics were meeting Asianized Europeans. The force consisted of some of those taken in boyhood in lieu of tax, mostly in parts of the Balkans, and war-prisoners prepared to embrace Islam. It was a fairly small élite force, though increasing from a muster of 30,000 during and after Sulaiman's reign; a disciplined infantry before Europe had anything of the sort in being, although there was some similarity between the two solutions found, Turkey conscripting non-Turks, Europe hiring foreign mercenaries. Janissary companies (*orta*) had a continuous existence and traditions, like the Spanish *tercios* when they came on the scene. Along with the Spanish and Swedish armies[33] they were in the van of progress in having a cadre of army chaplains. Non-Muslim by origin, they stood in need of religious instruction, and cultivated a relationship with the Bektashi dervishes which was made official in 1591.[34] From then on preachers were attached to all units, and after evening devotions the soldiers listened to their exhortations. A fervour akin to that of Gustavus's or Cromwell's regiments was the response.

They were, all the same, interested in pay and pillage as well as prayer, and were a corps certain to harbour praetorian impulses. Sulaiman's father, Selim I (1512–20), was the first prince set on the throne by the army, and his reign was punctuated by janissary tumults. Sulaiman was under compulsion to inaugurate his reign with grandiose expeditions, seizure first of Belgrade and then of Rhodes; when he then loitered at home for two years, indulging in the pleasures of the chase and the harem, an ominous outbreak in 1525 compelled him next year to draw the sabre again. Sultans were in some measure prisoners of their own erratic war-machine. Often clamorous for war with its excitements and opportunities, the

[33] G. Parker, *Spain and the Netherlands 1559–1659; Ten Studies* (London, 1979), p. 233, n. 13.
[34] Luke, pp. 26 ff. Cf. F. W. Hasluck, *Christianity and Islam under the Sultans* (Oxford, 1929) II, pp. 484 ff.

Ottoman army like the European nobility was at other times only too ready to jib at its hardships and ordeals.

There were inevitable discords between the two main sections of the army, and it was the *sipahis* who were the first to tire of long-range campaigns. As a fighting force they – like the *pomeshchiks* – were obsolescent, and they were not much use for siege warfare. Evolution was towards a bigger regular army, with the janissary corps growing but also being diluted by admission, from before Sulaiman's death, of sons of members, and born Muslims. Europe was moving slowly from foreign soldiery to national armies; the Ottoman empire, which was not and could not be a nation, risked falling between two stools. A national navy was still more unattainable by a race from inner Asia, strangers to the sea, whose governors' emblems of office were horse-tails. In its great days the empire did succeed in launching a powerful fleet, but it depended heavily on seamen from the Greek islands and miscellaneous renegades, and before the end of the sixteenth century was falling into incurable decay.[35]

On several frontiers the Ottomans were content to hold their own, and to treat dependencies as buffer provinces under loose control. This was the case with Transylvania, and Moldavia and Wallachia; a like status was given to the Crimea, the Maghrib or northwest Africa, and some Asian borderlands. Like the Chinese, the Ottoman sphere of influence was too vast to be governed from one centre. None the less, the Turkish war effort in Europe in the sixteenth century was astonishing; combined with the fighting on eastern fronts it was truly phenomenal. Only Spain, Turkey's mirror-image in some ways, waged war on so many fronts. Battles had to be fought at distances from Stamboul which demanded elaborate planning, testimony to the organizers' calibre. Losses were heavy. The attack on Malta in 1565 may have cost 30,000 lives,[36] of men not easily replaced. The empire's entire population seems to have been not more than 25 or 30 million,[37] fewer than the Habsburgs among them ruled, and inadequate to endure the incessant strain.

It was also very heterogeneous. Within it Muslims were probably a majority, but Turks a minority; yet the heaviest burden came in

[35] See Currey.
[36] Bradford, pp. 220–21.
[37] A. N. Kurat, 'The Reign of Mehmed IV, 1648–87', in Cook, p. 157. Shaw, p. 104, thinks the population under Ottoman rule nearly doubled during Sulaiman's reign, from 12 to 22 million.

time to fall on the Turkish-speaking regions.[38] They were the Castile of the empire, and suffered like Castile for their masters' greatness. Anatolia remained extremely primitive; yet among the villagers a rich folk-culture, much of it of pre-Muslim origin, lived on. One theme of the simple dance-dramas was a bullying governor caught and beaten. Eastward the arch-foe was heretic Persia, which by religious and political infiltration was always stirring up refractory elements in the debatable lands along the border. Arabs too gave chronic trouble. Compelled to face both ways, Turkey like Russia was debarred from true membership of any wider civilization, eastern or western. By and large it may be correct to view the massive marches up the Danube valley as at bottom only 'giant raids', and the empire as tilting, with the occupation of Egypt and the neighbouring lands, away from Europe towards Afro–Asia.[39]

A more total absolutism than any in Europe procured startling early success, and premature decline; the most superb of monarchies sank to the lowest degradation. Its power was based on a system too complex, like European feudalism of the high middle ages, and too unnatural to last for very long, at any rate when deprived of the afflatus of conquest. Sulaiman died finally, still on campaign, leaving only an incompetent heir, Selim II; his other sons had already perished in struggles for the throne, fomented by harem intrigue. In the next two hundred years there were very few able rulers, and several minorities. Before 1600 opinion was turning against mass fratricide, and succession by the eldest son or brother came in. European custom must have exercised some influence. To prevent strife, the royal brood were kept shut up until one of them was required, instead of as formerly being given provinces to rule by way of training. Clearly this was advantageous to ministers, who would have only ignoramuses to deal with.

Sokolli as grand vizir kept things going all through Selim II's reign and into the next. It was an odd instance of the mix-up of Turkish and European that his brother Sokolovitch was a monk, whom he made patriarch of a restored Serbian church.[40] But by now the whole fabric was showing signs of decay. Thanks to the Islamic ban on usury, the government was at least not piling up a debt, but the intricate financial mechanism was creaking. The two dozen bureaux attached to the treasury were less strictly audited.[41]

---

[38] Kurat, *op. cit.*, pp. 157, 160.
[39] Elton, *op. cit.*, p. 147.
[40] Temperley, p. 124..
[41] Lybyer, pp. 168 ff.; pp. 179 ff. are on the revenue system under Sulaiman,

Taxes were now habitually farmed out, often to local magnates. In Egypt the governor-general collected taxes to cover his costs, and remitted a yearly tribute,[42] a good deal of it paid in African gold, as America paid silver to Castile. Contracts were often subleased, and were managed more and more by non-Muslims of the commercial species.[43] Financially as well as politically and militarily, the Ottoman state was over-dependent on aliens.

Meanwhile its upper levels were being choked by the noxious byproducts that every irresponsible regime secretes. Venality of office started early, and went much further under Sulaiman, who, in need of money like all monarchs, made high dignitaries pay a toll on appointment; the practice rapidly spread downward. With it went the custom, familiar in Muslim India too, of every official having to extort money from those below him in order to be able to make handsome presents to those above. Governors borrowed money to purchase their posts, and then had to make ruthlessly quick fortunes out of their subjects, to the ruination of agriculture and future revenue. Bribery, 'the beginning and root of all illegality and tyranny', as a later treasurer called it, was rampant.[44] The army could not escape infection, and it began to be common for wire-pullers in the capital to own half a dozen fiefs, registered in imaginary names or those of their creatures.[45]

All the dead weight of the ponderous machine rested more and more heavily on the masses, chiefly as everywhere on the unfortunate race of peasants. In European Turkey hereditary succession to fiefs never hardened to the point of establishing a 'territorial aristocracy',[46] as it did in Russia. But there was an approximation to it in the growth of big estates, which must have owed something to contact with Europe. Exactions multiplied, until the seventeenth century saw a recrudescence of the serfdom which Ottoman sway had at first banished.[47] Rising prices stimulated production for the market, and the *ciftlik* demesne was 'tyrannically organized but productive', like an east-Elbian estate or a colonial plantation: there was technical advance, and use of neglected land, but with no

[42] Poliak, p. 46.
[43] Braudel, *op. cit.*, pp. 723, 816; cf. Poliak, pp. 47–50, on tax-farming.
[44] Sari Mehmed Pasha, introduction by W. L. Wright, pp. 52–3; and pp. 88–9.
[45] Sari Mehmed Pasha, p. 146; cf. J. S. Critchley, *Feudalism* (London, 1978), p. 120.
[46] Finlay, p. 51.
[47] A. de Maddalena, 'Rural Europe 1500–1750', in Cipolla, p. 289.

benefit to the cultivator.[48] Very much like Polish landowners, upper-class Turks desirous of western luxuries were exporting in exchange the food that ought to have been eaten by their peasants. This was not to the advantage of the state, any more than analogous developments in Europe. Here and there a conscientious pasha would give the tillers some protection,[49] but official energy for any good ends was running down. Urban life decayed, another parallel with Poland. Balkan towns had attracted numerous immigrants besides soldiers, such as Jews and Armenians, while in Bulgaria native inhabitants were turned out, in the interests of security.[50] Many of the newcomers were now going away, so that the towns, though smaller, were becoming more indigenous.[51]

Communications between them deteriorated. There had been efforts to improve roads, but they were breaking down by the second half of the sixteenth century, and the peasants made answerable for their upkeep were deserting. When Sulaiman himself was on his last march to Belgrade, his columns were harassed by bandits. In Bulgaria, where Turkish settlement was heaviest and most irksome, there were revolts in 1598 and later years. They were set on foot by the better-off strata, traders and priests and so on, hoping for Austrian aid, but there was a running accompaniment of guerrilla resistance by *haiduts*, village heroes and brigands with lairs in the mountains.[52] In Serbia too there were repeated risings: the biggest broke out in 1593, spreading into Bosnia and southern Hungary, and went on until the Austrian war ended in 1606. Its sponsor was the Serbian patriarch, national leader in default of any lay figure.

Inflation was an evil felt by all communities and classes. Where population was growing, it must have outstripped production, as it did in Europe; but the most obvious cause was the debasement of the coinage from about 1550, which might be called an Ottoman substitute for government borrowing and forced loans. Disorders about the close of the century were comparable with those in Russia. Distress was acute, in the capital and elsewhere; in 1589 and

---

[48] Braudel, *op. cit.*, p. 725. Cf. Shaw, p. 173; and P. Anderson, *op. cit.*, p. 386, on the 'practically unlimited control of the labour-force', and the expansion of demesne land at the expense of peasant plots.

[49] Temperley, p. 117.

[50] MacDermott, p. 25.

[51] See M. S. Anderson, *The Eastern Question 1774–1923* (London, 1966), pp. xvi–xvii.

[52] MacDermott, pp. 40–41, 49. Pp. 47–9 draw a sombre picture of Turkish oppression.

1592 the janissaries rioted, demanding donatives to make up for their pay standing still while prices soared. In Asia Minor rebellions broke out between 1596 and 1610, during most of which time the slogging war with Austria was bringing few gains. Foreigners were detecting the giant's feet of clay, and their reports dwelt on poverty and oppression which earlier in the century they had not been conscious of in any striking degree. That intrepid tourist Fynes Moryson found 'vast solitudes and untilled Desarts on all sides' (travellers were soon finding them in Spain too), because of the inhabitants being swept off by the wars or ground down by the despotism of quickly-changing governors 'and the general rapacity and licentiousness of the soldiers '.[53] Sir Thomas Roe, English envoy in the 1620s, had no doubt that the empire had passed its prime.

By then some Turks were realizing that things were going wrong, and trying to think of ways of rectifying them, much as in Spain, and as fruitlessly. They denounced intrigue, corruption, harem meddling. But the bold innovations needed to revivify the body politic would collide not only with vested interests but with a whole conservative habit of thought, whose custodians, the mullahs, were steadily tightening their grip. Something like a Counter-Reformation was taking place, a thick screen being erected against any ideas from the west. The government had to acquiesce, because clerical help in tranquillizing or stupefying the populace was indispensable. Some of the country's better features might now tell against it. Subsidized schools and colleges were more accessible than in most of Europe, but the pedagogic mind was stationary while the world changed, and education only broadcast its stultifying bigotry more widely. Katib Chelebi was an intelligent and a travelled man, but he showed little knowledge of foreign lands, and the topics he discussed suggest a scholastic, obscurantist atmosphere. One of the less abstract is bribery, which he felt that the public, ignorant of subtle shades and distinctions, condemned too sweepingly.[54] The earliest significant writing on Europe, by Evliya Chelebi, was the outcome of an embassy to Vienna which he accompanied in 1665. Some of the blame for this failure to learn must be laid on the empire's displacement towards the east, its deeper involvement in an Afro-Asia from which nothing useful was to be learned.

Radical reform being out of the question, explosive forces could

[53] *op. cit.*, p. 125.
[54] Katib Chelebi, pp. 124 ff.

only find an outlet in changes of a different kind, those of a desperate power-struggle fuelled by court faction but with the populace ready to take a hand. Vizirs, whose number grew to nine, jockeyed for the perilous elevation to the top place, whose occupant met with sudden death in 1622, 1644, 1649, 1653. Their master himself was not safe; Osman II was strangled in prison in 1622 (etiquette forbade any shedding of the sacred blood of Osman), partly because of fears among the janissaries that his government meant to put them down. Local administration was out of joint, pashas were shaking off control. Turkey like so many western lands was undergoing fresh upheavals about the ill-starred middle of this century. It was in fact experiencing, more protractedly than most, the interval of breakdown that all absolutist states went through at least once, and whose issue might be revolutionary change, or return to an old regime clothed with greater coercive force. Holland and England went one way, France and Russia the other.

Turkey's case was distinct from both, since it could neither mobilize energies capable of revolution nor return to the household-slave organization of its great days, if only because the supply of war-captives was drying up; and it had to adapt itself to standing on the defensive instead of conquering. Murad IV (1623–40), the last sultan for a long time to wield real power, made the first attempt to restore order, by methods not unlike those of Ivan the Terrible with whom he shared traumatic boyhood impressions of anarchy. It was in the nature of an obsolete system to be set in motion again only by violence, and with only spasmodic success. A more durable pacification was effected by the Kiuprili family, four members of which, starting in 1656, held the grand vizirate with some intervals for forty-six years. At first they practised the same terror as Murad, later there could be some relaxation. It might seem in those years that their rule was turning into a hereditary institution, like the Shogunate in contemporary Japan. This did not happen, but the regional shift of power marked by their advent long outlasted them. They came from Albania, and Albanians were increasingly prominent in government and army, transferring old tribal loyalties, akin to the pristine Ottoman, to a broader allegiance.[55] It was quite characteristic of Turkish, and indeed Islamic, history that the fresh vigour called for was not coming from the empire's more civilized centres, but from the untamed outskirts.

Old institutions were crumbling. Meetings of the Divan became

---

[55] Kurat, *op. cit.*, pp. 175–6.

merely formal, while decisions were taken by small groups in the background.[56] Madrid's juntas offer a parallel, while the *validos* in power there might be compared with the grand vizirs. Unable to subsist on their pay, janissaries were permitted to take up crafts, and turned into an unwarlike but obstreperous militia, as the *strieltsi* were doing at Moscow, while another kind of army was slowly taking shape. To the puzzlement of Europe, and of historians, the empire was to survive, inertly, into the twentieth century. It could do so thanks to its duality, its combining not kingdoms, like Spain or Britain, but continents, and its ability to borrow western techniques at least in the military field. From this point of view, though still more superficially than Russia, it was being Europeanized.

It was not without its own genuine loyalties. There was always in crises 'some sentiment for the well-being of the state'.[57] In its palmy days something like an authentic Ottoman patriotism can be discerned. It shows clearly in the memoirs of the admiral Sidi Reis about his expedition across the Indian Ocean, and his return home through India in 1556. He was a Turk by birth, with an interest in many things, navigation and theology among them, and 'unwavering faith in the power and the greatness of the Ottoman empire'.[58] He ends with an eloquent call for love of the fatherland and fealty to its sovereign.[59] State and nation were very far apart, but within the imperial state a Turkish nation was slowly being incubated; it was to reveal itself in 1918 when the empire vanished.

[56] Lamouche, p. 177.
[57] Alderson, p. 69.
[58] Vambéry, p. 111.
[59] *ibid.*, p. 107.

14

European Destinies

The Ottoman empire in its heyday, directed by bands of royal slaves, represents only an exaggerated form of a problem everywhere to be met with, of identifying 'ruling classes' and their relationship with the state. In some degree state power had always an aberrant character, a partial detachment from social moorings, with an accumulating ballast of vested interests of its own, and acted blindly or purblindly more than with clarity of deliberate purpose. Where monarchy survived down to 1914, this was a quality it never altogether lost. Its presence tended to perpetuate a medley of social groupings more or less archaic. Under its shelter capitalism, and with it classes of more modern type, might take shape, but only where an independent current of economic change was at work, as in England but not in Spain. Where this happened the fully national state was coming on the scene, in appearance the opposite of classes and their contradictions, but an opposite interacting with them; instead of either effacing the other, each accelerated the other's evolution. Only through very complex, very devious trains of development could this phenomenon, the nation-state, make its advent in the world it was destined to transform.

Over most of Europe aristocratic airs and pretensions were still growing, though often cultivated by upstart families aping their forerunners. An Armada must have a duke of Medina Sidonia to command it, whether he knew anything about salt water or not, because no one of lesser station could count on his orders being respected. But even the greater nobles were chronically hard up, like kings and for much the same reasons – the same reluctance to live within their incomes. Overblown estates with absentee owners could not be managed profitably. Their proprietors were borrowers, and might be lenders too, in debt to one another, a way of living that might be called aristocracy's version of commercial life, its initiation into capitalism. Some of the more enterprising took a hand in industry; all who could took more from the peasantry. But increasingly those with a footing at court utilized it to meet their liabilities at the public expense. To a striking extent they were coming to rely, in Spain conspicuously, on court favours and concessions to make ends meet. Centralized consumption on these lines was a late-feudal parody of the national economy forming in the more progressive countries.

Marx spoke of capitalist society as irrational, 'bewitched'; the same might be said with more obvious truth of this late feudal society. There was a fetishism of landownership: it was a badge of rank, eagerly sought, and widely protected by the much-debated custom of primogeniture at the cost of younger sons whose hard fate many writers deplored.[1] Yet landowners were more and more inclined to desert the countryside, where they no longer had any real place to fill, and enjoy the amenities of provincial town or capital. This must have helped to make a good many of them willing to part with their acres. A ban on purchase of land by non-nobles was resorted to in parts of eastern Europe, and would have defended nobility collectively in France or Spain, but to the prejudice of individuals of a large, heterogeneous class who wanted or were compelled to sell; of would-be buyers also, not seldom the same officials and lawyers who framed government policy.

Kings hesitated for long before deciding to bring the higher nobility to live with them at court. It was a practice only safe when monarchy was very firmly established, and even then had serious drawbacks. Nobles would never feel much gratitude to the crown, since whatever was given them they regarded simply as their due, and they could never be given enough. A court full of them and their wives and mistresses could for a long time be the focus of national culture, but it was also a sink of corruption and intrigue. As time went on, the worse side predominated, in England inviting denunciation of 'the Court'. by playwrights as well as preachers. Politically, the situation could lead to aristocracy becoming ambitious, though with only faltering success, of taking over direct control of the machinery assembled by the monarchy, thus upsetting the separation of government from highest class which was the hallmark of absolutism.

Courts drew gaping mouths, but – another facet of a bewitched society – they were also sources of profit for monarchy, by fostering

[1] See J. Thirsk, 'The European Debate on Customs of Inheritance, 1500–1700', in Goody, chap. 7.

the taste for what it had to sell, titles and distinctions of every sort, Keats's 'most prevailing tinsel'. All kings, even Louis XIV, who won acceptance by the upper classes, did so a great deal by playing on snobbery. Rulers in eastern Europe, where both a true feudal background and an aspiring bourgeoisie were lacking, were at a disadvantage here. In the west the squandering of wealth on costume and ornament was another sign of the times, of the trans-formation – rather than rational evolution – of counts into courtiers, merchants into marquises, all with an uneasy sensation of nudity which the tailor was called in to cover with his costly figleaves.

It was the peasantry, joined in the course of time by peasants of overseas colonies, that paid both for the perpetuating of the old order and the launching of the new. Rent-collector and tax-collector were rival cormorants, either of which might be the more voracious predator. In France, and more widely, seigneurial exploitation was the cause of more protest and resistance in the sixteenth century, royal in the seventeenth.[2] But the *intendants* sent out to superintend the fleecing of the peasants were also sent to shield them against their lords, who had it equally at heart to shield them against the crown.[3] A mainly natural rural economy was having a money economy superimposed on it. Taxation operated to bring this about, like the poll-tax in colonial Africa. It was reinforced by a growing drain from countryside to town of resources to support non-resident landowners, resources formerly consumed on the spot. Among peasants partible inheritance was customary; within family or kin they clung to an equality refused them by society. Population growth hastened subdivision of small holdings and worsening poverty, though in exceptional conditions this no less than capitalist agriculture might promote better production; chiefly where near-ness to urban markets, as in Flanders, favoured commercial apti-tudes, and intensive horticulture flourished.

Large-scale peasant insurrections, quelled in western and middle Europe in the first half of the sixteenth century, were less and less feasible as the military strength of governments improved. They still broke out further east, in Croatia and for much longer in the Ukraine and Russia. In the west revolt went on raggedly, locally, though still on a considerable scale in France in the first half of the seventeenth century; there were risings towards its end in Valencia. More massive agrarian upheaval might have been expected in some regions like central and southern Spain, where by 1600 the culti-

[2] See e.g. E. Le Roy Ladurie, 'Peasants', in NCMH XIII, p. 138.
[3] Brenner, 'Agrarian Class Structure', p. 71, citing M. Bloch.

vators were extensively proletarianized. On the other hand this may have had a reverse effect, by splitting their ranks. In Spain the rural well-to-do were a class 'facing at once towards past and future',[4] as might be said of them and divers other social strata in other lands too. Those reduced to wage labour might lack spirit to rebel; the ploughman is readier to take arms against his troubles when he ploughs soil that he can think of as his. Not much aid, moral or physical, was forthcoming from the towns. Artisans, though discontented, might benefit from urban privileges which checked rural competition, as well as from cheap food.[5] Just as the nation divided one people from another, the town, however internally divided, could cut off its poor from the village poor.

Less spectacular forms of resistance continued, evasion and obstruction, the 'silent' opposition of the oppressed that Engels spoke of.[6] Or the rustic might move away to another district, in the hope of bettering his lot. There is evidence of surprising mobility among countryfolk in England; it was the same in Russia until enserfment put a stop to it. Western governments seem to have perceived that it was safer to let peasants roam about if they wished; vagrancy might be worsened, but collective feeling and capacity for action were reduced. Many from derelict areas drifted into the towns, which they might hate as an incubus on the countryside but envied for their comforts and opportunities.

There was a kindred ambivalence in the more prosperous townsman's rancour against the nobility and eagerness to enter its ranks. There were some, and may have been many, who saw gentility as a useless encumbrance of society. Burton anticipated the *philosophes* of the next century when he paid tribute to China for admitting no nobility of birth, and choosing its magistrates for their learning and virtue.[7] He had a good word for the Turks as well, having heard that they all, from sultan down, learned some useful occupation, whereas 'amongst us the Badge of Gentry is idleness': hypochondria was the scourge of the upper classes because 'They know not how to spend their time'.[8] If he was right, nine tenths of Europe was being steeped in misery in order that the other tenth might be miserable. But not many plump businessmen would be visited by

[4] N. Salomon, *La vida rural castellana en tiempos de Felipe II* (1964, Spanish edn, Barcelona, 1973), p. 301.
[5] Brenner, *op. cit.*, p. 55.
[6] Cited by W. H. Shaw, *Marx's Theory of History* (London, 1978), p. 142.
[7] *The Anatomy of Melancholy* (Bohn edn, London, 1923), II, pp. 161–2.
[8] *ibid.* II, pp. 80–81.

such reflections; and it was another social emollient that the bourgeois could move up, as the peasant could move about.

In the later 1620s Thomas Mun enumerated the qualifications of a good merchant, and regretted that in England they were so little valued that the merchant was ready to throw up trade and go in for land.[9] It struck another English mercantile observer that the Dutch custom of sharing property among sons kept business activity alive and growing, whereas in England the sole heir too often set up as a gentleman and squandered his fortune.[10] Still, in England since much earlier times city men and squires were much the same people, at two stages of their life-history like caterpillar and butter-fly, and younger sons recapitulated the never-ending cycle. In such a society only the prospect of being able to buy an estate and the social consequence it brought with it was sufficiently alluring to induce men to hoard up wealth by toilsome effort, except perhaps when Puritanism instilled into them a love of work for its own sake. A class whose most energetic members are striving to work their way out of it will have less solidarity, but in English conditions businessman and squire could combine for action, as they did in the House of Commons. In other countries a one-way movement was likelier, commercial or professional families joining the landed gentry and never looking back, though along with older land-owners they might sink into penury.

Inventors were still labouring to transmute lead into gold; a noble thirst for quick profits and fortunes derived added inspiration from the torrent of American bullion. A stirring city like sixteenth-century Antwerp was full of promoters and speculators and wild-cat schemes.[11] On a more sober plane, expanding manufactures were a commonplace of the age. They drew on technical innovations of the previous five hundred years, in use of water-power for instance, more than on fresh discoveries.[12] In terms of management they were often capitalistic. Variants of the putting-out system, already old in some regions, were taking root in others; Castile may for a time have been one of them.[13] Textiles were their amplest field. Most of the activity was urban, but here and there in the countryside the poor were in one sense relieved, in another exploited, by cottage industry; very notably in England, where town and country were

[9] K. Glamann, 'European Trade 1500–1750', in Cipolla, pp. 519–20.
[10] J. E. Barker, *The Rise and Decline of the Netherlands* (London, 1906), p. 196.
[11] See, *Modern Capitalism*, p. 32.
[12] W. N. Parker, 'Industry', in NCMH XIII, pp. 49–50.
[13] F. Braudel, *The Mediterranean*, pp. 430–31.

thereby bonded together in another way.

Monarchy was not against capitalism in principle, but its closest ties were with the least wholesome sort of business – finance – while in industry its taste was for the old, easily regulated guild pattern. In one way and another the aristocratic state when it continued too long would pile up impediments to industrial advance. This was slackening by the late sixteenth century, and in the seventeenth decline set in. Underlying recession may be suspected a lack of adequate markets, which only a more flourishing countryside could have provided. Before 1600 urban population may have been growing more quickly than rural; after 1600 it fell off more quickly.[14] Industry organized by capital was coming to be concentrated very much in one sector of Europe, the northwest.

There could be only a stunted formation of a working class in its modern meaning. Workers like burghers were too heterogeneous to be a force by themselves. Many were scattered over the countryside. Specialization was only beginning; mining, especially of iron, was left a good deal to seasonal work by rural labourers. Migrants abounded. 'The artisan community in the sixteenth century was made up of many races, rarely native to the area.'[15] This made combination harder, and in most places the proletariat, so far as it existed, was capable of no more than a kind of guerrilla struggle. An 'endless subterranean revolution' smouldered through the sixteenth and seventeenth centuries in Venetia, Naples, the Mediterranean world at large; hatred, crime, harsh repression were endemic.[16] Such social maladies must have helped to inhibit economic growth, by frightening capital into its shell. In big cities mobs like Shakespeare's revealed a populace thrust out from citizenship, only in moments of hysterical excitement able to feel itself once more part of the commonwealth. It was in towns, in Flanders and northern Italy, that workers' movements had started in the middle ages; the interval between autonomous towns and the era of national market and nationwide struggle was for them a long-drawn disorientation.

In one way urban grievances could have more force than rural: fear of disturbances compelled those in charge of bigger towns to take careful measures to ensure food supplies, though they could not avert recurrent famine. Valencia, for example, had a department headed from 1555 by a specially elected magistrate, who might

[14] *ibid.*, p. 327; cf. de Vries, p. 149.
[15] Braudel, *The Mediterranean*, p. 433.
[16] *ibid.*, pp. 738, 745.

commission merchants to procure supplies, or send his own agents abroad.[17] Memories of the *Germanías* no doubt lingered. Such arrangements were most easily made by sea-ports. Yet for Venice or Naples and many like them, the expense entailed might be a 'crushing weight'.[18] The poor were levying toll from the rich. But over Europe as a whole impoverishment was the portion of the majority, and society was being polarized, more extremely, between the propertied and the penniless. It exhibited symptoms of moral as well as economic dislocation, among them the ravages of drunkenness.

In the polarizing of wealth and pauperism, the state had a major part. Braudel, it is true, calculated that taxation in 1600, from Castile to Turkey, amounted to no more than a ducat a head, and asked: 'Was the mighty state, striding across the stage of history, no more than this?' But, as he added, tax money was taken out of the exiguous cash flow of economies still largely pre-monetary.[19] More important, some paid much less than others, and too often it was those who could least afford it who had to pay most, for no return, while the well-off had manifold blessings to thank the state for. Again, the victims might be robbed less heavily by the state than by its agents. Governments were painfully slow in learning to improve their fiscal methods, which had the same strangulating effect as the harness of antiquity on the horse, but which too many vested interests did not want to see altered. Ferdinand and Isabella greatly enhanced their receipts, but by painstaking supervision, not by reconstruction,[20] and such an improvement could only be temporary; the same thing was to be seen over and over again, as in Sully's France. Inability to put revenue on a better foundation was intrinsic to the aristocratic state, only overcome, and never more than partially, as middle-class habits and instincts gained ground. Even in the Netherlands, the businessman's paradise, the East India Company was habitually cheated by ill-paid employees,[21] very much as kings were by their servants. Meanwhile in the seventeenth century, in spite of a shrinking European economy, governments were collecting and spending far more.

[17] C. Tilly, 'Food Supply and Public Order', in Tilly, pp. 438–9.

[18] Braudel, *The Mediterranean*, p. 331.

[19] *ibid.*, pp. 450–51. Cf. his remark that the state was 'increasingly emerging as the great collector and redistributor of wealth'. 'The Mediterranean Economy in the Sixteenth Century', in Earle, p. 26.

[20] J. Lynch, *Spain under the Habsburgs* I (Oxford, 1964), p. 11.

[21] C. R. Boxer, *The Dutch Seaborne Empire 1600–1800* (1965, Harmondsworth edn, 1973), pp. 226 ff.

Ministers were emerging out of councils or boards, as the principle of authority in a single pair of hands spread downward from the throne, and a premier or grand vizir was wanted to coordinate them. A gap was widening between flesh and blood monarchs and the popular image of the sovereign watching over everything that happened. Kings lived increasingly in a palace world of make-believe, and began to undergo the apotheosis that court artists and poets were fond of depicting in mythic guise. Rubens painted for Whitehall imaginary splendours of the late James I; Charles I routed his adversaries in fantasy, in court masques, before having to face them on the stricken field. Yet this too was part of the intricate process by which monarchy was evolving into state, a state of which the idea was growing faster than the reality. Naïve fancy came together with learned monarchical theory not much less naïve. Palaces themselves, and the rest of the buildings with which kings were adorning their capitals, were a visible manifestation of royal greatness, which was also the greatness of the nation. Official architecture has been among history's formative influences or teachers. It was a reflection of their relative situations that French kings did a great deal of palace-building, English sovereigns by comparison little.

A strong dash of the mystical was another aspect of monarchy evolving from personal to institutional. All French writers of the Gallican and Politique school dilated on the 'miraculous, super-human qualities of kingship'.[22] In a Europe caught up in a transformation as long-drawn and uncharted as its voyages of discovery, society was a mystery to itself, riddled with hatreds and jealousies not to be laid to rest by any merely human exorcism. In Calderón's religious play, *Life is a Dream*, the four Elements fall out and wrangle until 'Power', their presiding genius, bids them remember that they are at one in some attributes, though far apart in others. His allocution can be understood as a poetical sermon on harmony of classes under the aegis of the throne. 'Absolute' was one of the compelling words of the age, in theology as well as in political philosophy, for it stood for something shared by kings with God. It could be extended to anything perfect or peerless. 'His neigh is like the bidding of a monarch, and his countenance enforces homage', exclaims Shakespeare's Dauphin, lyrical in praise of his steed. 'It is a most absolute and excellent horse', replies the Constable, wearily humouring him. All overweening pretensions have their comic

[22] W.F. Church, *Constitutional Thought in Sixteenth-century France* (Harvard, 1941), p. 197.

side. Yet qualities illusory when ascribed to the poor forked creatures strutting in crowns were less so as emblems of the state, inheritor of their vague grandeur.

It was heir to much of their irrationality as well, and that of the social landscape they were embedded in. Monarchy was growing obsolete by the time that men like Olivares and Richelieu gave it a fresh impetus, and was keeping an old ruling class more and more artificially alive. This showed most glaringly in its addiction to war, in which Turkey, the conquest-state, was not un-European but ultra-European. During the seventeenth century pretexts for war regained some of the frivolity that had stamped them before the decades of civil and religious strife, though the conduct of war carried over from these their more grimly murderous visage. Hobbes saw all history in the colours of his own Europe, rulers 'in continual jealousies, and in the state and posture of gladiators; having their weapons pointing, and their eyes fixed on one another . . . and continual spies upon their neighbours'.[23] Heads of old-established dynasties no longer led their armies, as newer men like Henry IV or Gustavus did. But war was so much the breath of its nostrils that monarchy could only be fully itself when fighting or preparing to fight. Then it could feel that it was enjoying a freedom scarcely attainable in domestic affairs, where kings were hemmed in by the bureaucracy they themselves were conjuring up; in war lay an escape into a Don Quixote realm of adventure. Their chief amusement, in many cases their chief occupation, was the mimic warfare of the hunt.

Looking back from the Revolution, Barnave saw how war had both arrested internal progress and strengthened the hands of governments.[24] Whatever its supposed aims, its requirements had a potent effect on the shaping of administrative structures. The coming of the standing army was inseparable from that of later, more fully developed absolutism. Francis I's army was loosely put together, much of it foreign; he could take it equally for granted that his bureaucracy was far from completely at his beck and call. Stiffer regimentation of their subjects by rulers went with progress in the drilling and training of soldiers. In a country in course of reorgani-zation, as Brandenburg was from the early seventeenth century, army and treasury and officialdom grew together, inextricably intertwined. Civil and military hierarchies always interacted; *délégué* and *sous-délégué* under an *intendant* were much like lieutenant and

[23] *Leviathan* (1651), chap. 13.
[24] A. J. M. Barnave, *Power, Property and History*, ed. E. Chill (New York, 1971), p. 196.

sub-lieutenant under a colonel. With regular officer-corps, old feudal allegiance was being refashioned into a newer moral bond, the sentiment of personal attachment to the throne. It was fanned by the pomp and circumstance which were coming to surround military life and foster martial spirit and tradition.

Relations between the rank and file and their employer were of another sort. Most of Philip II's Catalan recruits were amnestied bandits, exchanging one profession for another divided from it by thin partitions. Any suggestion of a national militia was calculated to arouse, as it did in the Cortes in 1598, 'a general disinclination to place arms in the hands of such a great number of people'.[25] Where conscripts were made use of, as in England, their instinct was to desert: that of the professionals was to go on strike. Mutinies, chiefly over pay, or rather lack of pay, were incessant, but might be conducted in a style of orderly routine, as if by trade unions. German mercenaries, the *Landsknechts*, had a well worked-out organization and code, akin to those of a craft guild. In Spain's cosmopolitan forces in Flanders there were forty-six mutinies between 1572 and 1607, under elected leaders whom their superiors had to treat with.[26] It may be guessed that gentleman-rankers from Castile were to the fore on such occasions, as well as in battle. It is a sidelight on the condition of the poor that they were better able to defend their livelihood as soldiers than when struggling on their own account.

Tensions for which absolutism could find no solutions found some relief in war. Yet this deepened them by throwing heavier and heavier burdens on the tax-paying classes. In 1627 Richelieu frankly confessed that funds for pay were often diverted and troops left to commandeer from the people, who had to give them nearly four times as much as they were paying in *taille*. He confessed too that the budget could only be balanced in peacetime, and for war costs loans must be resorted to because of the danger of extra taxes breeding discontent.[27] It has been observed that the letters of statesmen, from Granvelle to Colbert, chronically nervous of tax-

[25] I. A. A. Thompson, *War and Government in Habsburg Spain 1560–1620* (London, 1978), pp. 141–2.

[26] G. Parker, *Spain and the Netherlands 1559–1659: Ten Studies* (London, 1979), pp. 106–7. Cf. an account of a mutiny in 1551 at a Spanish outpost in north Africa, by E. H. Currey, *Sea-Wolves of the Mediterranean* (London, 1913), pp. 261–2.

[27] A. D. Lublinskaya, *French Absolutism: the Crucial Phase 1620–1629*, trans. B. Pearce (Cambridge, 1968), pp. 309, 311. Cf. B. Behrens, 'Government and Society', in CEHE, p. 554: 'Even in peace all of them appear to have spent upwards of 70 per cent of their annual revenues on war purposes'.

revolts, throw a more realistic light on the outlook of governments than any formal documents or treatises.[28] Yet the risk had to be run. War was ruinous, but it could not be renounced, because of group pressures and interests, and patterns of collective psychology. Ministers had to trust to the armed strength made possible by higher taxation to crush the resistance it provoked.

Just as occasional voices were lifted in criticism of aristocracy, war too had its censors. Among the religious, not only the Anabaptists but Luther rejected it,[29] and his followers long continued to regard it as destructive and unchristian. By Rabelais, war is ludicrously burlesqued, and when he carries us to the next world and pokes fun at the kings and heroes of antiquity,[30] we can hear the voice of bourgeois rationality, well aware that what counts in the end is money. So too, in *Troilus and Cressida*, with Thersites' derision of war and lechery as the two chief occupations of courts. There was enough dissatisfaction among the literate to admonish governments of the need to justify their doings.

Charles V and Francis I were always publishing diatribes against each other. As time went on, propaganda had to be broadened from the pedigrees and rights of kings to their subjects' concerns. Some of the apologies produced have been much too readily accepted by historians, whatever taxpayers at the time made of them. It is hard to agree with A. D. Lublinskaya that wars like Richelieu's were 'waged in the interests of the nation as a whole',[31] a dictum on a par with the endorsement by Soviet historians of the entire expansionist record of the tsars. Richelieu himself was more realistic when he said that a people should not be allowed to feel too safe and secure, or it might start to kick over the traces.[32] In other words, it must be convinced that only royal vigilance stood between it and foreign attack. It was in a liberation struggle like the Dutch that the concept of national war could be most convincing, and thenceforward kings would have to look as patriotic as republicans. Coins and medals were a mass medium of propaganda for both. A coin of 1597

---

[28] G. Ardent, 'Financial Policy', in Tilly, p. 167.
[29] Luther's *Table Talk*, ed. W. Hazlitt (London, 1857), p. 332; H. Holborn, *A History of Modern Germany: the Reformation* (English edn, London, 1965), p. 266.
[30] Trans. J. Le Clercq (New York, 1944), pp. 133, 273 ff., 281.
[31] *op. cit.*, p. 91; cf. pp. 175 ff., 198, 276. For an opposite view see Pennington, p. 41. Cf. Glamann's view that trade came only third to religion and dynastic ambition as a cause of war, but 'governments sometimes tried to invent mercantile pretexts for their measures of foreign policy.' *op. cit.*, p. 427.
[32] Cited by A. Vagts, *A History of Militarism* (revised English edn, London, 1959), p. 341.

celebrated the battle of Turnhout with a dramatic effigy of Maurice of Nassau on horseback, a walled town in the background.

If defence offered one rationalization, national profit was another. Mercantilism was dawning, and lending new life to old notions of a government's duty to promote the economy. It was forming largely in official circles, in part at least as a device to prolong the established order by giving its head a fresh mandate. Commercial interests were swelling: monarchy would do well to convince them that it was championing them, that trade had need of an ally in shining armour. In reality the huge costs of the military system, even in time of peace, were what made it impossible for governments to spend much on construction, or to improve administration by paying better salaries. But in a social structure so distorted economics and militarism each infected the other. There were always some sections of capital to benefit from royal belli-cosity. Richelieu's foreign policy suited the financiers because war compelled him to borrow from them, at any rates they might fix.[33]

In suitable circumstances war could stimulate some branches of an economy, as it did with Swedish mining and metal-working. How little it could do to infuse industrial animation into a nation unapt for it is shown by the case of Spain, which imported weapons and armour from its Italian and Flemish dependencies, and never learned to breed gun-founders of its own.[34] For Spain the long endeavour in the seventeenth century to hold on to the southern Netherlands meant a heavy drain, instead of gain. On the other side, public opinion in the United Provinces had to be carefully tutored over the resumption of war in 1621, 'for which there was enthusiasm only in certain quarters': by 1624 riots against war taxes were breaking out.[35] But profiteers were firmly enough entrenched to keep going a contest out of which they made rich pickings. This was one strand of progress in England too, and the Anglo-Dutch wars can be considered more 'rational' and 'modern' than the scrimmages of the old monarchies.

Between the real or pretended blessings of war, and its theatrical appeal, literate Europeans were coming to feel an involvement in it not aroused by Asia's perpetual dogfights. In popular imagery a king was often seen as a conqueror, a heroic equestrian figure, ever

---

[33] A. D. Lublinskaya, *op. cit.*, pp. 270–71.
[34] Thompson, *op. cit.*, pp. 240, 244.
[35] J. I. Israel, 'A Conflict of Empire: Spain and the Netherlands 1618–1648', *Past and Present*, no. 76 (1977), pp. 35, 64.

'glorious', 'victorious', 'invincible'.[36] Even in England a peaceable, home-keeping ruler like James I could seem an anomaly, a scarcely authentic monarch. Elizabeth's reign had accustomed the country to glory, and this, disagreeably expensive as it might have been at the time, was now as Veblen said 'exposed to the slow corrosion of peace and isolation'.[37] It was from the grand designs of Henry IV, unfulfilled as these were, that Dr Johnson was to date the Frenchman's sense of belonging to a great people, 'masters of the destiny of their neighbours'.[38] Adding adjacent territories to France could seem more worthwhile than sparring in far-off Naples, and gradually enlist public approval. France is an example – Turkey only more obviously another – of a nation formed and moulded by a state;[39] and much of the formative energy was exercised through war, or the interactions of war with the social structure. But if the nation could only grow up under the aegis of the state, the latter could not evolve beyond a certain point without becoming a national state. As a non-national entity its future would be confined to parts of eastern Europe, with the Austrian Habsburgs as its presiding genius.

War was not Europe's only cross; starvation and pestilence helped to make the epoch one of the most frightful ever experienced. Amid all the rest of its turmoil the dementia of the witch-hunt, that sombre accompaniment of Europe's wandering in the wilderness, was a more faithful index of the depth of social and spiritual crisis than any fallings-out of Protestant and Catholic. Theologians of both camps urged on the persecution.[40] It was a cancerous renewal of the perishing social bond, allowing men to feel and act once more in unison, as they never could against the more tangible menace of the Turk. Every age can be seen by its successors to have contained a vein of madness, or delusion. In the Europe of that era it was very strongly marked;[41] Lear's broken mind led him into a collective abyss.

---

[36] Burke, *Popular Culture in Early Modern Europe*, p. 150.

[37] T. Veblen, *Imperial Germany and the Industrial Revolution* (1915, London edn, 1939), p. 173. Bacon thought England 'a nation particularly fierce and warlike', and Elizabeth's success in keeping it in order all the more remarkable. 'Queen Elizabeth', in *Works* (New York edn, 1878), II, p. 447.

[38] *The Political Writings of Dr Johnson*, ed. J. P. Hardy (London, 1968), p. 3.

[39] Even today a Frenchman can urge this against any merging of French sovereignty in Europe. 'La France sans État, son État sans souveraineté, et il n'y a plus de peuple français.' B. F. de Foucault, *Le Monde*, 14 July 1978.

[40] See Trevor-Roper.

[41] See M. Foucault, *Madness and Civilization*, trans. R. Howard (London, 1967).

With all this, the mystery is that Europe's unregenerate governments were unwittingly helping to drag it forward, and the rest of the world in tow to it, instead of backward. Pushed on by impulses mostly noxious or futile, they were yet somehow part of a disorderly advance towards a modern civilization which, to be sure, incorporates many of the same meretricious ingredients. India in the sixteenth century, China in the seventeenth, were coming under new regimes, imposed by invaders, but only to start on repetitions of outworn cycles. While Asia nodded over its drowsy syrups, Europe, or part of it, was full of self-questioning, chaotically on the move; as Carlyle said of England, there were 'multitudes of things confusedly germinating, which have since overshadowed the earth'.[42] Unlike Asiatic monarchy, absolutism was an unstable, transitional form, even if over wide areas it was prolonged for centuries. It set itself to prop up anachronistic social structures, by force and with the help of a religion which in many lands had to be revived by artificial respiration. Essaying to eliminate contradictions, amid multiple currents of change, it often accentuated them, or generated fresh ones. New methods and answers had to be sought for novel difficulties.

Undoubtedly the close proximity of many states, constantly acting on one another in all sorts of ways, peaceful as well as warlike, – a situation far more pronounced in Europe than in any other part of the world at any time – heightened their self-awareness and resilience. But the continent was being polarized between developing and stagnating regions, as well as socially between rich and poor. By 1600 its western zones were diverging from one another as sharply as west, centre, east had already done; problems were too complex now for any uniform prescription like that held out by early absolutism. Mass impoverishment, a potent force of change (though not by itself, as Asia reminds us), might strengthen dominant classes, as in Spain; or enable new ones to be forged on old patterns, as in Russia; or facilitate a transfer of power to classes of a new sort, linked with a process which was ushering in industrial capitalism.

Vitality was coming to be concentrated in the northwest, and secondarily Scandinavia; and, in an ominously different fashion, Russia, where monarchy if more tyrannous was less conservative than in the west because there was far less of an old social order to be conserved. Italy, and the whole Mediterranean arena, may not have

---

[42] *Historical Sketches*, ed. A. Carlyle (4th edn, London, 1902), p. 52.

decayed so hopelessly as used to be thought,[43] but decline was real enough; all Europe's southern fringe, Christian or Muslim, was suffering from a blight. A species of semi-feudal society, distinct in quality from that of the north, and less susceptible of modulation, was perpetuated in Italy by foreign or priestly rule. The commercialized aristocracy, or aristocratized bourgeoisie, which had once put northern Italy and cities like Barcelona into the lead, was falling behind now, while some regions formerly more heavily feudal were forging ahead. At the stage now reached, the absence of the antithesis of feudal and bourgeois to be found, even if blurred, in northwest Europe, deprived the south of a necessary tension, or propellant. In the deep south slavery reached a high-watermark about 1600,[44] and contributed to the semi-orientalism it shared with Russia. Clericalism fostered the mentality of the theologians consulted in 1630 – ridiculously enough – about a proposed canal to link the Tagus and the Manzanares, who replied that if God had wished those rivers to be joined He would have joined them.

Between the failures of the 1520s in Spain and Germany and the middle of the seventeenth century, it has been remarked, revolutionary consciousness appeared to decline, social discontent to grow more incoherent, even to degenerate into brigandage.[45] This may be credited to monarchy as one of the services it could render to aristocracy by camouflaging class domination. Clearly the revolt of the Netherlands was a grand exception, and attained a far higher level than any of the cluster of mid-seventeenth century outbreaks apart from England's. More remarkable than the fact of these happening about the same time (most of them were against the same Spanish Habsburg government) are the discrepancies of quality among them, which can be measured by their degree of ability to bring classes together for action while preserving the identity of each. Catalonia failed through imperfect cooperation between richer and poorer, townsman and rustic. The Netherlands were distinguished by the relative scantiness of their rural population, both gentry and peasant. Ireland stood at the opposite pole. In England almost alone, rebellion was ignited by social and

---

[43] Braudel came to think that general decline in the Mediterranean began later than had been supposed, perhaps as late as 1640–50. *The Mediterranean*, p. 894. D. Sella thinks that for Europe as a whole the seventeenth century may not have seen a steep industrial decline, though there was much redistribution of prosperity from area to area. 'European Industries 1500–1700', in Cipolla, pp. 389–90.
[44] There may have been 100,000 slaves in Spain in 1600. W. Minchinton, 'Patterns and structure of Demand 1500–1750', in Cipolla, p. 154.
[45] Braudel, *The Mediterranean*, p. 739.

constitutional frictions, without the factor of foreign oppression. It resembled others in starting from increased government demands, chiefly the result of war costs, colliding with an old framework of law and institutions. Kings everywhere had been called 'absolute' long before they really were so; it was when they tried to raise their real power to the level of their title that they provoked resistance. Parliamentarians could maintain with conviction that the crown was the innovator, not they. But to keep a movement going and gaining ground there had to be fresh ideas, images of future as well as past. Royal prestige was only slowly eroded, and rebels would cling as long as they could to a fiction that they were not fighting the king, only his wicked counsellors; but behind this lay the fact that the country was now ready to dispense with absolutism. Mass unrest both pushed forward, and was harnessed by, sections of the propertied classes, among whom landowners partnered by their urban cousins came out on top. English squires like Spanish nobles had kept a great deal of local power, and now like them were moving towards a more direct control of government, but in a different spirit, far more national and modernizing; more different still from the desire of the Polish gentry to get control of the state in order to paralyse it.

No revolution like the English was feasible in France. It required a long spell of internal peace and gestation, which France had not passed through. Recurrent disorders could only be quelled by periodic re-establishment of monarchy, under compulsion to learn greater efficiency and able, like the younger autocracies further east, to obtain technology from a more advanced Holland and England. It sustained the nobility, but also made it possible for the middle classes to improve their standing. French ideologists adhered more wholeheartedly than any others to the ideal of a perfect, untrammelled absolutism. It had an accompaniment in Descartes's conception of Deity, which 'emphasised power and truth rather than love and goodness'.[46] The vision of enlightened omnipotence floating before their minds was to be fulfilled at last – so far as it ever could be – by the Revolution and Napoleon.

Eastward lay the bulky agglomerations of Austria, Poland, Russia, Turkey, outer planets remote from the sun, each the consequence of dynastic accident and conquest, without natural attachments, and with no brisk circulation of trade or ideas to weld them together. Two of them were going downhill in the seventeenth

[46] H. Kearney, *Science and Social Change 1500–1750* (London, 1971), p. 152.

century, while Austria and Russia were still expanding, with the advantage lacked by the Spanish and Turkish realms of forming unbroken land masses. Coming later on the scene than Poland, the tsarist empire was still flexible enough to learn, within narrow limits, while it had far more of a national heartland than the Habsburg empire. All over this vast area religion continued to have a moulding influence; the later Prussia may be thought of as a Protestant version of absolutism, legalistic and impersonal, by contrast with the more arbitrary and capricious type represented by Catholic Austria. Despotism in Russia kept an Orthodox and Byzantine character, in Turkey an Islamic and Asiatic cast.

Such polities could contribute some novelties in fields like warfare, but very little to Europe's general advance. This was contingent on elements which western absolutism was for a while able to incorporate, but then tended to stifle. They flourished best within smaller political units, though smallness was no guarantee of development by itself. Of Europe's population, the northwestern areas where most progress was being made contained not much more than a tenth. In 1622 the province of Holland had no more than 670,000 inhabitants,[47] a tiny total for a land playing so historic a part. Republicanism was practicable only on so diminutive a scale. In both the United Provinces and Switzerland it lived on thanks to a local particularism which might imperil the defences of the federation.

Crucial to the future was survival, in whatever inchoate forms, of the representative principle; though except where expansive social forces could make themselves felt through elected bodies, these easily turned into mere shells. Government demands for money, chiefly for war, did most to wither them. By a kind of tacit bargain the state took on itself the invidious task of imposing taxes, on the understanding that the privileged orders would have nothing to fear. This happened in Spain, in France, and in seventeenth-century Germany where the shrivelling away of the Estates went with the stronger princes' participation in wars, which compelled them to gather in more cash to hire soldiers. Events in the advancing countries put a further damper on constitutionalism in the others. After the spectacle of revolution in the Netherlands and Britain, no rulers or ministers were likely to contemplate representative assemblies in their own dominions as complacently as they often did earlier on. Charles II, last Habsburg of Spain, is said by Voltaire to have

---

[47] G. Parker, *The Dutch Revolt* (London, 1977), p. 249.

thought of the Cortes with horror,[48] as if it were a kind of wild beast; not, clearly, on account of any teeth or claws displayed by any recent Cortes in Castile.

For translating national potential into useful energy, absolutism was a very inefficient mechanism; representative government had no need to fear comparison with it. That the Tudor state could function with so modest an apparatus shows how little the hyper-trophied Spanish or French bureaucracies were required for any reasonable purposes. Centralism carried as far as Philip II carried it was self-defeating; it was necessarily superficial, obscuring a location of power really very different. In 1587 work to make the Tagus navigable up to Toledo was completed, but it was badly performed, and use of the river was obstructed by a jealous Seville, and impeded by landowners' tolls, and by 1600 it had petered out.[49] Absolutism could control bigger territories than constitutional government, but less competently – a fact analogous in its way to the big estate's productive capacity, no better, or even worse, than the smallholding's.

Instead of solving or rendering soluble the problems of society, the state in Spain or France became itself a substitute for a solution, incorporating sections of the propertied classes in its hierarchy, affording them jobs, subsidies, security, investment chances and, for the men of the sword, excitement. The destination towards which all this might seem to be moving was Kafka's Castle. Sale of office and rank reached a reduction to absurdity when, as the Cortes complained in 1632, posts and patents of nobility were sold com-pulsorily to towns which could find no one to pay for them.[50] For the French bourgeoisie it was a further blockage, of the psychological order which has been as obtrusive in history as any physical obstacles, that it could in an illusory way suppose itself to be in power already. In England and Holland social relations, immobilized over most of Europe, were relatively free to evolve in accordance with what may be termed Europe's historical logic.

Sovereignty, Althusius wrote, belonged not as Bodin thought to the ruler, but to the people, 'the vital spirit, soul, heart and life' of the commonwealth.[51] But the People as a collective force was an

[48] *The Age of Louis XIV*, chap. 17.
[49] Vries, p. 169.
[50] Lynch, *op. cit.*, II, p. 85.
[51] *The Politics of Johannes Althusius*, ed. F. S. Carney, preface to 1st edn, pp. 4–5. Cf. pp. 10–11, the dedication of the 3rd edn, 1614, to the Estates of Frisia, congratulating them on their heroic resistance to Spain.

ideal concept, floating above the limbo of social divisions, and attempts to bring it down to solid earth, to realize it in action, were disappointing. Within the mass a very uneven development of the individuals composing it was taking place. It was, oddly, the Turks who led the way in demonstrating what the common man could be capable of; men of the humblest birth built their empire and commanded their armies. They were drawing on the talents of a handful of aliens, who could rise only in state service. In the west movements of rebellion gave opportunity of a less roundabout sort to some other plebeians. Western man as individual, distinct from acquiescent majority, was undergoing a complex evolution. He was being filtered out from the mass, acquiring for instance the taste for privacy that was dissolving the communal life of the great hall, or on another level the wish to choose his own religion. At the same time the rise of the state, of which the people had failed to gain possession, threatened him with heavier regimentation. An amorphous whole was dividing into another pair of opposites, human atom and state-and-church. Faustian man was being born, and his fetters weighed more painfully on him than any in Asia. Kropotkin was to lament, under the shadow of latter-day tsarism, the steamrollering of the human being by the modern barbarism headed by the state, military and priestly sway and Roman law.[52]

While Europe's nations moved apart, with religion to inflame their estrangement, there was conversely a heightened consciousness of Europe or Christendom as one whole, against the background of other continents now closer at hand, or known for the first time. Acosta the Jesuit's book of 1589 on the Indies, with its antithesis between primitive peoples and those reared in 'civill and well governed Common weales', had an English edition in 1604. Europeans were thinking of themselves as, unlike most if not all others, civilized. We may wonder why they thought themselves so – or why we think ourselves so. But Europe, with all its ailments, was having intoxicating glimpses of greatness. Religious exaltation was part of them, a sensation only known amid a clash of rival creeds. They were sharpened by the portentous rise of the state, as something – in Turkey too – outranging the antiquated, merely personal autocracies of most of Asia, and something which the individual could identify himself, even if he might also recoil from it.

Brightened by reviving memories of Rome, the illimitable claims of the state led men to believe it as omnipotent in fact as it was

[52] P. Kropotkin, *The State, its Historic Role* (English edn, London, 1969), pp. 31–32.

imposing in appearance. A dream of power haunted the mind of the age. It showed in Calderón's demiurge, in Milton's God and Satan, in the heroic figures of Rubens. In northwestern Europe early scientific successes tempted men to think of standing on the moon three centuries before they reached it.[53] From the seemingly rudimentary materials afforded by the Europe of 1600, advance in all spheres, technical and military, cultural and political, was astonishingly rapid. It was also lopsided, perilous, fraught with legacies of an unwholesome past. The State of Burke's rhapsody, that partnership in all virtue and in every science, is still a far-off vision.

[53] Dryden, 'Annus Mirabilis' (1667).

Bibliography

Abbreviations

Burke   P. Burke (ed.), *Economy and Society in Early Modern Europe* (London, 1972).

CEHE   *Cambridge Economic History of Europe* V, ed. E.E. Rich and C. H. Wilson (1977).

Cipolla   C. M. Cipolla (ed.), *The Fontana Economic History of Europe: The Sixteenth and Seventeenth Centuries* (London, 1974).

Cohn   H. J. Cohn (ed.), *Government in Reformation Europe 1520– 1560* (London, 1971).

Earle   P. Earle (ed.), *Essays in European Economic History 1500–1800* (Oxford, 1974).

Goody   J. Goody, J. Thirsk and E. P. Thompson (eds), *Family and Inheritance: Rural Society in Western Europe 1200–1800* (Cambridge, 1976).

NCMH *New Cambridge Modern History*, III (1968), IV (1970), XIII (1979).

Tilly   C. Tilly (ed.), *The Formation of National States in Western Europe* (Princeton, 1975).

CHAPTERS 1 AND 14: GENERAL

Allen, J. W.   *A History of Political Thought in the Sixteenth Century* (3rd edn, London, l951).

   Althusius, the Politics of Johannes, trans. F. S. Carney (London, 1964).

Anderson, P.   *Lineages of the Absolutist State* (London, 1974).

Aston, T. (ed.)   *Crisis in Europe 1560–1660* (London, 1965).

Braudel, P.   *The Mediterranean and the Mediterranean World in the Age of Philip II,* 2nd edn, trans. S. Reynolds (London, 1972– 3).

Capitalism and Material Life 1400–1800, trans. M. Kochan (London, 1973).

Brenner, R. 'Agrarian Class Structure and Economic Development in Pre-Industrial Europe', *Past and Present,* no. 70 (1976); symposium on this essay in no. 78 (1978).

Burke, P. (ed.) *Economy and Society in Early Modern Europe* (London, 1972).

Burke, P. *Popular Culture in Early Modern Europe* (London, 1978).

Cambridge Economic History of Europe V, ed. E. E. Rich and C. H. Wilson (1977).

Carus-Wilson, E. M. (ed.) *Essays in Economic History* (London, 1954).

Chudoba, B. *Spain and the Empire* (Univ. of Chicago Press, 1952).

Cipolla, C. M. (ed.) *The Fontana Economic History of Europe: The Sixteenth and Seventeenth Centuries* (London, 1974).

Clark, G. N. *The Seventeenth Century* (Cambridge, 1929).

Cohn, H. J. (ed.) *Government in Reformation Europe 1520–1560* (London, 1971).

Cooper, J. P. 'In Search of Agrarian Capitalism', *Past and Present,* no. 80 (1978).

Critchley, J. S. *Feudalism* (London, 1978).

Earle, P. (ed.) *Essays in European Economic History 1500–1800* (Oxford, 1974).

Elliott, J. H. *Europe Divided 1559–1598* (London, 1968).

'Revolution and Continuity in Early Modern Europe', *Past and Present,* no. 42 (1969).

Elton, G. R. *Reformation Europe 1517–1559* (London, 1963).

Figgis, J. N. *The Divine Right of Kings* (2nd edn, Cambridge, 1914).

Forster, R. and Greene, J. P. (eds) *Preconditions of Revolution in Early Modern Europe* (John Hopkins Univ. Press, 1970).

Fugger News-Letters, The, First Series (1568–1605), ed. V. von Klarwill (London, 1924).

Goody, J. *et al.* (eds) *Family and Inheritance: Rural Society in Western Europe 1200–1800* (Cambridge, 1976).

Grew, R. (ed.) *Crises of Political Development in Europe and the United States* (Princeton, 1978).

Griffiths, G. *Representative Government in Western Europe in the Sixteenth Century* (Oxford, 1968).

Hepburn, A. C. (ed.) *Minorities in History* (London, 1978).

Kamenka, E. and Neale, R. S. (eds) *Feudalism, Capitalism and Beyond* (London, 1975).

Kiernan, V. G. 'State and Nation in Western Europe', *Past and Present,* no. 31 (1965).

Koenigsberger, H. G. *Estates and Revolutions: Essays in Early Modern European History* (Cornell Univ. Press, 1971).

The Hapsburgs and Europe 1516–1660 (Cornell Univ. Press, 1971).

Kohn, H. *The Idea of Nationalism* (New York, 1945).

MacIver, R. M. *The Modern State* (London, 1926).

Mousnier, R. *Peasant Uprisings in Seventeenth-century France, Russia and China,* trans. B. Pearce (London, 1971).

Nef, J. U. *War and Human Progress* (London, 1950).

New Cambridge Modern History III (1559–1610), ed. R. B. Wernham (1968); IV (1609–1659), ed. J. P. Cooper (1970); XIII (companion volume), ed. P. Burke (1979).

Ogg, D. *Europe in the Seventeenth Century* (8th edn, London, 1960).

Pennington, D. H. *Seventeenth-century Europe* (London, 1970).

Renard, G. and Weulersse, G. *Life and Work in Modern Europe (Fifteenth to Eighteenth Centuries)* (London, 1926).

Rommen, H. A. *The State in Catholic Thought* (London, 1945).

Sée, H. *Modern Capitalism: its Origin and Evolution* (English edn, London, 1926).

Slavin, A. J. (ed.) *The 'New Monarchies' and Representative Assemblies* (Boston, 1964).

Swart, K. W. *Sale of Offices in the Seventeenth Century* (Hague, 1949).

Tilly, C. (ed.) *The Formation of National States in Western Europe* (Princeton, 1975).

Trevor-Roper, H. R. *The European Witch-Craze of the 16th and 17th Centuries* (Harmondsworth edn, 1969).

Vries, J. de *The Economy of Europe in an Age of Crisis 1600–1750* (Cambridge, 1976).

Wallerstein, I. *The Modern World-System* (New York, 1974).

CHAPTER 2: SPAIN

Altamira y Crevea, R. *Historia de España y de la civilización española* II (Barcelona, 1902).

Armstrong, E. *The Emperor Charles V* (London, 1902).

Brandi, K. *The Emperor Charles V,* trans. C. V. Wedgwood (London, 1939).

Bravo Morata, F. *Historia de Madrid* I (Madrid, 1966).

Cárdenas, F. de   *Ensayo sobre la historia de la propiedad territorial en España* (Madrid, 1873).

Carrión, P.   *Los latifundios en España* (Barcelona, 1975).

Casey, J.   'Moriscos and the Depopulation of Valencia', *Past and Present*, no. 50 (1971).

Chaunu, P.   *L'Espagne de Charles Quint* (Paris, 1973).

Chaytor, H. J.   *A History of Aragon and Catalonia* (London, 1933).

Davies, R. T.   *The Golden Century of Spain 1501–1621* (London, 1937).

   Spain in Decline 1621–1700 (London, 1957).

Defourneaux, M.   *La vie quotidienne en Espagne au siècle d'or* (Paris, 1964).

Domínguez Ortiz, A.   *The Golden Age of Spain 1516–1659*, trans. J. Casey (London, 1971).

Elliott, J. H. *The Revolt of the Catalans: A Study in the Decline of Spain (1598–1640)* (Cambridge, 1963).

   'Self-perception and Decline in Early Seventeenth-century Spain', *Past and Present*, no. 74 (1977).

Fernández-Santamaría, J. A.   *The State, War and Peace: Spanish Political Thought in the Renaissance 1516–1559* (Cambridge, 1977).

Guilarte, A. M.   *El régimen señorial en el siglo XVI* (Madrid, 1962).

Gutiérrez Nieto, J. I.   *Las comunidades como movimiento antiseñorial* (Barcelona, 1973).

Hamilton, B. *Political Thought in Sixteenth-century Spain* (Oxford, 1963).

Hamilton, E. J.   *American Treasure and the Price Revolution in Spain 1501–1650* (Harvard, 1934).

Hume, M. A. S.   *Philip II of Spain* (London, 1899).

   The Court of Philip IV: Spain in Decadence (new edn, London, n.d.).

Jago, C.   'The Influence of Debt on the Relations between Crown and Aristocracy in Seventeenth-century Castile', *Economic History Review* (1973).

Kagan, R. L.   'Universities in Castile 1500–1700', *Past and Present*, no. 49 (1970).

Kamen, H. *The Spanish Inquisition* (London, 1965).

   'The Decline of Spain: a Historical Myth?' *Past and Present*, no. 81 (1978).

Klein, J.   *The Mesta – a Study in Spanish Economic History 1273–1833* (Harvard, 1920).

Lynch, J.   *Spain under the Habsburgs*, 2 vols (Oxford, 1964, 1969).

Mackay, A. *Spain in the Middle Ages* (London, 1977).

Marañón, G. *Antonio Pérez*, trans. C. D. Key (London, 1954).

Maravall, J. A. *Las comunidades de Castilla. Una primera revolución moderna* (2nd edn, Madrid, 1970).

La teoría española del estado en el siglo XVII (Madrid, 1944).

Mariéjol, J. H. *Master of the Armada*, trans. W. B. Wells (London, 1933).

Merriman, R. B. *The Rise of the Spanish Empire* III and IV (New York, 1926, 1934).

Peers, E. A. *Catalonia Infelix* (London, 1937).

Pérez, N. *La Inmaculada y España* (Santander, 1954).

Pike, R. *Aristocrats and Traders; Sevillian Society in the Sixteenth Century* (New York, 1972).

Reglà, J. *Bandolers Pirates i Hugonots* (Barcelona, 1969).

Rennert, H. A. *The Spanish Stage in the Time of Lope de Vega* (New York, 1909).

Roth, C. *A History of the Marranos* (1932; reprint, New York, 1959).

Salomon, N. *La vida rural castellana en tiempos de Felipe II* (1964; Spanish edn, Barcelona, 1973).

Seaver, H. L. *The Great Revolt in Castile (1520–1)* (London, 1929).

Tapia Ozcariz, E. de *Las Cortes de Castilla 1183–1833* (Madrid, 1964).

Thompson, I. A. A. *War and Government in Habsburg Spain 1560–1620* (London, 1978).

Turberville, A. D. *The Spanish Inquisition* (London, 1932).

Uña Sarthou, J. *Las asociaciones obreras en España* (Madrid, 1900).

Valbuena Prat, A. *La vida española en la Edad de Oro, según sus fuentes literarias* (Barcelona, 1943).

Valencia, Pedro de *Escritos sociales* (Escuela Social de Madrid, 1945).

Valiente, F. T. *Los validos en la monarquía española del s.XVII* (Madrid, 1963).

Velarde Fuertes, J. 'Sobre la decadencia económica de España', *De Economia: Revista de Temas Económicos*, no.s 25–6 (1953).

Vicens Vives, J., with Nadal Oller, J. *Manual de historia económica de España* (3rd edn, Barcelona, 1964).

Vilar, P. *La Catalogne dans l'Espagne moderne* I (Paris, 1962).

Viñas y Mey, C. *El problema de la tierra en la España de los siglos XVI–XVII* (Madrid, 1941).

Wright, L. P. 'The Military Orders in Sixteenth- and Seventeenth-Century Spanish Society', *Past and Present*, no. 43 (1969).

CHAPTER 3: THE SPANISH DEPENDENCIES

Boxer, C. R.   *The Portuguese Seaborne Empire 1415–1825* (London, 1969).

Burke, P.   *Venice and Amsterdam: A Study of Seventeenth-Century Elites* (London, 1974).

Cochrane, E. (ed.)   *The Late Italian Renaissance 1525–1630* (London, 1970).

Cochrane, E.   *Florence in the Forgotten Centuries 1527–1800* (Chicago, 1973).

Coniglio, G.   *Il Viceregno di Napoli nel Sec. XVII* (Rome, 1955).

Hale, J. R.   *Florence and the Medici: The Pattern of Control* (London, 1977).

Hanke, L.   *The Spanish Struggle for Justice in the Conquest of America* (Univ. of Pennsylvania Press, 1949).

  'More Heat and Some Light on the Spanish Struggle for Justice', *Hispanic American Historical Review* (1964, no. 3).

  Spanish Viceroys in America (Houston, 1972).

Hazlitt, W. C.   *The Venetian Republic* II (1915; New York reprint, 1966).

Jamison, E. M. *et al.*   *Italy Mediaeval and Modern* (Oxford, 1919).

Koenigsberger, H.   *The Government of Sicily under Philip II of Spain* (London, 1951).

Lane, F. L.   *Venice and History* (collected papers; Baltimore, 1966).

Livermore, H. V.   *A History of Portugal* (Cambridge, 1947).

Madariaga, S. de   *The Rise of the Spanish Empire* (London, 1947).

Molmenti, P.   *Venice*, trans. H. F. Brown, Part 2, Vol. I (London, 1907).

Nowell, C. E.   *A History of Portugal* (New York, 1952).

Oliveira Martins, J. P.   *História de Portugal* (1879; 15th edn, Lisbon, 1968).

Parry, J. H.   *The Sale of Public Office in the Spanish Indies under the Hapsburgs* (Berkeley, 1953).

  The Spanish Seaborne Empire (London, 1966).

Procaccio, G.   *History of the Italian People* (1968; trans. A. Paul, Harmondsworth, 1973).

Pullan, B. (ed.)   *Crisis and Change in the Venetian Economy in the Sixteenth and Seventeenth Centuries* (London, 1968).

Salvatorelli, L.   *A Concise History of Italy* (1938; trans. A. Miall, London, 1940).

Shaw, D. L.   'Olivares y el Almirante de Castilla (1638)', in *Hispania* (Madrid, 1967).

Smith, D. M. *A History of Sicily: Medieval Sicily 800–1713* (London, 1968).

Smith, R. B. *Italian Irrigation* (Edinburgh, 1852).

Visconti, A. *Storia di Milano* (Milan, 1937).

CHAPTER 4: THE NETHERLANDS

Barbour, V. *Capitalism in Amsterdam in the 17th Century* (Ann Arbor, 1963).

Barker, J. E. *The Rise and Decline of the Netherlands* (London, 1906).

Bindoff, S. T. *The Scheldt Question to 1839* (London, 1945).

Boxer, C. R. *The Dutch Seaborne Empire 1600–1800* (1965; Harmondsworth edn, 1973).

Bromley, J. J. and Kossman, E. H. (eds) *Britain and the Netherlands* (London, 1968).

Caldecott-Baird, D. (ed.) *The Expedition in Holland 1572–1574* (London, 1976).

Carter, C. H. 'Belgian "Autonomy" under the Archdukes', *Journal of Modern History* (1964).

Febvre, L. *Philippe II et la Franche-Comté* (1912; new edn, Paris, 1970)

Geyl, P. *The Revolt of the Netherlands 1555–1609* (London, 1932). *The Netherlands Divided (1609–1648),* trans. S. T. Bindoff (London, 1936).

Griffiths, G. 'The Revolutionary Character of the Revolt of the Netherlands', in *Comparative Studies in Society and History* (Hague) II (1959–60).

Haley, K. H. D. *The Dutch in the Seventeenth Century* (London, 1972).

Harrison, F. *William the Silent* (London, 1931).

Hyma, A. 'Calvinism and Capitalism in the Netherlands 1555–1700', *Journal of Modern History* X, no. 3 (1938).

Kossman, E. H. and Mellink, A. F. (eds) *Texts concerning the Revolt of the Netherlands* (Cambridge, 1974).

Parker, G. *The Dutch Revolt* (London, 1977). *Spain and the Netherlands 1559–1659: Ten Studies* (London, 1979).

Pirenne, H. *Histoire de Belgique* III (1477–1567) and IV (1567–1648) (Brussels, 1907, 1911).

Renier, G. J. *The Dutch Nation: An Historical Study* (London, 1944).

Rowen, H. L. (ed.) *The Low Countries in Early Modern Times* (documents; London, 1972).

Swart, K. W. *William the Silent and the Revolt of the Netherlands* (Historical Association, London, 1978).

Tex, J. den *Oldenbarnevelt* (Cambridge, 1973).

Wedgwood, C. V. *William the Silent* (London, 1944).

Wilson, C. *Queen Elizabeth and the Revolt of the Netherlands* (London, 1970).

CHAPTER 5: FRANCE

Buisseret, D. *Sully and the Growth of Centralized Government in France 1598–1610* (London, 1968).

Church, W. F. *Constitutional Thought in Sixteenth-century France* (Harvard, 1941).

Davis, N. Z. *Society and Culture in Early Modern France* (London, 1975).

Doucet, R. *Les institutions de la France au XVIe siècle* (Paris, 1948).

Franklin, J. H. (ed.) *Constitutionalism and Resistance in the Sixteenth Century: Three Treatises* (New York, 1969).

Gately, M. O. *et al.* 'Seventeenth-century Peasant "Furies" ', *Past and Present*, no. 51 (1971).

Grant, A. J. *The Huguenots* (London, 1934).

Hanotaux, G. *Tableau de la France en 1614* (Paris, 1898).

Hauser, H. *La pensée et l'action économique du Cardinal de Richelieu* (Paris, 1944).

Hayden, J. M. *France and the Estates-General of 1614* (Cambridge, 1974).

Héritier, J. *Catherine de Medici*, trans. C. Haldane (London, 1963).

Knecht, R. J. *Francis I and Absolute Monarchy* (Historical Association, London, 1969).

Lewis, P. S. 'The Failure of the French Medieval Estates', *Past and Present*, no. 23 (1962).

Lodge, E. C. *Sully, Colbert, and Turgot* (London, 1931).

Lublinskaya, A. D. *French Absolutism: the Crucial Phase 1620–1629*. trans. B. Pearce (Cambridge, 1968).

Luçay, Comte de *Les Secrétaires d'État depuis leur institution jusqu'à la mort de Louis XV* (Paris, 1881).

Major, J. R. *Representative Institutions in Renaissance France 1421–1559* (Madison, 1960).

Michaud, H. *La Grande Chancellerie et les écritures royales au seizième siècle (1515–1589)* (Paris, 1967).

Monluc, Blaise de *The Habsburg-Valois Wars and the French Wars of Religion*, trans. I. Roy (London, 1971).

Mousnier, R. *L'assassinat d'Henri IV* (Paris, 1964).

Mousnier, R. et al. *Le Conseil du Roy de Louis XIII à la Révolution* (Paris, 1970).

Mousnier, R. *Les institutions de la France sous la monarchie absolue 1598–1789*, I (Paris, 1974).

Nef, J. U. *Industry and Government in France and England 1540–1640* (1940; New York edn, 1957).

Parker, D. 'The Social Foundation of French Absolutism 1610–1640', *Past and Present*, no. 53 (1971).

Porchnev, B. *Les soulèvements populaires en France de 1623 à 1648* (1948; Paris edn 1963).

Richelieu, *The Political Testament of Cardinal*, ed. H. B. Hill (anthology; Wisconsin, 1961).

Romier, L. *Le royaume de Cathérine de Médicis* (Paris, 1922).

Salmon, J. H. M. 'Venality of Office and Popular Sedition in Seventeenth-Century France', *Past and Present*, no. 37 (1967).

'The Paris Sixteen, 1584–94: the Social Analysis of a Revolutionary Movement', *Journal of Modern History* (Dec. 1972).

Society in Crisis: France in the Sixteenth Century (London, 1975).

Shennan, J. H. *The Parlement of Paris* (London, 1968).

Government and Society in France 1461–1661 (London, 1969).

Smiles, S. *The Huguenots* (6th edn, London, 1889).

Sutherland, N. M. *The French Secretaries of State in the Age of Catherine de Medici* (London, 1962).

Catherine de Medici and the Ancien Régime (Historical Association, London, 1966).

Tapié, V. L. *France in the Age of Louis XIII and Richelieu*, trans. D. M. Lockie (London, 1974).

Willert, P. F. *Henry of Navarre and the Huguenots in France* (1893; new edn, London, 1924).

CHAPTER 6: ENGLAND

Andrewes, L. *Sermons of the Conspiracy of the Gowries and of the Gunpowder Treason* (reprint, Oxford, 1841).

Aylmer, G. E. *The King's Servants: The Civil Service of Charles I* (London, 1961).

Barnes, T. C. *The Clerk of the Peace in Caroline Somerset* (Leicester, 1961).

Beier, A. L. 'Vagrants and the Social Order in Elizabethan England', *Past and Present*, no. 64 (1974).

Bindoff, S. T. *et al.* (eds) *Elizabethan Government and Society* (London, 1961).

Brookes, E. S. *Sir Christopher Hatton* (London, 1946).

Campbell, M. *The English Yeoman under Elizabeth and the Early Stuarts* (New Haven, 1942).

Carlyle, Thomas *Historical Sketches*, ed. A. Carlyle (4th edn, London, 1902).

Chamberlain Letters, The, ed. E. M. Thomson (London, 1966).

Clarke Papers, The, ed. C. H. Firth, I (London, 1891).

Cockburn, J. S. (ed). *Crime in England 1550–1800* (London, 1977).

Cruickshank, C. G. *Elizabeth's Army* (London, 1946).

Curtis, M. H. 'The Alienated Intellectuals of Early Stuart England', *Past and Present*, no. 23 (1962).

Dobb, M. *Studies in the Development of Capitalism* (London, 1946).

Elton, G. R. *The Tudor Constitution: Documents and Commentary* (Cambridge, 1960).

Everitt, A. 'Social Mobility in Early Modern England', *Past and Present*, no. 33 (1966).

Gardiner, S. R. *The Constitutional Documents of the Puritan Revolution 1625–1660* (3rd edn, Oxford, 1906).

Gleason, J. H. *The Justices of the Peace in England 1558 to 1640* (Oxford, 1969).

Gooch, G. P. *Political Thought in England from Bacon to Halifax* (London, 1915).

Harrison, G. B. *The Life and Death of Robert Devereux Earl of Essex* (London, 1937).

Hill, C. *Economic Problems of the Church from Archbishop Whitgift to the Long Parliament* (Oxford, 1956).

Society and Puritanism in Pre-revolutionary England (London, 1964).

Holdsworth, Sir W. S. *A History of English Law*, IV and V (London, 1924).

Ives, E. W. *Faction in Tudor England* (Historical Association, London, 1979).

James, Margaret *Social Problems and Policy during the Puritan Revolution 1640–1660* (London, 1930).

James, M. E. 'The Concept of Order and the Northern Rising 1569', *Past and Present*, no. 60 (1973).

English Politics and the Concept of Honour 1485–1642 (Oxford, 1978).

Johnson, A. H. *The Disappearance of the Small Landowner* (Oxford, 1909).

Kelly, J. T. *Thorns on the Tudor Rose: Monks, Rogues, Vagabonds, and Sturdy Beggars* (Univ. of Mississippi, 1977).

Kenyon, J. P. *Stuart England* (Harmondsworth, 1978).

Kishlansky, M. 'The Case of the Army Truly Stated: the Creation of the New Model Army', *Past and Present* no. 81 (1978).

Knappen, N. M. *Tudor Puritanism* (Chicago, 1939).

Lamond, E. (ed.) *A Discourse of the Commonwealth of this Realm of England* (anon., 1581; Cambridge, 1893).

Lambard, W. *Eirenarcha or of the Office of the Justices of Peace* (London, 1581).

Leonard, E. M. *The Early History of English Poor Relief* (Cambridge, 1900).

Leonard, H. H. 'Distraint of Knighthood: the Last Phase, 1625– 41, *History* (Feb. 1978).

MacCaffrey, W. T. 'England: the Crown and the New Aristocracy 1540–1600', *Past and Present*, no. 30 (1965).

McIlwain, C. H. *The High Court of Parliament and its Supremacy* (New Haven, 1910).

Manning, B. *The English People and the English Revolution 1640– 1649* (London, 1976).

Moir, T. L. *The Addled Parliament of 1614* (Oxford, 1958).

Morris, C. *Political Thought in England: Tyndale to Hooker* (London, 1953).

Neale, J. E. *Queen Elizabeth* (1934; Harmondsworth edn, 1971). *The Elizabethan House of Commons* (London, 1949).

Notestein, W. *The Winning of the Initiative by the House of Commons* (London, 1924).

Pollard, A. F. *Henry VIII* (new edn, London, 1905).

Prothero, G. W. *Statutes and Constitutional Documents 1558–1628* (Oxford, 1913).

Read, C. *Mr Secretary Cecil and Queen Elizabeth* (London, 1955). *Lord Burghley and Queen Elizabeth* (London, 1960).

Roberts, P. R. 'The Union with England and the Identity of "Anglican" Wales', *Transactions of the Royal Historical Society* (1972).

Rowse, A. L. *The England of Elizabeth: the Structure of Society* (London, 1950).

Schenk, W. *The Concern for Social Justice in the Puritan Revolution* (London, 1948).

Sharp, A. 'Edward Waterhouse's View of Social Change in Seventeenth-century England', *Past and Present*, no. 62 (1974).

Sharpe, R. R. *London and the Kingdom* (London, 1894).

Smith, A. G. R. *The Government of Elizabethan England* (London, 1967).

Smith, Sir Thomas   *De Republica Anglorum: A Discourse on the Commonwealth of England* (1583; ed. L. Alston, Cambridge, 1906).

Stone, L. (ed.)   *Social Change and Revolution in England 1540–1640* (London, 1966).

'Social Mobility in Early Modern England' *Past and Present*, no. 33 (1966).

The Causes of the English Revolution 1529–1642 (London, 1972).

Stow, John   *A Survey of London* (1603; ed. C. L. Kingsford, Oxford, 1908).

Supple, B. E.   *Commercial Crisis and Change in England 1600–1642* (Cambridge, 1970).

Tanner, J. R.   *English Constitutional Conflicts of the Seventeenth Century 1603–1689* (Cambridge, 1928).

Tudor Constitutional Documents 1485–1603 (Cambridge, 1930).

Tawney, R. H.   *The Agrarian Problem in the Sixteenth Century* (London, 1912).

Business and Politics under James I: Lionel Cranfield as Merchant and Minister (Cambridge, 1958).

Thirsk, J. (ed.)   *The Agrarian History of England and Wales* IV (Cambridge, 1967).

Trevor-Roper, H. R.   *The Gentry 1540–1640* (London, 1953).

Unwin, G.   *Industrial Organization in the Sixteenth and Seventeenth Centuries* (Oxford, 1904).

The Guilds and Companies of London (3rd edn, London, 1938).

Williams, P.   'A Revolution in Tudor History?' *Past and Present*, no. 25. (1963); other contributions to a debate during 1963–5 on G. R. Elton's view of Thomas Cromwell as a great administrative innovator, by G. L. Hariss (no. 25); J. P. Cooper (no. 26); Elton (no. 29); Hariss (no. 31); Williams (no. 31); Elton (no. 32).

'Rebellion and Revolution in Early Modern England', in *War and Society*, ed. M. R. D. Foot (London, 1973).

Willson, D. H.   *King James VI and I* (London, 1962).

Wright, L. P.   *Middle-Class Culture in Elizabethan England* (1935; London edn, 1964).

CHAPTER 7: SCOTLAND

Bingham, C.   *James V King of Scots 1512–1542* (London, 1971).

Cowan, I. B.   *Regional Aspects of the Scottish Reformation* (Historical Association, London, 1978).

Donaldson, G. *Scotland: The Making of the Kingdom, James V– James VII* (Edinburgh, 1965).
The First Trial of Mary, Queen of Scots (London, 1969).
Mary Queen of Scots (London, 1974).
Fergusson, Sir J. *The White Hind and Other Discoveries* (London, 1963).
Fraser, Lady A. *Mary Queen of Scots* (London, 1969).
Fyfe, J. G. (ed.) *Scottish Diaries and Memoirs 1550–1746* (Stirling, 1928).
Gillon, R. M. *John Davidson of Prestonpans* (London, 1936).
Grant, I. F. *The Economic History of Scotland* (London, 1934).
Johnston, T. *History of the Working Classes in Scotland* (Glasgow, 1920).
Lang, A. *A History of Scotland* II (3rd edn, Edinburgh, 1924).
Lee, M. *James Stewart, Earl of Moray* (New York, 1953).
John Maitland of Thirlestane and the Foundation of the Stewart Despotism in Scotland (Princeton, 1959).
Lythe, S. G. E. *The Economy of Scotland in its European Setting 1550–1625* (Edinburgh, 1960).
Mackenzie, W. C. *The Highlands and Isles of Scotland* (revised edn, Edinburgh, 1940).
Murray, A. C. *Memorials of Sir Gideon Murray of Elibank and his Times (1560–1621)* (Edinburgh, 1932).
Peterkin, A. R. (ed.) *The Booke of the Universall Kirk of Scotland* (Edinburgh, 1839).
Russell. E. *Maitland of Lethington, the Minister of Mary Stuart* (London, 1912).
Smout, T. C. *A History of the Scottish People 1560–1830* (1969; London edn, 1972).
Stevenson, D. *The Scottish Revolution 1637–1644: The Triumph of the Covenanters* (Newton Abbot, 1973).
Terry, C. S. *The Scottish Parliament: Its Constitution and Procedure 1603–1707* (Glasgow, 1905).
Wedgwood, C. V. 'Anglo-Scottish Relations, 1603–40', *Transactions of the Royal Historical Society* (1950).

CHAPTER 8: SCANDINAVIA

Andersson, I. *A History of Sweden*, trans. G. Hannay (London, 1956).
Berg, J. and Lagercrantz, B. *Scots in Sweden*, trans. R. P. A. Hort (Stockholm, 1962).

Gade, J. A. *Christian IV King of Denmark and Norway* (London, 1928).

Hallendorff, C. and Schück, A. *History of Sweden*, trans. L. Yapp (London, 1929).

Heckscher, E. F. *An Economic History of Sweden* (English edn, Harvard, 1954).

Larsen, K. *A History of Norway* (New York, 1948).

Lepszy, K. 'The Union of the Crowns between Poland and Sweden in 1587', *Poland at the XIth International Congress of Historical Sciences* (Warsaw, 1960).

Magnússon, S. A. *Northern Sphinx: Iceland and the Icelanders* (London, 1977).

Oakley, S. *The Story of Sweden* (London, 1966).

Roberts, M. *Gustavus Adolphus: a History of Sweden 1611–1632* (London, 1953, 1958).
  'Queen Christina and the General Crisis of the Seventeenth Century', *Past and Present*, no. 22 (1962).
  The Early Vasas: A History of Sweden 1523–1611 (Cambridge, 1968).

Stomberg, A. A. *A History of Sweden* (London, 1932).

Toyne, S. M. *The Scandinavians in History* (London, 1948).

CHAPTER 9: GERMANY

Armstrong, E. *The Emperor Charles V* (London, 1902).

Barraclough, G. *The Origins of Modern Germany* (Oxford, 1946).

Benecke, G. 'Labour Relations and Peasant Society in Northwest Germany *c.* 1600', *History* LVIII (1973).

Birnbaum, N. 'The Zwinglian Reformation in Switzerland', *Past and Present*, no. 15 (1959).

Bonjour, E. *et al.* *A Short History of Switzerland* (Oxford, 1952).

Brandi, K. *The Emperor Charles V*, trans. C. V. Wedgwood (London, 1939).

Carsten, F. L. *The Origins of Prussia* (Oxford, 1954).
  Princes and Parliaments in Germany (Oxford, 1959).

Clasen, C. P. *The Palatinate in European History 1559–1660* (Oxford, 1963).

Cohn, H. J. *The Government of the Rhine Palatinate in the Fifteenth Century* (London, 1965).

Demeter, K. *The German Officer Corps in Society and State 1650–1945* (English edn, London, 1965).

Engels, F. *The Peasant War in Germany* (1850).

Fay, S. B. 'The Roman Law and the German Peasant', *American Historical Review* XVI (1910–11).

Friedenthal, R. *Luther*, trans. J. Nowell (London, 1970).

Friedrichs, C. R. 'Capitalism, Mobility and Class Formation in the Early Modern German City', in P. Abrams and E. A. Wrigley (eds), *Towns in Societies* (Cambridge, 1978).

Holborn, H. *A History of Modern Germany: The Reformation* (English edn, London, 1965).

Journal of Peasant Studies III, No. 1 (1975); special number on the Peasants War.

Klassen, P. J. *The Economics of Anabaptism 1525–1560* (The Hague, 1964).

Ludloff, R. 'Industrial Development in Sixteenth-Seventeenth-century Germany', *Past and Present*, no. 12 (1957).

Marriott, J. A. R. and Robertson, C. G. *The Evolution of Prussia* (revised edn, Oxford, 1946).

Moeller, B. *Imperial Cities and the Reformation: Three Essays* (English edn, Philadelphia, 1972).

Oechsli, W. *History of Switzerland 1499–1914*, trans. C. and E. Paul (Cambridge, 1922).

Polisensky, J. V. 'The Thirty Years War', *Past and Present*, no. 6 (1954).

Rosenberg, H. 'The Rise of the Junkers in Brandburg-Prussia 1410–1653', *American Historical Review* XLIX (1943–4).

Rupp, E. G. and Drewery, B. *Martin Luther* (London, 1970).

Schiff, O. 'Die Deutsche Bauernaufstände von 1525 bis 1789', *Historische Zeitschrift* (1924).

Scribner, R. W. 'Civic Unity and the Reformation in Erfurt', *Past and Present*, no. 66 (1975).

Scribner, Bob (sc. R. W.) and Benecke, G. (eds) *The German Peasant War of 1525–New Viewpoints* (London, 1979).

Steinberg, S. H. *The Thirty Years War* (London, 1966).

Strauss. G. (ed.) *Manifestations of Discontent in Germany on the Eve of the Reformation* (Indiana Univ. Press, 1971).

Strauss, G. 'Success and Failure in the German Reformation', *Past and Present*, no. 67 (1975).

Wedgwood, C. V. *The Thirty Years War* (London, 1938).

CHAPTER 10: THE HABSBURG LANDS

Betts. R. R. *Essays in Czech history* (London, 1969).

Bromlei, Y. V.   *Krest'yanskoe Vosstanie 1573g. v Khorvatii* (The peasant revolt of 1573 in Croatia; Moscow, 1959).

Chudoba, R.   *Spain and the Empire 1519–1643* (Univ. of Chicago Press, 1952).

Coxe, W.   *History of the House of Austria* (3rd edn, London, 1847).

Evans, R. J. W.   *Rudolf II and his World: A Study in Intellectual History 1576–1612* (Oxford, 1973).

Hantsch, H.   *Die Geschichte Österreichs* I (Graz, 1951).

Jaszi, O.   *The Dissolution of the Hapsburg Monarchy* (Univ. of Chicago Press, 1929).

Knatchbull-Hugesson, Hon. C. M.   *The Political Evolution of the Hungarian Nation* (London, 1908).

Leger, L.   *A History of Austria-Hungary* (English edn, London, 1889).

Lützow, Count   *Bohemia: An Historical Sketch* (London, 1896).

Marczali, H.   *Hungary in the Eighteenth Century* (with an essay on earlier history by H. W. V. Temperley; Cambridge, 1910).

Myska, M.   Pre-industrial Iron-making in the Czech Lands', *Past and Present*, no. 82 (1979).

Schwartz, H. F.   *The Imperial Privy Council in the Seventeenth Century* (Harvard, 1943).

Sinor, D.   *History of Hungary* (London, 1950).

Thomson, S. H.   *Czechoslovakia in European History* (Princeton, 1953).

Watson, F.   *Wallenstein, Soldier under Saturn* (London, 1938).

Zarek, O.   *The History of Hungary*, trans. Prince P. P. Wolkonsky (London, 1939).

Zöllner,E.   *Geschichte Österreichs* (Munich, 1961).

CHAPTER 11: POLAND

Allen, W. G. D.   *The Ukraine, a History* (Cambridge, 1940).

Cambridge History of Poland (to 1696),   ed. W. F. Reddaway *et al.* (1950).

Dyboski, R.   *Outlines of Polish History* (London, 1925).

Étienne Báthory, Roi de Pologne (Académie de Science Hongroise and Académie Polonaise, Cracow, 1935).

Fox, P.   *The Reformation in Poland: Some Social and Economic Aspects* (John Hopkins Univ. Press, 1924).

Gieysztor, A. *et al.*   *History of Poland* (Warsaw, 1968).

Halecki, O.   *The History of Poland* (1933; English edn, London, 1942).

Hoszowsky, S. 'The Polish Baltic Trade in the Fifteenth to Eighteenth Centuries', in *Poland at the XIth International Congress of Historical Sciences* (Warsaw, 1960).

Hrushevsky, M. *A History of Ukraine*, ed. O. J. Frederiksen (Yale Univ. Press, 1941).

Kot, S. *Five Centuries of Polish Learning* (Oxford, 1941).

Kula, W. *Théorie économique du système féodal pour un modèle de l'économie polonaise 16e–18e siècles* (French edn, Paris, 1970).

Lednicki, W. *Life and Culture of Poland* (New York, 1944).

Malowist, M. 'Le commerce de la Baltique et le problème des luttes sociales en Pologne aux XVe et XVIe siècles', in *La Pologne au Xe Congrès International des Sciences Historiques* (Warsaw, 1955).

'Poland, Russia and Western Trade in the Fifteenth and Sixteenth Centuries', *Past and Present*, no. 13 (1958).

'A Certain Trade Technique in the Baltic Countries in the Fifteenth-Seventeenth Centuries', in *Poland at the XIth Congress.*

Zólkiewski, Hetman Stanislas *Expedition to Moscow*, ed. J. Giertych (London, 1959).

CHAPTER 12: RUSSIA

Avrich, P. *Russian Rebels 1600–1800* (London, 1972).

Blum, J. *Lord and Peasant in Russia from the Ninth to the Nineteenth Century* (Princeton, 1961).

Dukes, P. 'Russia and the "General Crisis" of the Seventeenth Century', *New Zealand Slavonic Journal*, no. 2 (1974).

Fennell, J. F. I. *The Correspondence between Prince A. M. Kurbsky and Tsar Ivan IV of 1564–1579* (Cambridge, 1955).

Ivan the Great of Moscow (London, 1963).

Fletcher, Giles *Of the Russe Commonwealth* (1591; Harvard edn, 1966).

Florinsky, M. T. *Russia: A History and an Interpretation* (New York, 1953).

Grey, I. *Ivan III and the Unification of Russia* (London, 1964).

Grobovsky, A. N. *The 'Chosen Council' of Ivan IV: a Reinterpretation* (New York, 1969).

Hellie, R. *Enserfment and Military Change in Muscovy* (Univ. of Chicago Press, 1971).

Herberstein, Sigmund von *Description of Moscow and Muscovy 1557*, ed. B. Picard (London, 1969).

Howe, S. E. (ed.)   *The False Dmitri* (London, 1916).

Howes, R. C. (ed.)   *The Testaments of the Grand Princes of Moscow* (Cornell Univ. Press, 1967).

Karamzin's Memoir on Ancient and Modern Russia,   ed. R. Pipes (1959; New York edn, 1966).

Kluchevsky, V. O.   *A History of Russia* II and III, trans. C. J. Hogarth (London, 1912–13).

Lowmianski, H.   'The Russian Peasantry', *Past of Present*, no. 26 (1963).

Lyashchenko, P. I.   *History of the National Economy of Russia* (New York edn, 1949).

Mavor, J.   *An Economic History of Russia* I (2nd edn, London, 1925).

Mousnier, R.   *Peasant Uprisings in Seventeenth-century France, Russia and China*, trans. B. Pearce (London, 1971).

Pokrovsky, M. N.   *Brief History of Russia* I, trans D. S. Mirsky (London, 1933).

Smith, R. E. F.   *The Enserfment of the Russian Peasantry* (Cambridge, 1968).

Staden, Heinrich von   *The Land and Government of Muscovy: A Sixteenth-century Account*, ed. T. Esper (Stanford Univ. Press, 1967).

Vernadsky, G.   *The Tsardom of Moscow 1547–1682* (V of *A History of Russia*; Yale Univ. Press, 1969).

Wipper, R.   *Ivan Grozny*, trans. J. Fineberg (revised edn, Moscow, 1947).

CHAPTER 13: THE OTTOMAN EMPIRE

Alderson, A. D.   *The Structure of the Ottoman Dynasty* (Oxford, 1956).

Bradford, E.   *The Great Siege: Malta 1565* (Harmondsworth edn, 1964).

Coles, P.   *The Ottoman Impact on Europe* (London, 1968).

Cook, M. A. (ed.)   *A History of the Ottoman Empire* (chapters from *Cambridge History of Islam* and *NCMH*; Cambridge, 1976).

Currey, E. H.   *Sea-Wolves of the Mediterranean* (London, 1913).

Eversley, Lord   *The Turkish Empire* (3rd edn, London, 1924).

Finlay, G.   *The History of Greece under Othoman and Venetian Domination* (Edinburgh, 1856).

Katib Chelebi   *The Balance of Truth*, trans. G. L. Lewis (London, 1957).

Keddie, N. R. (ed.) *Scholars, Saints, and Sufis: Muslim Religious Institutions in the Middle East since 1500* (Berkeley, 1978).

Lamouche, Col. *Histoire de la Turquie* (1934; Paris edn, 1953).

Luke, Sir H. *The Old Turkey and the New* (revised edn, London, 1955).

Lybyer, A. H. *The Government of the Ottoman Empire in the Time of Suleiman the Magnificent* (Harvard, 1913).

MacDermott, M. *A History of Bulgaria 1393–1885* (London, 1962).

Merriman. R. B. *Suleiman the Magnificent 1520–1566* (Harvard, 1944).

Poliak, A. N. *Feudalism in Egypt, Syria, Palestine and the Lebanon, 1250–1900* (London, 1939).

Sari Mehmed Pasha *The Book of Counsel for Vezirs and Govenors*, ed. W. L. Wright (Princeton, 1935).

Shaw, S. *History of the Ottoman Empire and Modern Turkey* I (Cambridge, 1976).

Temperley, H. W. V. *History of Serbia* (London, 1919).

Vambéry, A. (ed.) *The Travels and Adventures of Sidi Ali Reïs . . . 1553–1556* (London, 1899).

For references in Chapter 14, see the Bibliography to Chapter 1.

Index